The Marriage Relationship

THE MARRIAGE

(EDITED

BASIC BOOKS, INC. *Publishers*

RELATIONSHIP

Psychoanalytic Perspectives

BY *Salo Rosenbaum* AND *Ian Alger*

New York   London

To the memory of
William V. Silverberg
esteemed teacher, honored colleague and friend

THE AUTHORS

Ian Alger, M.D., Clinical Associate in Psychiatry, New York Medical College.

Irving Bieber, M.D., Clinical Professor of Psychiatry, New York Medical College.

Toby B. Bieber, Ph.D., Instructor in Psychology, Division of Adult Education, Cooper Union, New York.

Arthur M. Bodin, Ph.D., Training and Education Director, Mental Research Institute, Palo Alto, California.

Walter Bonime, M.D., Associate Clinical Professor of Psychiatry, New York Medical College.

Paul R. Dince, M.D., Clinical Associate in Psychiatry, New York Medical College.

Rudolf Dreikurs, M.D., Professor of Psychiatry, Chicago Medical School.

Marvin G. Drellich, M.D., Assistant Clinical Professor of Psychiatry, New York Medical College.

Aaron H. Esman, M.D., Director of Psychiatric Training, Jewish Board of Guardians, New York.

Alvin I. Goldfarb, M.D., Consultant on Special Services for the Aged, New York State Department of Mental Hygiene; Associate Clinical Professor of Psychiatry, New York Medical College.

Bernard L. Greene, M.D., Associate Clinical Professor of Psychiatry, College of Medicine, University of Illinois; Adjunct Clinical Professor of Pastoral Psychology, Garrett Theological Seminary.

Martin Grotjahn, M.D., Clinical Professor of Psychiatry, University of Southern California, Los Angeles, California.

Don D. Jackson, M.D., Director, Mental Research Institute, Palo Alto, California.

Abram Kardiner, M.D., Honorary Consultant, Columbia Psychoanalytic Clinic for Training and Research, College of Physicians and Surgeons, New York.

Theodore Lidz, M.D., Professor and Chairman, Department of Psychiatry, Yale University School of Medicine.

Sandor Lorand, M.D., Professor Emeritus of Psychiatry, State University of New York, Downstate Medical Center; Honorary President, Psychoanalytic Association of New York.

Max Markowitz, M.D., Director, Adult Therapy Clinic, Postgraduate Center for Mental Health, New York.

Judd Marmor, M.D., Clinical Professor of Psychiatry, U.C.L.A. School of Medicine; Director, Divisions of Psychiatry, Cedars-Sinai Medical Center, Los Angeles, California.

John A. P. Millet, M.D., Honorary Consultant, Columbia Psychoanalytic Clinic for Training and Research, College of Physicians and Surgeons, New York.

Lilly Ottenheimer, M.D., Associate Clinical Professor of Psychiatry, New York Medical College.

Alfred H. Rifkin, M.D., Associate Clinical Professor of Psychiatry, New York Medical College.

Salo Rosenbaum, M.D., Assistant Clinical Professor of Psychiatry, New York University School of Medicine.

Nathan Roth, M.D., Assistant Clinical Professor of Psychiatry, New York Medical College; Associate Professor of Clinical Psychiatry, New York University School of Medicine.

Andrew S. Watson, M.D., Professor of Psychiatry, Professor of Law, University of Michigan.

Alexander Wolf, M.D., Associate Clinical Professor of Psychiatry, New York Medical College.

PREFACE

The eclectic nature of the Society of Medical Psychoanalysts is reflected not only in the orientations of the editors, but also in the variety of chapters written by authors holding different theories. It is hoped that these multiple approaches will provide new perspectives for a psychoanalytic understanding of marriage.

Marriage is a fundamental institution in our society. It is an intimate relationship, as well as a legal contract. Many couples who join together by choice feel bound together by obligation. Some partners live together in a growing and mutually satisfying partnership, while others live in an apathy of resignation. Some first seek divorce, while others turn to psychoanalysis for insight into the causes of their suffering and for help in achieving a rational and mature resolution.

Factors which contribute to an understanding of marriage in our society are to be found in the psychodynamics of individuals, in the unique structure of their own families, and in the vicissitudes which are an inherent part of our society and culture. Many of these factors are explored in the contributions of the distinguished authors of this book. The chapters have been developed in a sequence which considers the approach to marriage and the problems of mate selection, then explores a variety of problems arising in marriage, and finally discusses the implications of various resolutions.

This book is published under the auspices of the Society of Medical Psychoanalysts, which also sponsored a symposium on the same topic in New York City in 1965. Some of the chapters are revised from papers presented at that meeting, while many have been written especially for this volume. The editors are extremely grateful to all the authors for their cooperation in making this multi-theoretical project possible. The editors also wish to express their appreciation to Drs. Irving Bieber, Walter Bonime, David B. Friedman, Joseph H. Merin, Simon H. Nagler, Lilly Ottenheimer, Alfred H. Rifkin, Nathan Roth,

Clifford J. Sager, and William V. Silverberg, all members of, or consultants to, the Society's program committee who provided us with inspiration and support.

SALO ROSENBAUM

IAN ALGER

New York
September 1967

INTRODUCTION

Salo Rosenbaum and Ian Alger

Marriage is an ancient social institution, whereas psychoanalysis is a relatively new science, and only recently have the new theories and insights of psychoanalysis been systematically applied to the union of husband and wife. Our intention in this volume is to present some of the current manifestations of this growing interaction.

There are, of course, many ways of approaching the problems involved—and we say problems advisedly. As in so many areas, we must concentrate, for the time being at least, on the pathological problems. Most probably, ideal marriages do not exist at all, but mutually rewarding and durable marital experiences certainly do. Sometimes they have been brought about by psychoanalysis. More often, the psychoanalyst has no professional contact with them, for usually it is the individuals in a troubled marriage who ask his help. Thus the attention of our authors is centered on problems—psychological and societal—whatever their topics.

The subject matter of this book provides as generous a survey of current thought as is possible in a single volume. Its province might be said to be the relationship and application of psychoanalytic treatment to the problems that people have as they contemplate marriage, experience marriage, and continue in it or divorce themselves from it —a wide-ranging province indeed. Generally speaking, however, it may be divided into four subprovinces: (1) the overviews; (2) some specific factors, such as age and sex, in relation to marriage; (3) specific therapies, their indications and contraindications; (4) the special problem of divorce and the psychoanalyst's peculiar relationship to it.

Throughout this book many of the authors emphasize that the psychoanalytic treatment of marital disorders involves special considerations. Many situations arise in which the psychoanalyst cannot always proceed readily with standard theories or clinical techniques, whatever they may be. Ultimately we will require clear and precise scientific formulations that will cover such contingencies as well. This volume attempts to answer some of the questions—and to raise many more—involved in the eventual attainment of this goal.

The monogamous marriage not only has positive social impact, but also allows for the greatest personal intimacy and involvement in a continuing collaborative endeavor. In addition, it goes a long way toward simplifying a person's existence by establishing efficient and dependable routines of living. The thousand details of everyday life can ultimately be ordered and the tasks of living shared. Companionship is readily available, and opportunities for satisfying sexual desires are easily arranged. The crucial questions are: How many among us really want this? For how long? And can we continue for a lifetime with the same person and obtain an adequate measure of satisfaction? Obviously some manage very well, whereas others fare miserably. Many settle down in their human trap by resolving to a kind of grim continuation; others develop psychiatric symptoms; and still others try to break out by hook or crook. However, in view of the prevalence of marital discontent, we must at least consider the possibility that there are aspects of monogamy in our society which tend to make it difficult for most and impossible for some to achieve even the bare minimum of fulfillment.

One cultural factor which has profound influence on the institution of marriage is the prevailing attitude toward the roles of men and women. In our society the attitude toward the role of women in particular has been undergoing major shifts since the beginning of the century. As a result, there is often confusion of identity, frustration, disappointment, and strife connected with one's role in marriage. This is a complicated subject, with far-reaching implications. It is therefore not surprising that it is considered from various angles throughout the book.

Whereas marriage primarily is a social expedient, and only secondarily may serve individual needs, psychoanalysis is essentially concerned with reducing specific individual neurotic suffering and expanding happiness. Since we cannot change the prevailing system to suit individual needs, our only hope is to alter the individual system through self-knowledge. "Happiness is not a goal in itself but merely the result of a job well done. Undoubtedly, many marital difficulties are linked to the culturally exaggerated notion of happiness and also the un-realistic attitudes that are a function of romantic love."[1]

Many married persons are emotionally immature and so neurotically conflicted that they cannot adequately adapt to the greater demands made on them in the marriage relationship. For both partners, mar-riage, among other things, represents an identification with the parents. Their experiences with them, their surrogates, and other significant figures greatly determine whom they will choose to marry and for what reasons. Subsequently they may perpetuate in their own mar-riage what they observed in their parents' or they may do the exact opposite. The greater the unresolved conflicts, past and present, which one or both partners import into the union, the greater the chances of exacerbations and repercussions later on.

If neurotic unconscious factors, although unobtrusive at the outset, are significantly dominant, then free marital choice is at best a theo-retical exercise. Moreover, neurotic choices are more likely to be compelling. Often their strength is derived from a powerful compul-sion to repeat in disguise earlier patterns and traumata that constitute nodal points of fixation, regression, or defense. They may be partly conscious or not; they may contain elements of reality or fantasy. For some, marriage is a series of chain reactions. This may indicate that for them neurotic mates are neither hard to find nor particularly dif-ficult to replace. The "normal" person usually profits from past experi-ence, whereas the neurotic is likely to perpetuate his mistakes.

Although psychoanalysts, no more than anyone else, cannot ac-curately define the state of "being in love," we are nevertheless able to recognize it and understand the feelings of our patients who are overwhelmingly in love. We neither can nor are inclined to quarrel with love, even in those cases where prevailing social prejudice places realistic handicaps to a particular union. Mature love generally will more than compensate for such additional difficulties. As is true of all areas of conflict, the patient and analyst first search for possible neu-rotic contaminants and, if they are present, work them through.

Love is intimately intertwined with sex. Sometimes it is virtually im-possible to consider one or the other as separate entities. Yet occasion-ally we hear from our patients that they have experienced sex as ab-

[1] Fredrick C. Redlich and Daniel X. Freedman, *The Theory and Practice of Psychiatry* (New York: Basic Books, 1966).

solutely ecstatic without the faintest trace of love. Of course, we wonder, and are somewhat skeptical, especially since we have every reason to assume that sex and love have highly synergistic properties. Therefore if loveless sex can be so wonderful, it should follow that in combination they are even more so. Sometimes two people love each other, but for one reason or another are deprived of sexual gratification. As would be expected, this is a most frustrating situation, and is likely to produce anxiety and other psychiatric manifestations.

Sex is often perceived as irresistibly and overwhelmingly important during the honeymoon phase or its equivalent. In a healthy marriage, by available standards, sex in time becomes somewhat more integrated and domesticated, yet still manages to be pleasurable, rewarding, and quite worthwhile. Therefore it is readily and eagerly pursued. A firm sense of one's sexual identity is essential to one's capacity to accept sexuality as a joyful human encounter, in contrast to the sense of alienation that is so often experienced by our patients during the sexual act. Complaints of sexual incompatibility in marriage often represent only the superficial layer of inner discontent which must be traced to its more hidden source. Sometimes we see marriages that appear to be quite hopeless; yet the partners claim to enjoy an absolutely exquisite sex life. The converse occurs as well. However, in marriages where sexual difficulties prevail, and the partners have a great deal in common otherwise, the prognosis for eventually preserving such a marriage is infinitely better than in the first example cited. Once again, the shifting sexual roles encouraged by our culture and misunderstandings at nodal points of development can play havoc with many who later emerge with serious confusion of identity.

A few general comments are in order concerning the role of the psychoanalyst with respect to marriage, about which there seems to be a great deal of misunderstanding. Ideally, our most effective role should be in evaluating marriages before they are contracted. From a practical point of view, this is hardly feasible. More and more, young people come to our offices before they marry or early in their marriage to ask pertinent questions and to seek advice rather than treatment. We are primarily therapists, and as such remain eternal students of human behavior in general, and of our patients in particular. No two individuals are sufficiently alike to be treated by the same formula, despite similarities in problems, circumstances, and diagnoses. Consequently, it is of the utmost importance that each psychotherapeutic attempt be designed for the needs of the particular patient. Knowledge about each analytic case must be assimilated patiently, synthesized, and then dispensed without personal bias.

The analytic goal is to seek the truth and encourage development of insight and awareness. Therefore, our purpose is neither to preserve nor to destroy a marriage relationship, but rather to enable the individuals involved to become free from distortions and conflicts (past and present) and to become more aware of the nature of complex situations and relationships in their lives, so that ultimately they may be able to make an independent and mature choice considering the circumstances at hand.

It is clear why society favors the preservation of marriage, why it makes it easy to enter and harder to leave, and why it is alarmed at signs of family breakdown and an increased divorce rate. Needless to say, to maintain a relatively happy marriage requires a constant collaborative effort on the part of both spouses, whereas the dissolution of a marriage can be accomplished singlehanded if need be. Moreover, separation and divorce are often spoken of as if they were the last stage of a poor marriage. This is not always the case. Some people may not separate in a poor marriage, whereas others will separate from a mediocre or even a fairly good marriage.

It is impossible to determine who will or who will not consult us with marital problems. Some relatively healthy persons will seek help, while others with obvious psychopathology may not. Many marriages are already broken and beyond repair when we are first consulted. Psychoanalytic effectiveness depends, among other factors, on strong motivation to obtain help and in the trust that our patients place in us. Those who seek psychoanalytic help early generally stand a much greater chance of successfully working out their difficulties, and then may remain in their present marriage, happily after all. Patch-up jobs generally do not hold. Evidently, something more durable is required to make a relationship work harmoniously for a lifetime.

CONTENTS

The Marriage Relationship

DON D. JACKSON *and* ARTHUR M. BODIN

Paradoxical Communication and the Marital Paradox

It is the authors' contention that monogamous marriage, while no doubt a worthy social institution, is an exceedingly difficult state for two individuals to maintain for any prolonged period. This may well be because we have no comparable enduring human relationships to compare to marriage.[1] It is not justifiable to attribute marital difficulties to the features specific to monogamous marriage in our culture. Nevertheless, beyond the fact that any prolonged dyadic relationship for humans is difficult, we feel that the chances for disharmony in marriage are increased by certain basic paradoxes peculiar to the marital relationship. Paradoxes inherent in the marital relationship will be reflected in people's communication. The expression of such paradoxes is often among the reasons why spouses seek psychotherapy, and can, we suggest, also be utilized in marital therapy much as in the old homeopathic dictum: "*similia similibus curabantur*" or "like cures like."

Paradoxes in the Marital Situation

THE BASIC PARADOX

In our culture the game of romance is played during courtship, and if frictions develop after marriage, the man-on-the-street or newspaper-columnist kind of opinion is that the couple should return more forcefully to the principles observed during the courtship. This is essentially the hot-black-negligee and the cold-dry-martini routine. That is, the woman is supposed to be "feminine" and the man is supposed to be "masculine," and the combination of these positively and negatively charged attracting bodies collide together and fuse into a remarkably new atom.

The paradox is that the male-female-atomic-attraction theory of marriage inevitably leads to the battle of the sexes. When something goes wrong in the marriage, each spouse simplistically and reductionistically believes that he can explain the problem by attributing the difficulties to the temperament or biological properties of the opposite sex.

Men and women have anatomical differences and are usually (but not always) distinguishable from each other on sight. In most cultures they dress differently, although, like the birds, it is not always the women who wear the perfume, beads, and colors. Since men and women differ in outward appearances, it is natural to suppose that they differ from each other significantly in temperament as well. However, evidence for this is puzzling and even contradictory. It is difficult to study male and female temperaments because we do not have a sufficiently developed science of personality to begin with. That is, scientists have not pinpointed personality traits that are fixed and enduring and could be attributed solely to hereditary or constitutional facts, such as hormonal differences. Among other things, the fact that women bear children and are usually expected to rear them and that this requires a very different way of life from that of men also colors the picture and makes it difficult to know what is "inborn" and what is social. There is also the problem that the system is constantly defining the individual as well as being created by him: since it is "feminine" to wear perfume, wearing perfume makes one "feminine." There is considerable evidence that the female personality is much or more conditioned by Madison Avenue than it is by estrogen or progesterone, and when a book like *The Feminine Mystique* becomes the best-selling hardcover nonfiction book of 1964 (80,000 copies), it is obvious that many people have considerable interest in maintaining the battle of the sexes.

The major paradox involved in the battle of the sexes, or male versus female, is that the idea of complementarity and equality making a monogamous marriage work is fairly obscured by the very process of romance and courtship. For example, girls are told that boys will be "after it" and that they should not sell themselves too cheaply. If a boy does not try to "make" the girl, he is being less than manly since he is not behaving according to the image that the girl's mother has warned her about and the one that his mother has told him all men are like except that *he* shouldn't be that way. If she doesn't have to defend her virtue, then she feels either he is not very interested in her or he is biologically inept. On the other hand, if she has to defend her virtue, she may feel slightly disgusted with all men and increasingly so if she has to continue to repel advances. Although this particular set of mores appears to be changing, it is not so dead an issue as some optimists would like to think. For example, in a recent David Susskind show on national television there were six successful and beautiful career women from New York City. Five of them stated that they had had to watch out from their very first date and that they did so because a man would think less of them (if they didn't); only one of the girls maintained that she didn't think men were interested only in sex. Interestingly enough, in no case did any of the women indicate her own sexual desires or interests, and if any had done so, the majority of the audience probably would have considered it vulgar, cheap, or, to say the least, unusual.

When the couple who has been caught up in the myth of courtship marries, they are supposed to drop their arms and under a flag of truce begin to engage in a collaborative relationship. But in any dyadic relationship there is always the problem of who should be first and who should do what to whom, and thus it is natural if the young married couple falls back on the sexual myth they observed during their courtship. For example, one of us (D.J.) saw a young couple who were brought to the office by the wife's insistence; having arrived and got herself settled, she blurted out, "I think my husband is a homosexual." The young man nearly fell out of his chair and then became so indignant that he started to get up and leave. It turned out that he had not been making sexual advances toward his wife because he was openly angry with her and was "damned if he would be the one who always had to be responsible for things." The wife, who observed all the rules in making herself "feminine," could only assume that the lack of interest was biological on his part; and when she withdrew in horror from the implications of her "discovery," he assumed all the more that she was leaving everything up to him and he withdrew further.

THE SPONTANEITY MYTH

Another paradox that stems from the overstressing of sexual roles in the courtship is the problem of spontaneity. One of the things to treasure about romance is the unexpectedness of it. Certainly *there* he or she is—in a matter of moments the intricate dance begins and each is thrilled to find that the other knows the steps and adds some of his own. In an hour they have shared years and the future holds promise never dreamed of. Now the young people become spouses and finalize the treasuring of their meeting by a ritual called marriage. The spontaneity of romance is partially chilled by such noble phrases as "till death do you part." This is apt to be a little different from any other contract they have entered into. Certainly neither has ever gone to work for an employer saying, "I shall work for you for the rest of my life." For one thing, the prospective employee would assume that the employer would take advantage of such a statement, and unions have led the way in such contracts by tying employees' time-bound promises to cost-of-living increases, fewer working hours per week, and longer vacations as time goes on.

Yet, in the concept of marriage so common in our culture, two people are supposed to be romantically spontaneous in a context that is clearly formal and sharply delineated by law, custom, and tradition. The sexual myth is exciting, spontaneous encounters. The marital myth is long-term security and being able to count on the other person through sickness, poverty, or any other disaster. The unexpectedness of romance—his showing up with a bunch of violets when she didn't even know he was coming over—is replaced by a cultural encouragement to plan. The proscriptions on behavior and the prescriptions as to what kind of behavior seem enormous when compared to the apparent carefree days of the romance. It is not surprising that young husbands in locker rooms will paint women as calculating and even mercenary, while women over the bridge table worry about men being reliable and, above all, faithful. In simple terms, the paradox is that the individual who fulfills the romantic sexual role makes a damn poor model for a mate and yet he or she is supposed to accomplish this metamorphosis during the course of a wedding ceremony.

The kind of implications that such a paradox has can be demonstrated in a very simple, practical example. A young engineer is on his first trip away from his bride after six months of getting used to each other. He is going several thousand miles away to the national meeting of the Society for Eager Engineers and Resolute Scientists, and he knows his bride is a little concerned about his partying with some of his old college chums or perhaps getting drunk with a possible client or his slightly lecherous employer, who, being older and wiser, will insist that they invite some girls over. He wants to write home and tell his wife that all is going well and that he has had a few somewhat boozy parties but nothing untoward has occurred.

What are the likely strategies by which he can attempt to convey this? (1) He can tell how much he misses her and play down the social-life aspects of his trip. (2) He can thoroughly describe the social aspects in order to "come clean" and show that he is hiding nothing. (3) He can attempt a combination of (1) and (2), although this is likely to result in a very long letter.

On the other end of the communication line, how will his wife receive each of these three kinds of letters? The "I miss you" letter may reassure her about her importance to him, but the question may occur to her later, "Why doesn't he say what's going on—surely he doesn't think that I think he is in his hotel at 8:00 every evening." With the "I'm telling everything" type letter she may feel an initial warmth at his candor, but she may have some rebound in the nature of "Why is he so careful about putting in every little thing he has been doing? He mentions here that they had only three or four drinks —I've never known him to keep track like that before." With (3), which in some ways seems the ideal—that is, the "I miss you and here's what I've been doing" combination—the length of the letter and its over-all balance may be reassuring, but the thought, unfortunately, can occur, "Is this the product of a guilty conscience?" Some of you may feel that thanks to Alexander Graham Bell there is a solution to this problem—but wait! What does she think about his spending the money to call long-distance? Is he feeling guilty? Is he too lazy to write? Does he want to be sure to get through to her before she hears it from somebody else? And if he sounds too nice and warm on the phone, then it means he's feeling good and isn't missing her enough, and if he sounds rather down, she may worry that he is not living up to the performance of his peers, or worse yet, that he is merely hungover.

These examples are deliberately overstated to make a point. They do contain, we believe, a basic truth. It is paradoxical to expect spouses to come together because they are romantically and sexually attracted to each other and yet to turn off this charm, thoughtfulness, virility, or whatever just because they have entered into a legal contract. If a woman feels that her husband is charming and attractive and therefore worthy of her marrying him, she must by the same token admit to herself that he may be attractive to other women. In fact, if he is not, she will feel deprecated. On the other hand, if the spouses turn off the romantic game as soon as they are married, each may be disappointed by the change of affairs in their lack of spontaneity, and the disappointment in each other may make itself felt through other humdrum items that marital couples can build up into a Peloponnesian War. It is interesting, as mentioned earlier, that the prescribers of How to Achieve Marital Bliss are often alike in recommending a return to the pre-married state as though that were not a contradiction of the very marriage vows that are supposed to keep the marriage secure and monogamous. If the husband falls for the martini and negligee bit with her, what is the wife to think when he is away traveling? If the husband demonstrates his commitment to the marriage by being thoughtful with little presents, what is the wife to think when, as inevitably it must, the thoughtfulness decreases or he just plain forgets? And if she sees this as a natural trait in him and one of the things that endeared him to her, then she can only assume that he is not now being thoughtful because the marriage has grown cold. Married couples are supposed to be equal and mutually respecting. How is this possible when the spouses have also been taught that the sexes are different, don't think alike, can never understand each other, that men are stronger and more dominating than women, that men are little boys when they get ill, and so on through hundreds of cultural myths?

Paradoxes of Marital Communication

CONTEXTUAL CUES

One of the main myths about marriage is its irrevocability, as is shown by the 70 percent divorce rate in San Mateo County, California, and by the incredulous reaction this statistic generally evokes. Yet the continuance of a marriage is evidence of a decision against its disruption, just as surely as the existence of an adult person is evidence of a decision against suicide. These existential truths were presaged by a

German proverb: "Keine Antwort is auch eine Antwort" (No answer is also an answer). Two principles are inherent in this saying: (1) the absence of manifest meaning does not preclude inferences about latent meaning; and (2), as Watzlawick pointed out, "One cannot *not* communicate."[2]

The covert meaning of ostensible "noncommunication" is qualified largely by contextual cues. For example, if a husband has been hiding behind a newspaper and his wife pleadingly asks him to show his face and converse with her, his continued silence is taken by her not as a "non-answer" but as a rejection of her appeal. On the other hand, she might be trying to concentrate on the crossword puzzle while he distracts her with a play-by-play recount of a football game from which he has just returned. If she asks him to stop chattering and he complies, his silence is taken by her not as a "non-answer" but as an acceptance of her appeal for quiet. In either instance the situational context contains cues essential to a correct interpretation of the husband's silence.

The marital situation itself may be an inescapable and crucial contextual cue in many husband-wife communications. Thus, a compliment may be met with a half-serious protest, "You're only saying that because we're married and stuck with each other!" Russell recognized the underlying paradox when he wrote, in *Marriage and Morals:* "There is another difficulty in the way of modern marriage which is felt especially by those who are most conscious of the value of love. Love can flourish only as long as it is free and spontaneous; it tends to be killed by the thought that it is a duty. To say that it is your duty to love so-and-so is the surest way to cause you to hate him or her."[3]

One salient feature of paradoxical communication in a workable marriage is the delicacy of its function, since the marital relationship is defined as one which is supposed to last and which is supposed to provide a degree of mutual respect and appreciation not to be counted on from other sources. Such a relationship has more to lose by disruptive derogation than does a casual gathering of strangers or of co-workers not dependent on each other for social satisfactions or a group of social friends not dependent on each other for team work in accomplishing any task beyond mutually enhancing the enjoyment of leisure.

While marital relationships have much to lose by disruptive communications, they have more trouble avoiding disruptive communication because of the following factors: (1) mutual expectations are high and easily disappointed; (2) prolonged intimacy provides a backlog of shared experiences which may suddenly come to mind as possible negative qualifications intended to nullify a covert message. Thus, a promise may be construed in marriage as a mere attempt at placation if similar promises have been broken in the past. This is obvious in marital therapy when one partner tries to change and the other maintains a negative skepticism such as suggested by the remark, "Well, why didn't you try that (or say that) twenty years ago?"

It is not merely the expectation of permanence that makes marital communication such a delicate matter. It is also the history of shared experiences, making for private traditions, which may make an ostensibly simple communication more ambiguous for the marital partners than for an outsider who is not familiar with the myriad details of daily living that have been shared by a couple and that may add covert dimensions or levels of meaning to even the simplest-sounding statement.

Thus, marital communication is complicated not only by the expectation of a shared future but also by the actual experiencing of a shared past. Both of these factors may be considered ramifications of the temporal continuity of the marital situation. Other properties, however, are inherent in the marital situation. For example, the couple, and eventually their children, comprise a very special kind of small group having many of the properties of a "system." What happens to one member or component of the system affects all other members of the system; disruptive chaos is reduced by the evolution of rules for decision-making and even rules for making rules about decision-making. It is with the evolution of these rules for interpersonal transactions that we must make the leap from the level of individual analysis to the level of interpersonal analysis. An individual may be thought of as being governed by roles, but related individuals must somehow dovetail their functions. Reciprocal role relation may be one way of obtaining such interpersonal integration, but there are other ways. Complementarity, which may be considered another term for reciprocal role relations, may fail as a mode of adjustment if both mates want the same role at the same time and they have not agreed upon procedure for deciding which one's wishes take precedence. In this case, their interaction seems to shift from a complementary basis to a symmetrical basis. The nature of a symmetrical relationship was vividly portrayed in the song in *Annie Get Your Gun* stating: "Anything you can do I can do better." When such a shift from a complementary to a symmetrical mode of relating has occurred, some couples are utterly unable to cope with the problem of interrupting the ensuing escalation. To do so, they would require a rule about making rules, i.e., a meta-rule. This is a difficult type of rule to agree upon, not only because people are generally emotionally excited when the need for one arises, but also because people are not accustomed to having discussions the *content* of which is the *process* of their other discussions. In work settings and other situations having clear role definition, job descriptions, and reward systems, there is less opportunity to confuse levels of meaning in intra-organizational or interpersonal communication than there is in the marital system. Since at least one of the mates is accustomed to the relatively clearly defined rules of the work-a-day world, the comparative ambiguity prevailing in the marital situation may be a source of confusion and frustration. In other words, the marital system is not a closed system; its members may also have membership in other systems with conflicting "demand characteristics,"[4] and they cannot help comparing their feelings in these two systems, though they may not be successful in analyzing the factors which make for less easily resolved conflicts in the marital situation.

BEYOND AMBIVALENCE AND AMBIGUITY

In order to appreciate exactly what is meant by paradoxical communication, it is important that this concept be differentiated from ambivalence. To begin with, the locus of ambivalence is within the individual, whereas the locus of paradoxical communication involves contradictory communication between two or more individuals, not by ambiguity within one logical level, but by inconsistency across levels. Weakland and Fry hinted at this fundamental distinction as follows: "Simple contradictions can occur only between two directly opposite messages at *the same level;* this is probably rather rare and not of major psychological importance."[5] Paradoxical communication derives its ambiguity from complex contradictions involving more than one level of meaning, and its locus is interpersonal, unlike ambivalence, which is intrapersonal.

A second distinction is that ambivalence implies bipolarity, whereas paradoxical communication implies at least bipolarity; the two poles of ambivalence are at the same logical level, whereas paradoxical communication may contain two, three, or an indeterminate number of additional logical levels, all of which may be contributing to the sense of paradox. One of the ramifications of the bipolarity of ambivalence is that it is generally associated with a conflict between two ends of an evaluative continuum such as has been found by Osgood, Suci, and Tannenbaum[6] in their research on the "Semantic Differential." Thus, ambivalence typically concerns conflicts which may be located on a good-bad, nice-awful, pleasant-unpleasant dimension. Paradoxical communication, on the other hand, contains a relationship message or command aspect as well as a report aspect, to use the terminology of Ruesch and Bateson in *Communication: The Social Matrix of Psychiatry.*[7] The report aspect of paradoxical communication is the facet that reflects the evaluative dimension; that is, a report on the good-bad differentiation being made. The command aspect, however, is more akin to the two other main dimensions found by Osgood, Suci, and Tannenbaum: the potency dimension and the activity dimension. In other words, the communicator is telling not only how he feels about something but what he feels the other person ought to do about it, if anything. He is indicating whether he thinks his evaluation calls for a strong or a weak response, an active or a passive response.

A third characteristic distinguishing ambivalence from paradoxical communication is the nature of the doubt involved. Ambivalence involves self-doubt, whereas paradoxical communication involves doubt from others, which, though it may have intrapsychic consequences such as self-doubt, arises from interpersonal causes, such as expressions of lack of confidence.

A fourth difference between ambivalence and paradoxical communication lies in the respective goals of these phenomena. Whereas ambivalence may serve to defend against one's own insight and action, paradoxical communication may serve to defend against the insight and action of others. For example, the doubt of an obsessive-compulsive person defends him against his own insight, and the vacillation of a Hamlet defends against the need to take decisive action; the doubt aroused by paradoxical communication occurs not so much in the communicator as in the recipient of his multilevel messages.

Everyday examples of paradoxical communication are likely to strike us as being a bit funny if we are not directly involved. In this respect, they have something in common with humor, which, through laughter, often provides an acceptable release from tension based on opposing ideas or impulses, at least one of which is forbidden. Humor generates tensions that are largely intrapsychic, though they may trigger simultaneous discharge of such tensions by members or individuals in a group. Paradoxical communication, on the other hand, appears to function as though it were designed to serve aims which at an interpersonal level are similar to those served by dream symbolism at an intrapsychic level: it represents without totally revealing, while it disguises without totally concealing. This delicate balance, attained intrapsychically by the distortions and elaborations of the "dreamwork," is achieved interpersonally by subtle disqualifications or complex contradictions and their resulting ambiguities in paradoxical communication.

There is something puzzling about paradoxical communication. Its powerful effects can best be neutralized by elucidating the processes by which it produces perplexity. A breakdown in metacommunication[8] (communication *about* communication) renders people prone to confuse discontinuous levels of meaning, such as the literal and metaphorical interpretations of a proverb. A well-functioning system of metacommunication, therefore, confers a specific immunity to confusion by paradoxical communication. In fact, from the phenomenological point of view, there must be something lacking in metacommunication in order for paradoxical communication to be experienced. There seems to be an inherently reciprocal relationship between these two types of communication that will be subject to empirical investigation when reliable techniques have been developed for identifying and rating these types of communication. In order to emphasize the complementarity of these concepts, it would be useful to have a term for paradoxical communication which is sufficiently parallel to the term *metacommunication* to indicate that both terms are disjunctive elements of a single set. For this purpose we had thought of inventing the term *paracommunication*, which combines the concept of *paradox* with that of *communication* while suggesting that the effect of such messages derives from something beside or beyond the content of the message *per se*, namely, the conjunctive relationship of two or more contradictory levels. The term, however, might easily be confounded with the term *paralanguage*, which Markel[9] describes as ". . . identifiable vocal phenomena that accompany the stream of speech . . . but cannot be analyzed as part of the phonemic or morphological structure of language."

Since our concern with communication involves increasing its clarity, we shall avoid introducing a term that might contribute a new source of confusion. Instead, we are coining the term *contracommuni-cation*, which suggests the integrally related ideas of *contra*dictory communication and of reluctance to communicate. Both these associations to the term *contracommunication* are appropriate individually, and to an even greater extent as components of the overall concept of contracommunication, which embraces the concepts of resistance to clear self-manifestation and paradoxical communication and, in addition, implies a causal relationship (between the former and the latter, in that order). If the hypothesis regarding this relationship is correct, then ratings of paradoxical communication (when these have been developed) ought to be positively correlated with scores on tests of "social desirability." Such tests have been variously interpreted as tapping "test reticence," "tendency to put one's best foot forward," and the "approval motive"—all of which have something in common with the term applied by Ford:[10] "defensiveness." Thus, a heuristic value of the term *contracommunication* is that it suggests the investigation of paradoxical communication as an interpersonal indicant of intrapersonal defensiveness.

THE SPECTRUM OF CONTRACOMMUNICATION

Having examined some of the paradoxical aspects of the marital situation, as well as their consequences in terms of increasing the potential for confused communication in marriage, we are ready to examine the vast range of contracommunication that typically occurs in marriage.

There are many shades of contracommunication, ranging from tact to sarcasm, from the gentlest kidding to the sharpest satire. Since contracommunication in marriage forms only one band in a whole spectrum of kinds of contracommunication, we must now try to identify some aspects of contracommunication in the marital context which distinguish it from contracommunication in other contexts.

Tact and kindness, motivated by benevolence and a little self-interest, stand at one end of the spectrum. Cunning and Machiavellism stand toward the other end of the spectrum, which is bounded by the suspicious and the guarded communication of a paranoid person, such as may be manifest in garbled speech or in a private language. Sometimes, only the passage of time will permit us to distinguish with any degree of confidence between the "normal" portion of the communicational continuum and the psychopathic or even psychotic end of the communication continuum.

Marriage, of course, is not the only situation in which such communication occurs. A very functional example of contracommunication outside the marital context is evident in the joke about the woman who seemed dissatisfied with the portrait a photographer had taken of her and asked him, "Do I really look as bad as this print?" to which the photographer replied, "Madam, the answer is in the negative." In this example, as in most puns, the nature of the split-level communication is obvious; it rests in the dual definition of a single word and the consequent *double-entendre* of the total message. It is not necessary, however, that one word contain the key to the multiple levels involved in contracommunication. For example, in the first session of a family whom one of the authors (A.B.) was seeing in conjoint therapy, the mother began by telling the son to tell the therapist what had happened that very day—namely, that the son had received a letter notifying him that he had flunked out of college. After dutifully acceding to the mother's request, the young man countered with a complaint of his own. He said, "I need more freedom, isn't that right, Ma?" The therapist wondered aloud why someone complaining about too little freedom would, in the same breath, concede that he had to ask his "Ma" whether his complaint was correct. With hindsight, the therapist appreciated another level of the son's message, namely, that he was demonstrating for the therapist his feeling that he had so little freedom that it was, in fact, necessary to ask his mother's permission to lodge a complaint against her.

CONCEDING VICTORY

The next example comes from some research on family interaction by one of the authors (A.B.).[11] A three-person negotiable game was being used to investigate coalition formation in family triads and accommodative versus exploitative strategies of play. The husband in the family in question was playing very accommodatively, much to the annoyance of his wife, who kept prodding him to become more aggressive. The husband was protesting in such words as "Why should I play for blood; this is my family, not a batch of strangers." His son, in coalition with the mother, was saying such things as "You'll never get ahead in business that way," which suggests that the son perceived his father's game behavior as analogous to some of his behavior outside the artificial laboratory situation. After some repetitive chiding from the mother-son coalition, the father finally said, "All right, I concede victory." Unlike a pun, the multiple levels of which are interpretable in terms of *semantics*, which explore the relationships between signs and significations, the father's message in this instance is interpretable in terms of *syntactics*, which explores the ways in which signs are combined. It is the peculiar combination of the word *concede* with the word *victory* that produces in the hearer the sense that something contradictory or paradoxical is occurring. The field of *pragmatics*, which explores how interpreters use signs in instrumental settings, holds the key to understanding this contracommunication. To dramatize the situation, the father might have said, in more explicit terms, "All right, *you win*, I concede victory." In other words, since the father clearly did not want victory in the game, his acquiescence in accepting a victory foisted upon him by his more overtly aggressive wife and son is tantamount to his losing the relationship struggle with them as to whether he should appear more aggressive than they do. A possible alternative interpretation of the father's statement at another level of meaning would run something like this: "Aha! I defeated you in something more important than the game. I demonstrated your inability to keep from pushing me into a one-down position which takes the form of my having to accept an unwanted victory."

CLAIMING DEFEAT

A common marital conflict takes the converse form of conceding victory. That is, each mate says, in effect, "I claim defeat." Classical mythology contains a prototype of this argument. According to Ovid, Jove, after drinking some wine, was "joking" with Juno as to which one got more pleasure from sexual intercourse, each one claiming to enjoy it less. They agreed to let their dispute be settled by Tiresias, the only individual qualified to ". . . know/ what love was like from either point of view," since he had spent a seven-year interlude as a woman. Unfortunately for Tiresias, he did not equivocate by paradoxically communicating his opinion: ". . . As umpire,/ He took the side of Jove and Juno/ Was a bad loser, and she said that umpires/ Were always blind, and made him so forever."[12]

The family therapist may do well to be cautioned by Tiresias's fate against introducing an extramarital coalition by taking sides when married couples vie to outdo each other in claiming defeat as indicated by such phrases as "I always get the short end of the stick," or "Sure you can stay calm! I've gotta knock myself out while you've got it easy," or, spoken with a broadening smile of triumph, "What do you mean I never smile? I think I have a perfect right not to be happy!" These complaints against the other marital partner were just a few of those voiced by a couple in conjoint therapy with one of the authors (A.B.). The mates seemed locked in a struggle characterized by an escalating series of symmetrical claims of being incontestably entitled to a feeling of defeat, in view of the spouse's lack of energy or appeal. Each mate, in turn, would dismiss the covert complaint by claiming that it was just such expressions of ingratitude that perpetuated and justified his or her own right to claim the deeper feeling of defeat. In an effort to enable these partners to arrest their endless escalation, the therapist told them the myth of Jove and Juno. The hope behind this approach was that the couple would find themselves laughing despite themselves and, in so doing, be forced to acknowledge that they had been cooperating, by tacit agreement, in playing games like those Berne[13] has named "If It Weren't For You," "See What You Made Me Do," and "Look How Hard I've Tried." What actually happened was more or less what the therapist had hoped. Husband and wife both burst out laughing, and when the husband regained his composure, he said, "I guess we've been playing the opposite of one-upmanship!" Thus he indicated his awareness that Potter's[14] principle of one-upmanship has a variant which is particularly difficult to counter decisively. We might name this stratagem the "Olympian One-Downsmanship Ploy" so as to highlight the paradox that underlies its potency.

Therapeutic Clarification of Contracommunication

The question will naturally arise at this point how the ability to recognize such contracommunication may be put to practical use in psychotherapy.

LABELING CONFLICTING LEVELS

One method of reducing the pressure of paradox is by clearly labeling its multiple levels *and* by exploring the implications of their having gone unlabeled for so long. Such an active form in intervention, of course, would hopefully be attempted as a jostling model only in the initial stages of therapy, being tapered off so that the family members could practice more overt and honest communication themselves in the later stages rather than relying upon the therapist for clarification.

INSTIGATING AWARENESS OF ABSURDITY

Another technique is to take the attitude that contracommunication in marriage is a defense against having to commit oneself to a potentially unpleasant or disapproved-of point of view. In effect, the communicator is straddling the fence. The best de-fence is a good off-fence! The confusing communicator may be induced to get his feet on the ground if the therapist reflects the absurdity of his fence-straddling position by paraphrasing it in exaggerated form so as to create an irresistibly ludicrous *reductio ad absurdum*. This tactic goads patients to some resolution of the paradoxes which paralyze their interaction. Similar approaches have been elucidated as *Strategies of Psychotherapy* by Haley, who wrote as follows: "The basic rule of brief psychotherapy would seem to be to encourage the symptom in such a way that the patient cannot continue to utilize it. One of the quickest methods is to persuade the patient to punish himself when he suffers from the symptom, thereby encouraging him to give up the symptom."[15]

SYMPTOM PRESCRIPTION

A third technique of intervention is that of "symptom prescription," based on asking one or more family members to carry out in literal, and therefore exaggerated, form one or another or perhaps even all of the apparent levels of the confusing communication. On its face this seems like a reasonable request since the therapist is merely asking the family member(s) to carry through on what has already been said by one or more of the family. But the patients may oppose the therapist's intervention on the grounds that it is silly to try harder to have symptoms that are already unpleasant enough. If this happens—fine. By the same token, if they balk at the therapeutic prescription because of their desire to remain independent of the therapist's influence, they must relinquish the symptom that he has prescribed and that they are already displaying. If the family dutifully follow the prescription to continue having and suffering from a designated habitual symptom—only more so—the situation soon becomes "runaway." When the exacerbated symptom exceeds the family's capacity for homeostatic tolerance, a severe "shake-up" occurs. When the dust settles, the air is finally clear enough for the family to see that a symptom has been brought under control the first time the family refused further toleration and substituted vigorous and determined opposition.

And finally, if they detect the therapeutic paradox and protest its imposition—wonderful: they have taken a significant step in learning to escape the effects of paralyzing contracommunication by exposing the nature of its "bind."

Conclusion

Paradoxical extremes constitute pressures for some kind of alleviating action by forcing a family to appreciate and deal with absurdities and their contracommunication, which has heretofore gone unquestioned, at least in the form of effective challenge. Thus, Eve did not have to let the matter drop when in response to her question to Adam, "Do you really love me?" he replied, "Who else?" As a masterful bit of obfuscation, Adam's reply is the father of all confusion between the intrapersonal level he had intended for Eve's comprehension and the broader interpersonal level he seems also to have had in mind.

A related incident occurred in the conjoint therapy of the same partners who practiced the Olympian One-Downmanship Ploy. The wife said that she could not get sexually excited by her husband because she was disgusted and angry about his having twelve bottles of beer every night. He retorted that he was "nerved up" by her habitually exaggerated calmness, punctuated by strident "hollering," and to embellish his gripe he asked, "Do you want a sick husband?" She countered symmetrically, "Do you want a sick wife?" Then she switched to a sympathetic tone and said she realized that he must really have been distressed, since "He didn't even touch a beer last night, and then you *know* he's sick." By this homeostatic[16] contracommunication, she told him that if he succeeds in ridding himself of one of his symptoms, she will consider its absence to be a new symptom. Soon the husband was telling his wife that one reason she could not excite him sexually was that she was too fat. Instantly she countered, "The only reason you woke me up in the middle of the night last Sunday is that I was the only thing around."

This article has been an attempt to develop a conceptual framework and to derive some technical tools for following, and perhaps disentangling, such confused strands of communication as those which have proved paradoxical and puzzling to therapists as well as their patients.

NOTES

1. Don D. Jackson, "Family Rules: The Marital *Quid pro Quo*," *Archives of General Psychiatry*, XII (1965), 589–594.
2. Paul Watzlawick, *An Anthology of Human Communication* (Palo Alto, Calif.: Science and Behavior Books, 1964), p. 2.
3. Bertrand Russell, *Marriage and Morals* (New York: Horace Liveright, 1929), p. 140.
4. Martin T. Orne, "On the Social Psychology of the Psychological Experiment: With Particular Reference to Demand Characteristics and Their Implications," *American Psychologist*, XVII (1962), 776–783.
5. John H. Weakland and William F. Fry, "Letters of Mothers of Schizophrenics," *American Journal of Orthopsychiatry*, IV (1962), 604–623.
6. Charles E. Osgood, George Suci, and Percy Tannenbaum, *The Measurement of Meaning* (Urbana: University of Illinois Press, 1957), pp. 1–20, 25–30.
7. Gregory Bateson and Jurgen Ruesch, *Communication: The Social Matrix of Psychiatry* (New York: W. W. Norton, 1951), pp. 179–181.
8. Gregory Bateson, Don D. Jackson, Jay Haley, and John Weakland, "Toward a Theory of Schizophrenia," *Behavioral Science*, I (1956), 251–264.
9. Norman Markel, "The Basic Principles of Linguistic Analysis," in E. P. Hollander and Raymond G. Hunt, eds., *Current Perspectives in Social Psychology* (New York: Oxford University Press, 1963), pp. 225–232.
10. LeRoy H. Ford, Jr., "A Forced-Choice, Acquiescence-Free, Social Desirability (Defensiveness) Scale," *Journal of Consulting Psychology*, XXVIII (1964), 475–476.
11. Arthur M. Bodin, "Family Interaction, Coalition, Disagreement, and Compromise in Problem, Normal, and Synthetic Family Triads" (Doctoral Dissertation, State University of New York at Buffalo, 1965).
12. Ovid, *Metamorphoses*, trans. Rolfe Humphries (Bloomington: Indiana University Press, 1955), Book III, lines 235–238.
13. Eric Berne, *Games People Play* (New York: Grove Press, 1964).
14. Stephen Potter, *Three-Upmanship* (New York: Holt, Rinehart and Winston, 1962).
15. Jay Haley, *Strategies of Psychotherapy* (New York: Grune & Stratton, 1963), p. 55.
16. Don D. Jackson, "The Question of Family Homeostasis," *Psychiatric Quarterly*, Suppl. Part I, XXXI (1957), 79–90.

A Psychoanalytic
Understanding of Monogamy

I propose to direct your attention to a point of view that we are not accustomed to think about in psychoanalytic theory or in practice: What are we studying when we study monogamy? Instead of using the microscope as we are accustomed to in psychoanalytic thinking, I shall invite you to use the telescope and survey the institution of monogamy from the point of view of social evolution. I ask you to do so, that you may get a new focus on what monogamy consists of—why humanity has elected it as the family pattern of choice. In connection with this, I make only one assumption, or invite you to make one assumption with me: different forms of patterning have different impacts upon all the participants in a marriage, including both statuses of sex differentiation and age. I shall try to account for the reasons why the monogamous form of marriage has persisted in spite of the many changes that have taken place in the past and are currently taking place within its structure. I am trying to discuss the problem from the point of view of social survival. It is not an irrelevant question.

In beginning a subject like this, we are sorely tempted to resort to what clues we can get from the study of our simian ancestors. Now, this can be very useful and it can be very misleading, because there must be differences; we are obviously not descended from our contemporaries. Evidently, things have happened to the human species, so that whatever we find among higher apes today does not necessarily have a bearing on man. Take as a brief example something that we know about simian social organization. An issue of *Life* magazine (February 19, 1965) carried an interesting description of life among monkeys and higher apes. The accompanying photographs of gorillas were of particular interest. From the description given by the author, who lived with the gorillas for a long time, it is apparent that they have no awareness of any form of social organization. Whatever organization they do have has no resemblance to a Cyclopean horde. The entire "organization" seems to be dedicated to the protection of the young. The female is of great importance during the time when she is the nutrient and the guardian of the young. After that, she ceases to be important. Another conspicuous feature is the absence of sexual jealousy. Males do not seem to mind the females around them having intercourse with other males. What does become important here, in this particularly rudimentary form of organization, is leadership. But leadership does not tend to preempt sexual privileges. If you wish, extrapolate from this. I shall show you evidence going back to the beginning of humanity (and humanity is very ancient: at least 1,700,000 years old) that the monogamous family suits humanity best, notwithstanding all the difficulties that arise from it. It therefore behooves us to find out the reason for its success.

Our simian ancestors worked themselves into a very serious predicament, biologically speaking. It is quite apparent from the life of the gorilla that if the female continued to have multiple births the chances of the survival of the individual unit, and of the group, would be greatly diminished. In the process of natural selection, and this is only a guess, those who had only single births stood the best chance for survival. The particular reason in simian life is that the motility of the young is severely restricted; the young have to cling to the mother in order to be carried with her and survive, because their life is divided into a nocturnal life, which is in trees, and a diurnal life, which is on the ground. Hominids and higher apes worked themselves into a serious predicament because there was no retreat possible from this pattern. The young were completely helpless, and a prolonged period of parental care was necessary while they developed a central nervous system capable of an infinite variety of adaptive patterns. (This was the reward for their prolonged infantile helplessness.) The hominid branch of the species undoubtedly had only one direction to go—by enhancing adaptability through a long protected period for the young in order to facilitate the development of this remarkable central nervous system. From this point on, I take the position that Dobzhansky does in his book *Mankind Evolving*. We do not speak of organic evolution as one thing and social evolution as another. They run concurrently.

Leaving our simian ancestors for the time being, let us look at the data furnished us by comparative anthropology. Familial patterning has infinite variety depending on a great many conditions that have nothing to do with sex. They have to do with conditions prevailing in the environment, and such conditions significantly affect function differentiation between male and female. Dobzhansky considers it highly probable that, going back 1,700,000 years, one can begin to recognize something that is human. Man was not accustomed to live in very large groups, and the easy accessibility of the female became an important factor. Once the likelihood of the accessibility of the female, or the proximity, or the constant being at hand all the time of the female has been lessened, the distribution of sexual opportunity also becomes important. Such a consideration as this makes it highly improbable that humanity originated with a Cyclopean horde. For purposes of human survival, the prime consideration that governed the homeostasis of a group, no matter how small, was cooperation. In a Cyclopean horde there is no social cooperation—at least not among the adult males.

The sea lion provides a beautiful illustration of a Cyclopean horde in operation. Some ten or twelve years ago, a motion picture was produced describing the life of sea lions during the mating season. It was a remarkable film and actually showed the primal father taking a beating and slinking off in disgrace. Several of the younger males then fought for the preemption of the females, and the strongest one won. The rest of them slunk around the periphery of the community. Why a Cyclopean horde among sea lions? It is a very effective way of propagating the species. You do not need families to propagate the species; families are needed for cooperation. The film also made the point that although the sexual privileges were preempted by the strong males, it was the female who went out hunting for food. One sequence in the movie followed a lone lion foraging for food and then returning to the community some hours later. The gathering of food is an individual undertaking and requires no cooperation. Under these conditions it is possible to have a Cyclopean horde, but not under the conditions that govern higher apes or humans.

When it became necessary to insure the protection of the helpless human for a protracted period, social organization had to follow. We do not know how many patterns of family organization have failed. We only know of those that succeed. If they succeed at all, they have to fulfill certain conditions. One is to distribute sexual opportunity with a fair degree of evenness, to insure the proximity of the female. Above all, the protection of the young must be insured, because the survival of the species depends on it. In the course of evolution, it is quite evident that some form of control over the sexual drive became necessary, particularly with respect to the young. The results were some form of sex custom, incest taboos, and particularly restrictions upon the sexually immature. Social control of sex became a necessity, because as culture developed, the requirements of what we can call by a euphemism "citizenship," or participation in the culture, became more and more complex. Today a serious discrepancy exists in man between the time of his sexual maturity and that of his social maturity. Sexual maturity comes at age eleven or twelve. There is no culture that I know of, however, in which social maturity is reached earlier than eighteen or twenty. In societies where fertility is high, the sexual behavior of the young during this interim has to be influenced in some way. In many of the primitive societies in the Pacific where promiscuity is permitted or even fostered among the young, fertility happens to be very low. The Trobriand Islanders, for example, do not begin to conceive until late in their teens, and of course they have no idea of the relation of sexual intercourse and paternity. When you mention that the two are related, they laugh at you. They say it isn't possible: they've been doing this all their lives; why suddenly do they impregnate somebody and a child is born as a result of this activity now and not before? They think it is a great joke. When you ask them what the true facts are, they will tell you that the ancestor opens the womb, etc.

Among fertile peoples (and they are particularly prominent in the Middle East, in contrast to the Pacific Islands), the necessity of training the young was soon discovered. How do you train the young? I suppose many expedients have been used to that end—and the one that proved the most effective was scaring the life out of them. Systematic discouragement was the norm, then; and in many instances, terrorization. That this practice existed very early in the cultures of the Middle East (those who are our immediate ancestors) was already on record in 2800 B.C. in *The Book of the Dead*, and at that time it was already considered to be very ancient. The prohibition of sexual activity to the immature (to say nothing of procreation) goes very far back in time. Masturbatory activity was discouraged as one of the things that made it impossible to enter the Halls of Osiris. These sex prohibitions have to do with the cohesiveness of the family; they have nothing to do with family patterning. Incest taboos, which are not altogether universal but very nearly so, also have to do, not with sex, but with maintaining internal harmony in the family and in the extended family. Monogamous marriage, with which Western society has been playing ducks and drakes for the past two centuries, may in the future present a special problem if we tamper with it: it has a high record of expediency for purposes of survival.

Let us now look at a society where circumstances have forced people into a form of marital patterning that has no resemblance to ours: polyandry as it exists in the Marquesan Islands. The system seems to work quite well and is in remarkable contrast to the monogamous family. Each woman has anywhere from three to six husbands. Only the poorest women are monogamous, and they are looked upon with contempt. The highest prestige goes to the family that has the highest wealth and therefore the largest number of husbands. Under these conditions, the female is the actual power in the community, because she has the right to withhold sexual opportunity. But she does not exercise this right. It is not in the interests of the group for any woman of a large male household to withhold sexual privileges from anybody. When she does that, she spoils cooperation, and the whole function of the family in this society is to preserve cooperation.

From psychoanalytic literature, it would seem that the hardest thing in the world to control is the sexual drive. As it turns out in this society, it is the easiest thing to control. One female shares five, six, as many as ten men, and the men accept this as natural. There are some indications, however, that this is not just a learned process. Under certain conditions the male wants exclusive use of or access to one female. This can be seen in the religious practices of these people. They have an institution called *Fanaua*, whereby, in exchange for exclusive sexual privileges after death, a man sells his magical powers, which a woman will use to destroy the fetus in another woman's womb. I remember telling a friend about this institution, and he said, "Well, that's no different from what it is in real life; this is the way they live. The female controls the whole situation: 'Now you do what I want you to and then you can have access to me.' "

But the female, in spite of all this, is held in very low esteem. She is looked upon with contempt and is treated with aloofness. Nobody bothers with her, because the survival of the community depends not on sexual satisfaction but on food-gathering; the cooperation of the males is of the essence. These people live largely by deep-sea fishing, which requires the cooperation of large teams, so there are all kinds of taboos that keep the males from fighting over females (though the men do get into fights when they get drunk).

Polyandry in these islands is the result of starvation. Periodically, there are two, three, or four successive years of poor fishing and consequent starvation; and although these people try to protect themselves by storing food in large quantities in great storehouses, the population is decimated during times of famine. One way they have figured out to survive is by killing off the female infants. When Dr. Linton was there and asked whether the female infants were really killed, it was denied. We know, however, that female babies are exposed and disappear, and that the tribes steal each other's children at night.

In this society, tensions do not exist among the males, as in Western society, but among the females. The women have a bitter time in their struggle for prestige, power, and what not, and they are furiously jealous of each other. One form of magic that they practice entails killing off the babies in the rival woman's womb. But in this society nobody suffers sexual want.

What are the weaknesses of this society? For one thing, the caretakers of the children are not the women. I feel this is a fatal weakness. The children are reared by the secondary husbands. The woman is too busy being courtesan to three or six males; she is primping and decorating herself, and spends very little time with the children. As a result, the relationship between the males and the children is very close, but the relationship between the mothers and the children is very poor. Moreover, children are educated very early in life in sensuality, but they develop no capacity for tenderness.

Other clues to the problems involved in this pattern of life are found in the folklore; for example, one-sided Oedipus stories: only incest between fathers and daughters; never between mothers and sons. The female is represented in folk tales as an evil creature who exploits the poor little boy sexually and threatens to annihilate him or devour him if he fails to satisfy. This is the equivalent of the Oedipus story in the Marquesan Islands. It may not be an accident that there is a high incidence of homosexuality in this society and that the activity of choice is fellatio.

I have great respect for the expediency shown by social evolution in the development of the monogamous family. This has been, ultimately, the basic pattern of all great societies that have survived—the Chinese, the Hebrew, the Greek, the Roman; I don't know of any great society that was polyandrous.

Polygamous societies must be considered a perversion of the monogamous pattern. Polygamy consists largely of the preemption of the females by the economically powerful males, as for example, in China, where the monogamous family is strongly entrenched, but concubines enjoy a special status. That is, there is the official wife and there are the concubines. Of course, the concubines have children: an easy way of creating a large family; in fact, to be plain about it, a slave class. What is the trouble with polygamy in these societies? The problems can be seen in the Middle East today. Polygamy does not offer equality of sexual opportunity nor does it foster cooperation among the males; and there are many males who stay on the outskirts of the society and do not take spouses. Because there are many bachelors, homosexuality is rampant.

I would like now to try to account for the success of monogamy, the family pattern that has been predominant in the great civilizations. It is the most plastic; it is capable of innumerable combinations into larger units—extrafamilial combines like clans, tribes, or phratries. And although many of these larger organizations have vanished, the family outlives all of them.

I believe that the monogamous family pattern has had the greatest success because it creates the most favorable conditions for the young. It favors development of those attributes that work out for the best interests of the society, notwithstanding the immediate difficulties it may create. The close proximity of the mother for a protracted period guarantees help for the child during the complicated process of growth. This fosters necessary dependency on the parent. It fosters the idea of the omnipotence of the child, as Ferenzi so effectively described it. The omnipotence of the child is an extremely important indicator that he has received good care, and children who lack this feeling do not fully mature, or they develop some very perverted form of omnipotent feeling. Close proximity of the mother also fosters the idea of the omnipotence of the parent and the subsequent idealization of the parent in religion—the antecedent of religion as an internal homeostat. In short, this style of family is best suited to the biological limitations of man.

The presence of one father is extremely important too. Monogamy makes him concentrate on his own group, which exercises a great egocentric pull upon the family as compared to nonfamilial societies. It makes for smaller but much more cohesive groups. Having many mothers and many fathers seems to have a confusing effect on the child, and probably prevents the development of strong attachments. Apparently children flourish best when they have one parent of each sex.

Here I must touch on a factor that has had a good deal of one-sided treatment in psychoanalytic literature. Freud pointed out some of the tensions that exist in a monogamous family, notably the Oedipus complex. The connotation attached to this complex is a sinister one—it's bad. Now, a family constellation can be found in every society, but not all such constellations have the configuration of the Oedipus complex. They differ according to social organization. For example, in Egyptian folklore there are no stories of father murders; there are sibling murders, however, because marriage between brother and sister was the prevailing form in Egyptian aristocracy (largely, I think, to perpetuate the inheritance of large estates).

As the social pattern varies, so does the family constellation. The Osiris saga deals with the struggle between two brothers. Set kills his brother Osiris, cutting his body into forty-two parts. Osiris's wife-sister Isis spends the rest of her life gathering together the forty-two parts, finding every one except the penis. In contrast, recall how the mother (female) is represented in the Marquesan folk legend—as a wicked, evil creature to be avoided.

Freud taught that the Oedipal complex in the monogamous family is the nuclear complex of all neuroses, but I am not altogether certain that this is the case. And Freud neglected to tell us some of the good effects of this monogamous family pattern: that it fosters dependency and encourages the development of effectiveness, that it is the basic factor in the formation of conscience, of ideal formation, and the process of identification with ideal formation, and that it fosters the feeling of omnipotence and religion. The chief boon of our monogamous type of social organization or social patterning is that it favors those emotions which make for the cohesiveness of society. All this in spite of the many tensions that exist within the confines of the family, including the Oedipus complex.

The point can be brought home by describing another monogamous society, one in which there is one mother and one father but in which the pattern fails. Owing to a capricious division of labor and the lack of ingenuity in inventing a cradle board, the mother abandons her child from sunrise until sunset, during which time the child shifts for himself or is taken care of by an older sibling, who, having been treated this way himself, has very little interest in taking care of his younger sibling. This systematic neglect on the part of the parent has disastrous results, both for the adaptation of the individual and for the society as a whole. We mentioned the idealization that is fostered by the monogamous family. The *form* of the family only offers the opportunity; it has to be filled by consistent parental care. *This* is the essence of the monogamous family. If that care is lacking, this pattern is worse than any of the others—people in the second monogamous society mentioned worship their ancestors. But do they? They do not have permanent figures of their deities; they do not have temples. Whenever an emergency arises, they get together, improvise an image of the deity, and, as soon as the emergency is over, throw it away. This practice has no resemblance to the Hebrew religion, none to the Christian religion; there is no permanent idealization. These are an anxiety-ridden people; they are filled with apprehension; they mistrust each other; and they are totally incapable of love.

The monogamous family pattern has favorable consequences for the family itself, for the offspring, and for the society as a whole. But monogamy carries no guarantee of permanent tenure. In the last two centuries, feminism and other influences have made serious inroads in our acceptance of monogamy as we have known it in the past. The role of the mother in the twentieth and twenty-first centuries has undergone many changes, for example. For the good of our society, we are going to have to remember the good that has accrued from the monogamous family and why, instinctively, society clings to it and raises as many obstacles as possible to its breakup.

I believe that Freudian psychology has had a good deal to do with the weakening of the family because it has emphasized not only pleasure but pleasure as the supreme objective of living—an idea which is not always in concert with the objective of a home. There social cohesion is of utmost importance—that is, the individual members of the family are not flying apart in all directions for their own ends.

In conclusion, then, let me say once more that monogamy has been one of the lucky strikes of humanity. A million and a half years of social evolution can't be wrong.

Changing Patterns
of Femininity:
Psychoanalytic Implications

There is probably no area in Freud's writings more fraught with theo-retical and clinical contradictions than his pronouncements concerning feminine psychophysiology. In what follows, I shall examine these pro-nouncements in the light of certain developments and changes in the behavioral patterns of twentieth-century women, with some considera-tion to the impact of these changes on the institution of Western marriage.

The exact nature of the relationship of primitive man and woman is shrouded in conjecture (the popular fantasy pictures a masterful cave-man dragging his willing and passively inert mate along the ground by her hair). We know, however, that since recorded history there has been no fixed pattern to this relationship. There is evidence to suggest that in most primitive nomadic communal societies, family descent was reckoned through the mothers (probably for the obvious reason that maternity, in contrast to paternity, could not be doubted), and clans were consequently organized along matrilineal lines. With the evolu-tion of agriculture, and the gradual development of private property, the transfer of property from father to son became a paramount socio-economic factor, and families began to be organized along patrilineal lines. The risk of false paternity was protected against by the development of the institution of wifely chastity, and gradually woman began to occupy a more and more subordinate role as a sexual chattel of man.

However, there has not been a straight line of social evolutionary development in the relationship between the sexes. The social status of woman has changed at various times both within the same society and in different societies. Thus, in ancient Greece up to the reign of Cecrops, families were matrilineal; women enjoyed considerable status and voted with men in the popular assembly. Yet subsequently, in the Platonic era, the position of the woman in the family became a degraded and depreciated one, and she was strictly confined to the home, without political or economic rights. There were important social and economic factors involved in these shifting vicissitudes, but they are beyond the purview of this chapter.

The Emancipation of Modern Woman

What concerns us more directly here is that in American and European history, up to the end of the eighteenth century, woman's position, for the most part, was distinctly subordinate to that of man. She was totally dependent upon him economically, had no vote and relatively few legal rights, and was denied access to formal education. Early in the nineteenth century, however, in the wake of the egalitarian spirit set into motion by the American and French revolutions and of the sociological changes engendered by the Industrial Revolution, women in England and America began, for the first time in modern history, to assert their prerogatives in relationship to men. Nevertheless, it was almost a hundred years before they obtained the right to vote and began to move toward fuller equality before the law. Even now, in the second half of the twentieth century, there are many states of the Union in which such equivalence does not exist; and the constitutional amendment on equal rights for men and women has repeatedly failed to pass Congress. Despite this, the decades since 1920 have seen remarkable changes in the status of women throughout the world. They are able to vote in most countries where voting franchises exist, to enter many professions previously reserved for men, and to move out of the confines of the home into the broader arena of social, cultural, and political life.

However, even within our lifetime there has been a discernible ebb and flow to this pattern. The "feminine revolt" that was so manifest in the twenties through the forties seems to have given way to the "feminine mystique" of the fifties. Where after World War I women were struggling to get out of the home, the current trend seems to be back to the home. A smaller percentage of college graduates today are women than were thirty years ago, and American women constitute a smaller proportion of the professional world today than they did then. (By contrast, women in some Eastern European countries have more than doubled their representation in professional occupations.)

The reasons for this apparent recession in the revolutionary upsurge of women in America are complex. Some classical Freudians would argue that the entire feminine revolution was essentially a neurotic outbreak of "penis envy" and that what we are now witnessing is a healthy return to "normal" patterns of femininity. Such a statement, however, merely attaches value-laden labels to the phenomenon without really explaining it. Indeed, there are those who claim[1] that the post-World War II popularity of Freudian theory in America has been in itself a potent factor in "pushing" American women back toward a more subordinate and passive role. While this view may have some validity, it seems more likely that certain broad socioeconomic factors have been involved, notably the gradual increase of automation and the pressure from men to push women out of the shrinking labor market except in those areas traditionally reserved for them (domestic work, secretarial and teaching positions, retail selling, and so forth). Friedan suggests that an additional factor may have been the increased awareness of American business and merchandising executives that "women will buy more things if they are kept in the under-used, nameless-yearning, energy-to-get-rid-of state of being housewives."[2]

Nonetheless, the increased emancipation of women that began in the twenties has left an important imprint on the relationship between the sexes that deserves our further consideration.

Changing Male-Female Relationships

What are some of the changes that have taken place?[3] By and large there has been a considerable relaxation of the social and sexual restrictions placed upon female children born after World War I. Little girls are now allowed to play more vigorously and competitively, with resultant greater muscular strength and athletic capability. During the preadolescent and adolescent years, contacts between the sexes have become freer, and adolescent as well as preadolescent petting occurs with much greater frequency than in previous decades. This increased freedom, both socially and sexually, has led to a higher degree of sophistication and self-confidence in young girls. This, combined with the earlier physiological maturation curves of most girls, tends to give them a considerable degree of relative dominance and mastery over boys of similar age levels, particularly during the adolescent years. Post-World War I mores have also accorded women greater freedom in taking the initiative in reaching out to men both socially and sexually, and as a result much feminine assertiveness that would have been dampened or totally inhibited by the convention of earlier eras has been enabled to flourish. Many other time-hallowed conventions have also changed. For example, it is no longer considered "unfeminine" for women to wear slacks, wear short hair, or smoke cigarettes.[4] Indeed, we are beginning to see evidences that before too long women will also be smoking cigars and pipes without loss of feminine status.

These changing conventions have been reflected in current patterns of marital relationships also. Women have tended to become more dominant in the home, in an interpersonal sense. Discipline, once the exclusive domain of the father, has been increasingly delegated to the mother. Indeed, in many homes it is now father rather than mother to whom the children turn for redress from discipline or as the "soft touch." Similarly, women are playing a more important role in family decision-making. The popular joke that wives make all the minor decisions (those concerning the family), while husbands make all the major ones (those concerning international relations), is a reflection of this shift in family dominance.

Another important indication of this shift in marital equilibrium has been the increasing emphasis upon female orgasm. In the Victorian era, "it was considered unfeminine for a woman to acknowledge or display sexual feelings of any kind, even in the conjugal relationship."[5] Now a significant proportion of women express their sexual desires quite openly and engage in the sexual act not as passive recipients but as active participants, indeed often taking the initiative in arousing the man. Sexual intercourse now is expected to culminate in orgasm for the woman no less than for the man, and failure to achieve orgasm is generally as disappointing to the woman as it would be to the man.

The changing status of women has had noteworthy reverberations outside the home also. The percentage of women in the American labor force (excluding the actual war years) has slowly but steadily increased in the past forty years. According to Bureau of Labor statistics for 1962, 24 million, or just over one-third of all working people for that year, were women.[6]

Thirty-six percent of all women were working women. Of these 24 million working women, moreover, less than 25 percent were single, and slightly over 20 percent were widowed, divorced, or separated. The remaining 56 percent, or 13½ million working women, were married and living with their husbands. These figures indicate that American women are assuming an increasingly important economic role in the family, not merely as the primary spenders of the family income, but also as wage earners. An additional factor in this growing economic importance is the fact that many women outlive their husbands and end up controlling their estates.

Because it is generally easier for Negro women to obtain work than it is for their husbands, the Negro woman in America is often the *only* wage earner in the family, and the Negro family therefore tends to be matriarchal, with the father occupying a depreciated status position. Although these effects are easily recognized in the Negro family, the corresponding, more subtle consequences in the white American family as a result of the economic factors described above are less easily recognizable but no less real.

Women who are not in the labor force also occupy a different psychological position than do men. The man who does not work in our society is apt to be left with a loss of identity and severe impairment of his morale; he generally becomes either depressed or apathetic, or aggressively antisocial.[7] The nonworking wife, however, still retains a meaningful identity as a wife and mother. She is thus able to use her leisure time more constructively. Increasing numbers of middle-class wives attend adult-education classes, read books, and participate in various artistic and creative activities. The result is that while many working husbands become progressively narrower in their areas of interest and knowledge, their wives become the chief purveyors of cultural and aesthetic interests in and outside the home. These factors tend also to increase the relative importance of the mother in the family vis-à-vis the father, and their effects upon the identifications formed by children in the family can be of great significance. It is possible.

for example, that they play a part in the increasing incidence of homosexuality in modern society; a common thread in the histories of many homosexuals is the identification with the "more cultured and aesthetically oriented mother."

The progressive technological development of society in the coming decades can be expected to have continuing important effects on the relations between the sexes. Not only does the increase in automation mean that women will become more and more able to do "men's jobs," but also the sharp decline in total jobs available is bound to mean an enormous increment in leisure time for both sexes, with profound changes in family relationships.

Psychoanalytic Implications

The classical psychoanalytic position on women as outlined by Freud[8] is too well known to require detailing here. Its salient features, however, can be outlined briefly as follows:

1. *Anatomy is fate.* The basic nature of woman is determined by her anatomy; most importantly by her discovery that she does not possess a penis.

2. *Penis envy.* All female children naturally envy males for having penises, and the desire for a penis is a universal fact of normal feminine psychology, only partially compensated for by giving birth to a male child. Helene Deutsch[9] asserts that penis envy is a natural consequence of the fact that the clitoris actually is "an inferior organ" in terms of its capacity to provide libidinal gratification, as well as for its lack of "the forward thrusting, penetrating qualities of the penis."[10]

3. *Masochism and passivity.* These are outgrowths of normal feminine development and are natural and essential components of healthy femininity.

4. *Faulty superego development.* Due to the fact that the feminine castration-complex (precipitated by the little girl's discovery that she has no penis) pushes the little girl *away* from her mother *into* an Oedipal attachment for her father, the little girl has greater difficulty than the boy in resolving the Oedipal complex. Consequently, she tends to develop a defective superego (because the latter presumably comes into being only as the "heir" of the repressed Oedipal complex). The result in women, according to Freud, is an inadequate sense of justice, a predisposition to envy, weaker social interests, and a lesser capacity for sublimation.

Let us now consider these formulations in the light of contemporary knowledge.

1. *"Anatomy is fate."* That the anatomical differences between the sexes must inevitably be reflected in some personality differences, regardless of variations in cultural patterns, would seem to be almost axiomatic. Differences in body image, in the experience of menstruation at puberty, in the subsequent monthly cyclical variations of endocrine function, and in the experiences of sexual intercourse, pregnancy, childbirth, and menopause are all aspects of bodily sensation and function that are uniquely different for the woman as compared to the man; and in the biological-environmental interaction that leads to personality formation, these *must* result in significant personality variances between the sexes. To deny this, and to argue, as some strongly oriented feminists have done, that personality differences between the sexes have *nothing* to do with biological differences but are *totally* a reflection of cultural factors is to miss the mark no less than do those who have overemphasized the importance of the biological factor.[11] The fact is that only by taking into consideration *both* the biological differences between the sexes *and* the variations in cultural reactions to these differences—that is, the *field situation*—can the personality similarities and dissimilarities between men and women, at any given time and place, be fully understood.

Even as sophisticated an observer as Erik Erikson tends to fall into the error of trying to derive some of woman's psychological characteristics *solely* from her anatomical structure. In his recent, beautifully written "Inner and Outer Space: Reflections on Womanhood,"[12] he advances the thesis that women are prone to be more concerned with "inner-space" as compared to men's greater preoccupation with "outer-space," and that this is somehow due to "the existence of a *productive inner-bodily space* safely set in the center of female form and carriage."[13] He presents as evidence for this conclusion the fact that in a study of 150 boys and 150 girls, aged ten to twelve, in which they were asked to construct a "scene" with toys on a table, two-thirds of the girls constructed *peaceful interior* scenes, while two-thirds of the boys constructed *aggressive exterior* scenes, or else structures with protruding walls. One need not question the accuracy of Erikson's observations to raise serious doubts concerning his conclusions that these differences derive somehow only from the anatomical differences between the sexes. What about the enormous multitude of acculturation factors—the toys, the games, the adult expectations, and so forth—that have played a part in shaping the fantasies, the perceptions, and the activities of these ten- to twelve-year-old children? Erikson himself notes that in almost one-third of the subjects the girls constructed "male" configurations and the boys constructed "female" configurations. Obviously these were the results of experiential, not anatomical, variations. The point, simply, is that to attempt to derive such differences solely from anatomical or physiological considerations inevitably results in oversimplifications. One must always take into consideration the interaction between these factors and the experiences they encounter in the environment—in time, place, family, and culture.

2. *"Penis envy."* It is, for example, a massive oversimplification to assume, as Freud did, that the lack of a penis must inevitably be considered as a defect by the female child, in all times and cultures. Clara Thompson[14] and others have quite correctly pointed out that the phenomenon of "penis envy" that Freud observed and described in his women patients was not a universal feminine occurrence but was related to the "culturally underprivileged" position that these women occupied. That this is so is confirmed by what has been happening to this phenomenon as the position of Western women has changed in the past four decades. Not only is it manifesting itself with much lesser intensity than it used to, but more and more psychoanalysts report that they do not even always find evidences of it. Meanwhile, another manifestation has begun to make its appearance with increasing frequency, a phenomenon in men which has been variously described as breast envy, womb envy, and woman envy, and which is derived from men's supposed jealousy of women's ability to bear and suckle children. In the past, when such a reaction was encountered in men, it was assumed to be deeply neurotic,[15] but now it is beginning to be described as a more "universal" phenomenon. But how is it possible that a clinical genius like Freud would have failed to recognize such a common aspect of male psychology? The answer, of course, is that it was *not* a frequent occurrence in his time, and has become so only as a consequence of the shifting equilibrium between the sexes. The fact is that womb envy, like penis envy, can only be understood by taking into consideration the total field situation in which it appears. The presence or absence of a penis may be regarded by the developing child as an asset *or* a deficit depending on the nature of the cues that he or she is getting from the environment. When a society places greater value on the birth of a son than on that of a daughter, children in the family become aware of this in a myriad subtle ways; the same is true when little boys

are accorded greater freedom of movement and play, and when fathers are accorded greater respect and deference than mothers. In such a society little girls, and later women, will inevitably manifest many indications of penis envy, while indications of woman envy in men will be relatively rare. On the other hand, when these conditions no longer hold true, or become reversed (as has begun to happen in Western society in recent decades), *then we can expect to find that unconscious manifestations of penis envy will begin to diminish, and those of woman envy will begin to increase.*

A male patient of mine—not a homosexual—grew up as the only boy and youngest child in a family of three children. The father was a relatively weak and incompetent person in contrast to the mother, who was a warm, competent, and dominant individual. The two older sisters were also extremely effective and assertive children. Little wonder that my patient recalled as a child strongly wishing he were a girl, and fantasying that the front of his body was smooth and penis-less just like his sisters'! *For his milieu,* his envy-reaction was no less "normal" than the penis envy of the little girl who grows up in a male-centered environment.

In this connection, Helene Deutsch's dismissal of the clitoris as "an inferior organ" in terms of its capability to provide libidinal gratification is a remarkable example of culturally influenced amblyopia, coming as it does from a woman. The actual fact, as Dickinson[16] has pointed out, is that although "the female organ is minute compared with the male organ . . . the size of its nerves . . . and nerve endings . . . compare strikingly with the same provision for the male. Indeed . . . the glans of the clitoris is demonstrably richer in nerves than the male glans, for the two stems of the dorsalis clitoridis are relatively three to four times as large as the equivalent nerves of the penis . . ." Little wonder that this "inferior organ" enables the orgastically potent female often to have multiple orgasms to every single orgasm of the male!

More recently, in the most definitive article to date on female sexuality in the psychoanalytic literature, Sherfey,[17] leaning heavily on the unprecedented and significant research findings of Masters and Johnson,[18] puts the finishing touch to the myth of clitoral inferiority. Not only is clitoral stimulation capable of producing multiple orgasms to an extent unknown in men (as many as twenty to fifty consecutive orgasms have been recorded within the span of an hour!), but also the average orgastic response in women is generally more prolonged than that of men and just as intense in terms of their muscular capacities.

3. *"Masochism and passivity."* The assumption that normal men are naturally dominant and aggressive, while normal women are naturally submissive and masochistic, is another myth that the changing patterns of relationship between the sexes has begun to dispel. Even the biological evidence has never justified these conclusions. It is well known that among lower animals the female of the species can be fully as vicious and aggressive as the male, while dominance per se, as biologists have long recognized, is not a simple sex-linked trait but depends on a number of variables, including relative size and strength, motivation, previous experiences, social setting, and so forth.[19]

A variant of this, the effort to justify this myth on the basis of the differences in roles in sexual intercourse, similarly fails to stand up under careful analysis. The common argument advanced here is that in the sexual act it is the male who must be the penetrator, while the woman is merely the recipient, and that the aggressivity of the male and the passivity of the female naturally follow from this.[20] The error here lies in confusing a *behavioral* phenomenon with a *motivational* one. A male can be a passive and submissive penetrator, while a female can be an aggressive and dominant recipient, in the sexual act. Indeed, recent researches[21] indicate that the female genital apparatus during orgasm is extremely active. Receptivity and passivity are not synonymous. It is a striking commentary on the power of a cultural prejudice that both male and female classical Freudians have always assumed that the vagina, as a hollow organ, *had* to be a passive receptacle, although they came to no such conclusions about either the mouth or the anus. "Oral" and "anal" aggression were readily recognized, but the same theoreticians, caught in the meshes of an unconscious common prejudice, were unable to see that, under certain conditions, the vagina too could be an aggressively seeking, grasping, holding, or expulsive organ. The analogy between the mouth and the vagina has, of course, been recognized unconsciously by many males in the symbolism of the "dentate vagina," but most psychoanalysts have tended merely to dismiss this as a neurotic construction, without recognizing the important kernel of truth that it contains.

An additional refutation of the myth of "normal feminine masochism" is that women who are passive and submissive in relation to men are *less* apt to be orgastically potent than those who are more assertive, self-confident, and dominant.[22]

It may be argued by some that one cannot ignore the impact of fantasy on character formation and that the sexual fantasies of men and women are inevitably different: the male adolescent's fantasies deal with penetration; the female's with presumably anxious fears of being penetrated, and deflorated. The experience of periodic menstruation with its bleeding also is supposed to contribute in some way to an inevitable masochistic inclination in women as compared to men. Perhaps. But here too I must caution that the psychological impact of what appear to be simple biological events in men cannot ever be divorced from their sociocultural context. Fantasies of being penetrated *may or may not* be associated with anxiety or masochistic implications. The little girl, relatively early in her life, under conflict-free circumstances, experiences the insertion of objects (or her finger) into her vagina as a pleasurable, not a painful experience. It is man, not woman, who assumes that to experience such penetration is painful and therefore masochistic. The fact that so many women in our culture are indeed apprehensive about their first sexual experience is not a biological inevitability but the result of a puritanical culture which in its effort to maintain a completely artificial sexual morality fills little children, and particularly little girls, with fears of sex as something dirty, sinful, and even dangerous. Even the bleeding of menstruation need not necessarily be anxiety-provoking. I have known a number of adolescent girls—and I am sure there are many—who welcomed their first menstrual period with tremendous elation and excitement and could not wait to tell their parents and friends that at last they had achieved the visible evidence of maturity. The fantasies and self-images of men and women are indeed different—and inevitably so, for both biological and cultural reasons—but these differences do not necessarily lead to sex-linked patterns of masochism or sadism.

4. *"Faulty superego development."* Nowhere does the cultural bias inherent in Freud's views about the nature of women become more apparent than in his bland assumption that women have less adequate superegos than men. (One is reminded of Professor Higgins's plaintive cry in *My Fair Lady:* "Why can't women be like men?") Certainly no objective mid-twentieth-century American behavioral scientist would seriously argue any longer that women inherently have a lesser sense of justice, a greater disposition to envy, weaker social interests, or a lesser capacity for sublimation than men. The record of women in England and America in the past four decades on behalf of social justice and human brotherhood compares more than favorably with that of men.

It is important to note, however, that Freud's views on women were not merely an outgrowth of his position as a nineteenth-century middle European male; they flowed quite logically from his theory about superego development. If they were in error, as they obviously were, his theory of superego development must also be fallacious. It simply cannot be that the development of the superego results only from the resolution of the Oedipus complex, as classical psychoanalytic theory has long held. This is not the place to enter into a detailed dissertation on how the personality phenomenon that Freud designated as superego comes into being, but suffice it to say that it is obviously an acculturation phenomenon that develops from the child's gradual incorporation of the do's and don't's from its environment—beginning from the time the child is first able to comprehend the significance of such interdictions. The impact of this acculturation process is felt by girls as fully and as early as it is by boys. Indeed, the evidence is that since, culturally, little girls are expected to be better behaved than little boys, the pressure of this process is *greater* upon girls than upon boys. As a result, as might be anticipated, females in our culture, at least in their early years, are apt to show evidence of *better* superego development than do males—the very reverse of Freud's theoretical assumption.

The Problem of Gender Role

Actually, much of what we have been talking about in this essay revolves around the problem of what modern social psychologists would call "gender role"—that is, what is considered "masculine" or "feminine" behavior. The fact is that gender-role patterns have varied widely in different times and in different cultures. As Opler[23] has put it:

> A Navajo Indian may be a he-man, a gambler, and a philanderer while dressing in bright blouses adorned with jeweled belts, necklaces, and bracelets. French courtiers in the retinues of effete monarchs were equally philanderers, though rouged, powdered, and bedecked with fine lace. The Andaman Islanders like to have the man sit on his wife's lap in fond greetings, and friends and relatives, of the same or opposite sex, greet one another in the same manner after absences, crying in the affected manner of the mid-Victorian woman. Like the Ute, they value premarital sexual experimentation and sexual prowess and technique in any later life period. Obviously, the style of social and sexual behavior is something of an amalgam and is culturally influenced.

Gender role and gender identity, although generally related to the biological sex of a child, actually are not shaped by biological factors but by cultural ones. Once the child's biological ascription is settled, a myriad of culturally defined cues begin to be presented to the developing infant which are designed to shape its gender identity to its assigned sex. Little girls are handled more gently than little boys, are given different toys to play with,[24] are expected to be quieter and cleaner, are spoken to in different tones, and are addressed in different terms. The little girl who wheedles is spoken of fondly as a "charmer" and a "coquette"; the little boy is told to stop being a baby and to act like a man. The little girl's clothes and hairdos are noticed, complimented, and fussed over. Not so the little boy's; he is more apt to be praised for his agility and courage. The girl is expected to help with "inside" chores (cleaning up, doing dishes); the boy, with "outside" ones (shoveling snow, mowing the lawn). So powerful are these acculturation processes that, as the Hampsons[25] have demonstrated, in certain cases of pseudo-hermaphroditism in which the child's biological sex is mistaken for that of the opposite sex the incorrect gender identity becomes so powerfully established by the age of two or three that it becomes psychologically destructive to the child to try to change it.

What is important to our present thesis, however, is not that this acculturation occurs, but that, as we have seen, its *content* can and does change. What we have been observing in recent decades is a gradual change in certain female gender-role patterns that have previously been traditional in Western culture.

The implications of these changing patterns extend beyond psychoanalytic theory to psychoanalytic therapy. Erich Fromm once observed that a psychoanalyst's value system would profoundly affect how he would treat a female patient who presented the problem of Nora in Ibsen's *Doll House*. If he held to classical psychoanalytical views concerning femininity, he would focus his interpretations upon her "penis envy" and her rejection of the "normal" feminine goals of wifehood and motherhood. On the other hand, if he were a feminist, he would, instead, focus upon her "healthy" rebellion against her husband's infantilization of her and would encourage her move out of the home as a laudable effort at self-realization. Still another alternative to these two extremes exists, however. One need not assume that motherhood and a fulfilling life in the outside world are incompatible, any more than fatherhood and such a life. In contrast to men, however, who are *expected* to combine these two aspects of life, women have alternatives now; they may or may not choose to combine them, and the choice is theirs. The task of the analyst is to help them make this choice, freely, without guilt, and in relationship to the realities of their specific life situations.

NOTES

1. Betty Friedan, *The Feminine Mystique* (New York: W. W. Norton, 1963).
2. *Ibid.*, p. 207.
3. The comments that follow refer to broad trends and are not intended as universal generalizations; obviously there are many individuals who do not fit into these patterns. The existence of these trends, however, regardless of their extent, is sufficient to document the points I shall be making.
4. An amusing sidelight on these changing patterns was afforded some years ago by a resolution passed by a Midwestern college fraternity forbidding cigarette smoking by any of its members on the grounds that it was too effeminate!
5. May Romm, "Sexuality and Homosexuality in Women," in J. Marmor, ed., *Sexual Inversion: The Multiple Roots of Homosexuality* (New York: Basic Books, 1965), p. 282.
6. Esther Peterson, "Working Women," *Daedalus*, Spring 1964, p. 672.
7. This fact may change in coming decades as increasing automation creates larger numbers of unemployed men. The traditional Puritan ethos associating personal identity with work identity may in time have to give way to a new ethos in which identities are based on other factors, such as specific cultural interests, or skills, and so forth.
8. Sigmund Freud, "The Psychology of Women," in *New Introductory Lectures on Psycho-analysis* (New York: W. W. Norton. 1933), pp. 153–185.
9. Helene Deutsch, *The Psychology of Women*, Vol. I (New York: Grune & Stratton, 1944), pp. 228 ff.
10. Freud believed also that genital erogenicity in the normal female, although first centered in the clitoris, eventually becomes transferred to the vagina, and that sexual orgasm in the mature, healthy female should be in response to vaginal rather than clitoral stimulation. I have discussed the reasons for questioning this theory in "Some Considerations Concerning Orgasm in the Female," *Psychosomatic Medicine*, XVI (1954), 240–245.
11. The reaction of feminists to the latter point of view, however, is under-

standable since the emphasis on innate differences has almost always been used to prove man's "inherent superiority."

12. Erik Erikson, "Inner and Outer Space: Reflection on Womanhood," *Daedalus*, Spring 1964, pp. 582–607.

13. *Ibid.*, p. 587.

14. Clara Thompson, "Penis Envy in Women," *Psychiatry*, VI (1943), 123–125.

15. As might have been expected in an androcentric culture, however, women's envy of men was always assumed to be normal and "natural"!

16. R. L. Dickinson, *Human Sex Anatomy*, 2nd ed. (Baltimore: Williams & Wilkins, 1949), p. 42.

17. Mary Jane Sherfey, "The Evolution and Nature of Female Sexuality in Relation to Psychoanalytic Theory," *Journal of the American Psychoanalytic Association*, XIV (1966), 28–128.

18. The researches of Masters and Johnson also explode with finality the fiction of the existence of a vaginal orgasm distinct from clitoral orgasm. Their studies reveal beyond a doubt that the nature of orgasm in the female is the same regardless of the stimulus that produces it, and consists of rhythmic contractions of extravaginal musculature against the greatly distended circumvaginal venous plexi and vestibular bulbs surrounding the lower third of the vagina. W. H. Masters and Virginia Johnson, *Human Sexual Response* (Boston: Little, Brown & Co., 1966).

19. According to Harlow (personal communication, 1965), in primates, *all other things being equal*, males tend to be dominant to females. If the female is larger and heavier, however, she may be dominant. In human beings, the significant variables in dominance behavior are much more complex and include social and psychological parameters as well as physical ones.

20. Even Erich Fromm, despite his strong cultural orientation, succumbed to this fallacy in his essay on "Sex and Character," *Psychiatry*, VI (1943), 21–32.

21. Masters and Johnson, *op. cit.*

22. A. H. Maslow, "Self-Esteem (Dominance-Feeling) and Sexuality in Women," *Journal of Social Psychology*, XVI (1942), 259–294.

23. M. Opler, "Anthropological and Cross-Cultural Aspects of Homosexuality," in Marmor, ed., *Sexual Inversion*, p. 116.

24. The assumption that all girls "naturally" prefer dolls to boys' toys is not borne out by objective studies. See Mirra Komarovsky, *Women in the Modern World* (Boston: Little, Brown & Co., 1953).

25. J. L. Hampson and Joan G. Hampson, "The Ontogenesis of Sexual Behavior in Man," in W. C. Young, ed., *Sex and Internal Secretions*, 3rd ed., Vol. II (Baltimore: Williams & Wilkins, 1961), pp. 1401–1432.

TOBY B. BIEBER *and*
IRVING BIEBER

4

Resistance to Marriage

Sociosexual behavior is regulated in all societies by one means or another, although standards may vary from casual permissiveness to extremes in restrictions and legalisms. In our own multifaceted culture, not only are there marked differences in courtship behavior, but the dating and mating practices open to young people may vary from family to family both in variety and in flexibility. Petting practices may start anywhere from pre-adolescence on; marriage may occur anywhere from adolescence on. There is no socially set time to marry, and, in general, one has a fairly broad choice of mate within certain age, class, and caste proscriptions. But for each socially evolved, sexually viable individual there is generally assumed to be a time to marry that is deemed appropriate. People are expected to marry and to continue to form the basic social unit, the family, which flows into the larger social organization ultimately comprising states and nations. Should an individual fail to follow the expected coupling pattern, the deviance may be rationalized by common sense or by magical explanations. We have found that failure to marry is rarely associated with the absence of marital opportunities per se; it is rather the consequence of conflict, fear, and inhibition. The thesis we shall develop is based on data derived from our experience over many years in clinical practice predominantly involving white patients of both sexes and on a systematic study of Negro unmarried mothers.

The earliest case report in the psychoanalytic literature illustrating resistance to marriage was contributed by Freud[1] in his paper "Those

Wrecked by Success." He described his own initial bewilderment with a patient who took ill when it became possible for her to fulfill a deeply rooted and long-cherished wish to marry her lover. Contrary to Freud's previous teachings, in which he had emphasized that the basic conditions for a neurosis were the deprivation and frustration of needs and satisfactions, he now found that the promise of *satisfaction* produced intense anxiety and severe psychiatric disturbance. His patient came from a sedate, middle-class family, and she found her life at home quite dull. Breaking away when very young, she proceeded to travel about the world and before long met an artist with whom she formed a relationship. They began to live together, and, after many happy years, the artist finally managed to reconcile his family who had been opposed to the match; he was then prepared to make the girl his legal wife. As Freud described it: "At that moment she began to go to pieces. She neglected the house of which she was now about to become the rightful mistress, imagined herself persecuted by his relatives who wanted to take her into the family, debarred her lover through her senseless jealousy from all social intercourse, hindered him in his artistic work and soon succumbed to an incurable mental illness."

This case had a great impact upon Freud, who, like most people, considered marriage to be particularly important for the woman and believed that she had a greater stake in it than the man, economically, psychologically, and biosocially. A belief still prevails that eager women must somehow skillfully coax and nudge hesitant men to the altar because they are reluctant to renounce their "freedom." Society has permitted men more leeway in sexual and marital conformities, largely because of their traditional role as economic provider. With insight emerging from psychoanalytic experience, it has become evident that men desire marriage no less than do women and that resistance to it reflects fears arising from beliefs associating marriage with danger and damage to self. Such fears keep a certain percentage of each sex from achieving marriage, although the view that women may neurotically resist marriage is less familiar.

The unmarried woman who enters treatment is usually concerned about her single state. She may wonder, "What do I do to spoil my chances?" Or she may be sensitively aware of her feelings of anxiety, uncertainty, or awkwardness when with men, but rarely suspects consciously that she fears and has been avoiding marriage. She may yearn for husband, home, and family, and in her own mind she is more than willing to marry—an accurate but only partial self-appraisal. The anxiety associated with marrying inhibits her and stymies the fulfillment of her wishes. The case histories of such women and their reports of current behavior reveal instance after instance of withdrawal from men. Dream content invariably exposes the anxiety, particularly about those men felt to be appropriate potential mates. Illustrative is the case of a young woman who showed the typical pattern of obsessiveness about finding a husband. A religious girl, she limited her choice to men who had similar interests in church activities. Her pastor and his wife were the patient's close friends. They arranged a date for her with a pastor of their acquaintance whom they liked and admired. The evening before the appointment, the patient had a nightmare in which she was being murdered. When she met the young man, he seemed unattractive and uninteresting to her. The following night there was no evidence of anxiety in her dreams. On the contrary, a feeling of relief was depicted in a scene in which she was being rescued.

Rationalizations among patients who have difficulties in marrying tend to consist of complaints that attractive, eligible partners are unavailable. The ratio of males to females in the United States is approximately even from adolescence through middle age.[2] At no age level is there the critical imbalance that may sometimes occur, as in France after World War I. A common rationalization noted particularly among women involves the conviction that one lacks the physical appeal necessary to attract the type of mate sought. Such a belief may be supported by failing to maximize physical assets or by sabotaging a sexually attractive appearance. Feelings of unacceptability may be painful, yet a self-image of sexual inferiority can be psychologically useful in that it may serve as a masochistic defense against fear of sexual involvement. This subtle but powerful mechanism of self-deception may occur where feelings of inadequacy are even more tolerable than is the anxiety about asserting frank sexual interest. Often patients unconsciously maneuver themselves into a position of being overlooked, so that, on the one hand, sexual fears may be concealed and, on the other, the resistance may be justified by invoking feelings of inadequacy. Some patients attempt to hold on to their self-esteem but will minimize the opposite sex by fault-finding and by hostile behavior that discourages contact. A frequent maneuver is the choice of a lover who is already married. But in some cases a satisfactory relationship may be developed as long as the liaison does not threaten to become binding in marriage, as Freud noted long ago. One case recently brought to our attention involved a couple with three children. They had been living together in a common-law arrangement for sixteen years. One might say that though they hadn't bought a ticket, they were surely on the train. All went well with them until they decided to move to a housing project, a move that required legal marriage. No sooner was this accomplished than the woman began to reject her husband, find fault with him, provoke discord, and finally demand a divorce. The husband's despair, confusion, and rage at this unexpected turn of events precipitated a depression that required him to be hospitalized.

The drama and inherent tragedy of illegitimacy have always attracted the attention of writers, humanitarians, and, in recent decades, social and behavioral scientists. The basic question underlying the vast literature and research has been: why the pregnancy? Conclusions have included the acting out of an unconscious wish to have a child, rebellion against authority, the combination of a weak ego and extreme dependency upon the man, and the need to gratify the Oedipal wish. In past clinical work, groups of married mothers were not systematically compared with unwed mothers to determine differences and similarities. Instead, the research was focused upon some given population of unwed mothers and generalizations were based upon the findings. The differences in motivation toward pregnancy between unwed mothers and comparison groups of married mothers were not evaluated. A married mother may bear children for neurotic motives, as seen in attempts to forestall the dissolution of a marriage, while an unwed mother may want a baby because she loves children. It is self-evident that unwed mothers are heterogeneous and that *the* unwed mother is a fictitious character. There are wide variations from sample to sample in background, personality, and motivation. In a formal study, T. Bieber[3] compared two groups of pregnant Negro women differentiated by a single variable: one group was married; the other was not. The average age was twenty and each girl was having her first child. Three salient findings emerged: (1) As soon as pregnancy became apparent, the unwed mothers showed evidences of sharp conflict and anxiety about having a permanent love relationship. The anxiety was displaced in a loss of interest in the putative father and in a resistance to marriage. (2) The unwed mothers showed evidences of shame and guilt about the pregnancy but nevertheless accepted the child, who was to remain with the unwed mother herself or with a close family member, i.e., mother, grandmother, sister (except in four of the forty-six unwed cases, where the child was being relinquished for adoption). (3) Significantly more of the unwed mothers came from broken, fatherless homes.

The relationship with the putative father as reported by the unwed mothers was hardly casual, yet more than half openly stated that they would not marry him. Most couples had known each other for two or three years; some had grown up together and had had very close affectional ties until the pregnancy. With this, the girls began to withdraw and cut themselves off from the man. In contrast, of the fifty-five married mothers studied, more than half had also become pregnant during courtship. But subjects in the latter group were psychologically able to marry their sexual mate and establish a nuclear family—father, mother, and child. Marital resistance among the unwed mothers was usually verbalized in vague and unrealistic terms. In a few instances the girls had had a liaison with a married man in which the possibility of marriage was remote or nonexistent. Undesirable characteristics in the lover seemed to become apparent to them only following the pregnancy. Some of the verbatim comments demonstrate the openness of the resistance and the need to minimize the man. "He's unreliable." "He's a Romeo." "He's not a man." One girl stated, "I had a chance to marry him but I wouldn't. He's a mamma's boy." Three girls in advanced stages of pregnancy, the youngest of whom was past seventeen, gave as a reason: "I'm too young to marry." Another girl said, "Oh, I keep putting off marriage." Several girls said, "I don't love him any more." Another said, "I couldn't stand him when I found out I was pregnant. If things get too bad, though, I might marry him." One girl was adamant: "I will not marry him under any circumstances." And another girl's comment was: "Married people, the way they act, the way you experience things you would rather be single yourself." The recurrent theme was: "I don't want to marry him; I can't stand him now."

It is sometimes argued that the high rate of Negro illegitimacy may be explained by their culture, which is said not to demand marriage; therefore, unwed motherhood is not looked upon with any particular disfavor. Consequently, without guilt, shame, and opprobrium as deterrents, young Negro women, more specifically those who are not members of the rising middle class, are deemed not to have anxiety about having an out-of-wedlock child.

This was hardly the situation found in this study of a low-income group. Toleration, among Negro families, of out-of-wedlock pregnancy is seemingly a myth and, like many myths, achieved widespread acceptance though it remained undemonstrated. These young women were ashamed, guilt-ridden, and depressed. For example, prior to pregnancy, about 80 percent in both the wed and the unwed group were regular churchgoers. Upon learning of their pregnancy, 60 percent of the unwed group discontinued church attendance, while less than one-quarter of the married subjects stopped attendance. The unwed girls felt ill at ease in the public setting of a church, with its halo effect of morality and virtue. Other emotional reactions included nervousness, worry, and preoccupation with delayed menses, reactions that significantly differentiated the unwed and the wed groups. Family disapproval was often bitter. "My father looks at me like I'm dirt." Or, "My mother will never forgive me." "My stepfather hates me . . . he disrespects me."

The unwed mothers did indeed feel themselves to be in an inferior, stigmatized situation; but even in many cases where the putative father was willing, the girls had too much anxiety about marrying to extricate themselves from the bind in which they found themselves.

The alienation between unwed mother and putative father may, of course, be reinforced by the man himself because of his own conflicts. Indeed, unwed fathers who share the same sort of fears of marriage may take off in panicky flight. However, when a pregnant girl panics about marriage and overtly or covertly blocks it, she cannot escape the biosocial consequences. In many instances, an unwed father would enter into marriage if encouraged to do so, in contradistinction to the stereotype that it is always the unwed mother who wants to marry while the man resists and defaults his responsibilities. In the Negro group studied, it was not uncommon for the putative father to pursue his reluctant pregnant sweetheart with offers of marriage. There is a prevailing idea that Negro men affiliated with the underprivileged stratum are unconcerned about abandoning their pregnant girlfriends. One case that was not part of the systematic study strikingly illustrates how erroneous this idea often is.

The patient came from the Harlem area rather than from Westchester, where the study was carried out. She was twenty-seven years old and gave the following history. At the age of fifteen she fell in love with a seventeen-year-old lad who, she said, reminded her of her father, to whom she was very attached. She soon became pregnant and gave birth to a girl. Her boyfriend was very eager to marry her, but she steadfastly refused, although her parents insisted she do so. When her father threatened to take the child from her, she married a much older man, with whom she did not cohabit. She continued her liaison with her lover and again became pregnant. Her marriage was annulled, but again she refused to marry her sweetheart, despite the fact that she knew she loved him. She wondered herself why she persistently refused to marry him. Again with family pressure, she relented, but announced that as far as she was concerned she was not really married. After marriage, her love for him waned. She consistently rejected him and tried to provoke him into leaving. She finally succeeded in driving him into an extramarital relationship and then proceeded to fight to get him back. Upon his return, she again began her rejecting, provoking behavior, and it was at this point that the couple sought help.

A proportion of the unmarried mothers comprising less than half the sample stated, often with ambivalence, that they wanted to marry the putative father. Despite their claims, however, these girls appeared to behave in ways similar to the girl in the case reported above, though the rejection of the man was less dramatic and far more subtly communicated. The way in which the putative father was informed about the pregnancy is telling. He sometimes found out about it from a friend, or he "guessed," or the girl might casually drop a remark that she was pregnant but not necessarily that he was the father of the child. One couple would meet each morning to travel together to their jobs. One day the girl informed her lover that she was not feeling well and would not be taking the train with him any more. They met once or twice after this, but the pregnancy was not discussed. Before long, the man left the city. More than a few expectant fathers respond to a cue of rejection with the nonverbal counterstroke, "You can't fire me; I quit!" It was mostly in such cases that the putative father abandoned the unwed mother. At least half the married women in the study became pregnant before marriage. Certainly during the period of pregnancy without benefit of clergy, they were, in a technical sense, unwed mothers. The critical difference between the two groups localized itself in problems surrounding marital decision. Despite the urgencies of a pregnancy situation, marital resistance was clearly manifest among subjects in the unwed group.

As stated earlier, there were significant differences in family pathology. In the unwed sample, 60 percent of the girls came from broken, unstable families, in contrast to the married-mothers group, where 60 percent came from intact homes. However, among the married group, even when the parents had separated, most girls continued to see their father, and each girl had had a relationship with at least one paternal figure who had influenced her in some positive way. Such a relationship was entirely lacking among many of the unwed girls, who in the main were very closely bound to and overtly partisan toward their mothers and grandmothers, their main source of support. Nonetheless, ambivalence and hostility to them would find covert expression.

Under certain conditions of maternal dominance, a daughter's fears about marital commitment may arise as a consequence of the pathologic dependency the mother has induced. When a girl is reared in a fatherless home or in a home with a sporadically appearing father, or when the father cannot be consistently depended upon because the mother also dominates him and he does not provide protective support for his daughter, need fulfillment then falls to the mother almost exclusively. As a consequence, need satisfaction becomes linked to feminine sources. In situations where the mother is overdirective, controlling, and inhibiting, a daughter's realistic needs for security guarantees may steer her into submission and into developing unrealistic fears of assuming an independent feminine role. Under these conditions the girl may become afraid to enter into any sort of competition—real or imagined—with her fearsome mother. The fears are then generalized to include other women. Such a girl remains overly fearful of her mother and distrustful of men, so that marriage represents a double-barreled threat unless the man appears strong enough to be a protective figure as a counterforce to the mother's power. Among many low-income Negro families, the dynamics outlined are clearly discernible. The prestige impoverishment of the low-status male articulates with family disorganization and structures a situation in which the mother assumes prime control. Thus, social and economic deprivation may wield more influence on the high rate of Negro illegitimacy than do the assumed laissez-faire attitudes toward out-of-wedlock pregnancy said to stem from the mores of slave society.

In the Negro families studied, there often appeared to be a singular kind of double bind promoting conflict about marriage. This pattern was established by a type of mother who was quite prudish in verbalized sexual attitudes. On the one hand, she inculcated the idea that women must be on guard against men. "They want only one thing."

On the other, she subtly communicated the message that the daughter provide her with a child but not with a son-in-law. In fact, the first child is often given to the mother as a placatory gesture, and the girl goes on to found her own family later in life. The mother who promotes conflict about love and marriage tends to be extremely competitive with women and too envious of her daughter to allow her the love relationship of which she, the mother, was usually deprived. Nor is she a wifely model for patterning and identification. In breaking new ground, the daughter must supersede her mother, and this is too formidable an attempt for many. In all, it can be safely assumed that when an unwed mother cannot bring herself to legitimatize her child, her fears of marriage are far more complicated and intense than is her anxiety about facing the consequences of unwed motherhood.

Counterposed to the group who resist marriage but not childbearing are those unmarried women whose fears of bearing and rearing a child are a central factor in their unconscious avoidance of relationships that might lead to marriage. Such women sometimes marry after they have passed their childbearing years since it is only following this seemingly dangerous period that they can relax with men and become psychologically able to marry. The child may represent the rival, the incestuous object, the pinnacle of achievement, the monstrous self, or a treasure that would be stolen by jealous female predators. Whatever the belief systems associated with the symbolic meaning of having a child, they are strongly enough associated with threat to inhibit the pursuit of marriage and family life.

The unmarried woman undergoing psychoanalysis may repress or obsess a desire to marry, but the wish is regularly observed. A yearning for a consistent, meaningful, heterosexual love relationship coexists with the neurotic fear of having to compete for it with other women. Sexual competition is perceived as dangerous and damaging to the self because of (a) the frightening aggression such patients have been exposed to in life history, in particular from maternal sources; (b) pathological dependency upon the mother, especially in fatherless families; and (c) unrealistic beliefs that desirable men are scarce but accessible to stronger, superior women. Fears about sexual competition are expressed in the idea that the attainment of a love object excludes and deprives other women. Guilt that marital fulfillment can be achieved only at the expense of another woman, who is also perceived as a competitor, precipitates anticipation of retaliation, physical attack, and/or rejection. Thus, guilt, fear of attack, and dread of rejection inhibit marital strivings. In order to ward off the threat of reprisal, goal achievement is sacrificed. Many such renunciatory women are pathologically dependent upon other women. They usually have had rejecting mothers and, as adults, have an exaggerated need for love, acceptance, and approval from women they value but fear and compete with. Guilt-provoking mothers not infrequently produce daughters who are incapable of tolerating any situation that stimulates guilt associated with the maternal figure. Similar psychodynamic constellations may be observed among married patients who are involved in disturbed marriages.

Now the question arises why many are able to marry despite the same sort of neurotic difficulties that prevail among those who resist marriage. We can answer this question only incompletely. A quantitative explanation seems, at best, partial. Psychodynamic common denominators are hard to tease out; however, we offer the following schema. Some individuals develop a range of defensive and circumventive attitudes and behaviors that others cannot adopt because the defensive strategies they would use as psychological safeguards against the fears about marrying are incompatible with their personality organization and/or group affiliation. Some women are able to short-circuit inhibiting fears of other women by marrying a man perceived as powerful. The cue may be physical, intellectual, or social, in terms of status. In any event, the mate they choose is felt to be strong enough to defend them against threatening females, and he appears able to meet security expectations previously sought from women. Such a resolution is sometimes available to White women in our society. The social structure with its comparatively fluid class lines offers them the opportunity to make a hypergamous marriage, a movement upward, which, by and large, has been closed to low-income Negro women in whose constricted class stratum men occupy low positions of social esteem.

The solution of settling into a pathologically dependent marital relationship with a male perceived as strong or superior is unavailable to women who fear strong men or who reject pathological dependency and its concomitants—submission, self-minimization, and inhibition of effective resources. Some individuals make an exogamous marriage in which the mate is perceived as less than desirable to prime rivals of the in group. Such a marriage is often a way of denying or avoiding anxiety about incestuous feelings seen particularly in mixed marriages—

religious or racial. This type of solution is untenable where religious or group affiliation represents an important aspect of security operations. Another example of the circumventive maneuver is that of women who, even on a conscious level, make a compromise: they marry a man who will provide enough gratification to make the arrangement agreeable, while believing they have not made the *most* desirable choice; the *most* desirable choice is relinquished to the stronger, superior women, and in this way attack from them is avoided. On the reverse side of the coin are those unmarried women who, because of deep-seated feelings of inferiority or deprivation, must have what they consider to be *the* best. A compromise is intolerable.

One must also take into account the many women who do not marry but who may have a more realistic sense of their psychological limitations than do the many who enter into a marriage but soon get into marital difficulties and separate or divorce as sequelae of the very fears that create marital resistance. Those who marry precipitously often blind themselves to their anxieties and limitations and plunge into situations they cannot mediate.

The view that some women avoid marriage because they fear men as a result of early trauma has not been supported by our experience. We find, rather, that women who have had a destructive, fearsome, or brutal father will nonetheless tend to marry, especially if they have had a reasonably good maternal relationship. Not infrequently, a paternally intimidated woman will marry a gentle person, the very opposite of her father. If she is a masochistic character, she may marry a replica of her father; but she *will* marry and sometimes very early in life. A possible exception is that small group of women who fear sexual relations so much that men are avoided. In this connection we have come across two or three cases of women who managed to marry, yet remained virgins.

In the main, the psychodynamics underlying marital resistance among men are parallel to those in women. Though much less true these days, the problem of providing economic support continues to be a factor in resistance but not in the sense traditionally understood, namely, that of avoiding the burden of supporting a wife and family. Rather, men whose work inhibitions seriously sap their confidence about consistent performance may fear the demands for effectiveness implicit in the founding of a family. Men who conceive of marriage as limiting occupational mobility may fear entrapment in economic servitude. Men whose sexual or creative functioning are contingent upon freedom from economic dependence on an employer may be particularly vulnerable to the threat of economic strictures. Such dynamics, however, play a relatively minor part or are used as rationalizations. The central and decisive determinants of resistance to marriage among men, as among women, involve the psychodynamics described—in brief, where commitment to a mate is perceived as aggressive or competitive, constellations of irrational fears of retaliative attack create inhibitions against marriage.

Fear of reprisals may be viewed as *the final common path* into which a multiplicity of dynamic components has entered. The many contributing pathogenic features stemming from family pathology include unresolved Oedipal conflicts, sibling rivalry, pathological dependency, and feelings of helplessness about coping with aggression against the self. The psychoanalytic aim is to help the patient resolve his irrational fears of competition through a delineation and working through of the variegated psychodynamic constellations that set off the fears of reprisal and have led to inhibition and avoidance behavior.

NOTES

1. Sigmund Freud, "Some Character-Types Met with in Psycho-analytic Work," in *Collected Papers* (New York: Basic Books, 1959), Vol. IV.
2. Population Estimates, U. S. Bureau of Census, Series P25, No. 311, July 2, 1965.
3. Toby B. Bieber, *A Comparison Study of Negro Wed and Unwed Mothers* (Unpublished doctoral dissertation, Columbia University, 1963).

Psychodynamics of the Choice of a Mate

Marriages, contrary to a widely held belief, are not made in heaven. They are made on this earth by human beings whose fallibility is manifold and manifest.

The practicing analyst is confronted with the dismal side of marriage. In fact, the discordant, unhappy marital relationship is frequently what brings one or both marriage partners to the analyst's office. In the main it is not possible to understand the complex difficulties as they are presented without understanding at least some of the dynamics involved in mate selection. The intention here is to make a contribution to this very interesting topic by describing *some* of those dynamics which have been seen by this analyst in the course of the years. As they are presented here, all my conclusions, with the exception of one, are drawn from the analyses of my own patients or of patients of students under supervision, from their dreams, fantasies, or transference material. It should be borne in mind that this chapter will not concern itself with the analysis of the nature of love, but neither can it be written without acknowledging love as a vital factor in the selection of a mate.

The cultural views of our time take for granted that love and marriage are unified; this is succinctly expressed in the popular song "Love and Marriage Go Together like a Horse and Carriage." Without a detailed review of the cultural history of marriage, which would be beyond the scope of this chapter, it is important to bear in mind the fact that this unity has not always existed, that it is a relatively modern development in the history of marriage. In medieval times, love was not given to the spouse. The troubadour did not consider his wife a suitable recipient of his romantic feelings, which were instead given and openly expressed to the lady of his choice. Hugo Beigel,[1] in his paper "Romantic Love," states that as late as the early part of the eighteenth century the English novelist Samuel Richardson (1689–1761) first mentioned that love is needed for marriage. In short, the integration of love and marriage is the outcome of a long history of development. This integration, however, makes it possible for me to use "mate," "spouse," or "love object" as synonomous terms.

My emphasis is on some of the determining factors in the choice of a mate. This selection determines the cause and the outcome of the marriage and, in the cases the analyst sees, the detrimental or unfavorable outcome of the marriage. This selectivity is also a singularly human feature, not shared by the species of the animal kingdom, where the sexual instinct seeks fulfillment without any discrimination. Kubie[2] expresses my own views with the words, "It is a difficult and complex thing to be a human," and "Part of the capacity to be a human being is the capacity of one human being to love another." The mate choices, however, as we encounter them in our offices are motivated by intricate and complex unconscious reasonings that replace the adult mature capacity to love.

Let me begin with Plato's legend, which has it that the inhabitants of the earth were originally of one sex until they were split into halves and these two halves were forced to seek each other in order to reestablish the original unity. Plato's idea expresses intuitively a wisdom that psychoanalysis through studies and observation has confirmed; namely, somewhere in the beginning, in the early years of life, there was the trauma, and the need for repair and restoration is the compelling force for the search of the other half, the mate. The growing-up process is never free from frustration and injuries. Some people carry very light scars, while for others there are injuries of everlastingly crippling consequences. A good marriage of the parents is clearly one of the most important factors in the development of a relatively healthy personality of the child.

People emerge from their childhood with certain convictions about themselves and others. These convictions are based on childhood impressions that may have been correctly or incorrectly interpreted. Very frequently these convictions are responsible for the selection of a particular mate, as I hope to be able to demonstrate in the course of this chapter. They are outside the awareness of the individual, and they are so complex that I can only discuss certain facets of these motivations. They are sometimes contradictory in themselves, as they can serve more than one purpose and may be derived from several convictions, but they all have certain things in common:

1. They are unconscious.
2. They replace reality gratifications, which could be derived from the marriage, by strivings for fantasy fulfillment.
3. They can be traced to childhood experiences and situations.
4. They reveal to the discerning ear the mark of their origin.

In one of his papers belonging to the group "Contributions to the Psychology of Love," Freud[3] deals with a very specific object choice of men. Some men will invariably select only older married or engaged women, with the purpose of replacing the rival. The origin of this choice—the Oedipal situation. The purpose is self-evident. In the same paper, Freud describes men whose choice depends on the urge toward the moral salvation of the beloved. According to Freud, the origin of this choice is also in the Oedipal situation, demonstrating a fixation on the mother. Not explicit, but implicit, in this example are several points that will help to illustrate my views.

1. The sexual activity of the parents has been perceived by the child.
2. This impression has led to several convictions: (a) that the mother is unwillingly engaged in an activity which is immoral; (b) that the mother should be rescued from this immoral behavior; (c) that the mother should be saved by him.

The child's conviction about himself—as a consequence of this rescue-fantasy—is not stated by Freud, but I can safely surmise that it must be one of inferiority, because each task the individual sets for himself which cannot be fulfilled leaves him with a feeling of inadequacy or failure. The later choice of women of "easy virtue" in order to save them is therefore meant to correct one's self-image of inadequacy and reestablish one's own self-esteem.

The division of the mother's image into the good, the pure mother, and the morally debased and bad woman is well known. This wish for the virginal mother is expressed in the religious belief in the Immaculate Conception. A choice of the mate deeply influenced by this wish must, of necessity, become a basis for marital difficulties, because there is no human being who can live up to the degree of purity demanded by this fantasy. This same wish is sometimes responsible for the selection of an extremely young girl, her youth being considered a guarantee of her virginity, or for the choice of a very frigid woman, in which case her frigidity is interpreted as respectability equaling virginity. Sometimes extremely youthful partners are chosen by men who derive a greater feeling of security through ascribing to the very young woman a lack of sexual experience that will make comparisons impossible; these young women offer less of a challenge to the man who dreads rivalry situations—a dread that is based in the main on a severe incest taboo.

A desire for the parent of the opposite sex that succumbs to a severe incest taboo and leads to a denial of one's own forbidden wishes or a denial of the parent's sexual aspects may sometimes be the basis of the choice of a mate of a race or a religious group different from the one of the parents. Abraham coined the expression "neurotic exogamy" for these selections because they seem to follow the exogamic laws of primitive peoples for whom all women of the same clan or tribe as the man are "untouchable." Dynamically, these interracial or interfaith marriages in our society very often represent a compromise between the original desire and the antagonistic tendency—a kind of negative demonstration.

Two cases will illustrate these dynamics. The first is the case of a Jewish man married to a Gentile woman. He came to analysis mainly because of marital difficulties. Although the need for help was felt by him, there were many complaints about his wife, the chief one being her frigidity. When one day he was asked what had originally attracted him to his wife, he answered: "Her daintiness." This somewhat enigmatic answer became increasingly understandable in the course of his analysis. Daintiness equals purity. Purity, however, was associated by him with being Gentile. It meant that the woman was different from the unconscious, debased image of his mother. These equations are based on the following:

1. A screen memory. He reported that from the apartment where he lived as a child he could look across the street into the apartment of two spinsters. The spinsterhood of these two women was, of course, of great importance for the understanding of this screen memory. At first, emphasis was given to the appearance of the apartment, which was described by the patient as very "dainty" and/or "immaculately clean."

This screen memory was a remembrance and a denial of his impression of the primal scene. The actual memory came later, in a dream in which the parental bedroom was seen with the beds unmade and soiled and was described as being "dirty and messy."

2. Transference dreams in which I appeared as a nun. My appearing as a nun in these dreams followed the same principle of denial described before. For *his* protection he had to deny what he knew to be true, namely, that I was Jewish and married. His choice of a Gentile wife served the same purpose.

The second case in this series is that of a Gentile woman from an old Puritan family. She herself, however, twice chose a Jewish man as spouse. Whereas in the first case I mentioned, the choice expressed a need for the pure and a denial of the sexual mother, the choice in the second case was also for an object different from, but not equal to, the father image. Anti-Semitism (outside her awareness), making for contempt for any member of the Jewish group, was the condition *sine qua non* of her choice. Her choices were a blatant negative demonstration toward the mother. The choices were made to let the women of her clan (substitute mother figures) know that she did not strive for the men desirable to them. I shall relate a dream that occurred in the second year of her analysis, a condensation of many of the dynamics that enter into the choice of her Jewish mates.

In the dream, she was in a house of prostitution; the madam wore a necklace of a certain kind, a piece of jewelry that actually belonged to the patient's mother. The madam offered her a slice of lemon and responded with a great big smile when she accepted the offer. But the patient looked over to the analyst, who was also in the room, with feelings of apprehension. With the lemon she associated tea with lemon, a combination she had had for the first time in the house of her in-laws; lemon as an additive to the tea was regarded by the patient as a specifically Jewish custom.

At this point I shall stress only a few aspects of this dream. First, her apprehension about the analyst was based on her fear that I would discover her anti-Semitic attitude. Second, the lemon, according to the colloquial use of the word, meant "not much," "nothing very desirable." In order to please her mother, she had to accept for herself a man who in her own mind did not amount to much. Comparisons between her husband and her father had come up before; her conviction as expressed in the dream was that she had to accept a "lemon" in order to maintain the relationship to her mother.

Her choice also represented a holding on by the skin of her teeth to a heterosexual adaptation, because although the Jewish man did not represent the very masculine desirable aspects of the father, he still was a man, albeit a "castrated" one. Complete submission to the mother would have meant giving up all heterosexual wishes, would have led to a homosexual adaptation. The fact that her husband was circumcised made it possible to ascribe to him a female identification. In a dream, she found herself in his arms and enjoyed his caresses, but both she and her husband were seen as toothless (associations leading to circumcision).

A certain amount of contempt for the future spouse, which is sometimes conscious to varying degrees, plays a part in the specific choice of the mate when this choice is predominantly made to gratify a need to revenge early humiliation. The revenge motive influencing the choice of mate is quite frequent and sometimes seems to give credence to the words "Hell has no fury like a woman 'scorned.'" Humiliations received from an older brother or the father, or ridicule, especially of the little girl's sexual approaches, make for hostility that cannot be expressed by the child, for fear of repercussions.

To be sure, those sexual approaches have to be rejected by the father. But the consequences of the father's rejection of the little girl's sexual approach depend on the way this rejection is carried out. If it is done with respect for the child as an individual, it may even support the child's conviction of the father's basic love for her; if the rejection is associated with ridicule or teasing, she is bound to consider him an enemy, intentionally thwarting her, with the detrimental effect of her loss of confidence in herself as a woman. A hostile, vengeful attitude toward the whole male sex may then be the outcome, with the persistent wish to repair her hurt self-esteem through revenge on men.

The form that the revenge takes follows the *lex talionis:* You destroyed my self-image as a woman; I shall destroy your self-image as a man. When such a woman chooses a spouse, he is unconsciously, if not openly, viewed as clumsy, helpless, awkward—in short, as nonmasculine. It is self-evident that the woman will not, and cannot, respond sexually to such a mate. But she may be responsive to the point of orgasm with other men, who quite frequently are compared with the spouse, to the latter's detriment. The subjects for these revengeful attempts at reparation of the injured self-esteem will quite frequently be very different from the masculine father image because they have to lend themselves to the purpose for which they are chosen. The choice of mate will therefore fall on a man who because of his own problem is not very assertive or masculinely aggressive to start with. Furthermore, his considerateness, tenderness, compassion, and even faithfulness are interpreted as weakness and lack of maturity. And so a "weak man" is chosen, against the woman's awareness that she wishes for a strong masculine mate, but she sacrifices these wishes in favor of her wish for revenge.

The counterpart of a woman who makes such choices is a man whose choice of spouse is predominantly determined by wishes for revenge toward his mother and later her substitutes. In the cases I have seen, the man sought out and married a woman who was considered quite superior by others around him and even by himself. His ensuing impotence was meant to express that as a woman he considered her anything but desirable, in spite of other people's high regard for her. In these cases, the mother's rejection of the Oedipal wishes and particularly her way of dealing with her son were bound to destroy his confidence in his masculine competency, leaving him with a feeling of inadequacy as a male. Such a man seeks a woman whose feminine desirability he can deny and whose confidence he can shake via their sexual life.

All the examples given so far are the outcome of the Oedipal situation; while Freud, by and large, considered the Oedipal situation the core of neurosis, he did not consider it the sole basis for object choice. In his paper on narcissism, Freud[4] postulates two types of choice of the love object: (1) the anaclitic, and (2) the narcissistic choice. By anaclitic, Freud means the choice according to the model of the one who first tended and protected the child. This formulation places the origin of the mate choice in a developmental phase which precedes the Oedipal situation. Elsewhere,[5] Freud says: "Not without good reason is the sucking of the child at the breasts of the mother the model of every love relationship."

Nobody, certainly, can accuse Freud of minimizing the power of the sexual drive; however, in this formulation, he acknowledges the human being's need for giving and receiving warmth, affection, and tenderness as an integral and normal part of his love relationships. Anticipation of a frustration of these needs is at the basis of the fear of having to lead a lonely life, a dread that sometimes leads to a completely indiscriminate mate choice.

The blissful, peaceful image of the child nursing at the mother's breast does not, however, always correspond to the reality of the given situation. There are those children whose mother's milk, figuratively speaking, went sour on them, who were rejected by their mothers from the day they were born. They emerge from childhood with needs for nurture that are so magnified that they appear in the character structure as "greed" and "insatiability," bringing with them the conviction that it should be possible to force an ungiving person into a giving mother—even if the object has to be devoured for this purpose. That these hopes and convictions can play a role in the selection of a mate, I shall try to demonstrate with a few simplified examples.

A young woman started treatment with a male analyst at a time when she and her husband had almost decided on a divorce. Her main complaints about her husband were his stinginess, his undemonstrativeness, and a lack of expressions of endearment. She was an only child. Her mother had died when the child was two and a half years old. When she was asked by her analyst what she thought had originally attracted her to her husband, she reported an incident: On their first date, when they were dining out, her future husband selected an especially nice asparagus stalk from his plate and placed it on hers. She reported that she was deeply moved by this gesture and experienced a welling up of feelings of warmth and tenderness.

Her first dream in analysis was brief and very condensed: "I am sewing a button on a man's sweater." This represented her wish to change a man's chest (i.e., penis, originally the father's) into a mother's breast. Her choice of her spouse was predominantly motivated by her search for the lost mother; the mother's death had reinforced the original trauma of the loss of the breast, leaving no hope for a reestablishment of the nursing situation. The patient's inability to accept this finality led to the conviction that it would and in fact should be possible to get from the father (and later his substitute: her spouse) what she had been deprived of earlier. Her husband's gesture on their first date was unconsciously interpreted by her as a promise for fulfillment of her conviction. On a different level, her first dream also represented her hope for the analysis and the analyst: to help her change into a motherly, giving woman. This hope was also present in her choice of a spouse to whom she looked for a deliverance from her greed and her devouring tendencies via identification with a person whom she considered altruistic and giving.

Shamefacedly, patients sometimes admit that they chose their spouse because of the lure of wealth. Dynamically, this turns out to mean a reestablishing of the nursing situation, in which they were given only, without any demands being made upon them. When a patient of mine once exclaimed with bitterness that "he who marries a rich woman has to earn every penny of it," he was expressing his failure to fulfill this fantasy.

In cases of a very disturbed early mother-child relationship, sometimes aggravated by marked preference for a sibling, the hostility against and need for the mother fuse to produce wishes to devour the mother or, later on, the love object substituting for her. In people with weak ego-organization, the fear that they may be overrun by these devouring impulses makes for a choice of a partner who will not permit these impulses to be acted out. They, therefore, will select love objects who are detached and aloof, not only so that they cannot be devoured (figuratively) but so that they cannot even be touched.

Since hostile and destructive wishes are always felt as punishable, many defensive attempts are made not to let them emerge. In the following case these defenses influenced the choice of a profession in an almost classic way and also influenced the choice of spouse. The patient was the eldest of three siblings; a brother two years younger was the apple of the mother's eye. When the patient was eleven and a half years old, her mother gave birth to another male child. How traumatic the birth of this child was in an already disturbed mother-child relationship can be seen from the fact that the eleven-year-old girl developed complete amnesia of the pregnancy of her mother. But shortly after the birth of the younger brother, the patient became the greatest help to the mother in taking care of this child. There was not a trace of rivalry in her conscious awareness, neither to the mother nor to the baby brother. The rivalry was completely warded off, but analysis revealed that the little girl who had taken over the care of the baby had entertained the fantasy that it was her own child.

A memory confirmed the existence of such a fantasy. Once, while nobody else was home and she was holding the child on her lap, she opened her blouse to nurse the child at her own breast—but, of course, reality interfered here; her breast did not yield any milk, an experience that increased the child's feelings of inferiority and inadequacy. Her fantasy, in which the child had become her own, also fulfilled an old wish of hers to have a child by her father. Her mother's pregnancy, at a time when she herself could have had a child (she was already menstruating), reawakened her feelings of rejection by her father, but her hostility and rivalry could be kept repressed because they were replaced by her going out of her way to help her mother and this brother. Since this defensive maneuver proved useful at that time of her life, it was applied to later decisions in life: her choice of profession and her choice of mate.

As regards her choice of profession: In spite of toying with the idea of studying medicine, she preferred to become a nurse. (This decision, in view of her unfortunate earlier attempt "to nurse" her young brother, is quite interesting, but outside the scope of this chapter.)

With reference to her choice of husband: She not only married a man several years younger than she, but a man who, by virtue of his boyish face and figure, looked even younger than he was. Her salary as a nurse made it possible for him to get settled in his profession and pursue his scientific interest. In becoming more a mother to him than a wife, she repeated her earlier pattern; in becoming a nurse, she withdrew from all rivalry with men.

The marriage went quite well for a while, but when her husband became successful in his own right and did not need her as before, the marriage became discordant and troubled. An event, trivial in itself, highlighted all the previous issues and was the beginning of an understanding of the dynamics involved in her choice of mate. Her husband was to receive an honorary reward, and before leaving, came to her bedroom to say goodbye, dressed in a dark suit. At that moment she felt as if she had not ever seen her husband before. He appeared to be "a complete stranger." The boy had become a man. Her husband's success and his pride in his ability to earn his own money made it impossible for her to repeat the sham mother-child relationship that at the age of twelve had been such a good solution. The husband's success also stirred up the old repressed rivalry. Until then, she very willingly and generously had supported the household, but she now retrospectively begrudged him everything she had done for him, just as she had begrudged what her mother gave to her brother.

Vestiges of the early relationship to significant people in one's life can be recognized in similarities of the spouse to these people. A certain degree of attractiveness of the future spouse can be based on such similarities as the color of the eyes, the hair, a typical gait, and other external features. It seems, however, that these preferences do not become the cause of disturbance in the marriage, although they represent remnants of early attachments. If the selection of the spouse is based on the dominant wish to correct infantile traumata and is much less concerned with the reality qualities of the partner, the marriage is threatened.

I have tried to show that the choice of mate is not accidental or random but is deeply influenced by unconscious factors. The complexity of these factors has been stressed. In this chapter, the emphasis is upon motivations derived from the Oedipal or pre-Oedipal phases of development, from the convictions which were formed during these early years. It is suggested that these convictions can become the nucleus for the choice of a mate in later years.

NOTES

1. Hugo G. Beigel, "Romantic Love," *American Sociological Review*, XVI (June 1951), 329.
2. Lawrence S. Kubie, "Psychoanalysis and Marriage: Practical and Theoretical Issues," in Victor W. Eisenstein, ed., *Neurotic Interaction in Marriage* (New York: Basic Books, 1956).
3. Sigmund Freud, "Contributions to the Psychology of Love: A Special Type of Choice of Object Made by Men," in *Collected Papers* (New York: Basic Books, 1959), Vol. IV.
4. Sigmund Freud, "On Narcissism: An Introduction," in *Collected Papers* (New York: Basic Books, 1959), Vol. IV.
5. Edward Hitschmann, "Freud's Conception of Love," *The International Journal of Psychoanalysis*, XXXIII (1952), 421–428.

Irrational and Realistic
Expectations in Marriage

The ambitions, the anticipations, and the aspirations with which an individual enters marriage, and which he generally nurtures with a fervid fondness, can be examined from many points of view: sociological, philosophical, ethical-religious, etc. The ensuing remarks will be made from the psychoanalytic standpoint, which undoubtedly has a contribution to make to the subject distinctive of that discipline alone. There is no other method by which the minutiae of a marriage can be scrutinized in such detail, while a survey of the larger aspects of the relationship is being simultaneously carried out.

When considering the rational and irrational expectations that an individual entertains with respect to his marriage, the psychoanalyst must of necessity carry out a series of comparisons between the strivings displayed by his patient and a set of values and realistic possibilities that he, the analyst, has constructed for himself. Whence are such constructs derived? For his view of the composition of a healthy marriage, the psychoanalyst has available to him, first of all, the data from all the sources commonly accessible; he has (usually) been exposed to the marriage of his own parents, to the marriages he has observed in his family and in his social life, to the teachings of his religious advisers; and he may have a good deal of specialized knowledge from sociologic and anthropologic studies, and so on. He brings to this task, in addition, a fund of information specifically his own, available to the investigators of no other discipline, and originating in his detailed knowledge of object relations. It is from this special area of study that he obtains the data to construct his values for a successful marriage, which is a particular type of object relationship. It is no exaggeration that this is the most useful body of knowledge available for the understanding and the betterment of the marital relationship.

The rational and irrational expectations from life in general and psychoanalysis in particular have already been discussed by me.[1] In general, one may anticipate the greatest satisfactions in life if one is free to employ one's talents and abilities in the largest possible measure and with the fullest abundance of energy with which one is endowed. In this chapter, the expectations with which people enter marriage will be discussed from the standpoint of how these possibilities are influenced by the marital situation.

It is proposed herein to consider the expectations that may be fulfilled in marriage around the cardinal theme of the begetting and rearing of children. As Hendrick[2] has put it: "Mature sexuality becomes . . . associated with the love for the potential mate, tenderness, a need for reciprocated pleasure, and, in its fullest development, the desire for one particular partner's children." Helene Deutsch[3] states that a mature woman's sexuality extends beyond coital orgasm and is completely fulfilled only by childbirth; Hendrick[4] says, concerning the female: "Not only is orgasm sought, but conception has become the ultimate aim of the mature woman, while the active aims of her libido are fully satisfied in childbirth, the care of children and home, or in substitutes for maternity."

Now this may be considered a trite approach to our topic; after all, every one "knows" that marriages are contracted for the purpose of having children. Yet the reluctance to enter into the specifically procreative act is much more widespread than is generally acknowledged, and as Erikson[5] says, in the adult male "the inventory of significant object relations must . . . give account of the presence or absence of a drive to create and secure personal children—a matter much too frequently considered merely an extension, if not an impediment, of genitality." The most important, single, all-embracing feature of the usual marriage is that it is entered into for the biologic and cultural purpose of founding a new family. This fact is determined by the most basic and utterly inescapable physiologic and psychologic dicta. The two partners to a marriage have the ineluctable duty of collaborating to carry out a task that is not voluntarily assumed. It has been imposed by the strongest forces of nature; it may be opposed only under the heaviest of penalties. Whether or not a marriage remains childless, it is the attitude of the partners to this prime issue that will eventually determine the outcome of their joint venture. Inasmuch as we have all been children and have identified with our parents, we feel a psychologic necessity to create and rear children and thus to repeat and improve upon the performance of our forebears. Inasmuch as we are organically structured and instinctually driven as we are, we experience a similar biologic compulsion to fulfill our somatic destiny in the role of parents. The choice lies only in the selection of the partner, not in the nature of the work.

Thus two individuals enter upon a new stage in their biologic and cultural development, designated as marriage, for which each singly is inadequate. The object relationship is forced upon them. No sooner have they matured into adult life and become ostensibly capable of relinquishing the preceding object relationships that have been so heavily colored by dependency features, than they must perforce enter a new type of relationship in which the need for collaboration has all the stringency formerly characteristic of dependency gratifications. It is possible to classify marriage and its pathologic variations on the basis of the partners' attitudes toward each other with respect to the creating and rearing of children. Two people are most likely to make this their prime responsibility and to carry it out successfully if they are functioning on a level of maturity characterized by a generosity and solicitude for others in which each partner is of equal importance, and by full genitality in the sexual area. It cannot be fully accomplished by one person whose partner is derelict in his responsibilities to any marked degree. It does not require making either partner less important than the offspring. Departures from the ideal attitudes and objectives take the form of pathologic object relations that are detectable, although not so prominent, in the premarital separate existences of the partners.

In the pathologic object relationships that characterize unhealthy marriages, irrational expectations make their appearance as more or less distant departures from the one basic objective of the undertaking. They are reproduced in the marriage with the same inevitability that pertains to the appearance of transferences in psychoanalysis. The same irrational expectations with which individuals hope to gain infantile gratifications in analysis are the disturbing elements of unhappy marriage. The successful analysis of marital unhappiness depends on the detection, within the transference, of infantile strivings, their isolation and clear delineation as the factors responsible for the marital failure, and the demonstration of the advantages to be gained from relinquishing infantile objectives and from their replacement by the goals of mature collaboration.

The psychoanalyst now finds himself on familiar ground. In marital disturbances he is confronted by all the deviations from healthy object relationships that he has examined in other contexts, but now set in bold relief by their departure from the primary purpose of marriage. The essential feature of the unhealthy object relationships of marriage is that they replace the solicitous and basically generous attitudes of very active cooperation by drives to achieve objectives of a different nature. The emphasis is put on reward when the task has been lost from sight, and the anticipated reward has nothing to do with the task at hand.

We may now proceed to illustrate some of the types of unhealthy object relationships of marriage that are distinguished by their irrational expectations. The simplest and most prevalent form of such difficulty occurs when one or both partners has more or less marked feelings of inadequacy to cope with the demands and requirements of child rearing. The fear that one cannot measure up to the responsibilities of parenthood makes itself felt immediately in the sexual area. A fear of conception results in sexual pathophysiology in both male and female. The varieties of these fears and anxiety-provoked responses are multitudinous, and only a few can be discussed here.

In the male, the tense and apprehensive state induced by a fear of impregnation leads most often to premature ejaculation, which can reach the degree of *ejaculatio ante portas,* and sometimes even a condition of spermatorrhea in a situation that is not actually sexual, but only symbolically so. The picture of frustration thereby induced in both sexual partners is familiar to all psychoanalysts. The irrational expectation of such a male partner resides in his insisting upon full sexual gratification while attempting at all times to elude the purpose and responsibility of sexual intercourse. The emphasis here belongs on the phrase "at all times," since every sexual act is not entered upon for the purpose of procreation, even though the pleasurable and health-promoting value of each act of sexual intercourse may rest ultimately upon its connection with procreation. The expectation of sexual gratification, while attempting to evade its responsibilities, is patently clear in premature ejaculation, whose unconscious and repressed purpose is so obviously that of avoiding conception, even though it has other objectives as well. This irrational expectation on the part of the male leads to a host of other such expectations, each in its turn provocative of further difficulty in the marriage. The naïveté and immature efforts on the part of some sufferers from premature ejaculation to correct the difficulty are often striking. The partner may be expected to correct the trouble or may be held responsible for it. Marital infidelity, with the intention of finding a partner who will not "provoke" the disorder, is a common outcome, accompanied by the further irrational belief that the marital partner can be expected to accept the infidelity. The mastery of the fear of impregnation is essential to the correction of the sexual difficulty, as well as to the demolition of the complex structure of unrealistic demands that is founded upon it.

A seemingly antonymous form of sexual difficulty in the male, but one actually interchangeable with it and based on the same unconscious motive, is that of retarded ejaculation. It is more likely to be accompanied by erectile impotence. It occurs in individuals of predominantly obsessive or depressive personality constitution, and as they are liberated by psychoanalysis from their neuroses, they are likely to pass through a period of premature ejaculation before finally achieving a satisfactory sexual adjustment. It is thus discernible that premature ejaculation is a less regressive form of behavior than retarded ejaculation. In the latter the irrational expectations reveal more serious deviations than in the former. The male suffering from retarded ejaculation is devoted to the principle of a more or less loveless life and to the defense mechanism of avoiding disappointment by not attempting to win love. This is a negation of all the purposes for which a marriage is contracted, and it dashes the reasonable expectations of the partner.

In the female, anxiety about the role of parenthood results in a whole gamut of sexual derangements constituting the various forms of frigidity and infertility. There is no need to enter here into detailed descriptions of the anesthetic form of frigidity with its interference with orgasm, of vaginismus, and of dyspareunia. What is important is that frigidity, like impotence in the male, is designed to have both alloplastic and autoplastic effects, viz., the elimination of sexual pleasure for both partners and the failure of conception. As impotence in the male is sometimes accompanied by oligospermia and azoöspermia, so frigidity is often the precursor of dysmennorhea, irregularity of the menstrual cycle, habitual abortion, and infertility.[6] Clearly, individuals who enter marriage with unwholesome attitudes toward parenthood cannot expect to manifest healthy sexual physiology. Shades of Charles Darwin and natural selection! Appropriately enough, when such couples do conceive, they are the ones most likely to be tormented by fears of malformation of the fetus.

A married person who is ambivalent toward children, or who decides not to have them, must go through the experience of object loss. Even if he becomes a parent, the ego is at least partially involved in the giving up of the child, and this, of necessity, requires an identification with the lost object.[7] How is it possible to identify with an unborn child whom one has never seen? It is an identification with a fantasied child, an unhappy and unwanted child. The married person who does not want children has himself in childhood had traumatic experiences of a severe nature, usually with his parents or siblings. He envisions his own children going through such traumata, and he dreads reliving his own childhood through them. In his decision not to become a parent he identifies with fantasied unhappy children, and these imagoes bear the stamp of his own childhood features and of other unhappy children he has known.

These identifications with fantasied unhappy children often take place very soon after marriage, and the dreaded anticipation of their occurrence occasions a fear of marriage. A patient of mine had had a miserably unhappy childhood in which he felt orally deprived and dangerously neglected, while threatened by the sexual seductiveness of two maids who substituted for his mother. He had expressed all the despair of his childhood by eating the dirt in the cracks of the sidewalk. In the latency period and adolescence he was much disturbed by the behavior of an older brother who was entering into a psychosis that later proved incurable. My patient had been urged into marriage by his parents, who thought it would promote his emotional health. Immediately after the marriage ceremony, there ensued a state of panic in which he pleaded with his wife to have the marriage annulled by the primitive procedure of tearing up the marriage certificate. He had quickly entered into identifications with unwanted unhappy children, and he began to reenact his own and his brother's childhood behavior.

He became sexually involved with women with whom he wished not to engage in coitus, but to repeat the performances he had engaged in with the two seductive maids, which consisted largely of exploring their bodies visually and manually. He became depressed and agitated in a manner showing an identification with his older brother and visited a series of psychiatrists as the brother had done. When he finally presented himself for psychoanalysis after the birth of his own two children, he feared he was in a hopeless condition, as his brother had been pronounced to be. His anticipation that his children would recapitulate in their development his own unhappy childhood induced him to seek psychotherapy for his five-year-old son, although not for his daughter. His own early oral deprivation was reflected in his continuous concern that his children were undernourished and would not grow properly, although his wife took good care of them. His ambivalence was especially expressed in his neglect of them, while from a distance he yearned to be a good father to them. He was markedly inhibited as a father because of his identification with the fantasied unhappy and unwanted children.

Such identifications with unwanted children give rise, of course, to pregenital regressions that are incompatible with a successful marriage. Orally demanding and sadomasochistic qualities are predominant in the partners of such unions, and there is no peace or happiness for them until their pregenital fixations are loosened.

According to Schlossberger,[8] "the concept of virtual endopsychic objects in the inner, subjective representational process, pivotal in the formulation of psychic reality, leads one to comprehend the processes of libidinal cathexis as a play of endopsychic forces affecting these objects. The same applies for concepts of binding by counter-cathexis and of repression that excludes these objects from conscious representation, relegating them to the system Ucs and its peculiar rules. The fact that the objects of the real world are thinglike (real), while the endopsychic objects are virtual and configurational is often inadequately stressed. . . . The real counterparts of these endopsychic entities, the objects and phenomena of the real world in which we live, engage the organism in the interplay of object relations." In the instance under consideration, there is a virtual endopsychic object, the imago of an unwanted and unhappy child, that plays a role in the object relationship of the individual with his marital partner. The reluctant parent has a hostile identification with this internal object, which he feels as a foreign body and which he wishes to project into his marital partner, upon whom he feels the responsibility for the unwanted object properly devolves. A reflection of this process is found even in happy marriages; when a child is unruly, one spouse will say to the other, "*Your* child is misbehaving."

This endopsychic object, felt as a foreign body, becomes enveloped with the libidinal and aggressive cathexes that are not being fused and discharged in a satisfactory sexual life and sublimatory activities and causes the marriage to become a stage for a drama of ill health. In particular, the identification with this internal object gives rise to a syndrome of hypochondriasis. Just as conflict about the role of parenthood gives rise to pathophysiologic processes, e.g., azoöspermia and habitual abortion, so a hostile identification with an internalized object gives rise to psychopathologic syndromes, of which the most prominent is hypochondriasis. The unwanted imago comes to reside in an organ that is actually a *locus minoris resistentiae*, or has been traumatized, or has attained a symbolic significance. Here the sexual life is played out in distorted form. As Schilder[9] has pointed out: "The hypochondriacal organ . . . receives as much attention as the genitals do normally. . . . As a rule, one can readily show that the tension and pulling, the hardening and stiffness refer to the male genitals, the female genitals are much less frequently symbolized by the hypochondriacal organ." Schilder[10] has pointed out that to scrutinize an organ hypochondriacally is also "to externalize it to a greater or less extent." When the internalized object is again exteriorized and projected into the marital partner, it gives rise to an anxious preoccupation with the physical health of the spouse. Continuous hypochondriacal concern with bodily health is the frequent lot of marital partners who have rejected parenthood. In a symbolic sense, hypochondriasis is a form of pseudocyesis in the female and of couvade in the male.

Another distortion of the marital object relationship consequent on the rejection of parenthood, and the repeated projection and reintrojection of the unwanted internal imago of the child, is the continuous presence of an atmosphere of guilt between the spouses. Each feels guilty in the presence of the other as a result of a sense of being derelict in a major obligation. Each spouse has a continuous unconscious need for punishment, which is supplied by the other. Instead of being helpmates, they defeat and gradually destroy each other. This is the exact converse of a healthy marital relationship in which each partner must serve as a benign superego for the other.[11] The unconscious need for punishment leads to the inevitable destruction of a marriage, just as, when it is unanalyzable, it leads to the failure of a psychoanalysis.[12] When an analyst sees an ineradicable sense of guilt in one marital partner, he is justified in concluding that the marriage cannot be saved and in communicating this opinion to the partners. This state of affairs is typical of those marriages in which one spouse becomes an alcoholic. No matter what the expectations of such people regarding marriage, their lot can only be pain and defeat.

The rejection of the role of parenthood due to traumatic experiences in infancy and the internalized imago of the unwanted child is a significant factor in the psychogenesis of latent and overt homosexuality It is not necessary to outline in detail here the difficulties provoked in a marriage by homosexual conflicts, or the manner in which such homosexual conflicts and their attendant expectations clash with what may reasonably be expected from a marriage. People who have rejected parenthood usually have memories of a long-standing dislike of children and of themselves feeling extruded from the main body of society; such characteristics are extremely prominent in homosexuality. The very fear of begetting children is sufficient to determine the abrogation of all heterosexual interests and a fixation in homosexuality. Conversely, mastery of the fear of begetting children is a most significant factor in therapeutic progress with a case of homosexuality.

It is particularly in cases of latent and overt homosexuality that one meets with statements that the patient abhorred the thought that his parents engaged in sexual intercourse. This is elaborated in the greatest detail; the father violated the mother, the mother was injured, the mother hated the father because of his sexual desires, etc. The relation between parental intercourse and the origin of children is especially disagreeable to such people. The child who is the product of such a reviled act considers himself a degraded individual and has a low self-esteem. That such attitudes lead to the rejection of parenthood is hardly surprising.

Of course, most married couples beget children, regardless of whether or not one or both partners is ambivalent toward them. Not all such marriages are disastrous by any means. A woman with healthy maternal attitudes may be very helpful in assisting her husband to achieve mature views about his offspring and to lead a more gratifying life in general. A secure husband may provide the strength needed by a woman who shrinks from the maternal role. But all too often such parents struggle with unconscious infantile problems that involve the child. It is not desirable here to enter into a discussion of the various syndromes to which this may give rise in the child, but one particular outcome of this state of affairs will be described. The parents are anxious lest the real child remind them of the endopsychic virtual object of the unwanted child with which they have a hostile identification. They do not want the real object to acquire the qualities of the internalized imago, the danger of which is an actual one. They fear they will not be able to carry out the step, described by Fairbairn,[13] who says: "It is important to distinguish the natural (biological) object and the incorporated object which is so largely substituted for it in psychopathological cases." They endeavor to escape from the situation by hastening the child's development, urging it to be grown up in its manners and attitudes. They do not want a child but a small adult, so that they will feel that they are not in the company of a child at all. In this process they overlook the real intellectual and intuitive powers of the child and become the victims of their own maneuver. Such children often sense the weakness in the parents and learn how to manipulate and exploit, as well as to guide, them. Eventually we find adolescent children directing the parents, who then appear more child-like than their offspring.

The expectations that marriage is intended to fulfill have been discussed here from the point of view of attitudes toward the begetting of children. The process is justified despite the fact that it necessarily entails a circumscribed and somewhat limited approach to the marital relationship. Its justification resides in the point that if this cardinal goal of marriage is not zealously pursued, all the other possible gratifications of marriage may be obstructed. Childless marriages may be happy and fulfilling if the attitudes of the partners toward children are not rejecting or ambivalent, and especially if the absence of children is not of the partners' own volition. It is one of the rare situations in which an actual frustration in reality is sometimes not so damaging as one determined by unconscious immature attitudes. The rational expectations in marriage are of almost limitless variety when the marriage is founded on the cooperative assumption of the common task of founding a new family. The fulfillment of these expectations results especially in an enrichment of the ego in both marital partners. While defects in the marital relationship are probably most easily detectable in the sexual area, the evidence of a good marriage is most easily discernible in this enrichment, which is the most important advantage accruing from a successful marriage. Both partners should find deep pleasure in established sublimations or in newly acquired interests, and all of this is dependent on the energetic pursual of the main task, the rearing of children. Departures from this objective, as determined by neurotic aversion to it, will bring in their wake many types of irrational expectations, the inevitable frustration of which causes much marital friction. Their nature is infantile and pregenital, giving rise to endless transference reactions, and they are usually altered only by the psychoanalytic procedure.

NOTES

1. Nathan Roth, "The Aim of Psychoanalytic Therapy," *American Journal of Psychotherapy*, IX (1955), 5–17.
2. I. Hendrick, *Facts and Theories of Psychoanalysis*, 3rd ed. (New York: Alfred A. Knopf, 1958), p. 49.
3. *Ibid.*, pp. 60–61.
4. *Ibid.*, p. 112.
5. E. H. Erikson, "The Dream Specimen of Psychoanalysis," *Journal of American Psychoanalytic Association*, II (1954), 5–56.
6. T. R. Harrison *et al.*, eds., *Principles of Internal Medicine*, 3rd ed. (New York: McGraw-Hill Book Co., 1958), pp. 643, 649.
7. Sigmund Freud, *The Ego and the Id* (1923) (London: Hogarth Press, 1961), pp. 29–30.
8. J. A. Schlossberger, "Deanimation: A Study of the Communication of Meaning by Transient Expressive Configuration," *Psychoanalytic Quarterly*, XXXII (1963), 479–532.
9. P. Schilder, *Introduction to a Psychoanalytic Psychiatry* (New York: International Universities Press, 1951), p. 27.
10. *Ibid.*, p. 25.
11. E. Bergler, *Unhappy Marriage and Divorce* (New York: International Universities Press, 1946), pp. 32, 55, 100.
12. Sigmund Freud, "Analysis Terminable and Interminable" (1937), in *Collected Papers* (New York: Basic Books, 1959), Vol. V.
13. W. R. D. Fairbairn, *An Object-Relations Theory of the Personality* (New York: Basic Books, 1954), p. 40.

Determinants of Changing Attitudes of Marital Partners toward Each Other

To the casual observer it is puzzling why two people should want to get married if they obviously seem to be unsuited. Even more baffling is the breakup of a marriage in which the partners seem to be exceedingly compatible, amicable, and harmonious. In between these two extremes is a wide range of marital relationships that seem to offend common sense, intensifying the mystery in which love and sex have been shrouded for ages.

The confusion is not much relieved by the outpouring of scientific and semiscientific literature, guiding the bewildered and explaining the seemingly irrational. Many interesting conclusions have been offered, both from experimental research and from clinical observations; so far, they all have failed to provide a reliable guide either to an understanding of the phenomena or to a prevention and correction of marital conflicts and discord. It has been reasonably well established that certain factors and qualities promise a high probability for success or failure in marriage; but no prediction, regardless of how accurate it may be, will indicate in which category of prediction any given couple will fall in identical circumstances. Even under unfavorable conditions there is some chance for success. In the same samples under investigation, other factors, neglected by the original investigators, are assumed to be perhaps even more accurate in permitting a valid prediction. Hall[1] took the thousand couples studied by Burgess and his associates[2] and demonstrated that family size and ordinal position in the family of each partner are related to success in engagement and in marriage, factors totally absent in the original study. Although Toman[3] demonstrated that dissimilarity of birth order in each partner's family constellation and opposite-sex siblings have a higher prediction of success in marriage, Levinger and Sonnheim[4] found no association between birth order of either partner and adjustment of the marriage, nor did they find that the person with opposite-sex siblings makes a better heterosexual partner. These are only a few aspects of the examples of existing uncertainties. The writer is fully aware that his interpretation of the dynamic factors in a successful or disrupted marriage is merely one of the many possible forms of analysis. It is based on his clinical observations, which here as everywhere else depend on their subjective evaluation by each practitioner.

One would assume that no single factor can be made responsible for success or failure in marriage. Upon careful scrutiny, however, one factor does emerge as a crucial variable. More important than real events and experiences, by far outweighing the impact of any favorable or disastrous contingent, is the attitude taken by the persons involved. The same set of circumstances may permit or even produce opposite attitudes and thereby change the behavior and reverse sentiments and emotions.

Choosing a mate or rejecting one is an expression of a favorable or an unfavorable attitude. We are usually more concerned with the reasons for *rejection*, because it has more ominous implications. When two people become engaged or get married, whether one considers the choice sensible or not, one wishes them success and hopes for the best. While the possibility of divorce is always in the background at a time when the divorce rate is steadily climbing, it is—at that moment—merely a faint and remote possibility. It is different when a marriage breaks up. In only a few cases has the union been so unfortunate that everyone is happy about its dissolution. Usually disruption, torture, suffering, and many financial, social, and parental hardships accompany the final act of mutual rejection. Then the questions arise: Why did this have to happen? Would it have been possible to avoid the breakup with all its accompanying agony? Efforts at reconciliation usually precede the final break, but frequently with little success. One can well understand the desire to comprehend the dynamics of marital breakup; hostility and misery seem so futile and destructive. It is sad to face the fact that so many marriages begin in heaven and end in hell. The height of happiness and fulfillment is in stark contrast to the sense of failure, frustration, and disappointment that marks the end of the single organic process called marriage.

The apparent contradiction of the happy beginning and the sad ending is actually far less contradictory than it seems. A better understanding of the mechanisms of attraction may lead to a clearer perception of the process of rejection.

A simple inquiry into the reasons why two people fell in love or why they now hate each other or cannot stand each other will generate an abundance of apparently reasonable explanations. In each case, the two people involved are the same human beings; but how different they are when viewed at one or the other time! It is obvious that factors exist of which the two partners are not aware. In general, no individual knows much about the real reasons for his actions. Explanations given are usually rationalizations. This fact should not be considered with misgivings. Our relative unawareness of our motivations is essential not only for the process of choosing or rejecting mates, but for any action we contemplate. We need a personal bias to choose, to prefer; without such predilections we could not participate in the give and take of social living. True objectivity would prevent any forceful action; action needs a personal bias. But we cannot be biased if we would know what we are and what our personal bias is. Therefore, we have to operate as if life were as we see it, not realizing that we interpret life and events only within the framework of our bias.

The same holds true for the game called "falling in love" or for "I can't stand you." If we were to be fully objective, in a dispassionate way, seeing the good and bad qualities in the other clearly and fully, probably we could neither love nor hate.

Let us examine the reasons people usually give for choosing a mate. If these reasons were valid, there would be no need for separation and divorce because usually little has changed in the person; only our views and attitudes have changed. Let us take one of the most frequently mentioned grounds—physical attraction. We know that sexual appeal comes and goes, without any appreciable transformation of the partner. Sexual attraction seems to be a poor excuse for marriage; it usually is a mere by-product of a choice made for deeper reasons, which, however, may not be any more trustworthy as a basis for marital bliss.

There is, then, the desire for companionship, the fear of loneliness, the assumption of being a failure if one cannot or does not get married. But in almost every case of a marriage for convenience, there was more than one possible candidate. Even the most incidental, impulsive, seemingly unpremeditated choice is usually based on deeper reasons for the attraction.

One of our patients, a young, pretty, unstable, and impetuous divorcee, went on a short trip. To our surprise, instead of returning, she sent us an announcement of her wedding. She had met a young man who fell madly in love with her and married her immediately. A short while later the boy's mother came to town and called for an appointment. She wanted to see me or one of my associates who had worked with me in multiple therapy with the girl. The mother could not understand why her son, who always kept free from entanglements with women, had decided to marry so suddenly; he did not know anything about the girl, what kind of person she was, and what he could expect from her. At this point my associate and I looked at each other and began to laugh. It was obvious to us that the girl looked exactly like his mother and was the same type of person, vivacious, aggressive, and seductive. It did not take him long to get to know her. He merely married his mother; she was mother's younger edition.

It is not always obvious what we seek and find. The moment of decision in favor of someone concludes a number of mutual interactions that preceded this final step. Two persons who meet for the first time communicate untold impressions, opinions, and promises without either of them being aware of his role in the transaction. They talk with their eyes, expressing admiration, consensus, support. Little movements of hands, facial expressions, tone of voice, the whole appearance reveal the entire personality and the reaction of one to the other. Whatever goes on between two human beings is reciprocal and promoted by *both*, although it may look as if *one* started the motion and hence is solely responsible for the established relationship. Such an assumption, however, is the result of inadequate observation.

We know more about one another than we realize. Our conscious impressions are only a small part of our actual knowledge, which is what we call intuition or, less flamboyant, a hunch. Acceptance or rejection of another person is based on much knowledge and agreement that may entirely escape our attention. As a matter of fact, whatever two people do to and with each other is based on mutual agreement and full cooperation. No relationship is possible without both partners' communicating to each other what they think and feel about each other, and without full cooperation, be it for the good or for the bad. We are so accustomed to using the term cooperation only for constructive interactions that we overlook the fact that one cannot even fight without the other's full cooperation. Without one man's communicating his intention to the other and reaching agreement, no fight would be possible.

This is a most important consideration if we want to understand why two people feel attracted or repulsed; in each case, the established relationship is based on a secret pact. Unfortunately, neither of the partners realizes his own role and contribution and each attributes to the other whatever happens between them.

When a wife complains about her husband or a husband about his wife, a mother about a child or a child about the mother, each is puzzled and confused about the other's being mean, unreasonable, inconsiderate. One could listen for hours to the endless recitation of the unbearable provocations to which each feels exposed. However, this recitation is like a dialogue in which only the lines of one actor are spoken. If the lines of one are omitted, the utterances and actions of the other make no sense. In order to understand, each must know what the other does. In all conflict situations we know only what our *opponent* says and does—and this makes no sense. No one knows the lines that he himself is speaking, the part that he is playing in bringing about the conflicts and hostile acts. We are influenced by our opponent as we influence him. But we do not know the influence that we ourselves exert, and therefore we usually feel like victims of forces and circumstances out of our control.

When we enter a relationship or when we break it up, we act in accordance with goals that we have set for ourselves and that are reinforced by our partner. We share secret aims and expectations which guide us like a compass. We respond only to those stimuli which fit into our plans and recognize only those opportunities which confirm our expectations. We feel attracted when we meet someone who offers us, through his personality and his intentions, an opportunity to realize our own goals. We play a very important part in evoking and stimulating in the other person precisely the behavior that we expect and need.

A great many people fall in love with or feel attracted to a person who offers the least possibility of a harmonious union. Often good marital prospects are neglected in favor of a very questionable choice. Two secret tendencies are chiefly responsible for this: the desire to maintain one's superiority, and the prospect of suffering. The one induces the selection of an inferior or inadequate mate; the other, the choice of someone who brings dissatisfaction or even torture, justifying pessimism and granting only the solace of martyrdom. The factors that induce the choice of a partner are identical with those which lead to conflicts later on. The relationship is not merely the result of a conscious choice and of logical considerations; it is more profoundly based upon the integration of two personalities. At the instant when two persons decide to marry, they sense the congruity of each other's life style.[5] Even a marriage contracted as a thoughtless incident of drunkenness and sexual excitement represents a deeper agreement of two personalities. Their general directions in life have merged, regardless of how long the agreement may last.

Matching of the life styles does not mean identity of the life styles. On the contrary, opposites often attract each other because they complement each other. An aggressive, determined person may want a mate who is willing to be led and supportive, just as a passive, submissive person needs one on whose strength he or she can rely. A creative person, who is likely to go astray, needs and wants someone who is solid and realistic, with both feet on the ground. One who tries to please in order to have a place will choose someone who demands, often in a selfish way, admiration and submission. It is the role that each one plays in life that fits him to the role which the other one plays. One may call it playing games.[6] In reality it is much too serious to be considered a "game," which implies the possibility of "not playing games." We all play the role that we unknowingly decided to play in our formative years; it was our movement within the family constellation into which we were born. In order to function, we follow our concepts of ourselves and the world, we take on certain roles and look for people whose roles provide what is missing in us, a role that supplements ours.

If it is true that deeper personality needs and patterns lead to strong attractions, how is it then possible that the same two people who fit so well to each other can come to the point where they can no longer tolerate each other? To understand this strange phenomenon, one must keep in mind that any human quality and trait—and it is true for every single one—can be seen in a positive or a negative way. The same person, in his characteristic way of life, appears either as economical or stingy; and the generous may be considered spendthrift and extravagant by those who do not profit from his generosity. One person is considered to be either kind or weak, another strong or domineering, depending on how one looks at him. We do not like a person for his virtues or dislike him for his faults. When we like him, we emphasize his good points, and when we reject him, we use his weaknesses as an excuse.

A girl falls in love with an unselfish man and then complains that he never thinks of himself and his family, only of others. Or a boy feels attracted to a girl who tells him what to do and is protective; but after a few years of marriage he cannot tolerate her dominance. Many a woman chooses a man who is gentle and considerate and wants to please. And then she is disgusted because he cannot stop submitting to the needs of his parents, trying to please them. Then mother and daughter-in-law fight for the loyalty of the hapless idealist. The wife seldom recognizes that, without his submissiveness to his mother, he would have never chosen her as a wife, nor would she have gained a compliant husband.

Naturally, attraction needs more than the difference in personality and character. The two partners must have something in common, be it interest, background, values, or preoccupations. It is a test of their positive or negative attitudes toward each other whether their common interests continue or disappear, or whether within the same field of interest a diversity replaces the previous congruency. As long as she is in love with him, she does not mind his interest in sports and joins him; but when their mutual good will disappears, she can no longer share his enthusiasm. Or they both love music and enjoy it together; and then comes the moment where their so-called "incompatibility" penetrates even the field of their previous common interest. He loves Wagner and she can't stand his music!

Before we enter into a discussion of the mechanisms that bring about a change of attitudes, turning the positive reaction to the mate's personality into hostility and eventual rejection, we may first investigate further the basis for the mutual attraction, the role that the life styles play when they meet.

The wife comes for help. She has been married for seventeen years and feels that something has been going wrong for a long time, at least for seven years. They were in love and perhaps still are. But he has utter disregard for her. He is very busy and takes on more than humanly possible. He thrives on pressure and has no schedule. He is so negligent that he may invite people to the house and then not show up. She can't take the tension any longer. He admits that he is inconsiderate. The accumulation of pressures bothers him, he says. His wife, he admits, is charming, attentive, a good wife, and he loves her. But she has a tendency now to scold him, and he is extrasensitive. He clams up. He is always late but hates to wait for others. He always undertakes too much, loves activity, but hates details. He always underestimates how long things will take.

What are their life styles?[7] She is the middle of three children, the only girl, in an extremely ambitious family. The older brother chose social success; she, intellectual and moral superiority; the younger brother, material gains. Each sibling was successful in some way, the woman stressing righteousness as her chief goal, patterning herself after a successful, effective mother who subdued and tamed a strong father. It was a family in which the pretense of harmonious relationship was mandatory; consequently, the family maintained that the father was the boss, while actually mother dominated him and them. The patient, not realizing her own success in being right, was impressed with the success of her two brothers. She was so bent on being always right that she despaired of ever being successful.

Her early recollections expressed her pessimistic attitude toward life. She believed that she had no chance to be right except when she could criticize others for doing wrong. Nothing she could do was right; everything she wanted turned out to be wrong.[8]

Her basic mistakes: (1) She sits in judgment on herself and others and the whole world. (2) She does not expect to find anything in life but wrongness. (3) She has no faith in her ability to do anything about it. (4) She uses criticism as a means to establish her moral superiority.

How does his life style fit into hers?

Family constellation: He was an only child, overprotected and overindulged by mother, but also put on a pedestal by his otherwise rough and belligerent father. He was the only good thing that happened in their marriage, and he relied more on their support than on his abilities. He lived away from the outside world, in a world of imagination, with fantasies of being a conquering hero. All his actual accomplishments failed in comparison with his ambitions and his parents' expectations, so that he could never feel satisfied with his accomplishments. He did not fight openly; but his rebellion came out in many devious ways, like bed-wetting and hypersensitivity. His criticism of others was concealed behind his self-criticism. The heaven that his family constituted for him made the outside world appear as hell. He lived in a fool's paradise, not wanting to see reality, but indulging in the compensation of fantasy.

His early recollections show that to him life is full of fight, unpleasant surprises, and dangers. Only if he is high up in the masculine world and in the driver's seat can he enjoy life and be sure of his place. But life isn't like that. He can't trust others or himself to find a solution, so he has to rely on pretenses.

His basic mistakes: (1) He overemphasizes the need for masculine superiority and his right to an elevated position. But they are all pretenses, beclouding his real opinion of life. His success can only be temporary. (2) Actually, he is a pessimist; he demands harmony and love but does not believe that he can get them except from his parents. (3) Even if he tries to be good, he can't be sure of approval. (4) He probably provokes discord and failure by his exaggerated idealistic demands and his unwillingness to accept reality's demands.

What did these two have to offer each other? First of all, the certainty of failure. Neither expected to get anywhere, and they chose each other to make sure of the failure that each one expected in life. But what really attracted them? He was on top of his family, she on the bottom of hers, in terms of status and success. She, too, believed in masculine superiority, and he gave her the picture of a successful, superior male. He, in turn, wanted admiration and support, which this "good," humble woman obviously offered him. Little did he know that her goodness also was a pretense, like his masculine superiority. Two overambitious idealists, full of pretenses of good intentions, met and found each other. And each provided the other with sufficient reasons to be disappointed. He arranged his whole life in such a way that, despite his best intentions and efforts, everything went wrong. And in doing so, he gave her a chance to look down on his wrongdoing and thereby gain her much-desired sense of moral superiority. As long as they united their efforts against a hostile world, they got along very well. But before long they recognized that the mate was part of that hostile and unfair world.

Here is another story, one about a couple who "had to get married," because the girl got pregnant. For years they considered divorce; but each time, as soon as they both agreed on it, they changed their minds. From the first mutual report about their consideration of a divorce, it was quite clear that neither really wanted one, although both had done their best to bring the marriage to a rupture. He was overpowering, verbally, intellectually, physically. Her only defense seemed to be passivity, withdrawal. It seemed that she looked for a superior male and at the same time resented and defeated him. He was thirty-seven years old, she twenty-seven. Now she felt that he was too old for her and complained about age discrepancy. But it was exactly his being so much older that had first impressed her. At seventeen she was proud of the attentions of an older man. Now he objected to her neglect of their child, her time spent either working or with her neighbors; she doubted his affection and complained about the lack of common interest. At the same time she called him a wonderful person, father, and husband, but she could no longer love him. She became interested in other men, having grown—according to her report—further apart from him, mentally and physically. He began to woo her again—they made up, but after a while they again discussed the possibility of divorce.

This pattern of wanting and rejecting each other had characterized their relationship from the beginning. Originally it was strictly physical attraction, they thought; but she was impressed by his intelligence, flattered by his being attracted to her, was in love with him, and wanted to marry him. He only wanted to make love, to prove his masculine prowess. While she had no orgasm, she could not stop the relationship because she was afraid of losing him. Her sex appeal was her power. She always wanted and hoped that he would propose, but he did not before she became pregnant. She was now happy, and he became a wonderful father, very proud of her, still adoring her.

What do they have in common, how do they fit together? Let us look at their life styles.

She is the younger of two, next in line after a successful older sister. She had her own way, by means apparently out of her control, like fears, temper, and oversensitivity. In her family, tensions were covered up and conflicts did not impair outwardly good relationships. Preferences were equally covered up, as was hostility between the members of the family. She tried to avoid looking beneath the surface, unable to admit to herself her own motivation, or the true picture of her relationships with the other members of the family.

Summary of early recollections:[9] I am passive, dependent entirely on what life is doing to me. I want the most intense pleasure and fear the most horrible dangers. I am small and weak and cannot admit my real intentions because I want to blame others for what is happening to me. I want excitement, but life is empty.

Basic mistakes: (1) She does not take into account her strengths and what she is doing. (2) She wants to be good, but only does what she likes. (3) She wants more from life than life can give her. (4) She tries to fulfill her life by *getting* more instead of seeing what she could *do*. She is an idealistic dreamer.

Let us look at his summary. He is the eldest of five, the older of a group of two (a sister two years younger), with a second group (one brother and two sisters) much younger. He maintained his superiority, primarily through intellectual and moral righteousness, following the superior picture of father, without being able to assert himself in reality, probably doubting his masculinity in comparison with his father. The family had high ambitions and exaggerated masculine standards, with all children except his younger sister striving for superiority. He was in a masculine alliance with father and younger brother against the women, trying to keep them down.

Summary of early recollections: In contrast to the air of superiority that he successfully maintained in life, his early recollections do not reflect any self-confidence in his masculine superiority. His recollections indicate that he is in the dark, seeking the sun; but even if he finds it, he will not get the benefits. Only with a woman can he be a man. But depending on a woman, he would become restricted by her. And he is sure that he will not succeed even if he were to fight the limitations. He believes that even a strong man can't succeed in this life, and he is not even that.

Basic mistakes: (1) He expects something special from life, but is sure he will never get it. He is an idealistic dreamer. (2) He is a pessimist, underestimating his chances to get anywhere. (3) He overestimates the significance of masculinity and at the same time underestimates his own power in a masculine world. Only through women can he have his place. (4) Things are not right; he gains status only by being the only one who knows what is right. Through his pessimistic criticism he gains moral superiority.

Now let us examine what they have to offer each other. Both are idealistic dreamers. (This statement in the summaries was made in interviews in which the life style of the other was not known. It was a spontaneous evaluation of each person.) Both underestimate their strength; but each one goes about it in a different way. She remains passive, blaming him for what happened to her, not seeing that she contributed to the events in her life. He, on the other hand, tried to maintain the fiction of his masculine superiority by looking down on her and criticizing her. She looked for a strong person to lean on and found it in the much older man; he looked for a woman to be superior to and found it in this apparently weak young girl. Both are pessimists, sure that they will not get anywhere, thereby pushing each other into actions that justify their pessimism. He demands domesticity, and she seeks pleasure from other superior men. Actually, they need each other and probably never will give each other up. Each contributes to the fiction that the other is unfair, and the constant alternation of acceptance and rejection creates excitement as well as despair.

The common bond between the mates is often an identical attitude toward life—unfulfilled idealism, pessimism, and certainty of failure, intellectual and moral superiority—which unites two people in a common stand against the rest of the world. When they discover that the partner also belongs to the rest of the world, they begin to look down on each other. This indicates the causes and circumstances in which positive attitudes become converted into rejection and hostility.

There are certain rules of cooperation, in line with the "ironclad logic of social living," which Adler[10] recognized. As was said before, all people when dealing with each other cooperate fully with each other. There is merely a distinction between constructive and destructive cooperation. It seems that the basis for each has been well established.[11]

The ability to cooperate is primarily based on a feeling of belonging. The extent and intensity of such a feeling determines the tolerance level for each partner. It implies confidence in the other as well as confidence in one's self within the given relationship. The limit of the tolerance is reached when distrust and suspicion enter into the relationship, when the certainty of being accepted and considered worthwhile disappears, and when fear and inferiority feelings undermine the willingness to participate and to contribute.

A universal tendency to regard a marriage as a fifty-fifty proposition leads inevitably to a breakdown in constructive cooperation, either temporarily or permanently. It is unavoidable, under this premise, to begin to wonder whether one gets only 49 percent and is expected to give 51. Then cooperation turns into conflict, undermining the harmony, the friendship, and eventually even the love. Differences of opinions and interests are unavoidable in any close relationship. They become a conflict, engendering hostility and "disjunctive affects,"[12] only if they stop being regarded as a common problem. Then each attempts to win. Losing would mean humiliation, losing face, losing status, losing a sense of equality that is essential in a harmonious relationship within the present social climate of democracy.

It was much easier to maintain a marriage and to find peace in one's home as long as the man was dominant. There was no conflict about sex; women considered their sexual role merely as one of satisfying the needs of their husbands. It made no difference whether he wanted much or little, or what he wanted; she was obliged to comply. Naturally, there were conflicts at times and in some cases; but they were not so widespread and general as they are today. Women now seek their own satisfaction and determine what they want sexually and what not. When both sexes reached a state of equality, free to decide what each wanted, sexual conflicts in marriage became almost unavoidable. It is impossible for two people always to want the same thing at the same time and to the same extent. As soon as one wants more than the other, the relationship becomes disturbed. The one who wants less feels imposed upon, and the one who wants more and senses reluctance in his partner feels rejected. This may not be true so long as both are still "in love" and are sure of the other one's respect and good will. Then discrepancies in interests and desires can be tolerated and evoke an understanding and mutual effort to overcome frustrations and to reach a satisfactory agreement.

The example of sex can be enlarged to any area of living together. It is not disturbing if each wants something different so long as each feels secure in his relationship. But this is difficult to maintain at a time when intensive competition pervades the fabric of our whole society, and especially the relationship of those who are close to each other, as are members of a family. Here everyone easily becomes the other's enemy, regardless of their love. This is the rule, occasional exceptions notwithstanding. Without realizing it, each one is afraid of losing status, and each in turn tries to establish his superiority over his competitor. In this atmosphere it becomes difficult to regard conflicts as a task for both. Instead, one pitches his strength against the other, and each feels victimized, not realizing that his opponent is equally afraid. If one could eliminate the question of status, the need for superiority, and the fear of humiliation, one could find ways to cope with inevitable problems. A mother-in-law becomes a source of friction only if a wife fails to unite her efforts with those of her husband and instead puts the blame on him for listening more to his mother than to her. Economic stress can either intensify the cohesiveness of the family or disrupt it. If it is a problem for both to face and to solve, they probably will come closer. But if the wife blames her husband for not earning enough, or he his wife for spending too much, then the problem becomes unsolvable.

It is amazing how insignificant the occasion may be to mobilize each one's hostile forces. The husband comes home tired; his wife, tied down with home and children, has been waiting all day for him for a moment of diversion, to go out with him. As long as their relationship is not disturbed, as long as they trust each other and feel understood, there is no problem: "All right, let us go out another time." But if he feels imposed upon by her demands, and she neglected in her needs, instead of going out or staying peacefully at home, they may quarrel the whole night.

This is the point at which most people are utterly unaware of the role they are playing. They remain united in their efforts; but what is their common goal? Regardless of the variations of the "game" that Berne[13] described, its nature is always the same. There seem to be only a few variations. The most frequent endeavor of each party is to demonstrate how wrong the other is. This is the reason that endless arguments indicate the collapse of harmony, friendship, and love. Why do the partners argue? In reporting their arguments, each often refers to the puzzling fact that usually they are about trivia, about insignificant little problems, not worth any attention or concern. They fail to realize that the issue is most important, in any single case. It is important for each to prove that he is right and the other one is wrong. Only by blaming the other one for what he has done to the relationship can each justify his or her own hostility and unwillingness to function. Each one knows that he is doing wrong, but he thinks it is always the fault of the other. Neither sees how his own behavior and attitude contribute to the wrongdoing of the other. Instead of realizing the psychological basis for their disputes, they remain on the logical level, each finding new proofs for his position.

Such concern with who is right and who wrong often yields to a much worse form of warfare. It is no longer a question of right or wrong, or whose faults are responsible for the marital conflict. Instead there is a desire to hurt each other, with no limits. Each one wants to punish the other for what he is suffering. One can truly say that they deserve each other; each punishes the other for the often inhuman way he is treated. The war of the sexes no longer is one of power and control, of superiority and status; each partner brings out the beast in the other, a hatred that has found cultural support in writers and philosophers from Nietzsche to Strindberg. The mutual antagonism between the partners can be so strong that it becomes impossible for them to agree on anything, even on the conditions of divorce. And often the fight may continue for a long while afterward, with children providing the battlefield. For each, agreement means giving in; and submission seems worse than death.

It is impossible to predict when a couple may turn against each other. All marital predictions merely indicate the lesser or greater *probability* of such an event, pointing to beneficial or harmful factors and circumstances. But even in optimal circumstances the fear of losing status and significance still hangs like the sword of Damocles over all men and women in our present cultural climate. Some are more insecure; others are sure of their place and value and therefore less vulnerable. Sometimes the disturbing aspects of the relationship are visible even before the wedding. Instead of facing them courageously, a couple may indulge in wishful thinking; after the wedding, things will straighten out. Sometimes they do, once fear and apprehension are overcome and mutual confidence and acceptance are established. However, because of the intense and general warfare between the sexes, each is only too susceptive to a feeling of neglect, abuse, imposition, and rejection. Such apprehensions are supported by our general concern with status and superiority.

One of the crucial factors in bringing about marital discord is the prevailing pessimism in regard to the prospect of a happy, lasting marriage. When a couple embark on marriage, they hope against hope. But the slightest incident may set off and evoke a condition that they feared from the beginning. Little do they realize that fear usually brings about what we fear the most. Anticipation is still one of the strongest motivations. We move toward what we expect, without being aware of what we expect or what we are doing to actualize it. It is interesting to note that a broken home is more inducive to marital failure among the children than the loss of one parent through death.[14] The latter makes marriage desirable; the former is a confirmation of its hazards. Such hazards are constantly impressed upon our children so that it is almost impossible to eliminate apprehension and anxiety about marriage. They certainly sensitize the spouses to an exaggeration of all conflicts of interests and desires.

One has to distinguish between the individual's capacity and preparation for marital fulfillment and the pitfalls of situational perils. Many "ideal" relationships go on the rocks after a child is born; the father may resent sharing his wife's attention and service, and she may switch her loyalty from husband to child. Or a husband's earning capacity may diminish and put a burden on their relationship, forcing the wife to go back to work when she got married to avoid working. In our time of equality between the sexes, the possibility of infidelity is always there. In an autocratic era, the wife would not have dared to commit adultery, but in turn took it almost for granted that a man needed extramarital satisfactions. Any predicament may tax the spouses' morale and tolerance and thereby provide the turning point in their relationship, from love to indifference or even hate.

The most frequent source for marital breakup seems to be the nature of attraction that originally drove the couple into each other's arms. Whether the mate was chosen for his faults or for his virtues, the crucial factor is whether they can continue to use them for mutual supplementation or decide to turn against each other. It is this decision which spells success or failure in marriage, although neither of the partners is usually aware of having made a decision and why. Nor do they know that they have it in their power to change their negative attitude into a positive one, if they only would be willing. Many efforts at reconciliation fail because nothing is done to help the partners recognize the reasons for their attitudes and change them.

Shifting attitudes toward each other, the ups and downs in mutual satisfaction and dissatisfaction, are unavoidable at a time when people are concerned more with what they like and dislike than with what they have to do. The best definition of a good marriage is still the statement that the mother in the film "The Best Years of Our Life" makes to her daughter, who thought her parents did not know anything about the tribulations and tortures of love: "We never had any trouble? [To father:] How many times have I told you I hated you—and believed it in my heart? How many times have you said you were sick and tired of me—that you were all washed up? How many times have we had to fall in love all over again?"

Hardly any marriage can avoid a serious crisis; but most crisis situations would not need to lead to a marital breakup if the people involved knew how to extricate themselves or had the courage to let themselves be pulled down by the whirlpool of life and be spilled out safely, if they only could hold their breath and wait.

The following example shows dramatically to what extent attitudes can change and reverse rejection into acceptance. A patient (this happened in Europe) was suffering from various nervous symptoms. He could not stand any pressure and was unable to go to a dentist even for the most urgent needs. He had to be in complete control. He was the younger of two, and dominated his older sister and his mother, imitating a domineering father. While he strove for "masculine superiority," he was constantly on guard, not sure that he was enough of a man. He developed a peculiar system of tyrannizing and charming others to give in to his every whim, avoiding very carefully any situation where his dreaded inferiority might become apparent. He remembered an incident at the age of eight, when he was walking along and encountered a man who gave no indication of stepping aside. So he did the same and consequently bumped into the man.

He married rather young, when he found a girl deeply devoted to him and willing to do anything he wanted. She took care of him and provided him a kingdom where he reigned supreme. After a few years, however, he became apprehensive and rebelled. She exerted certain pressures on him—for his comfort and benefit, to be sure, but nevertheless pressures. She brought him his house slippers when he came home, made him put on a housecoat, etc., etc. This threatened him and increased his fear of being dominated. Abruptly he decided to leave her. She became hysterical and literally fell on her knees, embracing his legs, imploring him to keep her as his slave. He could do whatever he wanted as long as she could stay with him and serve him. His feeling of superiority was restored and he stayed. To test his power, he ignored her domestic efforts by entering the house with dirty or wet shoes and ignoring any order. It broke her heart, but she suffered in silence. He went further: he had a number of mistresses, and told her of the gifts he received and of other exploits and successes. She was hungry for his love and affection, so he denied her both.

During therapy he not only began to understand his mistaken concept of dominance and rebellion against pressure; he began to change. First, his nervous symptoms diminished. Then he dropped the multitude of girlfriends in favor of one. And then something strange happened to him. For years he had found his wife sexually repulsive. One night, while lying awake in bed and looking at her, he suddenly thought that she was not so unattractive, even younger and better looking than his mistress. He felt sexually aroused, had intercourse with her, but could not understand what had happened to him. It came so unexpectedly. As he began to understand, he gave up his girlfriend, whose admiration and gifts he no longer needed as proof of his masculine superiority.

Such changes from negative to positive are not infrequent; but they are not necessarily all for the good.

A young man fell in love. The girl did not respond and rejected his proposal of marriage. But he was used to getting what he wanted. He was unwilling to take no for an answer, particularly since his ardor was so great. So he persisted; but she remained adamant. He became desperate and threatened suicide. At this point she weakened. He had proved how much he loved her, and they were married.

Soon afterward he lost his interest in her and neglected her, even sexually. When she complained, he merely told her that he was no longer in love. She had not really cared for him, and they were divorced. Whereupon he "fell in love" with her again. He discovered that he could not live without her. This time he was really in love with her. He again pursued her, with even greater urgency than before. To escape his pressure, she married someone else.

Now he was truly challenged, determined to have her back as his wife. He began to threaten the life of her husband. To protect him, she divorced him. Now the intensity of her first husband's pursuit increased. He convinced her that his divorce had taught him a lesson. Knowing how much he needed her, he was a "changed man," and his love was now deep and eternal. They were married again.

It was not long before he again began to neglect her. Of course it was not his fault. He could not help being again out of love.

It is obvious that this was a man who merely wanted to have his own way and particularly wanted to impose his will on a reluctant adversary. When she did not want him, he forced her into submission; and when she expected love and affection from him, he denied it. In many a marriage, the basis for attraction, physical and personal, may be of a very questionable nature. In such a case, falling in love again, changing rejection into acceptance, may merely serve to prolong the agony. It is important not only that we love but also whom we choose to love. Changing negative into positive attitudes in a marriage is not desirable in itself. Sometimes the rejection is long overdue; it may be more constructive than continuing a marriage that saps the strength and courage of each partner, provides the children with a conviction of hostility between the sexes, and intensifies the marital pessimism characteristic of our times.

If any one attitude may be considered conducive to a marital breakdown, it is this latent pessimism, which increases with the percentage of marital failures. The decisive factor for considering divorce and refusing a reconciliation is a defeatist conviction that nothing good can come of a continued union. It is this pessimism which makes one or both partners look at every shortcoming and inconvenience, regardless of how small, as a sure sign of doom. Such an attitude precludes any glimpse of hope. The breaking point occurs precisely when hope fades and pessimism prevails.

Which attitudes, then, permit a continuation of marriage despite all conflicts, differences, and disappointments? First of all, courage, belief in one's ability to cope with whatever problems may arise. The courageous person can succeed where the timid is bound to fail. Beyond that, the willingness to contribute, to be useful, instead of the increasingly prevalent concern with pleasure and getting.

Marriage is one of the most difficult assignments for modern man. It is easier to keep a job than to maintain a marriage. Once it was a haven to which a man could return from his struggle in a hostile world to find peace and comfort. Today, many a man prefers working late at the office to coming home to friction and demands.

These difficulties, which discourage and demoralize husbands and wives alike, are partly due to this new relationship of equality, which developed as part of the democratic evolution. There is no tradition that teaches us how to live with each other as equals, in mutual respect and trust. We have not learned to solve problems through agreement, without winners or losers. It is this lack of technical knowledge in problem-solving on the basis of confidence in one's self and the other which undermines the feeling of belonging that is the source of tolerance, good will, and optimal participation.

NOTES

1. Everette Hall, "Ordinal Position and Success in Engagement and Marriage," *Journal of Individual Psychology*, XXI (1965), 154–158.
2. E. W. Burgess and P. Wallin, *Engagement and Marriage* (Philadelphia: J. B. Lippincott Co., 1953).
3. W. Toman, "Family Constellation of the Partners in Divorced and Married Couples," *Journal of Individual Psychology*, XVIII (1962), 48–51.
4. George Levinger and Maurice Sonnheim, "Complementarity in Marital Adjustment: Reconsidering Toman's Family Constellation Hypothesis," *Journal of Individual Psychology*, XXI (1965), 137–145.
5. The concept of the life style is basic to Adlerian psychology. The life style is the unique configuration of an individual, indicating his pattern of concepts about himself and others and his movements through life. It is based on the ideas, convictions, and goals that each person develops in his formative years. The recognition of a person's life style permits a holistic perception of him as a unit. Adler provided us with a technique for determining a person's life style (*Social Interest: A Challenge to Mankind* [London: Faber & Faber, 1943]). An analysis of the family constellation permits an understanding of the way in which the person found his place within his first group. The sociogram of his family indicates the role that each member of the family played. Early recollections then indicate clearly how the person looks at himself and life. An individual remembers from all the myriads of early childhood experiences only those which fit in his outlook on life. If he changes his personality pattern in psychotherapy, his early recollections change accordingly. When we know on which principles he operates, we can

then visualize the basic mistakes which he makes in his evaluation of himself and life.

6. Eric Berne, *Games People Play* (New York: Grove Press, 1964).
7. We are presenting here only the conclusions of the information that was gathered about each person, as described in note 5.
8. *Ibid.*
9. *Ibid.*
10. Adler, *op. cit.*
11. Rudolf Dreikurs, *The Challenge of Marriage* (New York: Duell, Sloan & Pearce, 1946).
12. Alfred Adler, *Understanding Human Nature* (New York: Greenburg Publishers, 1927).
13. *Op. cit.*
14. G. Gurin, J. Veroff, and Sheila Feld, *Americans View Their Mental Health* (New York: Basic Books, 1960).

shows us the basic mistakes which he makes in his evaluation of himself and life.

6. Eric Berne, Games People Play (New York: Grove Press, 1964).

7. We are presuming here only the conclusion of the information that was gathered about each person, as described in note 5.

8. Ibid.

9. Ibid.

10. Adler, pp. 76.

11. Rudolf Dreikurs, The Challenge of Marriage (New York: Duell, Sloan & Pearce, 1946).

12. Alfred Adler, Understanding Human Nature (New York: Greenberg Publishers, 1927).

13. Op. cit.

14. T. Garcia, J. Verrill, and Sheila Feld, Americans View Their Mental Health (New York: Basic Books, 1960).

Marital Problems
of Older Persons

Discordant aged married couples frequently present a serious problem to themselves, to their families, and to the community at large. In general, the marital conflicts that come to psychiatric attention stem from personal social, economic, or environmentally determined difficulties previously experienced by one or both parties to the marriage. Under the stress of physical, psychological, and social losses incidental to aging, the earlier emotional difficulties acquire new scope and significance. The type and urgency of marital difficulties in old age range from seemingly simple problems of maladjustment, through depression and brain syndromes, to such extremes as attempted double suicide in relationships verging upon *folie à deux.*

Because a quarrelsome older couple often turn to their children for emotional support and comfort, the entire family may soon find itself involved in the conflict. Attempts to enlist the aid of offspring usually represent a reversion to old patterns of parental behavior. Old family rivalries are revived and reinforced, new alliances formed, the aged parents become the focus of bitter intrafamilial warfare. Consequent socioeconomic changes in the family, and the disturbed behavior of individual members, may involve the outside community and suggest a need for social action.

The marital problem is usually presented to the psychiatrist or therapist in the form of a complaint. One partner feels that the other *is not* or *does not do* what he (the complainant) wants; conversely, it may be that the complainant *cannot be* or *cannot do* what his mate wants. In either case, one of the pair feels that the other demands too much and gives too little.

Such complaints may be entirely justified. More often, they contain merely a kernel of truth. Behind them lie feelings of frustration and a festering grievance that the marital partner is failing to gratify the "plaintiff's" sexual, social, or emotional needs.

Marital complaints by an older individual often reflect an effort by the complainant to avoid recognizing his own feelings of depression, "nervousness," helplessness, fear, or anger—often elaborated in such a manner as to warrant the label of "mental disorder." In some instances the person appealing for help is the more rationally oriented of the pair; in others, he is impelled by his partner to seek assistance, with varying degrees of justification. This may represent a sincere desire to obtain help for the troubled individual or couple; or it may be a manipulative maneuver, a tactic to obtain an ally in the person of the physician.

Even when psychiatric disorder of major significance is present, it is not always easy to answer the question: "Who is the patient?" The individual appealing for help may be less seriously ill, from the psychiatric viewpoint, than his marital partner; if equally or even more severely ill, he may be more rationally oriented. It is often easier to determine who suffers most than who originally was at fault.

Fortunately, the psychiatrist need not be greatly concerned with who is at fault, which partner is failing in terms of mutual marital gratification and cooperative social behavior. His job is to understand the complaints and their origin, so that he can effectively resolve the conflict by modifying the attitudes of one or the other partner, or the conditions under which the couple lives.

If the basic problem is diagnosed as mental disorder in one of the pair, then if circumstances have not progressed to a "point of no return" the marital conflict may be resolved by treating it. Fears that psychiatric improvement of one may make the relationship worse by exposing the other to realistic demands are greatly exaggerated. However, all too often the mental problem, rather than *aetiologic*, is *embedded* in the relationship, and close attention to the personal interaction is required during its resolution. Because the therapist must use whatever rational and ethical methods are most effective, he may find that the only way to treat the "stronger" partner is by emphasizing that the interviews are an essential part of treatment for the "weaker" partner. At times, the only feasible approach to the patient is through environmental manipulation by way of family, friends, or community agencies.

Major or basic personality changes are seldom the therapeutic goal. The principal aim is to improve the immediate situation by bringing about a beneficial change in the relationship, as the result of psychiatric intervention.

General Considerations

Pangloss said that noses were made for spectacles; hence we have them. Similarly it has been said that man was made for marriage; hence we have it. According to sociologists, the contrary is true: marriage became an institution because it made provision for man's basic biosocial needs, and its form has varied in accordance with man's social and economic demands.

Historically, the marital relationship undoubtedly has provided a number of important services to the individual and to society. It was a cooperative arrangement for the division of routine duties and necessary labor—wage earning to the husband, housework to the wife. It assured a readily available and relatively willing sexual partner and companion. It established a stable setting for reproduction and child rearing, insuring the preservation of human knowledge and its orderly transmission from generation to generation. It served to replenish self-esteem and self-confidence which might suffer attrition in the outside world. It offered a reason for existence and for work by providing pleasurable, supportive, affectively charged relationships. Last but not least, through the family and its social extensions it offered an effective mode of protecting and caring for the young, the weak, the ill, and the aged.

However, the functions of marriage that led to its evolution as a monogamous union in our culture, with the male as nominal head of the family, appear to have been steadily decreasing in importance. Technologic change, woman's need for gainful employment and her new place in the labor force, changing attitudes toward sex and companionship, the growth of the community's role in the education and rearing of children, together with cogent reasons for population control and widespread dissemination of information and techniques of contraception, are making serious inroads into the stability and functions of marriage. Adult male and female roles appear to have altered in such a way that even the benefits of family life to the healthy social development of children are being questioned by some observers.

Many authorities now believe that there is little reason for the continuation of the present type of marriage as a social institution, other than for its capacity to provide a convenient and pleasurable relationship between adults. It is this potential, the mechanics of which may become more clear with advancing years, that is tested in old age when the importance of other factors may decline.

The patterns of marriage that persist in old age do not reflect human and biologic propensities so much as they do cultural influences. It appears, however, that emotional relationships do play a central part in holding together elderly marital partners. The relationship may be affectionate, or an admixture of obligation, feelings of guilt, duty, and fear combined with pleasurable expectation—called "love"—a bond based more upon patterns of domination and submission rather than on mutual affection. In short, despite the obvious lack of harmony in most of these marriages—and the extreme discord in many—their preservation appears to be less a result of human instinct and immediate social pressures than it is a product of cultural influence upon personality development and habits of reaction.

Individuals who manage to preserve their marriages because, wittingly or unwittingly, they recognize the convenience and usefulness of marriage, can be categorized as fairly well adjusted. They appear to be healthier, more content, and longer-lived than the widowed, separated, or divorced. They have fewer complaints, cause less social friction, are more congenial and socially engaged, have better work and better productivity records, a higher opinion of themselves, fewer depressive reactions, and proportionately fewer mental disorders as measured by hospital admissions and clinical experience. Similarly, persons who remarry after the death of a spouse tend to be somewhat better adjusted than those who do not remarry—although, admittedly, many of them enter into marriage again only because they are unable to tolerate a nondependent way of life.

The statistically established advantages of marriage in old age must rest partly on selective factors: the sick, the handicapped, and the maladjusted are less likely to get married, stay married, and remarry. However, the advantages are also a consequence of the social effects of the marital relationship. Even in old age, marriage definitely contributes to morale and continued activity. This is especially true in a society such as ours, which favors the development of dependent personalities who derive gratification from their attachments to specially delegated (by themselves) persons, rather than by way of independent interaction with society.[1] Under such circumstances, the marriage of an aged couple can be seriously disturbed emotionally even while it exerts a protective influence upon health, the family, social relations, and economic and living conditions. Conversely, mutually dependent relationships may contribute to marital contentment.

It has been observed that marriages that were good to begin with generally tend to improve, whereas those marred by early strife and discontent tend to grow worse. It is also true, however, that many marriages that seem good at the start decline precipitously in the later years, and conversely, many highly disturbed marriages settle down and turn out surprisingly well. Bad marriages improve not only because of personality changes; they may get better as habit, the force of economic circumstances, and cooperation in the sharing of duties and living accommodations make themselves increasingly felt. Relatively good marriages, on the other hand, may be disrupted by illness of the wife. This is especially true when the husband is already ill or is unable to cope with the task that suddenly devolves upon him. Wives are much better equipped to handle problems posed by a husband's illness; they often manage to do so despite illness and impairments of their own.

The departure of children "from the nest" may improve good marriages. On the other hand, it may accentuate the defects of bad marriages as the common interest in child rearing is lost, or a scapegoat escapes and husband and wife are thrown back upon each other for emotional gratification, companionship, diversion, and purposeful activity.

Sexual interests can and do persist into very old age. Here again it is a matter of prior emphasis. Those who were very much interested in sex and were sexually active continue to be so, whereas those who were uninterested, passive, and inhibited use aging as an excuse to desist from sexual activity and to discourage the more active partner. Here again the good marriages tend to remain good or get better, whereas the bad get worse. However, it is also true that in marriages where sexual activity has been distasteful to one of the pair—usually the wife—diminution of interest by the other partner may lead to new-found harmony and contentment.

Not all married couples have a "lifetime" union. Many persons marry, commonly for the second time, relatively late in life or even in old age. Such marriages, though usually of economic benefit to the woman, are also highly advantageous to the male in many ways. In some instances they make parenthood possible relatively late in life. In the long run, marriage late in life offers the husband a distinct advantage: because of a shorter life expectancy, it is likely that he will require nursing, personal assistance, and other services for a relatively lengthy period before his death.

For these reasons, it appears that an old man is wise to seek a wife younger than himself. In some societies where sequential marriages are the rule, young men marry older women, who teach them the facts of life—not only sexual—and provide them with material assistance. Upon the death of the woman (or in her old age, if the society is polygynous), the aging man takes a young wife to assist him in his failing years. On his death, the widow completes the cycle by taking a younger man for a husband.

Personal Needs and Marital Conflict

Marital conflict in the older age group almost invariably can be understood in the context of the dependency construct. Dependency is primarily an exploitative maneuver performed by an individual who is weak—or believes himself to be weak—with respect to a person whom he regards as strong and potentially helpful. In other words, the "weak" individual seeks to manipulate and dominate the "strong" one —sometimes directly, at other times, paradoxically, by emphasis on his own subservience and submission.

This personality trait is not incompatible with coexisting feelings of sincere affection; however, in the absence of a capacity for affection, the elaborated maneuver often serves as a substitute designed to attract and hold the interest and help of another. Furthermore, the dependent relationship may be mutual; that is to say, each of the marital partners may simultaneously look to the other for gratification of his basic need to feel emotionally secure and comfortable.

The chosen protective person or parental surrogate need not be aware, or accepting, of the delegated role. Open refusal to accept this role is not necessarily regarded as a rejection by the dependent person; indeed, he often expects and desires the other to fulfill this role reluctantly and grudgingly, or regards rejection as a challenge to more effective action. However, in the event the delegated person fails to show promise or to fulfill the role, a state of intensified "search for aid" is at once instituted within the dependent person, which is reflected by subjective mood change and altered behavior.

This concept, which equates much maladjusted behavior with a "search for aid,"[2] does not replace psychodynamic theory; it supplements it. Dependency is the persistent need for a parental figure based upon the legitimate needs of the infant and child carried into maturity and elaborated and modified in attempts to repair the ensuing adaptational inefficiencies. The persistent dependency and ineffective behavior is usually based upon fear, ignorance or misinformation, failure to acquire skills, and feelings of inadequacy which originate in the early dependency period through the interaction of temperament and environment. Dependency can be reinforced and exaggerated by events of later life. The genetic-dynamic events behind these fears—which can usually be traced to the biological dependence of the infant upon his parents—and their permutations constitute a large body of psychodynamic observations. Treatment procedures, however, seldom require the complete revelation of how psychological inhibition was favored and how this led to, and tends to perpetuate, dependency. Instead, a recognition of the dependent person's pattern of search for aid can lead to an understanding of how the helplessness from which it stems can be decreased, how its manifestations can be made less troublesome, or how its target—a protective person—can be provided, so that its intensity and the accompanying distress subside and the behavior is improved.

In the interests of rational and effective treatment, individuals can be classified by whether their "life style," "way of life," "mechanisms of psychological (or emotional) adaptation," or "habits of reaction" reveal them to be more or less socially cooperative or socially dependent. Clinical experience suggests that many personality traits, while considerably influenced by genetic factors, can be understood as part of a cluster of dependent or nondependent social behavior evolved in the process of individual socialization. The behavior can be classified as it appears to have been polarized by, or tends to contribute to, four major psychodynamic constellations. These are the modes of maintenance of: (1) the sense of purpose, or meaning, of life ("Who am I? Where am I going? Why?"); (2) the feelings of self-esteem, personal worth, or dignity; (3) feelings of self-confidence ("I can do it!"); (4) the capacity for pleasure through the achievement of gratification and through relief from tensions arising from biologic or acquired needs.

The manner in which these clusters are integrated suggests whether the person can be categorized as relatively nondependent or dependent. Further, the two general types of persons can be subdivided according to how these characteristics are elaborated and emerge as differing patterns of maintaining social relationship because of the individual's constitutional differences and variations in cultural exposure. (See Table 8–1.) This scheme, then, serves as a bridge between intrapsychic and psychodynamic patterns of functioning and interpersonal or sociodynamic behavioral patterns.

It is apparent that dissimilar intrapsychic constellations may give rise to different or similar interpersonal behavioral patterns. Consequently, prediction of behavior cannot be based upon knowledge of psychodynamics alone; cultural opportunities, culturally determined personal values, and pressures make direct contributions to the manner in which psychodynamic adaptational and homeostatic maneuvers emerge into personal action.

In these terms, the characteristics of the two major types of personality can be briefly outlined as follows:

TYPE I. THE NONDEPENDENT PERSONALITY

A. Personality Characteristics

Sense of purpose. Depends upon internalized desire for self-realization combined with biologic urges toward survival and reproduction; thus, self-assertion necessary for survival also serves for the improvement of the individual and his social conditions.

Self-esteem. Enhanced and maintained by recognition of one's self as effective and capable of survival, of provision of pleasure to the self, and of cooperative work and play with others, and by such effective action.

Self-confidence. Established and augmented by recognition of one's ability and achievements, and by effective action.

Table 8–1

Influences on Personality	Adaptive Integration	Psychodynamic Constellations	Sociodynamic Constellations
Family Culture Temperament Experience	Sense of purpose →Self-esteem Self-confidence Pleasure	Clustered around finding and holding another or others ↗ ↘Accented toward problem-solving and self-realization with others or alone	Simple dependent Masked dependent Pseudo-independent Antisocial dependent Pseudo-dependent Masked independent Independent Asocial independent

Pleasure. Obtained through the suitable recognition of tensions and needs and the identification of means of achieving gratification within a socially and self-approved context; and by suitable effective action in which "feelings of mastery" accompany satisfaction. Also, obtained by pride in self as capable of recognizing the need for, and contributing to the relief of, tension and gratification of others in a mutually cooperative sensual, problem-solving, or creative context.

B. Subtypes and Social Characteristics

1. *Independent.* Rational, cooperative, and efficient in social functioning, and in personal relationships in which the person neither develops nor provokes emotional overreactions: action is attuned to individual needs and if not socially beneficial is at least harmless.

2. *Masked independent.* Same as above, but characteristics are unobtrusive.

3. *Pseudo-dependent.* Rational social functioning modified by outward conformity to dependent behavior to avoid interpersonal

complications. Since the nondependence is disguised, it is not easily recognized even by the clinician.

4. *Asocial, antisocial.* Openly exploitative behavior, the direct aim of which is gratification of the individual without regard to its effect upon the group. This behavior may be incidentally concordant with social views, but it is without affectional ties. It can be argued that this is nonsocialization, rather than a type of socialization; but it is included here for comprehensive coverage of all types.

TYPE II. THE DEPENDENT PERSONALITY

A. Personality Characteristics

Sense of purpose. Centers upon a search for and the holding of others, on winning and controlling other persons who are regarded as having strengths and useful attributes.

Self-esteem. Because approved of by others; conviction of value gained by such approval; belief in worth by way of class, clan, or family association.

Self-confidence. Based on belief in one's ability to identify, search for, and win others.

Pleasure. From services to another or efforts to perform such services, or through accomplishments believed to please another —the delegated important other; from the belief of success in dominating or triumphing over another or others; from the belief that an ally, friend, or help has been gained, especially if attributable to one's own efforts.

B. Subtypes and Social Characteristics

1. *Simple.* Open, transparent, obvious dependent relationships or strivings, easily recognized by others and often freely admitted by the dependent person, usually without guilt or shame and sometimes with pride: "Isn't that the way people should be?"

2. *Masked.* Highly elaborated disguised search, control, and exploitation of others: as service which is rationalized as a cultural value, a virtue, or good, although its intent—whether recognized or unrecognized—is to bind another; by projection the individual views his self-imposed service as martyrdom at the hands of the delegated other; through religious beliefs which yield conviction of worth, of ability to command aids, and which provide an illusory parental figure.

3. *Pseudo-independent.* Brave and heroic show of "masculinity," "femininity," or maternal behavior usually with controlled anger; effective self-assertion depends for breakthrough upon accessions of anger that provide "strength" and courage for necessary or desired action.

4. *Antisocial dependent.* Tries to take by force what is not given willingly or can't be "won" from the other. Seeks protective care via drug-induced illusions, and wishful thinking about special states or powers with consequent privileges. Addiction to gambling, speculation, and chance-taking, all as misguided expressions of magical practice or masked dependency.

The dependent person derives a sense of pleasure and security from serving another, and he usually is proud of his subservience. His self-confidence and self-esteem depend on evidence that he can win and hold another individual in a personal relationship, or gain approval. He is highly vulnerable to the loss—or threatened loss—of the "other" individual. Such a defeat invariably is accompanied by loss of purpose; all his pursuits seem meaningless in the absence of the special human "object." To paraphrase Rado, he *"works and studies for the teacher, and not for the love of the subject or the tasks."* He is frightened by anything that threatens his ability to attract and hold a "love object"— such as deterioration in personal appearance, in potency, or in earning capacity. The nondependent person derives pleasure and security from problem-solving and "effective effector synthesis."[3]

Each of these major types is the clear-cut end product of social interaction during growth and development. In therapeutic attempts it must be recognized that to achieve a shift from dependent to nondependent functioning, or vice versa, is extremely difficult and perhaps impossible. Shifts between subtypes, however, appear to be easily influenced or may occur spontaneously. Such shifts may make profoundly important differences in relationships, in the tolerance of one marital partner, and in social integration.

One influence which can promote a shift from one "subtype" of social functioning to another is psychotherapy. Implementation of such a shift may be the most effective way of decreasing marital discord.

For example, an openly dependent person, by way of counsel, guidance, or psychotherapy, can be aided toward interpersonal patterns which mask his dependency and make him more acceptable to his mate.

Cynical as it may seem, and transparent as the device may be, a therapist's suggestion that one catches more flies with honey than with vinegar is little more than an attempt to explain to a demanding, angry, dependent spouse that consideration, kindness, and even gifts may elicit the responses that sulking will not.

Further, masked dependency may be converted to pseudo-independent behavior when controlling service on the part of one partner has become onerous to the other. Explicit or implicit advice ("What about you—where do you come in?") from the therapist which converts controlling solicitude to behavior that appears to be pleasure-seeking may elicit favorable responses to the new enthusiasm, "self-assertiveness," and "strength."

Occasionally, a pseudo-independent dependent person with social difficulties may, in therapy, find a supportive relationship through which he can find more direct ways of achieving gratification, first within the therapeutic alliance and later with his spouse. Displaying less anger and more self-assertion, as his self-esteem and self-confidence rise, he will shift toward greater nondependence and increased awareness of—but less frequent and more effective use of—pseudo-independent social behavior. Conversely, pseudo-independent behavior which has been regarded by the partner as selfish, inconsiderate self-seeking may helpfully be toned down to "masked dependent" ways.

How many individuals in our society are truly nondependent is not easily determined. Many who are capable of functioning independently function in a dependent manner out of conformity or in order to obtain social advantages. Psychotherapy may help them to understand that excessively conforming dependent behavior is actually a disadvantage, and an independent nondependent person with "problems" may acquire information which enables him to behave in a pseudo-dependent manner more in keeping with the needs of his spouse.

All types appear to be helped by techniques that encourage socialization with emphasis on affectionate relationships and cooperative attitudes of nonharmful independence or of constructive pseudo-independence. Assistance toward such a shift may be the most effective way of decreasing marital discord.

Encouragement that patients make such shifts in behavior is common in counseling, guidance, and psychotherapy. Unfortunately, very often the therapist is unaware that this is what he does. Greater awareness of the cultural molding which occurs in attempts to resolve marital problems may be helpful.

This is not to say that the therapist plays God and tries to convert the patient to a new way of life; rather he helps new ways of behavior to emerge for the patient who, needing help, comes to the therapist groping toward them and in need of support for their achievement.

Statistically speaking, dependent persons in the "masked" and "pseudo-independent" categories probably comprise the majority of our population and their study probably has led to generalizations about "human nature." Because persons with simple or masked dependency frequently require assistance toward more effective pseudo-independent functioning, and because their desire to please a therapist can be utilized to their benefit, many effective techniques of encouraging increased quasi-self-assertion have evolved.

Although somewhat dogmatically stated, this scheme is proposed not as an ultimate truth but as a framework for increased understanding of personal reactions and their potential for modification. This point of view has made it possible to assist aged persons with marital problems by decreasing the troublesome aspects of their elaborate search for aid, in the first place by providing them with a suitably supportive individual in the person of the therapist, and second by providing guidelines for the spouse or family.

Conclusions

The marital problems of the aged cannot be dismissed merely as the meaningless bickering of old and cantankerous individuals. Their difficulties are a reflection of significant adaptive maneuvers during periods of suffering. Underlying their disturbed and disturbing behavior is an attempt to manipulate and master the social environment, in order to decrease feelings of helplessness and fear at a time when certain essential needs are not being met. Whether these needs are biologically determined or socially acquired is not important; the significant factor is the individual's feeling of inability to cope with tension-producing situations.

Such feelings of helplessness are related to the loss, with aging, of protective or adaptive resources—physical, psychological, social, or economic. Attitudes of helplessness, anxiety, and anger give rise to a search for aid or support from others. Where marriage is expected to fulfill these supportive, reassuring functions, failure to find such gratification and feelings of security by way of this social relationship leads to "marital problems"—a state of struggle and manipulation.

Of special interest to the psychiatrist is the fact that a disturbed marital relationship may occur in any situation in which customary modes of achieving self-esteem, self-confidence, and a sense of purpose are threatened—especially when the threat occurs within the family setting. In numerous cases the problems directly involve children, and one partner may be manipulated by the other in order to obtain the moral support of the child. At times the marital problem is incited by a child. In many cases where children are present, the problem is aggravated by their inability to understand or tolerate the dependent behavior of the parents.

Although aging couples present a wide variety of marital problems to the psychiatrist, almost all of these can be understood in terms of a successful or unsuccessful search by one or both partners for aid or support from the other. This search, while occasionally a new development, usually emerges in a setting of lifelong episodic or chronic feelings of helplessness and anxiety.

The concept of dependency as a binding as well as a disruptive force in marriage helps to explain the seemingly pointless behavior of many older married couples. Success in achieving and maintaining a dependent relationship has become a source of pleasure to them; this is frequently achieved by gaining emotional mastery of other persons, in this case the spouse, who are fantasied pleasure providers even though they may be required to do little. The pleasure is derived, therefore, not from an affectionate, compassionate, cooperative association but from the manipulation of another and the feelings of strength and pleasure that come from a sense of mastery. Complicated efforts to control, or which are conceived of as promising to control, another provide purpose to an existence in which an individual's capacity for self-realization through productivity, achievement of status, and fulfillment of life roles has been impaired or destroyed, or has failed to develop. By substituting success in the manipulation of others for that successful cooperation with others which is impossible for him, and for the mastering of challenges to constructive biosocial action, the individual finds meaning for existence.

Thus marital closeness is often comprised of interlacing pain-filled personal relationships in which manipulative maneuvering is mistaken for affection and in which guilt, crushing sense of obligation, and compulsive need for social compliance—joined with fear and inability to act with rational independence—constitute a reciprocal bondage miscalled "love."[4] Family cohesion in such households is based upon the social interplay of dependent individuals whose pleasures are all contingent upon the feeling that a parent surrogate is always available.

Individuals can develop as dependent persons and manifest their dependency in a variety of ways throughout their lives, contingent only upon changing personal needs and situational demands. Therefore it is incorrect to characterize their transparently dependent behavior as "regressive" when a lifelong trait emerges with greater clarity at a late stage of life. It has become obvious or troublesome either because it is less elaborately disguised or because it is displayed in a form that is socially or personally less acceptable than before.

The problem-causing dependent behavior provides a therapist with a potent lever. Frustrations in an irrational search for aid often bring the "searcher" to the physician. By recognizing and skillfully accepting the role thus thrust upon him, the psychiatrist can utilize his delegated status in the best interests of the patient—to increase the latter's self-esteem and self-confidence, and to restore a sense of purpose which can lead to improved behavior and improved relationships to the remaining years of the patient's life.

NOTES

1. Alvin I. Goldfarb, "Psychodynamics and the Three Generational Family," in Ethel Shanas and Gordon F. Streib, eds., *Social Structure and the Family: Generational Relations* (Englewood Cliffs, N.J.: Prentice-Hall, 1965), pp. 10–45.
2. Alvin I. Goldfarb, "Patient-Doctor Relationship in Treatment of Aged Persons," *Geriatrics*, XIX (1964), 18–23.
3. Alvin I. Goldfarb, "The Rationale of Psychotherapy with Older Persons," *American Journal of the Medical Sciences*, CCXXXII (1956), 181–185.
4. Alvin I. Goldfarb, "Intimate Relations of Older People," in Seymour Farber, Piero Mustacchi, and Roger H. L. Wilson, eds., *Man and Civilization: The Family's Search for Survival* (New York: McGraw-Hill Book Co., 1965).

The Effects of Children on Marriage

The arrival of the first child transforms spouses into parents and turns a marriage into a family. A new cycle in the endless drama of life starts with the leading roles filled by players who had learned the parts while waiting in the wings during the preceding performance; but the old lines do not quite fit and constant improvisation is required. From spouse to parent, and from marriage to family—these are the topics I wish to explore in discussing the effects of children upon marriage.

In becoming parents, the marital partners enter into a new phase of life—indeed, as Therese Benedek has amplified, into a new developmental phase.[1] The tasks with which the parents must cope, the roles they occupy, their orientation toward the future alter profoundly. They are offered opportunities for new satisfactions, opportunities to achieve a greater sense of completion and to live through experiences that had been fantasied but frustrated since early childhood. They need no longer play at being "Mommy and Daddy"—they are. However, this simple step into parenthood, so often taken as an inadvertent misstep, provides a severe test of all preceding developmental stages and the consequent integration of the individual parent. The inevitable changes in the husband and wife will, in turn, alter the marital relationship and place strains upon it until a new equilibrium can be established.

The birth of a child, actually perhaps the awareness of conception, changes the marital partnership by the need to make room—emotional room—for a third person. The product of their unity can be a strong bond, a source of common interest and shared identification, but children are also a divisive influence; in varying proportions in each marriage, a unifying and separating force. The spouses who properly have transferred their major object relationships to each other and wish to be the focal point of the partner's emotional and affectional investment now find the other intensely cathecting a newcomer. Further, a family unit is not so plastic as a marital union. A childless couple can relate in a great variety of ways and the marriage will remain adequate if both partners are satisfied or even if they simply believe it more satisfactory than separating would be. The preservation of the equilibrium of a family, however, and even more clearly the adequate rearing of children require the achievement and maintenance of a dynamic structuring of the family in which each spouse fills fairly definitive role allocations. Deficiencies of the marital partners in filling their requisite roles lead to conflict and family imbalance, which I shall examine presently. On the other hand, the structure and role allocations that are an inherent part of family life can provide greater security to the spouses and increased stability to the marriage.

I shall first consider the changes in the individual parents and their capacities to move into the phase of parenthood, because it is the immaturities, fixations, and regressions uncovered by the need to be a parent that usually interfere with a spouse's acceptance of his or her respective parental role allocation or with the capacities to fill it adequately.

Speaking of the ideal, which reality occasionally approaches, the partners who married have each achieved an individual identity, have shown themselves capable of intimacy, and have rescinded independence for the benefits of interdependence and its security of knowing that one's welfare is as important to the partner as his own. They hope to achieve the completion that could not be gained within their own families, where sexual satisfaction could not be permitted and in which they must remain children. Each spouse seeks resolution to his own particular version of his frustrated and incompleted family romance. The incompleteness of the male or female roles and skills is balanced by the mate. The task of self-creation is virtually over for most. The energies that went into sexual repression, or into seeking ways of satisfying sexual drives, and into the search for the mate who could bring completion to the imbalance of being a man or a woman are released for investment in a creativity that transcends the self. The conception of the child is an act of mutual creativity during which the boundaries between the self and another were temporarily eradicated more completely than at any time since infancy. The child can be a continuing bond forged by that creativity; a focus of mutual hopes, interests, and efforts; and a blending of two personalities as well as of genes. Whereas each parent grew up the product of different family lines with differing customs and identifying with different parents, they are now united by a child whose experiences they will share and with whom they both identify. We must also recognize that they have willingly or unwillingly been turned into parents, and here, as in other spheres of life, many persons grow through finding the abilities to meet the responsibilities that are thrust upon them.

Particularly for a wife, a sense of fulfillment only comes with the creation of a new life. Her biological purpose seems to require completion through conceiving, bearing, and nurturing children, and strong cultural and educational directives have added impetus to this drive. Feelings of incompletion and deprivation in being a girl have been compensated by realization of her innate capacities for creativity, but the realization requires actualization. Childhood fantasies of displacing mother and providing a child for father are now symbolically realized. The birth of a child turns her into a woman by setting her on a par with her mother. Her love for the husband who has made such completion possible deepens. She does not wish the child just for herself but as a meaningful outcome of her relatedness to her husband, pleasing him with a gift that is part of him that he has placed in her to nurture but also something of herself that the husband will cherish. To some extent, the baby is herself loved by a benevolent father.

The husband—the idealized husband whom we are considering— also has strong drives for an offspring and can be transformed by it. The child provides a continuity into the future that mobilizes ambitions. An offspring constitutes an important sign of virility. Even though it does not require much virility to impregnate a wife (one father I know replied, on being congratulated, "Don't congratulate me. It was the easiest thing I ever did—and besides I wasn't even trying"), he has gained the status of "father," something that for many years could only be fantasied. The child's admiration and adulation of him will provide narcissistic satisfactions too. Paradoxically, even as paternity secures and heightens his masculine self-esteem, he also gains the opportunity to express the feminine nurturant qualities derived from his early identification with his mother that previously had few acceptable outlets and had required repression.

When such maturing influences upon the two parents occur, the marriage will be stabilized and deepened, and different concepts of family and parental roles, or of child-rearing techniques, are not likely to be disruptive. The child provides new sources of interest that both share. Any slack in their lives that permitted boredom and any doubts about the marriage that may have arisen after the initial ardor passed now vanish. For many, the child rather than marriage itself produces the critical change in existence.

However, every transition into a new developmental phase of life presents a test of the solidity of the passage through the prior stages, and parenthood sets one of the most difficult tests. It not only disrupts many marriages but produces psychiatric and psychosomatic casualties among the parents—and eventually, of course, among the children. Because the parents are now again facing the beginning of the life cycle and its gradual progression through each psychosocial phase, weaknesses in the various stages in the parents' development that had been covered over, compensated for, defended against can now be exposed. The parent now must fill the guiding role in the child's development, the opposite of that which he experienced earlier in life, and the shortcomings of his parents as well as his hostilities toward his parents can interfere with his capacity to fill such a role. The confrontation with the need to cope with the child's oral phase may precipitate regressive provocation of oral problems rather than simply regression to a preceding developmental phase. I can here consider only a few of the more common difficulties that are likely to arise, using them as representative of a number of different problems.

The woman's capacities to provide maternal nurturance to her infant are related to the quality of the nurturant care she herself received in her infancy and childhood. If her needs were met with reasonable consistency and she did not experience chronic frustrations and rage, she now has confidence that she can properly satisfy her own child. We might hazard also that her own feelings and responses were properly programmed in her childhood and she can now empathize with and understand the needs and feelings of her children. The mutuality established between herself and the child increases her self-esteem, her pride in her motherliness, and her assurance of her femininity. She can transcend the inevitable difficulties and periods of frustration without self-derogation or distorting defenses against loss of self-esteem. In contrast, the woman who was deprived in early childhood responds to a child's dissatisfactions and refusals to be placated by increased feelings of inadequacy. Regrets at having married and hostile feelings toward the child disturb and must be undone. A vicious cycle sets in between a frustrated child and a frustrated mother. The mother's inadequacies and despair soon spill over into the marital relationship: she may become depressed, place unrealistic demands upon her husband for support, or erect defenses, including projection of blame, that upset the family equilibrium.

A woman whose concerns about her capabilities as a wife were heightened by a long period of sterility had her pleasure in having a baby turn into desperation when she found that she could not quiet her infant, who would become rigid and shriek when she picked him up seeking to comfort him. Her husband's attempts to be helpful were taken as criticism of her adequacy. Her mother had been an aloof woman who had avoided physical contact with her children and had never been able to convey a sense of warmth and protectiveness. The young wife now felt herself even more inadequate than her mother, whose attitudes she had resented. As becoming a more adequate wife and mother than her own mother had formed a major motif of her life, the foundations of her integration were being undermined. She turned the old hostilities toward her mother against herself—she had not rid herself of the resented internalized mother—and became convinced that her husband wished to be rid of her.

Parapartum difficulties are by no means confined to the wife, though the relationship of a husband's problems to childbirth are often overlooked. The increased responsibilities, the deprivation of maternal attention from his wife, a blocking of sexual feelings toward a wife who has become a mother, unconscious fears of a rivalrous son, etc., can provoke a wide range of emotional and behavioral problems.

Concerns over displacement by a child can affect either parent, but the husband is more vulnerable because the early mother-child symbiosis requires some withdrawal of the wife's cathexis of her husband. However, intense rivalry with a child that can disrupt a marriage reflects serious and unresolved sibling rivalries in childhood. Fears of the child as a hostile rival are projections of the father's childhood death wishes toward his own father.

I wish to emphasize, even if only in passing, that the problems that the child's developmental transitions pose to a marriage are not confined to the readjustment to having a child or to the first few years of his life. The Oedipal transition can create profound difficulties when a mother needs the child to complete her life or when, because of her own Oedipal frustration, she cannot frustrate the eroticized components of her child's attachments to her. It seems evident that contemporary parents encounter particular difficulties with the adolescent, leading to situations that can create serious friction between spouses. The advent of puberty in a daughter can lead a father to flee from his attraction to her into extramarital affairs that wreck the family life. The superego lacunae of parents of delinquent children become particularly noticeable at the time of the offspring's adolescence, directing the adolescent to act out what the parent had suppressed but not properly repressed. Perhaps some of these difficulties arise when the adolescent no longer supports and bolsters the parents by admiring and considering them omniscient, but begins to see through pretense and becomes critical of parental behavior.

Even though failures to cope with a child's developmental needs can be disorganizing to parents and to their marriage, particularly when the parent feels more of a failure than his own hated parent, similar situations in more stable persons can provide a maturing experience. The individual gains a new understanding and tolerance of his own parents, seeing them now from the perspective of an adult rather than from that of a child. He recognizes that the parents he blamed and resented were also caught in the web of their fates, that they had been spouses as well as parents, that they too had been beset by problems that had interfered with their capacities as parents. The new perspective of the parents, who had been major influences internalized in the superego, modifies the superego and permits greater tolerance of the self and sometimes even of the spouse.

We have been considering how the personality changes, emotional difficulties, and regressions of a spouse following difficulties in some phase of parenthood can upset the marriage. The manner in which either of the couple relates to the child can in itself create problems. The wife, whose beauty flattered the husband's pride and whose vivaciousness delighted him, turns into an ogress to the husband, who empathizes with the son, whom she treats as a nuisance and mistreats when she feels annoyed with his need for attention. Ethnic or social-class differences in role expectations, which had been inconsequential in the marital partnership, become more troublesome when they concern child-rearing practices. A woman of Irish descent accepted and even admired her Polish-American husband's domination of her and his decision-making for both of them, but she could not tolerate his expectations that their three-year-old son would be strictly obedient or receive a thrashing, or his insistence that she docilely accept his decisions concerning the child's upbringing.

In a marital relationship, harmony depends essentially upon the couple's finding reciprocally interrelating roles, but one spouse may forego his desires or needs to support the partner and maintain harmony. But a family subserves functions other than the satisfactions of the spouses; it must also provide for the protection and care of the children, and it also serves society by preparing its new recruits to live in the society and carry on its culture. Even these minimal functions of the family can and often do conflict and cause marital disharmony.[2]

Further, reciprocally interrelating roles are far more difficult to achieve for three or more persons than for two. Whereas the relationships between a husband and wife, even though complex, can be understood in terms of a dyadic interpersonal relationship, the family forms a group in which the action of any member affects all and produces patterns of reaction and counteraction. Its functioning must be considered in the complex and indefinite terms of small-group dynamics. Small groups tend to split into dyads, and in a family such splitting disrupts the essential functioning of the group. Maintaining unity and the ability properly to carry out its several functions simultaneously requires a dynamic structuring of the family. The achievement and maintenance of the essential structure require in turn that parents fill their allocated roles and do not permit the malleability of role relationships that can suffice in a marriage without children.

The implicit but essential demands that the spouses fit into specific roles and carry out role-bound functions can cause serious strains and even disrupt a marriage. The stresses can be particularly insidious, as the couple may be only dimly aware of the functions and obligations of their roles. Indeed, they may be unaware that, with the acquisition of children, the transition into a family has imposed a demand for a more definitive structuring of their relationship and a more rigid adherence to their allocated roles.

Now, the basic structure of the nuclear family is established by the biological division of the family into two generations and two genders, each with prerogatives, needs, limitations, obligations, and role assignments of its own.[3] The division into four role allocations according to generation and sex reduces role conflict within the family, though it does not provide freedom from role conflict between children of the same sex. Each sex has different roles and functions that can interrelate and be mutually supportive. But the family, like any group, requires leadership to provide unity of purpose and direction of behavior. In a family, however, there are two leaders, a mother and a father, who must complement each other. The mother is the leader and expert in child rearing and has a primary concern with intra-familial harmony and reduction of family tensions, whereas the father is the instrumental leader, providing for the family and establishing its status in the community. Even though these leadership functions are complementary, dual leadership presents problems. It requires that the parents form a coalition and support each other in their roles and in carrying out their tasks. Further, the parental role of giving of oneself so that the children can assimilate from, identify with, and gain direction from the parent can conflict with the marital roles and needs. To form and maintain a family that can function harmoniously, the spouses must fill a few requisites—they must form a coalition as parents, maintain the boundaries between the parental and childhood generations, and adhere to their respective sex-linked roles. Elsewhere, my colleagues and I have outlined how filling these few requisites is critical to the harmonious development of the children. I cannot enter upon this aspect of the problem here—but, of course, disturbances in the children's personality developments are almost certain to have adverse effects upon the marriage. However, failures in these areas will also adversely affect the marital relationship directly.

To form a parental coalition, to maintain the boundaries between generations, to adhere to sex-linked roles—assignments that sound simple enough, but their implications are extremely complex, and few couples achieve or manage to maintain them consistently over the years. Yet, in fitting into these implicit requirements of parenthood, the spouses can achieve a greater stability and security—for the ensuing delimitations provide direction, and the role allocations furnish a more definitive pattern of behavior. The mutuality of parenthood and the needed coalition foster a supportive interdependence for the spouses as well as guidance for the children. But the capacities to assume the roles depend upon the earlier development of the parents within their families of origin, as we have already seen; the ability to consider the needs of another on a par with one's own; and also the support of the spouse.

Children are likely to disrupt the parental coalition because a parent can form a dyadic relationship with a child that tends to exclude the spouse. Such use of a child breaches the generation boundaries. Similarly, the inability of a parent to tolerate the normal and desirable attachment of a spouse to a child—as when a father feels excluded when his wife must devote time and attention to a child—can create rivalry between parent and child that also violates the generation boundaries. The efforts or demands to remain a child of a parentified spouse also cause conflicts that cannot but affect the marriage. A young wife whose husband, before they had children, permitted her once or twice a week to retreat into her mother's bed could not mother her child, as she resented giving the mothering that she herself still sought. She expected her husband to assume much of the responsibility for the baby's care and fell back upon her mother to care for the baby when her husband was at work. The husband could no longer continue to placate her, and he found that he was being forced to renounce all outside interests and become a mother. When he ceased to treat his wife as a child, she felt rejected by him and resentful of the baby, upon whom he lavished affection. This young woman could not be parental, could not assume her share of the parental coalition; she was rivalrous with her child—and even though she did not impinge upon the prerogatives of the male, she sought to force her husband to fill the female parental role. We might note that whereas gender-linked role-reversals between husband and wife are not altogether incompatible with harmonious marriage, after a child is born disturbance is almost inevitable: the husband cannot properly be a mother, and if he manages, the later resultant distortions in the child's personality will create difficulties.

The effects of failures to adhere to the few requisites that we are considering can be far reaching and subtle—and the origins of the ensuing marital conflict may be difficult to ascertain. In a family in which the husband's alcoholism had become a significant problem, it appeared as if the wife had excluded her husband from the family interaction by forming a dyadic relationship with her son. However, this man had required constant adulation to bolster his self-esteem and insecure masculinity. He could not tolerate the attention his wife had to give the child, and soon he sought a new source of admiration extramaritally. He felt and acted as if he had lost a wife rather than gained a son. The wife, who had tried to support him, now felt deserted and invested more and more attention in her son, seeking to find a substitute source of gratification and a reason to continue the marriage.

In discussing the effect of children upon marriage, I have inescapably touched upon the impact of the parents' marriage upon their offspring. It is my contention that all too commonly child rearing is discussed in terms of techniques, of what parents do for a child and how it should be done—how to hold, feed, bowel train, etc.—or in terms of the mother's nurturant capacities and emotional stability. I believe that who the parents are, their personal characteristics and how they interrelate with each other, and the nature of the family they create are also fundamental influences upon the child—as we all know in practice. The parents as models for identification, their interaction as an example of mutuality, the importance of the family structure in structuring the children's personalities are examples of topics that demand careful scrutiny if we are to learn what produces stable and unstable children. Perhaps when parents learn that their behavior as individuals and as a couple is of prime importance in determining their children's personality development, they will be in a better position to raise happy and stable children.

A psychiatrist tends to think of his patients and therefore to think of unhappiness in marriage and of difficulties created for children and by children. The rewards of parenthood are, of course, great. The current trend toward larger families is not due to flaws in contraceptive techniques but rather to the fact that in an insecure world in which values and purposes are obscure, people realize that tangible, meaningful values can be found in relationships between parents and children. Couples are willing to give hostages to fortune by having children. Children provide objects whom parents are free to love and from whom they gain the satisfaction of being close and being necessary—a relationship that may well be fundamental to happiness and that is worth much pain and sacrifice. Each new phase in the child's life brings not only new tasks for the parents (as well as for the child) to master, but also change, variety, and new adventure into the parents' lives. The children are a force that keeps a marriage vital through constant renewal and challenge.

NOTES

1. Therese Benedek, "Parenthood as a Developmental Phase: A Contribution to the Libido Theory," *Journal of the American Psychoanalytic Association*, VII (1959), 389.
2. Theodore Lidz, *The Family and Human Adaptation* (New York: International Universities Press, 1963).
3. Talcott Parsons and R. Bales, *Family, Socialization and Interaction Process* (Glencoe, Ill.: Free Press, 1955).

Marital Psychopathology: Its Effects on Children and Their Management

In the first recorded case of the psychoanalytic treatment of a child, the case of Little Hans, Freud[1] describes in great detail the intrapsychic conflicts of a phobic boy struggling with his Oedipal impulses and fantasies. He also elaborates on a number of highly significant environmental circumstances that predisposed the child to the development of his neurotic disorder, and on those circumstances that precipitated its outbreak.

It is only on a close examination of the case report, however, that we note the fact that but two years after the events reported by Freud the child's parents separated and were subsequently divorced. At no point in his narrative does Freud direct our attention to any possible impact on Little Hans of the marital discord that must have reigned in the family at the time of his neurotic illness. No more does he address himself to the possible effect of modifications in parental behavior or interactions on the boy's psychopathology.

It is most unlikely that so sophisticated and perceptive an observer as Freud would deal with similar material in this manner today. In the sixty years that have intervened since Little Hans's phobia wrought a revolution in the understanding of childhood psychopathology, we have become increasingly aware of the influence of intrafamilial conflicts on the emerging personality organization of children, and we now incline, if anything, to overemphasize such considerations at times to the exclusion of the intrapsychic conflicts to which Freud first drew our attention.

Flugel, in his *Psychoanalytic Study of the Family*,[2] was perhaps the first psychoanalyst to center his attention on the dynamics of family interaction. His discussion of the influences of parents on their children, published almost forty-five years ago, has a remarkably modern ring and still repays careful reading. In more recent years, many psychoanalysts, psychiatrists, and other students of family pathology have continued to alert us to these issues. Lidz,[3] for instance, has contributed a series of papers focusing on the patterns of interaction in the families of schizophrenics, delineating such matters as the differential roles of fathers and mothers and specifically the contributions to pathology incident on marital schism. I have myself described[4] the deleterious consequences on ego development of deviant role-patterning in the families of psychotic children. Similarly, Wynne and his associates[5] have investigated the influence of disordered patterns of communication in the families of schizophrenics on the development of thought processes and cognitive modes as well as the individual differences among siblings in such families. Bateson, Jackson, and their collaborators[6] have also contributed notably to the knowledge of disordered communication in the families of schizophrenics and have particularly emphasized the role of the "double bind" in disorganizing the child's patterns of expectation and reality assessment.

Perhaps the most familiar and certainly the most influential work in this field has been that of Ackerman,[7] who, along with a group of co-workers, not only has attempted a systematic study of patterns of family interaction and pathology in a wide range of disturbances, but has developed a methodology of treatment that has achieved a considerable degree of acceptance. I shall have a few words to say on this subject later in this presentation.

It is, of course, a truism that a secure, mutually gratifying marriage provides the optimal soil for the growth and development of the child. It is equally obvious that marital conflict engenders tensions that can adversely affect the child's growth. What may not be fully appreciated, however, is the extent to which specific aspects of marital conflict and pathology may induce specific aberrations in the child's fantasy formation, identifications, and defense organization. I should like, therefore, to describe a few instances of such influence to illustrate my thesis.

1. In the course of his psychotherapy, John, the depressive nine-year-old son of divorced parents, began to raise questions about sex and procreation. His therapist pursued John's fantasies on the subject to the point at which John was struggling with the method of paternal influence on the process of conception. Having rejected the idea of parthenogenesis, he was still convinced of the oral basis for impregnation, and he was at a loss to explain the manner in which the father influenced the child to resemble himself. Finally, it occurred to him that the father must shout into the mother's mouth, "Hey, you down there, look like me!" It was apparent that this fantasy reflected the child's notion of goings-on between the parents during the violent verbal battles that had occurred in the bedroom at night before they had separated. These battles had distorted John's concept of the primal scene into this bizarre fantasy that at once denied genital activity and reflected his oral-sadistic view of the sexual act. At the same time the boy's depressive quality was a response to the affective withdrawal of his narcissistic mother, an attitude that had contributed strongly to the conflict between the parents and had led to their ultimate divorce.

2. Jeremy was brought to a child-guidance clinic at six because of his effeminacy, transvestism, rebelliousness, and irritability, and regressive trends such as thumb-sucking. His most aggravated problems—the effeminacy and transvestism—were first noted as early as age two, when he began walking around in his mother's shoes and showed a great interest in her dresses and lingerie. Gradually he took to wrapping towels around himself to simulate low-cut dresses, putting on lipstick and makeup, and swishing around the house. At first, his parents were unconcerned about this behavior, but gradually they began to discourage it as it continued unabated.

As Jeremy grew older, he became concerned that his mother would grow old and fat and that she might die. He often saw his mother nude and asked her why women don't have penises and why little girls don't have breasts.

Jeremy's parents were separated seven months before he came to the clinic. They had, however, been essentially unrelated to each other since shortly after their marriage, when each began having extramarital affairs. Mrs. T, a narcissistic, vain, exhibitionistic woman, who sought a career as an actress, constantly exposed herself to Jeremy and clearly fostered his interest in her clothes and in her dates, sharing with him details of her social life and asking his advice about her dress. After the separation, which she instigated, Jeremy expressed fears that she, too, would leave him as his father had.

Mr. T, a rough-hewn immature man, whose gambling and involvement with "the boys" bespoke his unconscious homosexual trends, repeatedly emphasized his manliness in his interviews. He had, ever since the separation, urged Mrs. T to have sexual relations with him and on many occasions had induced her to do so during what were supposed to be his visits to the children on weekends, but only after prolonged arguments on the subject in the presence of Jeremy and his older brother. (Jeremy described his parents as "fighting in bed each morning.") Indeed, throughout the marriage he had insisted on intercourse on virtually every possible occasion; Mrs. T complained both of his insatiability and of his inability to satisfy her.

In his highly dramatic play, Jeremy repeatedly, almost perseveratively, enacted scenes in which the mother doll or puppet was represented as rejecting, frightening, murderous, and cruel on the one hand and seductive and teasing on the other. She was also represented as being involved with several men at once. Such play alternated with elaborate efforts on Jeremy's part to make gifts and cards to present to his mother.

Different as these two cases are in diagnosis, structural details, psychodynamics, and genesis, both John and Jeremy serve, I think, to illustrate the ways in which specific aspects of the marital relationship and its pathology can influence the child's psychosexual and ego development and the quality of his deviations. In the first instance the content of the child's sexual fantasies was decisively affected by the nature of the parents' conflictual behavior, while his major symptoms were responses to the mother's characteristic modes of defense. In the second, as in those cases of sexual pathology reported by Johnson and her associates,[8] the boy's basic conception of himself was distorted by a pathological identification with his mother. This originated in an excessive early pre-Oedipal involvement that was encouraged by the mother's narcissism and was consolidated partly by his fear of losing her as he had his father and partly on the basis of an identification with the aggressor. Jeremy saw his mother as the dangerous, castrating figure in the family constellation. At the same time his erotic excitement and therefore his confusion and anxiety were kept at a high pitch by the overt sexual behavior of his parents and his mother's seductiveness; his tantrums and irritability were in part defensive reactions to this anxiety.

These two children fall, of course, within the range of neurotic conflict and illness. Even more extensive deviation can be seen in situations, sometimes more subtle, where the role patterns and expectations of the family are confused, inconsistent, or deviant. In such cases, as I have described elsewhere,[9] the child's conceptions of reality as mediated to him by the parents, and of his place in relation to it, may be profoundly distorted.

A case in point is that of David, whose parents, both barely compensated paranoid schizophrenics, were in a constant silent war with each other in which David was used as a pawn. Primarily, Mrs. Y involved herself in an intense, nonverbal union with David, which walled them off from the angry withdrawn father, who resembled in many ways the father depicted in that reborn modern classic, Henry Roth's *Call It Sleep*. Mrs. Y literally did not speak a word to David for the first two years of his life, "because he couldn't answer me if I did." As a result, David did not speak at all until age three, and at six, when he came to the clinic, his speech was limited in quantity and deformed in quality, despite superior intelligence as measured by nonverbal tests. He was, in effect, his mother's phallus, her weapon in the interminable war with the father, an undifferentiated portion of her self-representation, her solace, her husband-surrogate. David and his mother were fixed in a persistent symbiosis that verged on maternal parasitism and that precluded David's emergence into separation-individuation. Small wonder that he had no conception of an autonomous self, that he could not communicate verbally, that he anticipated that his wishes would be magically understood by adults without his having to express them. Similarly, it is small wonder that as he improved in therapy his mother's illness became overt, so that she ultimately required hospitalization.

All these cases exemplify the delicate balance that all too often exists in families in which deviant modes of interaction and communication between the parents ramify into the development of their children. Of course, the nature and extent of the influence of such conflicts on the child's development will depend, among other things, on their timing and on the quality of their effects on the parents themselves. In some instances, for example, the mother may respond to a deterioration in the relationship with her husband with a reactive depression or with emotional withdrawal and unavailability. Should this occur during the early months of the child's life, it is likely to have adverse effects on the development of what Erikson[10] has termed "basic trust," may lead to oral fixation, or even to what Spitz[11] calls "anaclitic depression" or a depressive diathesis, with persistent defects in the capacity for object cathexis and in the development of other critical ego functions. If such issues arise during the phallic phase, as in the case of Little Hans, disruptions of Oedipal development may occur with less profound impairment of basic ego development but with potential for fostering of neurotic symptoms or deviant character formation.

In any case, these illustrations offer testimony to the prime requisite in the management of such cases—a coordinated concept of treatment of the family system as a whole. By this I do *not* mean "family therapy"—at least, not necessarily. Family therapy, as described by Ackerman,[12] Satir,[13] and others, involves, as I understand it, the joint treatment of all members of the family—or at least the critical triad of child, mother, and father—simultaneously and together, focusing attention to the interactive phenomena of the group in preference to, if not to the exclusion of, intrapsychic and individual conflicts and their consequences. Though it is undoubtedly a valuable technique, I consider it a method with very special indications, and I believe its uncritical application to all cases of family pathology is as unwarranted as would be the treatment of all infections with penicillin, or all fractures with open reduction. It is particularly useful, in my experience, with those adolescents who, while in full rebellion against parental directives, experience sufficient conflict to long for some sort of resolution of their difficulty. Needless to say, in such situations there are often conflicting messages from the two parents involved, and their open clarification can be of great therapeutic value.

Even where "family therapy" is not clearly indicated, however, it is unquestionable that many couples cannot see the pathological interactions that go on between them unless they experience them directly in the presence of an objective observer. For such couples, conjoint therapy is of great value and may be of critical importance in interrupting behavior that is pathogenic to their children.

For example, Nancy, at six and a half, was brought for treatment because of her negative, oppositional behavior, tantrums, nail-biting and thumb-sucking, poor peer and sibling relations, and sleep difficulties. Her parents, a young professional couple, were both dependent on their own parents and highly immature. Mrs. R appeared to be emotionally labile, depressive, and self-accusatory; her husband was rigid and constricted and emotionally withdrawn, with typical obsessive-compulsive defenses. They were locked in a mutually accusatory, complaining relationship in which each saw the other as the culprit. They rarely communicated, though there was a lot of talk. On the basis of this pattern, revealed in individual interviews, it was decided not only that they should be seen conjointly but that Nancy be left untreated to emphasize the view that her illness was a symptom of the marital tension.

In conjoint therapy these parents were able to experiment on safe ground in the direct communication of feelings and wishes. They were able to become aware of the stereotypy of their patterns of conflict, and to learn how often their assumptions about each other were wrong. In this way the mutual scapegoating was diminished, and, with the aid of individual sessions that focused on the personal problems of each, they were able to modify their behavior greatly. Mr. R became a more active, involved father, while Mrs. R was able to give up an extra-marital affair she had been conducting for some months before treatment began. Nancy, faced with consistent and unified parental attitudes and behavior, ceased to be Mrs. R's reincarnated bad childhood self and began to adapt to normal expectations. She is no longer seen by them as a "problem" child.

As this case demonstrates, it is not necessary that every member of the critical triad must himself be in treatment in situations of this kind —at least, not where one's primary focus is the child and his welfare. What I have in mind is that the treatment plan must be developed with an awareness of the impact, not only on the child-patient, but on the family structure as a whole, of all therapeutic interventions and of the influence in turn of such impact on the child.

Take, for instance, the case of Billy, whose parents brought him for consultation at age nine at the recommendation of the school. He was described as listless, involved in fantasy, tense and fearful in school, and sullen and rebellious at home. In the course of the evaluation it was learned that the parents had long been emotionally estranged, that the mother, totally frigid in her sexual life, had been moderately depressed for several years and had recently become involved in some tentative, sporadic, and unsuccessful extramarital affairs in flight from her depression and feelings of worthlessness. The father had withdrawn almost totally into his business and had never been interested in his children to begin with.

This case is a classic instance of the way in which children serve as symptoms of the marital pathology of their parents and as their entering wedges into treatment. The mother had for years been considering seeking help—had on one occasion gone for a few sessions to a psychiatrist. But she could not have done so at the time the family came to me had not her son's difficulties provided her with a pretext and an opportunity to save face. It was immediately evident that the urgent need here was a referral for analysis of the mother, whose depression and affective detachment from her children was a principal cause of her son's disorders. The boy himself, as is so frequently the case at this age, was rigidly defended, reluctant to acknowledge difficulties, and highly resistant to the idea of treatment. It was apparent that only when the mother's illness could be relieved to the degree that she could again involve herself positively with the child could he be successfully approached therapeutically. Ideally, the father too should have been analyzed, but he was unavailable for such treatment; his absorption in his work served him as an effective basis for denial of pathology. Subsequently, however, as his wife improved, he developed acute potency difficulties and, after a protracted period of typical obsessional doubt and indecision, began his own analysis. This very shortly led to a significant shift in his involvement with his family; much of the bickering that had characterized the relationship between the two parents stopped (at least insofar as it concerned the management of the children), and they united in the decision to press for treatment of Billy. The lapse of almost two years had not, unfortunately, undone Billy's rigid projective, denying defense pattern, and he remained an almost impenetrable mass of resistance—but at least the environmental setting became conducive to the support and maintenance of a therapeutic effort.

In the case of Jeremy, on the other hand, intensive psychoanalytically-oriented therapy was immediately instituted with the boy, with both parents being involved in weekly interviews with a caseworker (though the father soon made himself unavailable). As indicated above, Jeremy actively played out his anxiety-laden fantasies of destruction of and by the aggressive, phallic mother. His father rarely appeared in his overt or disguised communications, except as one of the mother's many victims. Sexual confusions were rife throughout. Interpretations of his anxiety and the conflictual nature of his relationship with his mother were at first met with denial, but soon were confirmed and discussed openly. In the course of this process, his transvestism stopped, and he seemed more capable of relating appropriately to peers.

Mrs. K rejected joint sessions with her husband, but at first participated willingly in her own weekly interviews. It became quickly apparent that her narcissism, sustained as it was by her acting aspirations, left little room for significant change in her relationships with men or with her son. She soon began canceling appointments, bringing or sending Jeremy late, and, subsequently, failing to call for him, so that he had, at age eight, to travel home by bus himself. The pathological relationship between the parents continued more or less unabated. Finally, the pursuit of her theatrical career led her to move with her son to California, thus prematurely terminating Jeremy's therapy. Though she gave lip service to the idea of resuming after her move, it seemed unlikely that she would do so.

Nonetheless, Jeremy showed remarkable gains in treatment. It seems as though he is one of those children who have the capacity to modify, under appropriate therapeutic auspices, behavior that is in large measure the reflection of, if not consequent on, the pathological marital relationship of highly deviant parents. There does not seem to be much hope for significant impact of the treatment process on the parents or on their marriage, but there does seem to be some prospect for salvaging something of Jeremy's exceptional endowment.

The cases cited here lend support, I think, to the observation that the child psychiatrist or the child-guidance clinic is often the first professional resource to learn of marital psychopathology. The emotionally disturbed child is frequently the most blatant—or perhaps the most acceptable—manifestation of intrafamilial tension and is used in many cases as the instrument through which the parent or parents can find their own way into treatment. I want to make it clear, however, that I do not wish to indulge in the ever popular sport of parent-baiting. Many children develop various sorts of psychopathology on the basis of genetic factors other than parental misbehavior. There is, after all, still such a thing as trauma, and we see, occasionally, that *rara avis*, the case of a classical neurosis engendered by intrapsychic conflicts alone—and we owe all our families a thorough assessment of all possible contingent factors before slapping the label "pathogenic" on any parent or parental pair. We must include in our assessment that group of constitutional determinants of later behavioral style to which Fries,[14] Chess and her associates,[15] and others have helped to direct our attention.

But in the average run of cases, we find that the child's problems tend to reflect, in one way or another, aspects of the personalities, unconscious conflicts, and behavior of his parents, and that this often includes such strains in the family equilibrium that we have come to speak of as "marital pathology." Management of such children must include a sensitive family diagnosis and a treatment approach that takes cognizance of the relevant—and remediable—aspects of such pathology.

NOTES

1. Sigmund Freud, "The Analysis of a Phobia in a Five-Year-Old Boy" (1909), in *Collected Papers* (New York: Basic Books, 1959), Vol. III.
2. J. C. Flugel, *The Psychoanalytic Study of the Family* (Vienna: International Psychoanalytic Press, 1921).
3. Theodore Lidz, Stephen Fleck, and Alice Cornelison, *Schizophrenia and the Family* (New York: International Universities Press, 1966).
4. A. H. Esman, M. Kohn, and L. Nyman, "Parents of Schizophrenic Children," *American Journal of Orthopsychiatry*, XXIX (1959), 455–459.
5. L. Wynne and M. Singer, "Thought Disorder and Family Relations of Schizophrenics: I, A Research Strategy; II, A Classification of Forms of Thinking," *Archives of General Psychiatry*, IX (1963).
6. G. Bateson, D. D. Jackson, J. Haley, and J. H. Weakland, "Toward a Theory of Schizophrenia," *Behavioral Science,* I (1956), 251–264; see also D. D. Jackson, ed., *Etiology of Schizophrenia* (New York: Basic Books, 1960).
7. Nathan W. Ackerman, *The Psychodynamics of Family Life* (New York, Basic Books, 1958); see also Nathan Ackerman, Frances Beatman, and Sanford Sherman, eds., *Exploring the Base for Family Therapy* (New York: Family Service Association, 1961).
8. E. M. Litin, M. Giffin, and A. Johnson, "Parental Influence in Unusual Sexual Behavior in Children," *Psychoanalytic Quarterly*, XXV (1956), 37–55.
9. *Op. cit.*
10. Erik Erikson, "Growth and Crisis of the Healthy Personality," in *Iden-

tity and the Life Cycle (New York: International Universities Press, 1961).

11. René Spitz, "Anaclytic Depression," in *The Psychoanalytic Study of the Child*, Vol. II (New York: International Universities Press, 1948).

12. *Op. cit.*

13. Virginia Satir, *Conjoint Family Therapy* (Palo Alto, Calif. Science and Behavior Books, 1964).

14. M. Fries and P. J. Woolf, "Some Hypotheses on the Role of the Congenital Activity Type on Personality Development," in *The Psychoanalytic Study of the Child*, Vol. VIII (New York: International Universities Press, 1953), p. 32.

15. S. Chess, A. Thomas, and H. Birch, "Characteristics of the Individual Child's Behavioral Response to the Environment," *American Journal of Orthopsychiatry*, XXIX (1959), 455-459.

PAUL R. DINCE

General Considerations
of Major Sexual
Disturbances in Marriage

The marital sexual relationship is a reflection of and a major determinant of the capacity of the marital partners to engage in a collaborative commitment to a heterosexual relationship. The quality of an individual's sexual function is an indicator of the degree of maturity that has been attained in individual development and, consequently, of the capacity to love as a husband, wife, or parent. Since individual development does not cease at the time of marriage, but continues within the context of the marriage, the contribution made to the established fabric of the marital relationship by the sexual aims and activity of the individual partners is of primary importance. Personal growth is facilitated by a positive marital experience and tends to be impeded by a poor one.

There are very few generalizations that can be made concerning the relationship of sexual disturbances to the presence or absence of harmony within the marital relationship. Whether a marriage endures or terminates, is relatively harmonious or turbulent, depends upon a complex of factors of which the genital relationship is only one. No marriage terminates because of a sexual difficulty alone. On the other hand, disappointment, frustration, overt and covert resentment consequent to an unsatisfying sexual relationship do affect the general course of a marital relationship, its potential intimacy and richness, and, indirectly, the relationships of each partner to the children of the marriage.

A major sexual disturbance may be said to exist when either or both marital partners avoid sexual activity for prolonged periods of time or when attempts at sexual engagement fail because of severe inhibitions of function. A representative classification of marital sexual disturbances is that offered by Eisenstein under the headings of frigidity in the female, potency disturbances in the male, preference for masturbation, preference for sexual perversion, hypersexuality and lack of sexual interest. A general approach to sexual function and dysfunction predicated upon the degree of deviation from optimal heterosexual adaptation is more useful for the achievement of the aims of this discussion. Consideration of the specific forms of deviation would require extensive and separate study; only a brief preliminary consideration of potency disturbances in the male and frigidity in the female can follow here.

Potency Disturbances in Males

Potency disturbances in the male may be classified as total or partial. Full potency may be said to exist when a male is able to achieve full erection and maintain that erection during heterosexual genital relations until satisfying ejaculation and detumescence take place, accompanied by feelings of tenderness toward a valued and respected female. Total impotence may be said to exist when a male is unable to experience arousal and erection in genital relations with any woman in any circumstances, as in many homosexual and fetishistic disorders. The majority of nonhomosexual, married males seeking psychoanalytic treatment are found to experience some form of partial impotence.

One form of partial impotence is illustrated by those men who are able to approach their wives infrequently, requiring intervals of a week or more between sexual encounters. These prolonged intervals of avoidance are rationalized as due to fatigue, disinterest, or concern for their wives. However, the fatigue proves not to be physical fatigue but a transient state of depression and apathy consequent to conflict and anxiety. An individual who is not inhibited by sexual conflicts is quite capable of sexual activity even when physically induced fatigue exists. Sexual disinterest proves to have similar determinants, while those men who explain infrequent sexual approaches to their wives on the basis of their *wives'* disinterest often reveal that their wives do not, in reality, reject their advances or will respond to a moderately persistent approach. In many instances, the male is consciously or unconsciously aware that he can achieve mechanical potency only when these prolonged intervals occur and that more frequent sexual activity will evoke failures of function and embarrassing exposure. The apparent disinterest in sexual activity is thus often seen to be a defensive attempt to cope with the potency problem by avoidance.

Those men who do not rely upon avoidance as the primary means of escaping the sexual encounter and its attendant anxiety may experience transient or periodic inability to attain satisfactory erection, although motivated and emotionally aroused. Others may achieve a partial erection or find that a complete erection subsides to a partial erection or flaccid penis following insertion or during coital movement. Ejaculation prior to insertion, immediately upon, or very soon after insertion are other examples of partial impotence. A less frequently observed form of partial impotence is the inability to achieve an ejaculation and orgasm although arousal, erection, and prolonged coital stimulation have taken place. In other instances, ejaculation and expulsion of seminal products may take place without the psychologic relief from tension and muscular contractions of the orgasm.

A most common form of partial impotence is observed in men who are mechanically potent with their wives so long as their wives are devalued as love objects. The absence of feelings of tenderness, the presence of overt or covert minimizing attitudes constitute for them a necessary requisite for mechanical potency. Thus a transient disturbance of mechanical potency may take place in the course of psychoanalytic treatment of a male married patient when more positive and affectionate feelings toward his wife emerge. Some men can be mechanically potent with their wives when they, in effect, deny the existence of the real sexual partner and engage in fantasies. Within such fantasies, the sexual object may be a woman other than the wife, may be homosexual, and the interaction may be sadomasochistic in nature. Other men require for their mechanical potency that the wife behave in ways that act out the male's fantasies, as, for example, the man who insisted that his wife parade before him in her underclothes, silk stockings, and high-heeled shoes. As long as he could view his wife as a prostitute, mechanical potency and, therefore, some illusion of masculinity were possible.

Frigidity in the Female

Optimal sexual function in the female requires arousal and excitation deriving from the mutual stimulation of foreplay, preparedness for coitus through the production of lubricating vaginal secretions, and relaxation of the musculature of the introitus. Mounting excitation following penetration and coital movement culminates in the orgastic discharge of tension and peristaltic contractions of the vaginal musculature accompanied by affectionate and tender feelings toward a valued male sexual partner. Total frigidity is defined as the inability to achieve orgasm in the act of coitus with any male in any circumstances. As in the male, disturbances of sexual function may be intermittent or partial.

The psychophysiological sequence of arousal and discharge described above may be interfered with at any point within that sequence. There are women whose sexual function has suffered such extensive and pervasive damage that they must avoid all sexual contact with males or who are unable to experience any awareness of arousal should sexual contact take place. These women either avoid marriage or marry men whose sexual needs are minimal and whose sexual function has been damaged in comparable fashion. Some women are able to experience arousal during foreplay that involves parts of the body other than their genital region, but are unable to sustain their arousal if the partner attempts specifically genital stimulation. In other women, foreplay and clitoridal stimulation may induce arousal, which subsides when penetration takes place, or arousal may continue following penetration and subside at some later moment in anticipation of and before the point of orgastic experience.

As in some males, orgasm may be dependent upon fantasies during coitus in which the actual partner is replaced by some other person, in which a homosexual act is depicted, or which contain sadomasochistic elements. In other instances the sequence of arousal and orgastic discharge may be achieved only when widely spaced intervals occur between coital activity.

There are women whose capacity for orgastic coital activity is dependent upon the avoidance of impregnation. If those instances in which enlargement of the family comes into real conflict with limited economic resources or poor maternal health are excluded from consideration, *fears* of pregnancy are consequent to irrational psychosexual conflict. For many women, the fear that impregnation will take place is an important, if not decisive, determining factor in their avoidance of or cautious approach to coital activity. In the marital relationship this problem may become overt prior to the birth of any child or it may become manifest following the birth of a child.

An illustrative example is that of a young woman in her twenties who was capable of orgastic coital activity with her husband up to the birth of her first child. The postpartum period was characterized by symptoms of depression and a gradually increasing fear of sexual relations with her husband. An escape into an extramarital relationship provided her with satisfying sexual activity with a partner who could not expect of her that she bear his child. When she contemplated remarriage to the extramarital partner, she was overcome with anxiety and the impulse to flee this relationship, for she might now have to face the prospect of further childbearing. Analytic exploration revealed that childbirth was associated with overwhelming fears of mutilation and death, fears that she had successfully denied in the early years of her marriage, for they conflicted with her image of herself as fearless and capable of meeting any challenge.

Full potency of the male partner and full sexual responsivity of the female partner therefore allow for the development of an optimal marital sexual relationship. When the marital couple is able to engage in relatively frequent sexual activity, each achieving orgastic satisfaction and increased feelings of tenderness and value for the other, an optimal sexual relationship may be said to exist. This capacity signifies the ability to sustain sexual pleasure without significant anxiety, an ability that permits the psychophysiological sequence of arousal, stimulation, and orgastic discharge to occur without inhibition of sensory and motor functions. It also implies the presence of that ample degree of confidence in one's autonomy which is necessary for the flexibility to adapt to the partner's idiosyncratic needs and the ability to proffer gratification to the partner. Finally, it implies an acceptance of the partner as a separate, although related person, as opposed to a view of the partner as an extension of one's self to be exploited in a narcissistic fashion.

The foregoing concept of the optimal marital sexual relationship can merely serve as a flexible guideline, for ubiquitous intrapsychic and external forces periodically interfere with the sexual sequence in the most stable of sexual relationships. However, in an optimal relationship, such periods of interference will be the exception rather than the rule. Departures from this optimal sexual relationship may be considered on a scale that, in effect, reflects the degree of psychopathology of the marital partners and therefore the degree of disturbance within the sexual relationship. Such a scale would portray the entire range of individual psychopathology; the defensive and developmental maladaptive formations that obstruct the capacity to sustain heterosexual gratification and love.

All aspects of the marital relationship, including the sexual, must be viewed and reflected against a background provided by several factors. Each of the partners brings to the marriage a character structure and individual neurosis that will mesh in some ways and clash in other ways with the character and neurosis of the other partner. There is the additional factor of object choice: the role which each partner plays as a transferential object, representing one or more members of the nuclear family of the other, and the consequent expectations and unconscious fantasies directed toward each other. In a marriage of some duration there is a further factor, provided by the accretions of time: the continuing sequence of interaction and mutual adaption, the regulatory functions which serve to maintain the marital equilibrium.

Marriages are observed in which some level of intimacy is attained on levels other than the sexual level. Conversely, there are relationships in which intimacy of some sort is achieved only through sexual activity, with other areas of relatedness characterized by a lack of intimacy. There are marriages in which one or both partners experience no sexual satisfaction within the marital relationship but do achieve sexually satisfying relationships with extramarital partners. In some marriages it is the husband who is incapable of participating sexually as often as expected; in others it is the wife who avoids and rejects sexual intimacy. There are those marriages in which, by tacit or explicit consent, sexual activity is avoided and rejected by both partners. Some women are threatened by a husband's sexual disinterest or impotence because it represents to them a potential abandonment. Sexually frigid themselves, they require occasional sexual activity as proof of the husband's commitment. There are husbands whose need for sexual activity is very intense, not on the level of sensual gratification per se, but in order to restore continually wilting confidence in their masculinity or to reassure themselves that their wives will not become sexually interested in other men. Others, with similar underlying pathology, fear the sexual demands of their wives, for they are thereby exposed as sexually inadequate. Disturbances of potency may be present from the inception of marriage or may appear consequent to life changes such as the birth of a child. Even chronic disturbances of potency are variable and tend to fluctuate in intensity. Among women, frigidity may be present from the beginning and remain chronic throughout married life, or it may be replaced by sexual responsivity, not infrequently after childbirth. Conversely, a woman who has been sexually responsive prior to childbirth may become frigid afterward. Changes in sexual potency of the husband or responsiveness in the wife may lead to increased sexual difficulty in the partner. A man who has been mechanically potent with a frigid partner may become less potent when she becomes more responsive. A woman who is sexually responsive as long as her husband approaches her infrequently may become less so if his sexual demands increase. These are but a few of the variations observed in the sexual disturbances in marriage as reported by patients in psychoanalytic treatment.

Whether these and other variations threaten the harmony or continuity of a marriage is dependent upon the many factors that make up the totality of the relationship. However, the libidinal needs of human beings are such that the failure of satisfaction within the marital context necessitates the institution of adaptive measures. The adaptive efforts are primarily oriented to the repair of damaged self-esteem and may range from the attempt to suppress and deny sexual strivings to the pursuit of sexual satisfaction with a partner other than the mate. This is true whether the failure of satisfaction is due to the sexual unresponsivity of the partner or to psychosexual pathology that prevents the individual from achieving sexual gratification with a marital, valued sexual object.

In psychoanalytic practice, it is relatively rare to encounter a marriage in which one or the other partner is completely unavailable for sexual activity. Nor do we encounter patients whose marriages are characterized by relatively frequent, uninhibited, anxiety-free sexual relations accompanied and followed by feelings of increased tenderness for the mate. We observe most frequently the range between these extremes—relationships in which sexual activity does take place, but in an atmosphere of anxiety and overt or covert mutual resentment. It is not the purpose of this discussion to explore the causes of sexual anxiety, but rather to touch upon some of the consequences of sexual anxiety in the marital setting.

In order to pursue this aim, I would like to offer the concept of the sexual refractory period to denote a pattern seen in many disturbed marriages, wherein an instance or period of sexual activity is followed by a period of sexual avoidance by one or both partners. When a wife withdraws sexually from her impotent husband, or a husband from a wife who is sexually rejecting, the significance of the withdrawal is reasonably clear. When, however, we observe sexual avoidance following sexual activity in a couple in which the husband is potent and the wife capable of achieving orgasm, the avoidance takes on something of a paradoxical character. This pattern, observed in many disturbed marriages, is based upon conflict and anxiety related to genital function and genital pleasure. The anxiety is often rationalized in the form of derogatory attitudes toward the partner, who by this means is made the scapegoat for the individual's distress.

To illustrate this point, I would like to offer the instance of a woman in her early thirties, married for a number of years and the mother of several children, whose presenting complaints included a recurrent inability to respond sexually to her husband. Included in her history are considerable fear and guilt connected with active childhood and adolescent masturbation and a fearful Oedipal conflict. Orgasm posed for her a considerable threat, for it was an experience that deprived her of her overvalued control. Following intercourse, she experienced a refractory period of ten days to two weeks in which she was angered by the sexual advances of her husband. Psychosomatic headaches made their appearance; she became compulsively involved in household tasks, which kept her busy until the late hours of the night or rendered her physically exhausted; deliberate delaying tactics were engaged in, which ensured her retiring later than did her husband. She berated herself for her failure to be a good wife, but could feel only resentment toward her husband, resentment that she rationalized as due to one or another aspect of her husband's behavior. These feelings would gradually subside, intercourse would take place, and another refractory period would ensue. The refractory period is, in fact, a depression of moderate proportions, a depression which for this patient would begin with a painful, tearful feeling of isolation following immediately upon the orgastic experience.

Many of the mechanisms described in the chapters devoted to resistance to marriage, choice of marital partner, and simulated orgasm were operant in the dynamics of her illness. Multiple transferential distortions required that she view her husband as an embodiment of her mother, a withholding and narcissistic woman, who had abandoned the care of the patient to a series of surrogates when the child was two years of age, and who had been consistent in her subsequent insensitivity to the patient's needs. As a transferential substitute for the father, who reacted to her childhood efforts toward intimacy with ridicule and unmerciful teasing, the husband was viewed by the patient as demanding and impossible to please. In truth, her husband was not a depriving or withholding person, nor did he have expectations of the patient that were in any way unreasonable. She reported the memory of an early childhood fantasy that had been accompanied by anxiety-ridden masturbatory activity: she was attacked by a faceless adult male while her arms were tied and her back arched as if on a rack. The fantasy constituted a screen memory which obscured the primal scene. In the sexual relationship, she frustrated and deprived her husband, her unconscious motivations including the impulse to castrate him.

Following an attempt to alter her pattern of sexual avoidance, the patient reported the following dream. There is a large dog tied to a dog sled by reins that are held by a man who is behind the dog. The man is holding the reins in his left hand, while in his right hand he holds a whip or staff with which he prods and torments the dog. The dog struggles to free itself, works itself loose from the reins, turns around, and bites off the man's left hand, the hand holding the reins. The dog runs loose. There are people in the background of the dream who are frightened of the dog.

Her associations to the dream clearly identified the man as the analyst who sits behind her and holds the reins in the analytic situation. To the whip or staff, she associated her husband's erect penis approaching her from behind as she lay in bed with her back to him, and her thought, "He thinks he's such a man with his erection . . . I'd like to tell him what I really think about his penis." To the reins, she associated her feelings consequent to the analyst's interpretation of the pattern of sexual avoidance. She had viewed the interpretation as a demand that she give up her behavior at once and felt that failure to do so would risk the analyst's anger and ridicule. She felt that she was in a trap and was furious with the analyst, as if he had created her dilemma. The taboo libidinal drives, activated by the psychoanalytic transference, are crystallized by the dream, as is her view that she can achieve gratification of these drives solely in a sadomasochistic relationship. Her escape is to destroy partially the object of the drives, to destroy his "hold over her."

In the marital relationship, her need to castrate the husband is over-determined. She gains revenge for the deprivation for which she inaccurately holds him responsible, and gains an illusory restoration of equality with the envied male. But of nuclear importance is the need to defend herself against the consequences of the repressed incestuous wish toward her sadistic father. Her reservoir of rage originates from her early, persistent deprivation, but is used maladaptively to destroy that which she inaccurately perceives to be the source of the danger, the male (father's) genital. Her pattern of sexual avoidance protects her against the uncontrolled eruption of her sadistic aggression, the retaliation of the male, and the retaliation of the mother she wants to replace.

Another young woman, also unable to allow her husband to reach her sexually during her refractory periods, became obsessed during these weeks of sexual avoidance with thoughts that she had married the wrong man, that he was not sufficiently handsome or cultured, and with fantasies of romantic liaisons with other men. With the subsidence of the refractory period, she would view him more realistically; in truth, he was not unattractive and was above average intellectually and most devoted to her. Sexual intercourse would take place with orgastic satisfaction, only to be followed by the next refractory period.

Male patients report the same pattern. One man described his feelings as follows: "After we have sex, I go off into my own little world. . . . I don't want her to touch me physically or emotionally. . . . Mentally, I want to get as far away from her as possible." Another man reported that after intercourse he has the feeling that he is "circling" around his wife, fearful of touching her or feeling anything in common with her. This is accompanied by vague feelings of guilt and shame, as if he had just done something to his wife that wasn't very nice. He experiences quite prolonged refractory periods, which eventually cause him to feel concerned about his masculinity. At such times he will plan to make a sexual approach to his wife, but before his impulse can become a reality, he compulsively begins to derogate her in his fantasies, focusing his thoughts on one or another of her failings, thereby working himself into such a rage that he provokes an argument with her, thus avoiding the sexual encounter.

These instances are but a few of many. For some individuals, the refractory period takes the primary form of retreat and withdrawal; for others, defensive rage aimed at distancing the partner is the most obvious phenomenon. Some combination of withdrawal and rage is consistently observed. Much of the rage seen in marital disturbances is misunderstood, for an individual's rationalizations may serve to obscure the significance of the rage as a defensive response, a maladaptive effort to ward off sexual anxiety.

Where husband and wife tend to experience refractory periods of relatively similar proportions, the potential for conflict in the sexual sphere of the marriage is minimized. When it is the wife who is subject to a prolonged sexual refractory period, the husband may respond to the castrating implications of her avoidance by retreat or aggression. When it is the husband who experiences the prolonged sexual refractory period, the wife doubts her feminine sexual attractiveness and may respond in like fashion. This process can lead to considerable friction and disharmony, leading to a very real problem in living together, which obscures and replaces the neurotic one. It is in such circumstances that the marital partners may turn their libidinal strivings toward their children, who represent safer libidinal objects, thereby contributing to the forces that will help create the next generation of sexual and marital disturbance. These circumstances may also foster a search for resolution through extramarital sexual activity, divorce, and, at times, multiple marriages.

Some comments about extramarital sexual relationships: For some individuals, the extramarital relationship represents a purposeful, though not necessarily deliberate, effort to escape from a wretched marriage. For others, its meaning differs, for they evince no genuine intention of terminating their marital relationships, as proven by their unwillingness to do so when given the opportunity. The extraordinary efforts to maintain the secrecy of the extramarital relationship attest to the need to avoid jeopardizing the marriage. While some men with potency problems have similar difficulties in extramarital sexual activity, others find themselves to be extremely potent with an extramarital partner whom they see once or twice a week. There are women who are unable to respond sexually to their husbands but who are uninhibited and orgastic with a lover. Frequently the initiation of an extramarital relationship constitutes a masochistic act following upon a successful fulfillment in a major life area.

The structure of the extramarital sexual relationship obviates many of those forces that tend to promote sexual anxiety and consequent inhibition. The partner is not so easily subject to the Oedipal taboos as is the mate, the necessarily clandestine nature of the relationship provides a protective mantle of secrecy for the sexual activity and sexual relationship, and the demands for intimacy on levels other than the sexual are minimal or absent. In addition, the stake in preserving the marriage requires that contact with the extramarital partner be periodic so that intervals are established that correspond in quality to the sexual refractory period mentioned above. It is quite possible that the defensive mechanisms of sexual avoidance need not be brought into play since realistic considerations determine continuing interruptions of intimacy. In many instances where an individual divorces to marry the extramarital partner, the same sexual problems that existed in the first marriage recur in the second.

If there has been any primary theme in this discursive appraisal of sexual difficulties in marriage, it is the concept that sexual interaction can have a divisive effect not only on the bases of disappointment and frustration, but also on the basis of sexual anxiety consequent to sexual fulfillment and orgastic pleasure. The factors that determine and perpetuate injury to the sexual function and its potential maturation in marriage are manifold, complex, and beyond the scope of this discussion. The consequences of such injury must inevitably affect the course of a marriage, however, and in some instances will contribute to its demise.

The Significance of the Orgastic Pretense

The orgastic pretense is a complex clinical entity, being not merely a subordinate, or a variant, of frigidity, but having significant and special implications for the problems of acting out, faulty identifications, and body-image pathology. Over the years, the pertinent literature on frigidity has increased enormously. This increase may attest to our deep interest and concern with this problem, as well as to our frustrations and disappointments with our clinical results. Recently, the topic of frigidity has been aptly and concisely reviewed by Moore[1] in a published article of twenty-six pages. For reasons of expediency, I must dispense with a detailed summary of the classic writings on this subject. In surveying the extensive literature on frigidity, however, I was unable to find a single contribution on the topic of the orgastic pretense per se—remarkable indeed, in view of the likely prevalence of this condition. Therefore, I have formulated this material in this chapter from what I have been able to observe and extract from five interesting cases that share the symptom of orgastic deceit as part of their frigidity.

All five were stunning and talented married women in their thirties, who were sufficiently motivated and integrated to be able to attain an eventual symptomatic cure of their frigidity, thereby rendering the orgastic pretense obsolete. Their frigidity was without vaginal anesthesia, yet they experienced varying degrees of both psychic and physical arousal, which then suddenly disappeared as they were about to reach the orgastic peak. The psychoanalytic literature on frigidity notes the various gradations, but essentially uses the absence of the vaginal orgasm as the sole criterion.[2] Moore[3] explains in this connection that "What is probably important is not the presence or absence of sensitivity but the cathexis of the organ as the site of erotic satisfaction."

Sexual arousal in women and the female orgasm are infinitely more subtle phenomena than the undisputable manifestations of male erections and emissions. Consequently, the female orgasm lends itself much more readily to incorporation of sexual intrigue, mystery, challenge, teasing, and deception—so much so that in many instances orgastic potency can be denied when it is present or passed off as present when it may be absent. The over-all greater feminine talent for intuition and sensitivity has been amply emphasized and is readily conceded at the very outset. It develops early in life and is fostered and reinforced all along by the inherent vicissitudes and many nodal points of female identifications, as well as the nature of our culture.

Suffice it to say, the female orgasm most plausibly represents nature's gift to femininity, and not primarily women's bonus to masculinity, as the current vogue tends to emphasize. Therefore, it is not surprising to find that many women who cannot attain orgasm through their own efforts produce an allegedly reasonable facsimile thereof, often as a protective tribute to their mates' virility. This disguise may also serve as an effective smoke screen for significant psychopathology of their own. The women who practice this fraud regularly are inclined to view it as the perfect crime. Upon repeated sexual contact with the same lover, this dubious "art of loving" often is further refined, whereby the woman will permit her true frigidity to appear intermittently. As far as I have been able to ascertain, this is not done because she has suddenly decided to drop the pretense. On the contrary, it is done in order to make the "ersatz" appear more genuine. One of my patients who all along insisted that she was absolutely convinced of her perfect falsification in this respect, as well as her husband's complete gullibility, became very anxious when she was able to achieve real and full orgastic satisfaction after all. She was then convinced that this man was going to find out what she had done to him during all those years. The answer is: he didn't. He merely remarked to her that "things are going still better now," which of course was absolutely correct. I hasten to add that this patient thereafter referred to her genuine orgastic feats as ejaculations. When I had the opportunity to question her about this, she professed to be completely naïve on the subject, this despite her otherwise great worldliness and good intellect. She simply assumed that her profuse lubrication during orgasm was equivalent to the product of the male emission.

In this connection, Almansi emphasizes that "the highly bisexual makeup is at the root of their frigidity and their orgastic pretense." They are so fixated on the level of imitative gestures that, as part of their tendency to identify with the male during intercourse, they display "a strong need to emulate the motions and thrusts of the male."[4]

Because of limitations of space, I will have to forego the opportunity of describing in detail the men who fall prey to these women. They would fill a chapter in their own right. Although these men are generally successful and spectacular in some endeavors, the weakness that they display for beautiful women most certainly is not their only one.

"Nowadays beautiful women are counted among the talents of their husbands."[5] Freud speaks of beautiful narcissistic women and the fact that "it is only themselves that such women love with an intensity comparable to that of man's love for them."[6] He also observed that "such women have the greatest fascination for men, not only for aesthetic reasons . . . for it seems very evident that another person's narcissism has a great attraction for those who have renounced part of their narcissism and are in search for object love." According to Freud,[7] " 'Beauty' and 'attraction' are originally attributes of the sexual object. It is worth remarking that the genitals themselves, the sight of which is always exciting, are nevertheless hardly ever judged to be beautiful; the quality of beauty seems instead to attach to certain secondary sexual characters."

Although orgastic deceit may be seen as part of various disorders, the cases under consideration here are patients who not only manifest "as if" orgasms but display personalities to match. They are "neurotic characters"[8] for whom pretense in general and the senseless repetition thereof for the purpose of mastery constitute a way of life. They are striking women who basically have keen intellects, an enormous ambition for status, and strong masculine strivings. Still, they are highly seductive and ultrafeminine in dress, appearance, and behavior. Beauty props to complement and implement their charms favorably are used with cunning strategy. They are highly narcissistic and have a low frustration tolerance because of their oral predisposition.[9] According to Waelder,[10] "as if" personalities "are suffering from a feeling of emptiness or nothingness and are trying to fill themselves up, as it were, through appropriating from others without it ever becoming fully their own." "Their efforts to be feminine are incessant and futile, just as their efforts to be masculine."[11] These patients are forever in search of identity" as described in Erikson.[12] They "identify with the aggressor,"[13] and "struggle against identifications."[14] They are prone to run to and from successive "fleeting identifications."[15] In the circumstances at hand, it is no surprise that the cases described here were prone to multiple marriages or to successive similar arrangements.

According to Greenacre,[16] in acting out, "such people often believe that to do a thing in a dramatic or imitative way—to make it look as though it were true—is really the equivalent of making it true. It is obvious that this works also to ward off with magic activity as well as to produce by imitative approximation." Reich[17] feels that "fixation on the level of imitative gestures leads to a lack of internalization in the ego ideal and constitutes the basis for the 'as if' personality." "The externalization of such an ego ideal, and its fusion with a love object represents a form of narcissistic object choice in women."

As I have already indicated, these patients were greatly preoccupied with their shapely bodies. However, the greatest emphasis was given to their well-formed breasts. They endowed these organs with particular magic and irresistibility. The penis-breast equation is of course well known, and so are many other combinations and permutations of symbolic equations pertaining to the various erogenic zones. Schilder[18] states: "It might almost be said that the erogenic zones of the various body images are closer to each other than other parts of the body, or that intercourse between the body images takes place especially through the erogenic zones." Greenacre[19] describes patients of beauty and talent, both frigid and not, who in their psychic representations "disregard the penis and fixate on the testicles, while the breast is exalted over any male genital." Thus "both male and female genitals [are] represented in the breast." The male testicles are eclipsed by the larger breasts of these women, which simultaneously represent the proud prototype of their own ambivalently cherished femininity.

To the extent that the orgastic pretense constitutes an imposture, it implies imposture of a mature woman. As a result, she tries to cover up her orgastic defect and pretends to be more complete than she is. Only at first glance, if at all, may this appear as a benign imposture. The imposture of a mature woman in a sense signifies an adult way of "playing house"; however, because it is generally agreed that these "as if" patients are the product of phallic mothers[20] to begin with, what is acted out here cannot be the role of the mother they had, but more likely represents the feminine image they wish and strive for. Therefore, we are primarily dealing with acting, rather than identification with a real object. This phallic feminine constitution seemingly mirrors maternal indoctrination plus, since it is highly questionable that the phallic mothers also indulged themselves in this additional refinement of the orgastic deceit.

According to Hartmann and Loewenstein,[21] "the ego ideal can be considered a rescue operation for narcissism." It may serve a restitutive function to the extent that it maintains the object; however and most of all, it is a form of denial through the magic of action.[22] Here the imposture appears as acting out of an otherwise normal ego ideal. Reich[23] explains that "the degree of pathology of the narcissistic object choice depends on the normalcy or pathology of the ego ideal." Moreover, on the basis of current information, we are probably correct in postulating that the orgastic pretense entails considerable gratification of sexual aggressive wishes that are not based on past relations or affectionate cathexis and as such are prone to be incestuous in nature. Part of the pathology may rest with the fact that the sexual act here is perceived as a humiliating and submissive experience. This humiliation is self-perpetuating, since the fear of humiliation leads to orgastic inhibition, and this failure evokes an additional humiliation. Beyond this, it neither gratifies the phallic ambitions of these women nor, because of their frigidity, do they ultimately emerge sexually satisfied and complete as the women that they are. Therefore, the acting out and pretense of the "as if" orgasm serve to ward off the painful feeling of humiliation in this predicament.

To assume that the orgastic pretense is performed as an act of great kindness and charity, done for the benefit of the male partners, is of course possible, but highly unlikely. More plausibly, these women wish to hide this defect for fear of incurring the man's wrath, because for them to be orgastically impotent is equivalent to emasculating the man. Withholding an orgasm from oneself and the partner may be one thing, but additionally pretending to have one is something else, which may be viewed as orgastic misbehavior. It constitutes a sexual tease whereby the woman ambivalently wants the man to have the sensitivity to know what she is perpetrating upon him and feels contemptuous of him if he does not. To these phallic women, orgasm is experienced as merging with the man. This they both wish and fear. Climax and the attainment thereof here document full acceptance of their own womanhood and relinquishment of the illusory penis. To be fully gratified by a man's penis is also perceived as dangerous, since it no longer provides them with either sufficient control over themselves or over the man. Moreover, it is blocked by their crossed sexual identifications and confused identities. They pretend to be active as a denial of their inability to accept the passive role.[24]

That orgasm itself, instead of intercourse, may readily become equated with the fear of pregnancy, since pregnancy constitutes further documentation of womanhood, has occurred to me. However, I have no evidence from my patients either to refute or to corroborate this. Similarly, I had to rule out in these cases the possibility that the orgastic pretense might simply be a device to end the torture of the sexual act. Most of the time, all these patients experienced varying degrees of pleasurable vaginal arousal, except when an orgasm was imminent.

Like other frigid patients, and more so, they are participant-observers during coitus. This attitude is not restricted to sexual activity. In an almost compulsive manner, this tendency pervades many aspects of social intercourse as well. Since much of their lives deals with one pretense or another, they are forever busy ruminating about their next move. Constant self-observation in the presence of significant individuals is indispensable in order to maintain the exquisite control required. Emphasis on visualization[25] is so cardinal a factor to this pathogenesis that, for this reason alone, satisfactory surrender during the sexual act, or any meaningful interpersonal relationship, is practically impossible. These patients feel absolutely lost unless they can visualize themselves in action.

This need for visual surveillance may at least in part account for the frequent, if not universal, complaint of insomnia, as well as the comparatively greater or absolute disinclination to assume the reclining position during psychoanalysis. The meaning of the fear of annihilation during sleep has been described by Lewin[26] as part of the oral triad. Freud said that "the seat of anxiety is in the ego."[27] Brodsky further explains that "to be meaningful as a psychic danger situation, extinction of the ego must be understood as extinction of the self-image."[28] In such individuals the ego is largely equated with the eye. What cannot be seen is perceived as dangerous and gives rise to anxiety, or as Brodsky put it, "not to have a stream of preconscious-conscious thought is not to have a self image."[29] Their identities are perceived as so fragile that visual reassurance is observed most of the time like a ritual. Dressed or undressed, these women live up to the façade-images and goals that they have erected for themselves. The fear of possibly not looking just as beautiful as usual during climax is paramount, but even more dreaded are the fears of loss of sphincter control, an epileptic seizure, or running rampant and other aggressive acts. "When the body is used to symbolize the phallus," as described by Lewin,[30] "the mouth may represent the urethra, and the ejection of fluid from the mouth an ejaculation or urination." "The fantasy of one's whole body being a penis is symbolically a passive feminine fantasy, the equivalent of the phallic level of castration."[31] Therefore, these patients are terrified of losing control even for a single moment, and for this reason do not attempt to have orgasm, because of the dangers that are anticipated as a result of such liberty. What is feared is injury, castration, disintegration, fusion,[32] and ultimately annihilation.

That there must be secondary gain aspects in this and other deceits is unquestionably true. However, the gratifications from this component are likely to be contaminated by the already mentioned fears, which cannot be counted on always to be repressed or otherwise detoxified. What may perhaps contribute to the additional maintenance of this practice occurs because of the chronicity and intensity of the pretense. As a consequence, the achievement of an orgasm may become idealized to a point where reality no longer can compete with it, thus reinforcing both the pretense and frigidity.

By the time a young lady reaches full sexual bloom, she is already effectively sensitized to penis envy, has developed submissive masochistic feminine identifications,[33] and has been subjected to the prevailing cultural and parental prejudicial attitudes, which reflect the moral "blue laws" (Lewin) of our society toward sexual freedom in women. Therefore, her fully developed biological equipment seemingly arrives too late to convince her readily of its comparable value. The hostility of frigid women is originally and foremost toward their mothers, but then it becomes transferred to men.[34] Lampl-De Groot[35] has established the phallic activity of girls toward their mothers. Mother is not only "a creature who is without a penis,"[36] but, as Lorand[37] points out, the envy and aggression was aimed at the mother's body which contained the father's penis. He observed that although they expressed a wish to be as different as possible from their own mothers, in most cases they turned out to be exact replicas of the mothers. Oscar Wilde revealingly said, "All women become like their mothers. That is their tragedy. No man does. That is his." Lorand further stresses that the important factor in the frigid reaction is the patient's idea that the mother's sexual life with the father cannot be one of pleasure. Only when she accepts the idea in analysis that her mother may have enjoyed this relationship can she permit herself to experience pleasurable sensations.

Freud in his essay on female sexuality writes: "With many women we have the impression that their years of maturity are occupied by a struggle with their husbands, just as their youth was spent in a struggle with their mothers." "Their hostile attitude to their mothers is not a consequence of the rivalry implicit in the Oedipus complex, but originates from the preceding phase and has merely been reinforced and exploited in the Oedipus situation."[38] Knight[39] explains that while hostile feelings toward men may not be evident, or easily elicited, their disguised derivatives may be apparent. Therefore, despite their insistence, these women are not all that they claim to be, namely, man's best friend.

Interestingly enough, in the case of the orgastic pretense we find no open manifestations of hostility toward the male partner, which is so often seen in complete frigidity and appears as outright attempts to humiliate the man, to disappoint him sexually, or to destroy his potency. In the case of the orgastic pretense, the revenge is infinitely more camouflaged and lacks the characteristics of open "genital warfare" (Deutsch), since the gratification afforded by the deceit modifies the experience of anger. These women render only token service to the virility of their partners. They virtually dare the man who knows to accuse them that they did not achieve orgasm, thereby exposing his weakness, his deficiencies, and his helplessness.

One's biological destiny and the acceptance thereof have horizons far beyond anatomical differences, particularly for the woman. According to Sarlin, "anatomical reality may dictate an identification which emotional factors reject." "It is of fundamental importance for the reality testing function of the ego that these identifications be established in conformity with anatomical reality."[40] While the male penis, for better or worse, at all times leaves no doubt as to its various shapes, activities, and functions, the vagina, by comparison, is perceived primarily as a dark, obscure cavity and something of a mystery.[41] Be-

cause of this, it often gives rise to feelings of utmost intrigue as well
as mortal fear in members of both sexes. Evidently, these parts of the
body which are least accessible to vision provide greatest uncertainty
about structure and boundaries of the body image and therefore are
most poorly integrated into the concept of the self.[42] Because integration of these vaginal representations, despite their paramount importance, is relatively poor to begin with, their subsequent surrender during orgasm becomes additionally difficult. However, it is the fully erect
penetrating penis that outlines, fills, and confirms most clearly for the
woman the boundaries of her sexual apparatus. Shortly before she at-
tains vaginal orgasm, she is definitely presented with the naked fact of
her unmistaken feminine image. This moment of truth constitutes her
last chance to relinquish her illusory penis in exchange for her true
orgastic femininity. Whether it is this enforced picture of her femininity that causes the anxiety that interferes with orgasm or whether it is
the fear of castration is a matter for speculation. The orgastic pretense
obviously hides either one, or both, equally well.

You may wonder, as I did, why these highly narcissistic women with
strong oral predispositions and such perfect bodies considered analysis
for themselves to begin with, and even more so, why they continued.
These five cases are the good-looking and the gifted acting-out patients. When they consulted me, they were in their early thirties and
had already suffered incredible boredom from leading shallow lives
for many years. They had been riding the crest of the waves on their
beauty alone for quite some time. They obviously had been long aware
and in fear of the fact that "beauty is the first present nature gives to
women and the first it takes away" (Méré). They came for analytic
treatment, and continued, in order to acquire the courage to pursue,
in addition to their standard feminine occupation, a spectacular masculine one as well, such as a respectable profession, or a flourishing
legitimate business of their own. Although in all these cases frigidity
never appeared as a presenting symptom, they could not reconcile it
much longer with their "aggrandized, wishful self-images,"[43] which
required both the greatest of looks and the greatest sexual potency to
go with them.

As I have indicated all along, these women suffered from relative
frigidity[44] and only experienced sudden cessation of excitement shortly
before orgasm was impending. Therefore, the orgastic pretense was
required only during the very final phase, the brief period before the

summit, when orgastic feelings were suddenly lost. Whenever this sequence applies, the orgastic deceit is facilitated, since both effort and strain along these lines are required for exceedingly short periods. By reason of this brevity, it becomes so much more difficult for the male partner to detect the fraud. Lorand[45] ascribes this last-minute flight from sexual pleasure due to "fear of losing the penis before achieving orgasm, that coitus will end and they will be compelled to surrender the male organ." "When orgasm is inhibited, it is because of fear of losing this love (breast, penis, affection, etc.) and of being left alone, apart and empty." The fear of post-orgastic emptiness is caused, according to Agoston,[46] by: (i) traumatic predisposition: strong castration anxiety,[47] (ii) acute traumatic experience: physical and emotional discharge, frightening beyond control.

Although my patients were predisposed to oral regression, they were not fixated on that level. Nor were their ego boundaries so vague and their sense of identity so precarious as those of the frigid patients whom Keiser[48] describes. He states, "The body ego based only on oral gratification is too weak and insufficiently differentiated from external reality to achieve genitality because the normal loss of ego boundaries during orgasm is too great a threat." While my patients feared the loss of identity and could not readily surrender to orgasm, their need to achieve their ego ideal ultimately triumphed.

One woman, a physician, was in the habit of arriving late for her sessions. When I inquired repeatedly, I eventually learned that it was my prerogative to end the hour, and hers to begin the session. The orginal batch of elementary interpretations did not alter this habit one bit. She simply smiled when I explained her wish to control, to be the doctor herself, and her inability to accept the passive role. Then when I confronted her with her wish to treat our appointments like dates, for which she religiously arranged to be late too, I drew fire. She was infuriated; it did indeed represent a partly conscious fantasy. This interpretation miraculously stopped the lateness. My therapeutic intervention presented the patient with her unconscious fantasy of intimacy and closeness of our relationship, which she had heretofore viewed as impersonal. The real fear in the therapeutic situation is very similar to the sexual one; namely, the fear of submission to a significant man, or any meaningful person. These women come close only momentarily, like hit-and-run drivers, because of the intolerable fear and frustrations. The fear of coming close is ever present, as is its opposite desire. Any attempt to come close is primitive and in the direction of taking over the entire person; coexistence is fraught with dangers and consequences.

Since pretense is the modus vivendi in these patients, the analytic situation cannot be expected to escape exclusion. I have already indicated that orgastic deceit was not a presenting symptom as far as I was able to determine. Furthermore, those fortunate ones who succeeded in attaining a cure of their frigidity neglected to report this blessed event to their therapist for several weeks or more. Contrary to what might be expected, there were no exclamations of "Eureka" to anyone. They were stunned, frightened, and feared that by talking about it they might cease experiencing orgastic pleasure in the future.

This clinical observation, especially if it can be corroborated in the same context, would have significant and interesting implications in terms of the transference reaction. Acting-out patients are notoriously inaccurate reporters in the therapeutic situation. This important omission may be viewed as another form of acting out, since it has been said that the patient who can report his acting out with complete unconcern must be in some sense acting. Greenacre[49] points out that frequently the acting out that occurs away from the analysis remains unknown to the analyst for a long time, sometimes forever, unless he happens to hear of it from other patients or learn of it from some other incidental and unexpected source. Silverberg[50] clarifies that in acting out the patient is not at all trying to show us what he means; rather, he is impelled, by motives he does not understand, to behave in the specific way involved.

As could be easily anticipated, the respective marriages of these patients sooner or later became studded with rather volatile emotional scenes. Similarly, the clinical course in all these cases turned out to be rather stormy, particularly in view of the patients' competitive and narcissistic predispositions, the proclivity for acting out, their enormous seductiveness, and last but not least, their deceit, all of which had to be frustrated in the analysis. Needless to say, these ingredients make for an explosive mixture, and this is precisely what happened. Almost from the first visit, there was evidence of an overwhelming positive transference, which had to be viewed with both a healthy respect and a great deal of suspicion, just in case it was part of the type of show that the patients were so adept at putting on elsewhere. They knew from what they had heard and read before entering analysis that they might fall in love with their analyst. Most likely, they had to make sure here too, as they did with other men, that they fully lived up to a positive transference, or else they pretended to do so. Habitual acting out of the orgastic pretense progressively alienates the patient from reality with respect to true orgastic fulfillment, to a point where it becomes tinged with a flavor of pseudologica fantastica, which in part only may account for the fact that it is not reported readily during the analysis. These women behaved toward the analyst in a most seductive and provocative manner. Two hundred years ago, a mathematician had already figured out, and I think correctly so, that "the most successful and therefore the most dangerous seducers are the 'deluded deluders,' "[51] which seems to apply here. There can be no question that these patients had grandiose fantasies and embarked upon what they perceived as a course of action that had a realistic potential. Consequently, they tried their utmost to have the analyst "fall for them," so that they could add him to their long list of conquests. I firmly believe that they nevertheless preferred the analyst to be different, although such a preference must have been a highly ambivalent one.

After this initial phase, the honeymoon of the questionable erotic transference was definitely over. The transference pendulum now tended to swing far over in the other direction and to stay there for a while. They had apparently given up on the analyst, since he was not likely to succumb to their charms. For several patients this allegedly was the first time that they had not been able to get their man. They felt frustrated, rejected, and depressed, and they threatened to interrupt treatment. Now that the analyst was perceived as invulnerable, they could for the first time reveal to the doctor their orgastic frigidity and the deceitful way in which they tried to negate it. This revelation was coupled with their genuine desire to be cured and become fully effective orgastically. Gradually, as their problems in other areas began to resolve, and confidence in themselves and the analyst increased, the transference reaction ceased to manifest its strong hourly vacillations and settled on a mildly positive, and only hesitantly ambivalent, tone. Ultimately, orgasms were achieved. Despite their protestations to the contrary, it would seem that the attainment of an orgasm occurred as part of the positive transference. At least unconsciously, the analyst must have been substituted for the lover during the sexual act, since they all had previously fantasied their orgastic fulfillment as if the analyst were their lover. To the patients, orgasm constituted a gift to the analyst, a monument to his theraupeutic omnipotence. The fact that it had to be withheld, for a short time at least, was again the equivalent of the orgastic pretense, except in reverse. No more than they could previously accept dependency and gratification from the male penis could they now willingly concede the therapeutic potency of their male analyst. Significantly, when the orgastic miracle was finally reported, it was stated with little affect and "as if" it had only little significance. Perhaps they expected me to have the sensitivity to know about it anyway, without having to be told, and were therefore disappointed.

On the basis of what has been said so far, one might expect a tendency to switch analysts as well. The fact that this did not constitute a serious problem soon became clear, and then was most helpful in deciding on the best clinical strategy to pursue with these challenging cases. Once the secret of the orgastic pretense was revealed to the analyst, the patients soon confessed their absolute disinclination of ever going through this painful and humiliating revelation with another person. I rather doubt that the transference alone could possibly account for the otherwise unexpected therapeutic faithfulness in these patients. One can only assume that there must have been a considerable number of dropouts among those patients who never reached the point in therapy where they could bring themselves to level with the analyst with respect to their practice of orgastic deceit.

In contrast to this unequivocal antipathy toward switching analysts, there was a most marked proclivity for terminating the analysis prematurely. For reasons just stated, resumption with another analyst was definitely out and considered impossible. Therefore termination was presented as a permanent break with psychoanalysis. Because of their narcissistic predisposition, it appeared highly questionable that they could return to therapy in the event that they changed their minds at a later date. These recurrent threats to quit usually occurred at particularly strategic points in the analysis. In several instances they were actually acted upon. Fortunately, these premature terminations were merely brief interruptions. In one patient there were multiple "terminations" of this type. Eventually I was informed by the patient that this practice on her part would definitely cease in the future. Subsequently, she put her prediction into effect. The reason given for this resolution was that she finally came to the conclusion that it was much more difficult for her to have to return and then face up to the problems of why and when treatment was discontinued. Again, it was perceived as too painful and humiliating. This response is identical to what was verbalized regarding the pros and cons of changing analysts. In this particular case these pseudo-terminations ultimately were exposed during the course of the analysis and then essentially turned out to have been just another pretense that operated from the very beginning. Ambivalence, although present, was never sufficiently intense during these episodes to account for these brief interruptions. Upon resumption of the analysis, the patient displayed an almost irresistible curiosity to ascertain whether the therapist had known all along that "deep down" she never meant to discontinue. Needless to say, the answer was never given her. Instead, I could not help wondering out loud why it was of such vital importance for her to know whether or not she actually had succeeded in deceiving the therapist as well.

This presentation attempts to expose the subject of the orgastic pretense and to introduce this clinical entity into the field of psychoanalytic investigation. On the basis of the case material at hand, it is depicted as a form of denial through the magic of action, and appears as an imposture that attempts to act out an otherwise normal ego ideal.

Only a special group of cases was available for illustration. The patients described were highly attractive, married, and successful career women who habitually pretended to experience full orgasm as a denial of their frigidity. During intercourse they originally were able to achieve adequate sexual excitement, which, however, regularly vanished when climax was perceived as imminent. They were gifted, narcissistic, phallic women who made the most of their beauty. Their frigid behavior was particularly complex and sophisticated, as was their pretentious style of life. Their makeup was essentially "as if" in nature. Concern with bodily appearance and sex appeal was excessive. Moreover, there were almost magic-like qualities and exaltations ascribed to their breasts. At all times they were participant observers and attempted to maintain visual surveillance of themselves. Insomnia was a universal complaint and is equated with their fear of annihilation. Orgastic satisfaction during intercourse was feared primarily because it signified intolerable loss of control and represented unmistakable documentation of their ambivalently perceived femininity. Motivation for psychoanalysis was sufficiently strong to withstand a stormy therapeutic ordeal and attain a symptomatic cure of their orgastic inhibition, thus rendering the pretense obsolete. Reasons were offered to account for why and when the information pertaining to their habitual practice of orgastic deceit was withheld and relinquished during psychoanalysis.

I am eager to emphasize that persons with different personality constellations may also indulge in orgastic pretense. Some do so only occasionally or for special reasons. Still, they would have to share obvious characteristics with the group of patients that has been described. In this connection Almansi[52] states that "it is logical to assume that the orgastic pretense is a very complex phenomenon in which various libidinal and aggressive factors are subtly blended and interwoven in varying proportions; in which substantially different ego attitudes may exist, and in which—in different cases—different motivations may be prominent. As in all other psychological structures, the principle of multiple functioning and over-determination hold full sway here; but the accents and emphasis may be displaced from one case to another." Therefore it would seem that the most important determining factor in each case is whether the aggressive component in the orgastic pretense is primary, which applies to the clinical material presented, or whether it is secondary and thus defensive in nature.

From the evidence available so far, only the habitual and compulsory need to practice orgastic deceit would mitigate strongly for the existence of significant psychopathology. This estimate may well require revision as our knowledge concerning this problem increases. The efforts and risks involved to accomplish this feat appear remarkable. By comparison, in the absence of such pathology it must be infinitely easier and more rewarding to strive for and achieve real orgasm instead. The conjecture that the orgastic pretense constitutes an ancient practice that enjoys considerable prevalence remains, as it has been all along, strictly hearsay.

NOTES

1. Burness E. Moore, "Frigidity: A Review of Psychoanalytic Literature," *Psychoanalytic Quarterly*, XXXIII (1964), 323–349.
2. This yardstick for frigidity is an arbitrary one. It seems unduly harsh. Obviously, the term needs descriptive qualification in actual usage. This presentation does not concern itself with the current controversy as to the significance of vaginal versus clitoral orgasm. Because of limitation of space, the reader is referred to the following contributions to this subject which are not quoted in the text: Judd Marmor, "Some

Considerations Concerning Orgasm in the Female," *Psychosomatic Medicine* XVI (1954), 240–245; William H. Masters and Virginia E. Johnson: *Human Sexual Response* (Boston: Little, Brown & Co., 1966); Mary Jane Shefrey: "The Evolution and Nature of Female Sexuality in Relation to Psychoanalytic Theory," *Journal of American Psychoanalytic Association*, XIV (1966), 28–128.

3. Moore, *op. cit.*
4. Renato J. Almansi, special communication.
5. George C. Lichtenberg, *The Lichtenberg Reader* (Boston: Beacon Press, 1959).
6. Sigmund Freud, "On Narcissism: An Introduction" (1914), in *Collected Papers* (New York: Basic Books, 1959), Vol. IV.
7. Sigmund Freud, "Civilization and Its Discontents" (1930), *Standard Edition*, Vol. XXI (London: Hogarth Press, 1961), pp. 59–145.
8. Franz Alexander, "The Neurotic Character," *International Journal of Psychoanalysis*, XI (1930), 292–311.
9. Otto Fenichel, "Neurotic Acting Out," *Psychoanalytic Review*, XXXII (1945), 197–206.
10. Robert Waelder, *Basic Theory of Psychoanalysis* (New York: International Universities Press, 1960).
11. Erik H. Erikson, "The Problem of Ego Identity," *Journal of the American Psychoanalytic Association*, IV (1956), 56–121.
12. *Ibid.*
13. Anna Freud, *The Ego and the Mechanisms of Defense* (New York: International Universities Press, 1946).
14. Ralph Greenson, "The Struggle against Identification," *Journal of the American Psychoanalytic Association*, II (1954), 200–217.
15. Helene Deutsch, "Some Forms of Emotional Disturbance and Their Relationship to Schizophrenia," *Psychoanalytic Quarterly*, XI (1942), 301–321.
16. Phyllis Greenacre, "General Problems of Acting Out," *Psychoanalytic Quarterly*, XIX (1950), 455–467.
17. Annie Reich, "Narcissistic Object Choice in Women," *Journal of the American Psychoanalytic Association*, I (1953), 22–44.
18. Paul Schilder, *The Image and Appearance of the Human Body* (1935) (New York: International Universities Press, 1950).
19. Phyllis Greenacre, *Trauma, Growth and Personality* (New York: N. W. Norton, 1952).
20. Greenson, *op. cit.*
21. Heinz Hartmann and Rudolph M. Loewenstein, "Notes on the Superego," in *The Psychoanalytic Study of the Child*, Vol. XVII (New York: International Universities Press, 1962), pp. 42–81.
22. Edith Jacobson, *The Self and the Object World* (New York: International Universities Press, 1964).
23. Reich, *op. cit.*
24. Greenson, *op. cit.;* and Alan Parkin, "On Sexual Enthrallment," *Journal*

of the American Psychoanalytic Association, XII (1964), 336–356.

25. Greenacre, "General Problems of Acting Out."

26. Bertram D. Lewin, *The Psychoanalysis of Elation* (New York: W. W. Norton, 1950).

27. Sigmund Freud, "Inhibitions, Symptoms and Anxiety" (1926), *Standard Edition*, Vol. XX (London: Hogarth Press, 1959), pp. 75–175.

28. Bernard Brodsky, "Self-Representation, Anality, and the Fear of Dying," *Journal of the American Psychoanalytic Association*, VII (1959), 95–108.

29. *Ibid.*

30. Bertram D. Lewin, "The Body as Phallus," *Psychoanalytic Quarterly*, II (1933), 24–47.

31. *Ibid.*

32. Moore, *op. cit.*

33. Sylvan Keiser, "The Fear of Sexual Passivity in the Masochist," *International Journal of Psychoanalysis*, XXX (1949), 162–171.

34. Sigmund Freud, "Concerning the Sexuality of Women," *Psychoanalytic Quarterly*, I (1932), 191–209.

35. Jeanne Lampl-De Groot, "The Evolution of the Oedipus Complex in Women," *International Journal of Psychoanalysis*, IX (1928), 332–345.

36. Sigmund Freud, "Female Sexuality" (1931), in *Collected Papers* (New York: Basic Books, 1959), Vol. V.

37. Sandor Lorand, "Contribution to the Problem of Vaginal Orgasm," *International Journal of Psychoanalysis*, XX (1939), 432–438.

38. Freud, "Female Sexuality."

39. Robert P. Knight, "Functional Disturbances in the Sexual Life of Women: Frigidity and Related Disorders, *Bulletin of the Meninger Clinic*, VII (1943), 25–35.

40. Charles Sarlin, "Feminine Identity," *Journal of the American Psychoanalytic Association*, XI (1963), 790–816.

41. Karen Horney, "The Flight from Womanhood: The Masculinity Complex in Women, as Viewed by Men and by Women," *International Journal of Psychoanalysis*, VII (1926), 324–339; Sylvan Keiser, "Body Ego during Orgasm," *Psychoanalytic Quarterly*, XXI (1952), 153–166; Judith Kestenberg, "Vicissitudes of Female Sexuality," *Journal of the American Psychoanalytic Association*, IV (1956), 453–476.

42. Sylvan Keiser, "Female Sexuality," *Journal of the American Psychoanalytic Association*, IV (1956), 563–574.

43. Jacobson, *op. cit.*

44. Edward Hitschmann and Edmund Bergler, *Frigidity in Women: Its Characteristics and Treatment* (New York: Nervous and Mental Disease Publishing Co., 1936).

45. Lorand, *op. cit.*

46. Tibor Agoston, "The Fear of Post-Orgastic Emptiness," *Psychoanalytic Review*, XXXIII (1946), 197–214.

47. Equivalent to the traumatophilic character described by Fenichel (*op. cit.*) with respect to acting out.
48. Keiser, "Body Ego during Orgasm."
49. Phyllis Greenacre, "Problems of Acting Out in the Transference Relationship," *Journal of the American Academy of Child Psychiatry*, II (1963), 144–172.
50. William V. Silverberg, "Acting Out Versus Insight," *Psychoanalytic Quarterly*, XXIV (1955), 527–544.
51. Lichtenberg, *op. cit.*
52. Renato J. Almansi, special communication.

The Problem of Infidelity

Kazantzakis, the famous Greek writer, regarded a young man in his twenties as one of the great philosophers of Spain. This young man believed that all the problems of the world might be solved if only one could solve the problem that has always existed between man and woman. Unfortunately, this philosopher died when he was thirty. He drowned himself. Over a woman.

Of course, as knowledgeable analysts, we suspect that this specific woman could hardly have been the sole cause of his tragedy. Undoubtedly there were other complications. Apart from the psychopathology that engages certain couples in mutually destructive patterns, the problem between man and woman is eternal and hardly to be solved in one man's lifetime, let alone in a few pages. But since I am dealing with the same eternal problem today, swimming in the same dangerous waters, so to speak, I am prepared, wearing an imaginary Mae West. I may not reach any shore in the pages allotted to me, but I hope I can at least remain afloat.

Infidelity. How does one begin discussing so broad and yet so intimate a subject? Marriage, or the legal commitment to one mate, seems to be for many less than a highly gratifying state. If I had more regard for authority, I might quote more experienced hands on the question of fidelity. One such authority, Elizabeth Taylor, makes the cogent observation "that our society today finds illicit love more attractive than married love. Our love," she says [that is, the love between her and Richard Burton], "is married love now. But there is still a suggestion, I suppose, of rampant sex on the wild."[1] It is this "suggestion . . . of rampant sex on the wild" that leaves us waiting expectantly for her next move.

If I were a comedian, I might say that marriage, long described as a ball and chain, is for some really more like a hot bath: if you stay in it long enough, it's not so hot. If I were a religious philosopher, I would perhaps offer a solution to the problem of infidelity by citing the Ten Commandments and demonstrating the ruin in the sight of God that follows on the heels of broken marriage vows. Or I might emphasize the Judeo-Christian ethic, which demands monogamy. If I were a moralist, I would call on conscience and point out that most people feel that fidelity is good and infidelity is bad; that if we make our bed, marital or extramarital, we lie in it, whether in virtue or in vice. If I were a jurist, I would call attention to the fact that the law supports the faithful and punishes the unfaithful. I would emphasize that extramarital liaisons are certainly not uncommon in our society, but that our laws prohibit adultery and that the lawbreaker may be jailed. Even if he is not discovered, he is usually plagued by anxiety and guilt. If I were an economist, I would observe that money and power talk: a king, a sultan, a rich man may have many wives or mistresses, and a rich woman may have many husbands or lovers. If I were a sociologist, I would take note that in some families or societies a future wife and husband may be committed to each other at birth by parental prearrangement. I would bear in mind that other people, the French and Italians, for example, are much more tolerant of infidelity than we are. I would observe that in Mexico it is not uncommon for men to have children in parallel families, a sort of "Captain's Paradise." I might detail the role of different societies in fostering or condemning marital infidelity and make a plea that each individual make up his own mind whether it is better to conform or to deviate from the norms of our society.

And if I were an anthropologist, I would ask: How are we to deal with the challenge of polygamy or polyandry? Is the man with multiple wives or the woman with multiple husbands to be regarded as incapable of fidelity? Or are they faithful so long as they do not cohabit outside their polygamous or polyandrous households? I would note that families do not necessarily exist in all primitive societies. I would remark that husband and wife in certain cultures do not live together in physical intimacy, that even among us there may come a time in the lives of many couples even at the height of their sexual powers when sexual intimacy ceases. I would recall that the Samoans welcome an extramarital affair so long as it in no way threatens to destroy the family or social order by being too passionate.[2] I would observe that only the fact of fatherhood and motherhood is unalterable; marriage is not. Marriage is a social institution, a social contract. Western Judeo-Christian culture introduced the idea of limiting sexual relations to the marital partners. Similarly, the double standard exists only in our tradition. Modesty, chastity, and other asexual virtues are not virtues among non-Judeo-Christians. They marry largely in order to have children. For those who do not want children, they may ask: Why get married—why limit sexual freedom?

As a psychoanalyst, I, of course, practice none of the above-mentioned disciplines, though I believe that all of us, especially when dealing with the man-woman problem, must at times use the approaches of the humorist, the philosopher, the historian, the anthropologist, the sociologist, and even the economist, the jurist, and the animal behaviorist. For the problem of infidelity in the man-woman relationship is, I believe, not a symptom of individual emotional disturbance alone, but also a symptom of society's traditional as well as rapidly changing fashions, mores, and values. Though we do not generally interject such intellectual factors during psychoanalytic treatment, I believe that we as therapists should be aware of them, so that we may help the patient see his problem in proper perspective at the proper time.

The evidence for fidelity among animals other than man is meager indeed, and very likely not too appropriate to our discussion. There is likely to be only pseudo-monogamy among the lower mammals, which is probably adventitious. Among the higher orders, polygamy is much more prevalent, and Darwin believed the higher species to be more polygamous than the lower because they are more intelligent. There is a South American marmoset (the *Nyctipithecus vergatus*) that is reputed to be monogamous, possibly because its habits are entirely nocturnal, and it is quite unable to see clearly in daylight.[3]

In contemporary cultures, marriage is viewed, at least theoretically, as the only kind of basis for an acceptable intimacy between man and woman. Extramarital intercourse is pretty generally disapproved of as improper. However, in the more primitive stages of cultural development, marriage does not exclude coitus with others.[4] Wedlock is not regarded as the exclusive means of access to a sexual partner. In less developed cultures, unmarried women who are not regarded as property are not restrained as to whom they may or may not practice coitus with, feeling quite at liberty to engage with whomever they please.[5] In some cultures, then, there is not necessarily a connection between marriage and sex. In the light of these anthropological studies, the title of this chapter may contain a prejudice.

The Veddahs of Ceylon are often reported to illustrate the prevalence among primitive peoples of ethical sexual values not unlike those in the contemporary Western tradition. Unlike most underdeveloped people, the Veddahs are monogamous and their marital contracts unseverable. But the marital commitment of the Veddahs is a direct consequence of their hand-to-mouth existence and is in fact neither stable nor steadfast.[6] Don Mas reports that the continence imposed on Igorot young women of Botoc in the island of Luzon is so severe that, incapable of subduing their sexual needs, they flee into the forests and cohabit with monkeys.[7]

Extramarital relations are acceptable among primitive people who, due to their *economic poverty*, are more or less monogamous, although dyadic marriage is not general among them. On the contrary, such aborigines are conspicuously unbridled in coitus with different partners. The importance of infidelity as sexual transgression appears first in those stages of cultural evolution in which a privileged order of persons has emerged.[8] In our own society, for example, the rich can support secret lovers or can divorce more easily than the poor, who are often bound to one another by the ties of straitened circumstances.

In many societies the husband-wife relationship is not looked upon as sealed until they have a baby; childlessness may be grounds for annulling the marriage or for divorce. Marriages in primitive cultures are often as short-lived after as before the arrival of children. Occasionally, the birth of a child, instead of holding the marriage fast, becomes the precipitating element in its breaking up.[9]

In contemporary Western culture the father competes with the child, who has taken his wife from him, as he experiences it. For the father the child may represent a sibling or his own castrating father. The wife who has a child offers the man more freedom. Where there are no children, there is a greater need on the part of the wife to control her husband. The Iroquois and Delaware Indian women also desert their men, after having received many gifts from them and knowing that they can expect to obtain no more. They then marry another man, from whom they can extract more presents.[10] Some women in our own society are similarly incapable of constancy and marry a succession of wealthy men, whom they exploit for financial gain. Curiously, many men lend themselves to this sadomasochistic interaction, work themselves to death for their wives, die early of heart attacks, and leave their widows with large incomes but without men. This self- and other-denying commitment on the part of men to their wives is generally an acting out toward the mother and father in which men reenact their enslavement, servitude, and hostility toward one or the other parent.

The Vaertings selected the historic cultures of Egypt, Libya, and Sparta as their primary source material for a study of the sociology of sex differences.[11] Klein, in reporting their work, points out that at certain times in these civilizations when the society was female supremacist the husband was subordinate to his wife. In ancient Egyptian marriage, the husband was obliged to promise to be subject to the will of his wife. Virtue, continence, and marital faithfulness were required of him, and his infidelity was dealt with harshly. The double sexual standard, which appears where one sex dominates the other, favored the ruling sex, so that the duties of the woman were less rigid than those imposed on the man. The prevailing female took sexual liberties that were rigidly denied to the subject male by common practice, by unspoken and implicit ethical precept, and often by formal statute. Even the general principle of monogamy was unable to stop the development of a double sexual standard that gave women extramarital privileges. In Sparta, despite a manifest commitment to monogamy, polyandry was a common practice, and Plutarch tells us that the Spartans tended to make a merit of women's unfaithfulness. In Egypt, the promise to keep one's marital vows was not demanded of women, and no censure was imposed on either the mother of a bastard child or the child itself.[12]

There is less infidelity among women in a patriarchal society. Apparently in a matriarchy, women are equally unfaithful. In a male supremacist culture, women are forced, by economic needs, social forces, and biological dependency, to be faithful. In Western society, there is a tendency to keep the mother and children "pure-blooded," chaste.

Their bearing the father's name, his title, and their being inheritors of his property tend to make them his possessions, dependent, enforcedly faithful. A woman pays a much greater price for infidelity and takes more serious risks in chancing impregnation and threats to her social and biological security. Her having to submit to a double standard leads her to resent man's "freedom" to choose. The development of contraception gave her more room for infidelity. Mothers teach their daughters about men's greater freedom and try to keep them virginal, asexual. A woman's sexual acting out may represent a rebellion against the mother or against male supremacy.

It is almost impossible to find records in the period before Christ in which multiple or extramarital sexuality is regarded as unsavory or offensive. Sexual promiscuity might have incurred ritualistic disapprobation, but in and of itself it was not seen as evil. This view of infidelity is in accord with the Greek view, which saw no innate proclivity as wicked. Sexual gratification was regarded as natural as eating and drinking.[13]

The institution of marriage in the Christian view is based on neither economic nor social factors. The monogamous relationship is established here in order to control sexual intercourse by limiting it as much as possible. In early Christian times, marriage was generally derided as incompatible with an ethical existence, and total sexual abstinence is still believed in devout Catholic circles to be a higher state of virtue. Christian monogamy, which was incorporated from Roman marriage forms, was conceived as an attempt to adjust the conflict between the Christian standard of goodness, namely, the denial of sexuality on the one hand and on the other a yielding to natural instinctual and social needs. These Christian tenets were not derived from archaic concepts of the evil or forbidden character of sex but from notions regarding the danger of any kind of physical pleasure or human fulfillment. Bodily enjoyment and emotional happiness are in most cultures believed to excite the jealousy of divine, all-powerful forces, of apparitions, and of gods.[14]

The pious, cabalistic commitment that elevates sexual abstinence to the supreme virtue, the ideas of lust and moral looseness, did not prevail in ancient Rome or in any other culture of the time, savage or refined. These values grew out of the Christian faith. By superimposing puritanical disavowal of sexuality, which arose at first in order to

avoid the envy and wrath of mystical powers, by elevating sexual ab-
stention to the noblest ethic of human existence, Christians were the
first to make sexual self-denial a mark of goodness.[15]

In most cultures there is a reliance on a stable marriage; it should
continue for as long as the couple lives. This is so regardless of how
easily divorce may be achieved or how readily marital ties are broken.
No culture has devised a kind of marital tie durable enough to last
that did not contractually commit the partners to a lifetime together.[16]

When we examine most cultures, we discover in them some family
structure, some stable plan in which men support women in providing
for their offspring in infancy and childhood. Generally the men provide subsistence for their wives and children.[17] While there are some
exceptions, most societies are dependent on the *acquired training* of
men in sustaining their families.[18] But this scheme of things can be
qualified, and the variations demonstrate that the supportive role of
men is not instinctual.[19] In fact, the impetus of men to support their
children is so fragile that it can be easily demolished by other familial
and cultural organizations.[20]

A considerable number of Negro families consist of grandmother,
mother, and children, with grandfathers, husbands, and fathers in desertion. When the Negro was a slave in this country, he was brought
up largely to reproduce and increase his numbers. He was valued to
the extent that his labor could be freely exploited. His family was often
auctioned off and separated from him. The scars of the white man's
superimposing absentee fatherhood on him are still to be seen among
poorer Negroes in America. Here the main supports of the family are
the mother and grandmother. The father and grandfather may join
the family unit without assuming any financial responsibility. However, among educated and middle-class Negroes, the father assumes a
characteristically responsible position in the family.[21]

In order to guarantee the constancy and uninterrupted sequence in
marriage that enable family life to proceed, every culture is obliged
to resolve the problem of rivalry among men for women so they will
not destroy each other; or so few males command a large number of
women that there are hardly any mates for the remaining men, or
ostracize too many of the younger men, or abuse the women and
children too seriously during the contests of courting.[22]

At bottom, incest taboos are a means by which the family can be
maintained and the interconnections, alliances, identifications, and rel-

ative positions within it developed and defined. The expansion of taboos against incest to many aspects of the care of all children in a given culture as a defense against every misuse of and cruelty toward children is only one example of the way the preserving, security-insuring maneuvers of man's development operate as a prototype for more extensive appropriate social conduct beyond the family.[23]

Every culture must protect its children from incestuous acting out. The identification of the young with the parent of the same sex is associated with certain tensions and taboos with regard to the parent of the opposite sex. The security of the child from the father and mother is related to the necessity to render the parents safe from the child as well. The safety of a ten-year-old child from her father's seduction is a critical determinant of their adequate social development. The defenses that evolve in the young against sexual yearning for the parent are the natural antithesis to the position assumed by the parent in order to take care of the child. Generally, prohibitions against incest are extended so that the young are in no danger from adults, although their safety may be inadequately assured.[24]

The primary taboos against incest involve three basic relationships within the family, those between father and daughter, mother and son, and brother and sister. Since the fundamental work of any culture is to enable men to execute their labors in some kind of voluntary participation with one another, any difficulty that propels them into mutual antagonism is deadly in its effect. If a father is to continue to be a supportive husband and parent, he must feed, educate, and sustain his needy sons, nephews, and dependents. If he is to participate in joint social endeavors with other males in his community, he needs to relate to them in ways that exclude too dangerous sexual rivalry.[25]

There are three telling blows in the psychological development of a child that make him feel his mother has betrayed him, that tend to make him in turn revengefully unfaithful. From the start the child experiences his mother as the original sexual object in oral erotism, through the breast, through body contact, through being fondled, diapered, bathed, powdered, and loved. The first disappointment to his assumed exclusive possession of her is his awareness that she has been unfaithful to him with his father, with whom he must now contend. It is only a later rationalization that he was conceived by immaculate conception. The second disillusionment comes when a younger sibling is born, and the elder child sees the younger one getting erotic gratification at the breast, an experience that is also fulfilling to his mother. The third maternal act of infidelity is the child's recognition that his mother gets pleasure from a variety of people. The betrayed child, become the neurotic man, sees the mother surrogate as virgin or whore. If his mother has been unfaithful, he becomes so out of retaliation. The therapeutic struggle with him is in part to give up the illusion of absolutes, the division of women into the two categories, the virginal mother who is asexual or the betraying prostitute.

Briefly, the sequence of events with a male child are: (1) Mother and I are one. (2) Mother and I are separate, a dyad. (3) We are three: mother, father, and I. (4) Mother is related to everyone; she is promiscuous. (Betrayal has begun at stage 3.)

The female child experiences: (1) Also that mother and I are one. (2) Mother and I are separate, a dyad. (3) We are three: mother, father, and I. (4) She feels betrayed by both mother and father. (5) Her father is related, as mother is, to others.

Where a man's wife is experienced as the mother, he avoids sexual contact with her because of the incest taboo and seeks gratification elsewhere. Unfaithful, he is repeatedly "getting even" with the inconstant mother projected on his wife. He may act this out by trying to seduce successive women (mothers) away from their respective husbands (fathers), a sadomasochistic Don Juanism in which both mother and father are punished. With some men who identify with the mother, their promiscuity is largely an unconsciously intended assault on the father.

The view of a spouse as the ball and chain is a perception of her as a parental figure, demanding, controlling, castrating. Men tend to marry the mother figure and, either unable to be incestuous or projecting betrayal, are in turn unfaithful to her. They can love a stranger until they marry her, when the same projective process and acting out occur in order not to be sexual with the mother surrogate. Women who are unfaithful cannot be sexual with their husbands seen as father. Men fear the father and women the mother, forming neurotic alliances with the parent of the same sex. Infidelity may be judged manifestly as deliberate faithlessness by a possessive or controlling wife, when, in fact, the husband may be acting out a latent homosexuality or may be appropriately struggling against strangulation and castration and trying to achieve genuine heterosexuality elsewhere.

Infidelity, then, may be an acting out in retaliation against the projected parent in one's spouse, a mother or father figure experienced now as in childhood as unfaithful. This acting out may be Oedipal or pre-Oedipal in origin; a reflection of split ego problems in which the patient submits to and rebels against the incorporated negative ego of a parent; derived from oral, anal, or phallic compulsion; a consequence of faulty ego or superego development. Seen as acting out, infidelity may be dealt with as transference, resistance, or acting out a defense against heterosexuality. Infidelity needs to be understood in terms not only of sexuality but of violence and homosexuality. The homosexual equivalent is seen among men who join each other in clubs, lodges, bars, and sports, leaving their wives, sweethearts, or mistresses isolated.

A minority of promiscuous men compulsively seek out virgins to deflower. Their aim is to be the first, to precede or change places with the father. Some may wish to degrade the virginal mother who betrayed them by falling from a chaste, idealized image. Some may be testing every virtuous mother figure they can find, to prove her lewd. After a man has succeeded in seducing a woman, he may try to arrange for her marriage to another man in order to keep her virtuous, with the assumption that then she will not be available to other men. At the same time he feels himself superior to her spouse (the father) because he (the patient) has had her first.

One curious and seemingly contradictory source of infidelity lies in the extent to which one partner interferes with the other's masturbatory experience during the act of intercourse. If two onanistic personalities marry and, instead of making intercourse the center of their sexual experience, they take turns giving each other masturbatory gratification by whatever means—even in the act of intercourse itself, for it may be so used—the two may remain faithful to each other, in their fashion. But if one of them tries to engage the other in a more mutually interactive response, the compulsive masturbator will find his erotic pleasure reduced, if not nullified completely. He may then seek out a female who herself prefers a masturbatory act to whom he can then be "faithful." Here the threat to fidelity is a fear of closeness, of intimacy, of interaction, and seeming devotion is possible where there is distance and isolation and perhaps only a fantasied, sadomasochistic, or masturbatory gratification.

Infidelity may be seen as reflecting a neurotic incapacity to love another person based on an emotionally ambivalent transferential attitude toward one's spouse. The spouse is generally viewed as the bad parent or as the idealized parent, so defensively desexualized and sanctified as to be sensually unapproachable. The lover is equally transferentially endowed with romantic and sensuous investments that make him or her the physically desirable parent, sibling, or extrafamilial representative, partly because they are not possessed. Once won, they too soon became the transferentially unlovable parental figure. Until the right to love the parent of the opposite sex is remembered, affectively reexperienced in the course of analysis, and worked through, the patient is incapable of liberating himself toward the new freedom of loving commitment to another person.

The current generation of adolescents and adults, despite their sexual promiscuity, seem strangely alone, even when they are in groups. They grope hungrily for a variety of sensuous experiences, as if physical contact might remove their loneliness. Despite the frequency of one-night stands, the struggle against insularity is generally lost. Every such searcher for a sexual adventure hopes to find with his partner that consummate passion which will last forever, only to discover disappointment. Separated in introspective or distorted projections, they seem unable to break through their basic disconnection. Their sexual union is an attempt to resolve the barrenness of their existence, their inability to communicate. They seem to reject the way of life of their forebears, seeking a way of their own, but unable to find it. They overvalue mere sensuous pleasure and reject the value of love. They use their sexual experiences to storm citadels and regard love as a form of capitulation, unfreedom, and stupidity. There is increasing detachment, pride in their affective wasteland, and contempt for tenderness. They prefer an easy resort to sense experience to the obligations of marriage.[26]

Perhaps we of an older generation, in unconscious revolt against the standards of our parents, have unknowingly got our children to act out our own wish to rebel. Perhaps we have foisted on them a compulsion to protest against and reject the disciplines once imposed on us. Perhaps we have disillusioned them with the successive sadomasochistic crises in our own marriages. Perhaps we have not given them adequate inner models to govern their behavior. Too many of the present generation, of good intelligence, have difficulty applying themselves to any constructive endeavor. Their promiscuity is partially intended to sadden and wound their parents. The current lack of principle and dependency on the flesh take precedence over the pursuit of the good life. Underneath, one senses anxiety, depression, and perplexity, and a manifest suggestion of gaiety conceals an underlying painful reserve. Their sexual acting out, like a narcotic, helps them momentarily but repeatedly to evade their more basic inner disturbance and the realities of our cultural problems. One idea seems to be to curb hopeful expectations, because they will undoubtedly be frustrated. It becomes poor style to show spirit or fervor or commitment to anyone else or any thing. Nonchalance, even coldness or apathy, is being cultivated. "Play it cool" seems to be the vogue.[27]

But this generation surely has as much latent feeling as its elders. Perhaps it feels betrayed by the duality of what we say and do. We talk of integrity and justice while we remain neutral or participate in dishonesty and deception. Our misrepresentation of the realistic difference between thought and deed is enough to make our successors the victims of an impossible contradiction. Under the promiscuities of modern times probably are imbedded aborted longing for a more ethical and fulfilling way of life, indignation at what ought not to be, and acute mental suffering. The young seem alien, apart, and angry with their parents and the society that left them such an unpalatable heritage. Their sexual indiscrimination is not simply wantonness or debauchery, but their despairing protest and escape from a society they find wanting. Their apparent rejection of love and affirmation of physical contact points up the extent to which they feel bewildered, exposed to dangers around them, and screened off from one another. It may well be that their protest contains the seeds of a search for more human and rational purpose in their lives than we have yet found.[28]

Modern young people may be acting out their parents' disillusionment with love, romance, and the longed-for freedom to be merely sensuous without emotional ties experienced as exorbitant demands. The young also identify with their elders who cannot lovingly commit themselves to one another, who separate and divorce. If fathers and mothers do not care for each other, the child also becomes unconcerned, phlegmatic, or frigid. If his parents do not treasure marriage, why should he estimate it too highly? Somewhere, latent under this cynicism, our young are still eager to remake the world into a better place. Somewhere, in repression, is their wish to know, understand, change, grow, and pursue more gratifying human values, to believe again in man, in his incorruptibility, gallantry, and tenderness.[29]

Having considered some psychological and other reasons for the bullish trend in the sexual marketplace, let us take a brief look at the marketplace itself and the stresses it imposes on the institution of marriage. Margaret Mead[30] points out that American culture offers very little middle ground between continuous attention to other people's wishes, desires, hopes, thoughts, and feelings and complete indifference to everything except one's own desires. Without that middle ground, most people fear that if they don't show active concern for others or for another, they will be committed either to isolation or to a life of excessive self-indulgence. Many, therefore, see marriage as their only alternative—as a haven, so to speak, against meaningless promiscuity or frightening disconnection and loneliness. This, by the way, is the argument Grotjahn uses to stress the value of monogamy for modern man.[31]

Mead, however, disagrees with this solution. She feels that marital infidelity as practiced today is also rooted in our culture, because our society is also supposedly built on freedom of choice, freedom to change houses, states, jobs, and political parties. So, some reason, why not change bed partners as well? Thus the conflict is set up: on the one hand, marriage as security haven with its price of confinement; on the other hand, so-called freedom with its price of isolation or sexual intemperance. These contradictory attitudes toward marriage and eternal freedom of choice have their psychological analogues, and it is with this area that we need to occupy ourselves. Many of the patients we treat are caught in just such a conflict between what they see as the black and white of the all-exacting "security" marriage and the emptiness of neurotically acted-out impulsive or compulsive gratification rationalized as freedom of choice.

Usually these contradictory attitudes parallel the way these patients are emotionally caught in some pre-Oedipal or Oedipal relationship to parents of the same or the opposite sex. It is during these developmental stages that the emotional seeds of contentment, trust, and hope or of infidelity, mistrust, and despair are sown. It is then that mother is most likely to be seen as vestal virgin or whore, father as priest or roué. And unless insight into the nature of each individual transference is achieved and worked through, marriage for these patients will continue to be projected, in A. P. Herbert's words, not as holy wedlock but as unholy deadlock, and infidelity may be seen as the only way to resolve the conflict. For when true heterosexual gratification in terms of commitment as well as libido is cut off, relief is often sought elsewhere.

To describe the promiscuity and marital infidelity we see all around us today as due to transference alone is to give a widespread social difficulty too pat a label. In our society very real problems exist in the man-woman relationship that cannot be solved by insight into and the resolution of transference alone. Let me cite for you here a relationship, begun thirty years ago, that was a marriage and still not a marriage, where the rejection of monogamy was perceived by the partners as a fight against society's rigidity and as a fight for freedom. It is a relationship open to study by all: that of Jean Paul Sartre and Simone de Beauvoir. These two highly verbal people have given us detailed accounts of their early lives and of their lives together.[32] Whatever transferential elements they may have been acting out, it is clear that society as a whole was also a leading character in their personal drama—the antagonist. They both believed that society's demand that cohabitation have legal sanction was outmoded and unreasonable. And they enforced those beliefs by their individual excursions with sexual partners outside their relationship. Until, after thirty years together, they both fell in love with others to a point where their own long, close-knit relationship was threatened. When eventually both decided to forego the new alliances, they did so on the basis that characterologically, culturally, and ideologically, the new unions could not work so well as the old. That part of this decision was emotionally, even transferentially determined, I do not believe there can be much doubt. Even in this instance, in what is perhaps the most sophisticated relationship ever publicly documented, the question of infidelity eventually became a painful, festering sore, once the sensual, romantic, casual encounters developed into something serious enough to threaten their deeper ties to each other.

Simone de Beauvoir, in making out a case for infidelity, describes it almost as a tit-for-tat proposition.[33] "Often prescribed, rarely practiced," she writes, "complete fidelity is usually experienced by those who impose it on themselves as a mutilation. They console themselves for it by sublimation or by drink. Traditionally, marriage used to allow the man a 'few adventures on the side.' Without reciprocity, nowadays, many women have become aware of their rights and of the conditions necessary for their happiness; if there is nothing in their own lives to compensate for masculine inconstancy, they will fall prey to jealousy and boredom." Better infidelity, she seems to be saying, than jealousy and weariness with one another.

Society today has caught up with the protest that Sartre and Simone de Beauvoir made thirty years ago. Today more and more people agree with them. Many factors contribute to these changes in attitude. Women, for example, outnumber men, and this ratio is increasing. Women are becoming more and more independent financially and emotionally, and this includes both married and single women. In contemporary cultures in which polygamy is no longer tolerated and women are less restrained and suppressed, a new dilemma has emerged, namely, the contention among women for men. This is a difficulty largely produced by the dictates of society, an issue superimposed on a preceding instinctual and physiological necessity.[34] In more primitive societies, men in constant gravitation toward women, with their superior bodily vigor, and free from the demands of children, were in an intrinsic struggle with one another for women. The women were largely prizes of the victors. As society has evolved and advanced to replace physical might with the strategies of authority, status, and fame, the difficulty created by male competition for a single female has become increasingly severed from its instinctual design. As a result, in those cultures where females outnumber males, as in our own, and where dyadic marriage prevails, we see masculine competition for women changing to admit also a contest among women for men. It may be that there is no clearer evidence of what can be achieved by societal forces than this contemporary change in courtship, which demands aggressive struggle among women, who are physically less well equipped than men to compete with one another.[35]

At the same time, the male is becoming, willy-nilly, more and more the organization man whose mate is expected to conform to the image of the organization wife. This imposes still another control over marriage which can further increase the frustration of the people involved. Added to all this, for the majority of people, work on the one hand is becoming more routinized, while leisure time is becoming more plentiful. In both work and leisure, men and women alike are coming face to face with what can only be called stark boredom. One could go on enumerating these dilemmas of our changing society, perplexities which are bringing about concurrent changes in sexual relationships both for the good and for the not so good.

As for the good, we see sex more freely discussed, sexual gratification more openly demanded, and, especially among the young, much less sexual hypocrisy. As for the not so good, we see the meaningless and self-destructive practice of key parties and wife-swapping. Newspaper and magazine accounts tell of wife-exchanging in certain suburban areas. Thirty-two couples were involved in one such arrangement. The setup was regarded by the membership as practical because it made it unnecessary to go to bars to seek sexual partners. One couple, finding familiar extramarital relations tedious, put an advertisement in a newspaper to attract, invite, and develop a new sexual community. An assistant district attorney in one city remarked that private wife-bartering was not a criminal offense.[36] We see semiprofessional housewife call-girls prostituting themselves for hire while their husbands stay home watching television and minding the babies. We have handbooks on the best-seller lists telling girls how to get a man into bed with or without a marriage license: any man, single, married, divorced, or a bigamist. And, by the way, men are reading these books as avidly as women to find out their proper ploy when the improper play is made.

There is a good deal of diversity in people's handling of the question of which males are to be related to which females, under what specific conditions and for what length of time, and the more recent question of which females are to win which males. Certain cultures allow times for sexual laxity when individuals who feel they can handle more members of the opposite sex than are generally accorded them have an opportunity to realize their fantasies without destroying the family and the society. In some cultures, men accommodate other men with their wives, or spouses are switched among friends, so that reciprocity and concord among the men is buttressed by sexual connections.[37]

Very few of us are Simone de Beauvoirs or Sartres. Most of us live our lives on much less sophisticated levels. With so many myths about human nature, morality, marriage, and what-have-you proving inadequate, the majority of us can turn neither to fundamental principles nor to rules nor to sophisticated rationalizations. We can only ask questions. And among the questions concerning conflicts around marriage is this one: "If not infidelity, then what?"

Many critics of Freud have accused psychoanalysts of approving and encouraging sexual promiscuity. It would do us all good to recall what Freud actually did say. About infidelity, he said it was something to be understood but hardly to be praised. As Philip Rieff[38] puts it: "If from Freud we may infer that monogamy is not a very satisfactory arrangement, the results of his science may also be taken to show that man is a naturally faithful creature: the most inconstant sexual athlete is in motivation still a toddler, searching for the original maternal object." If Freud were alive today, I believe he would agree that though we have not exactly upset the romantic, sexual applecart, we have certainly removed a wheel and scattered the apples all over the place. Scattered apples need to be picked up and put in order again. And many of us are trying to do just that, no matter how experimentally or blunderingly.

Our problem as analysts is not merely to understand infidelity, its manifestations, and its causes, but to sympathize with those who are propelled into it by the forces of a complex society, both rigid and changing. Though some few indulge in infidelity to be in fashion, many more do so as the only expression they can find of an unnamed, unformed inner drive toward freedom. Unfortunately, freedom achieved in this way does not and cannot last, for it is, in fact, the pursuit of limitlessness motivated by impulsion or compulsion, both leading to unfreedom. As analysts we know that identity, goal direction, structuring, and limits are necessary for the healthy individual to exist even in an unhealthy setting and for the striving individual to help make his environment more healthful.

There is no quick answer to how this can be accomplished. But starts have been made toward speculating on and investigating the process by which the human being develops the attribute of fidelity. Many interesting experiments in education are also being undertaken with the specific aim of teaching the child conceptual views of life, science, and the world about him so that true intellectual competence can become associated with his emotional and characterological development.

Erik Erikson[39] is one of the few psychoanalysts who cites *fidelity* as part of the psychodynamic process. He calls it an ego quality that emerges with and from adolescence and is built on hope, trust, and competence achieved in earlier stages of development. This is his definition of fidelity: "Fidelity is the ability to sustain loyalties freely pledged in spite of the inevitable contradictions of value systems. It is the cornerstone of identity and receives inspiration from confirming ideologies and affirming companions." Erikson makes the further point that "identity and fidelity are necessary for ethical strength but they do not provide it in themselves."

It is not easy to paraphrase Erikson, but I shall make a stab at it. What I believe he is saying is that fidelity is not an instinct. It is a human attribute that develops as the human being develops and is largely dependent on the success of his earlier developmental stages. Once fidelity becomes a conscious process in adolescence, it must be implemented throughout adulthood. In other words, fidelity must be fought for and it must be worked at. And the way the individual chooses to exercise fidelity can be traced by the number and the quality of choices he makes, choices of friends, mates, and co-workers. Erikson calls this the person's "style of fidelity." And Erikson believes that only when the style of fidelity has been decided on can the adult truly love and care for another person. When applied to marriage, the implication seems to be that fidelity, freely pledged, can absorb the many differences and conflicts that must inevitably occur in any close relationship. And that when differences cause breaks over and over again in a person's history, one can say that his style of fidelity either has not been decided on or is not very sound.

Erikson's theoretical position on the positive development of the human being is an interesting one. I wish I could also believe it were easy to achieve. However, the changing methods of formal education are also going in that direction, and for that I think we can be grateful. Jerome S. Bruner of Harvard, for example, has reported on the fascinating experimental work he and others in his department have been doing. He has found that very young children, eight to ten years old, are capable of understanding concepts of mathematics, physics, and chemistry if they are presented in their broad structures first, with details and facts to be filled in later. He also believes, and I quote, that "any subject can be taught in some intellectually honest form to any child at any stage of development."[40] Bruner feels this principle can be applied to the teaching of history, the social sciences, and the humanities as well as to scientific subjects.

As a psychoanalyst, I can only wish he had mentioned some attempt to include sexual teaching. I think it might be a good idea to have the whole area of sex taken out of the hygiene department and put where it belongs, with the sciences and the humanities. If children show themselves to be old enough and capable enough to understand principles of economics, government, sociology, psychology, and the sciences, I say they are old enough to know and understand the complicated place of sex in their lives. And I say the sooner this work is begun, the better. By sex I do not mean merely the literal practices that lead to sensuous gratification. Nor do I mean the limited fulfillment that is derived from indiscriminate sexual contact. I mean the day-to-day, tender and responsible reactions on the part of parents to the growing child's curiosity that enable him to bind together love, sexuality, and allegiance so that they develop as a unified triad, sturdy guarantors of a freely chosen and freely given fidelity. No matter how much we improve our methods of teaching the sciences, the social sciences, and the humanities, important as this advance certainly is, as long as our children remain burdened with feelings of confusion, guilt, and shame concerning sex, the new generation will be as defective emotionally as the present generation. It will do us little good to land men and women on the stars who carry with them an outworn, earthbound morality.

As for those of us who must remain behind, treating our fellow earthlings, beset by the eternal problem of the man-woman relationship, I believe that an excellent method of treatment is that which is conducted in groups. Insight into the causes of individual infidelity is implemented when the group, projected as a surrogate family, helps the patient to see his activity both subjectively and objectively. In psychoanalysis in groups, infidelity can be seen, examined, and discussed not only in its intimate details but also in its broad, social implications. The shared fantasy life of group members lifts the burden of personal mortification and guilt. The patient learns that acting out which takes the forms of promiscuity and infidelity, when fully discussed with a diminishing sense of shame or culpability or fear of retribution, meets a dramatic response in the group that is direct and spontaneous.

I have invariably found therapeutic groups to be health-striving, and not in the sense of conforming either. Individuals in the group may go through periods of impulse gratification, of compulsive acting out, or of rigid conformity to existing codes. But they generally return to the deeper search for goals that are meaningful and personal relationships that are, for the most part, lasting. And the experience in groups teaches us that modern man, beset though he may be by the historic slings and arrows and the current atomic weapons of outrageous fortune, still strives toward his ultimate fidelity to Eros, which we analysts know to be not merely sexual gratification but life itself.

NOTES

1. Elizabeth Taylor, interviewed by Associate Editor Richard Meryman for *Life*, December 18, 1964, pp. 74–75.
2. Margaret Mead, *Male and Female* (New York: William Morrow & Co., 1949), p. 114.
3. Robert Briffault, *The Mothers* (New York: The Macmillan Company, 1931), p. 9.
4. *Ibid.*, pp. 226–227.
5. *Ibid.*, p. 220.
6. *Ibid.*, p. 221.
7. *Ibid.*, p. 222.
8. *Ibid.*, p. 261.
9. *Ibid.*, pp. 223–224.
10. *Ibid.*, p. 224.
11. Mathilde and Mathias Vaerting, *The Dominant Sex: A Study in the Sociology of Sex Differences* (London: Allen and Unwin, 1923).
12. Viola Klein, *The Feminine Character* (London: Kegan Paul, Trench, Trubner and Co., 1946), pp. 118–119.
13. Briffault, *op. cit..* p. 268, referring to the work of W. H. S. Jones.
14. *Ibid.*, p. 257.
15. *Ibid.*, pp. 271–272.
16. Mead, *op. cit.*, p. 195.
17. *Ibid.*, p. 188.
18. *Ibid.*, p. 189.
19. *Ibid.*, p. 190.
20. *Ibid.*, p. 191.
21. *Ibid.*, p. 193.
22. *Ibid.*, p. 195.
23. *Ibid.*, p. 200.
24. *Ibid.*, pp. 198–199.
25. *Ibid.*, pp. 199–200.
26. Samuel Grafton, "The Twisted Age," *Look*, December 15, 1964, pp. 37–46.
27. *Ibid.*
28. *Ibid.*
29. *Ibid.*
30. Mead, *op. cit.*, pp. 354–358.
31. Martin Grotjahn, "The Academic Lecture: Merits of Monogamy," *Psychiatric Spectator*, I (1963), 4–6.
32. Jean Paul Sartre, *The Words* (New York: George Braziller & Co., 1964); Simone de Beauvoir, *Memoirs of a Dutiful Daughter* (New York: World Publishing Co., 1959); Simone de Beauvoir, *The Prime of Life* (New York: World Publishing Co., 1962).

33. Simone de Beauvoir, "The Question of Fidelity," *Harper's*, November 1964, pp. 57–64; December 1964, pp. 111–122.
34. *Ibid.*
35. Mead, *op. cit.*, pp. 196–197.
36. Grafton, *op. cit.*, p. 39.
37. Mead, *op. cit.*, p. 197.
38. Philip Rieff, *Freud: The Mind of the Moralist* (New York: Anchor Books, Doubleday and Co., 1961), p. 183.
39. Erik Erikson, *Insight and Responsibility* (New York: W. W. Norton, 1964), pp. 125–127.
40. Quoted from Jerome S. Bruner, *The Process of Education,* by Andrew T. Weil, "Harvard's Bruner and His Yeasty Ideas," *Harper's,* December 1964, pp. 81–89.

Homosexuality in Marriage

Homosexuality in marriage is a problem of considerable theoretical interest but uncertain practical dimensions. Psychoanalysts do not often see married homosexuals and there is little opportunity to explore the psychodynamic structure of their marriages. This circumstance is worthy of note, for according to Kinsey's studies,[1] as many as 10 percent of males and 3 percent of females who are married also engage in homosexual activity. The form in which Kinsey's data are presented does not permit any accurate estimate of the percentage of homosexuals who marry, or of the nature or extent of homosexual activity among those married individuals who also engage in homosexual activity. Presumably, the figures stated include the entire range of hetero-homosexual balance from occasional acts to frequent and continued relationships. Homosexual patients in analysis sometimes mention contact, usually transient, with married persons. Kinsey notes that some of his informants made similar comments. The pseudonymous Daniel Webster Cory[2] avers that he is married and discusses "gay husbands" as though they are quite common. It is said that there are stable unions between male and female homosexuals which are marriages of convenience indeed, each partner giving the other full freedom to continue the preferred activity. A comprehensive study would require the pooling of data from many analysts. The use of such pooled data was demonstrated in a study of male homosexuality by the Research Committee of the Society of Medical Psychoanalysts,[3] but the task would, in this instance, be more difficult because of the scarcity of married homosexual patients. Relying on cases I have seen, or of which I have direct knowledge through their analysts, I will attempt here to discuss only certain aspects of homosexuality in marriage which were illuminated by the patients about whom I have sufficient information.

Male Homosexuals

Several features of the sexual behavior of this group of married homosexual men are of special interest. These include the episodic quality of the homosexual activity, the role of nonsexual factors in their sexual behavior, and the preoccupation with sexual adequacy.

A noteworthy finding of the study of male homosexuality conducted by Bieber and his colleagues[4] was the evidence of heterosexual strivings in many of the most confirmed male homosexuals. In some instances, homosexual activity was seen to be the aim-inhibited outcome of heterosexual interest or stimulation. The married homosexuals who are the subjects of this chapter have, of course, given clear indication of their heterosexual interests. For these patients, heterosexual stimulation was an omnipresent factor, while their homosexual activity was episodic. In the course of analysis of such patients it soon became clear that homosexual activity was a signal of stress that was both specific and nonspecific. In some respects, these patients resembled alcoholics or drug users who resort to a previously established technique in dealing with anxiety. Two levels of stress could be distinguished: long-term, chronic stress patterns, and acute, relatively short-term stress situations. During prolonged stress there were many indications of anxiety, such as mounting irritability and quarrelsomeness, depression, drinking, and disorganization of work patterns. These nonspecific features were accompanied by heightened homosexual interest and diminished interest in heterosexual activity. Only one wife knew of the husband's homosexuality. She surmised what the husband was up to during such periods. She had married to prove that he could be wooed to heterosexuality and regarded the homosexual acting out as one would a period of relapse in a chronic disease. The other wives seemed unaware of the husbands' homosexuality and reacted mainly to the decreased sexual activity and the husband's increasing quarrelsomeness, irritability, withdrawal, and rejection.

In addition to the more or less extended periods of crisis and homo-sexual activity just described, there were also sporadic single incidents, usually casual pickups in previously familiar homosexual haunts. In these instances the accompanying disruptions in general behavior were variable. Sometimes there was obvious, conscious anxiety, but in other instances there was little alteration in the over-all routine of daily ex-istence. The homosexual episode appeared as a more or less isolated event for which the patient could at first offer no explanation.

The factors which precipitated the extended episodes of homosexual acting out were of several varieties, but with a common denominator: a situation that threatened the patient's sense of adequacy, compe-tency, or potency. The extended periods of acting out were mostly associated with extended crises in job or business situations. Most often such situations involved conflict with superiors or competitors which could not be easily resolved. In one instance the competition was with the wife in terms of professional standing and prestige. These circum-stances brought a flood of homosexual fantasies which followed the previously established preferred patterns of homosexual activity, whether the offending agent was male or female. Subjugation and humiliation of the partner were prominent in the fantasies and the sexual acting out that followed had, essentially, the same dynamic significance.

The sporadic single homosexual acts were more often the outcome of problems in the home or family. Routine household chores and the division of labor and responsibility within the family became foci for serious conflict. The issues included such matters as who should attend to a crying child during the night, sleeping late on holidays, shopping, and so on. These issues are, of course, not specific for, or characteris-tic of, the homosexual men; it was the intensity of the reactions and the element of infantile petulance which accompanied their complaints which was noteworthy. Almost invariably the issue was perceived in terms of control and dominance, and the men expected that their needs would receive unquestioned priority. When this was not the case, the reaction was immediate and sharp. All these men had some difficulty in their sexual relations with their wives. While these diffi-culties were not always severe, the men themselves were invariably preoccupied with their sexual performance. They demanded initiative on the part of the wife, and were bitterly disappointed if she did not give evidence of great gratification. They were quick to respond with hostility to the wife in the face of any problem, sexual or nonsexual. The sporadic homosexual act grew out of this hostility and was thus primarily vengeful. It demonstrated the theme "I can get along without you," but was, at the same time, a symbolic replenishment of potency from the transient male partner. There was never any interest in the partner, but only hostility and exploitation. Potency was clearly an issue of continuing doubt and sensitivity, requiring repeated bolstering and reinforcement.

These men were quite competitive, sometimes overtly, more often subtly and covertly. They made great demands upon everyone in the environment; wife, children, relatives, friends, co-workers. They not only manifested a low frustration tolerance, but their competitive demands for position, recognition, attention, and gratification were such as to guarantee that they would meet disappointment. Competition with children, especially male children, for the wife's attention was noteworthy. The events which triggered off homosexual fantasies and acting out were not necessarily sexual, actually or symbolically, but consisted mainly in the failure of the situation to conform to what was being demanded. Descriptively, the demands might be labeled oral, but the homosexual fantasies were not necessarily oral, following instead the patient's preferred pattern. The subsequent homosexual acts aimed at fulfilling the fantasies, but were modified often in accordance with the preference of the partner.

This summary of the conditions under which homosexual fantasies and activity waxed and waned has many implications for the theoretical understanding of homosexuality. These patients highlight the multiplicity of factors that determine the level of homosexual activity. There is evidence in the histories of the patients that multiple determining factors operated also in the genesis of the homosexuality.

The reversion to homosexuality in the face of stress deserves further comment. The dynamic content of the homosexual acting out consisted mainly in hostility, vengefulness, and replenishment of the sense of adequacy and potency. What requires explanation is the need for a homosexual rather than a heterosexual object. Both in fantasy and in actuality, these men were capable of giving expression to hostility toward women. They could be, and were, challenging and critical toward their wives, as well as petulant and demanding, and, on occasion, they acted out the hostility forcefully. Nevertheless, full restitution seemed to require the homosexual channel. Subjugation of a female was not sufficient. Only conquest of a male could relieve anxiety and restore confidence and potency.

What kinds of women did these homosexual men marry? To begin with, these men sought especially attractive and sexually stimulating females. The fact that they were making off with an attractive, desirable prize was a significant inducement toward marriage and provided strong reinforcement to their shaky masculinity. Also, they sought women who would make minimal demands and present little challenge in the marriage. This, however, did not always prove to be so. In all the cases homosexual activity had begun during adolescence and was well established as the pattern of sexual relatedness as these men entered into adult life. Turning toward women was, therefore, a reversal of pattern which required much support. The women these men married had to meet them more than halfway. In several instances the men reported that they had been pursued. One patient had had several affairs with older women before venturing into relationships with women his own age. He finally married a girl considerably younger than he was. She had come to work in an organization in which he was an important executive and for her he was what is popularly known as a "good catch." She admired his rugged, virile appearance and gave every indication that she would be a dutiful wife. He had many doubts and hesitations about marrying, saying that he feared he would be engulfed. Even during the courtship there was ample evidence of his hostility. He was late for appointments, inattentive when they went to parties together, and generally negative and critical. He recognized the significance of this negative behavior, and her continued devotion was convincing reassurance that he would be safe. In this situation, safety meant that he would not be rejected, that she had seen him at his worst and was prepared to put up with him. After they were married, his behavior varied as has been described, according to the pressures on him at work and at home. Eventually, the wife developed numerous psychosomatic complaints which led her to seek analysis. This patient's heterosexual potency had already been established by the time he met the girl he married. He did not have potency difficulties after marriage, but his negative attitudes toward his wife, and toward women generally, persisted.

Another patient established the safety of his prospective marriage by gradually making the fact of his homosexuality known to his prospective wife. She had literally seduced him and was quite accepting of his initial failures sexually. As his potency improved, he worried more and more that he was becoming too seriously involved. He dropped hints, introduced her to his "gay" friends, and broke a date to stay overnight in the apartment of one of his homosexual acquaintances. She blandly accepted his halfhearted excuse that he had had too much to drink and wanted to rest.

These patients had tested their heterosexual potency before marrying, which on the whole would seem a reasonable precaution under the circumstances. In contrast, a third patient ventured into marriage without having made any previous heterosexual attempt. After marriage he had continuing potency difficulties, but he complained that his wife did not stimulate him sufficiently. After their first child was born, she developed dyspareunia. When under pressure in his work, he would stop at a "gay" bar on the way home. Although displeased, the wife did not raise any open objection to his late return.

These homosexual men had sought support and reassurance for their masculinity by choosing attractive, safe, nonchallenging wives, but their hopes were largely disappointed. Although the wives originally seemed compliant and accepting, they gradually made their needs known and eventually became angry and resentful when these needs were not met. Characterologically unable to take bold, assertive stands, the wives engaged in subtle sabotage or fell back on somatic illness. The net result was a state of chronic dissatisfaction with the marriage, punctuated by periods of sharpened conflict. During these periods, the men returned to, or intensified, homosexual activity, while the wives suffered from anxiety and a variety of somatic symptoms.

These married homosexual men provide some interesting insights into the attitudes of at least some homosexuals toward women. Popular belief has it that homosexuals avoid women and are hostile toward and afraid of them. Part of this belief was borne out by the research study of male homosexuals conducted by Bieber and his associates.[5] Seventy percent of the homosexuals studied were reported to show fear of women. On further analysis, however, it was found that almost as many (60 percent) sought out some social contact with women, and almost 30 percent idolized them. Taken along with other evidences of heterosexual interest and of inhibition of this interest, the conclusion drawn was that the expressed fear of women was specifically sexual and that homosexuals do not avoid all contact with women but only that which is manifestly sexual. Thus, a male homosexual will, on occasion, be quite friendly with a married couple, in which case he is likely to be closer to the wife, or he will be friendly with an older woman, with the mother of a friend, and so on. The married homosexuals who are the subject of this report did not fear women, nor did they express fear or aversion for the female genitalia. Such fear and aversion was frequently reported by the men studied by Bieber *et al.* The primary concern of the married homosexual men was with their own adequacy. Though preoccupied with their sexual performance, they were equally vulnerable with respect to their performances in their jobs or professions and with respect to the impression they made in social gatherings, and so on. They made great demands on others but did not tolerate demands made upon them. They were concerned with the wife's sexual gratification mainly as proof of their own potency and masculinity. In nonsexual matters, they were narcissistic, competitive, and exploitative. They attached great importance to their heterosexual marriage in a fashion reminiscent of Bernard Robbins's description in the "Psychological Implications of the Male Homosexual Marriage."[6] They displayed toward their wives many of the attitudes displayed toward the male partner by the males in the homosexual "marriage."

In the usual course of events, a male homosexual may maintain social contact with women which not only is nonsexual in manifest content but is in practical terms quite superficial. Even though a homosexual may make a confidante of a woman friend, the actual relationship is limited and distant. It is this lack of involvement and the peripheral nature of the interaction which permit the relationship between the homosexual and female friend to remain formally friendly and correct. The close, daily interaction entailed in either a heterosexual or a homosexual marriage provides the arena for narcissistic and exploitative maneuvers. In two patients, who married during the course of analysis, it was clear that attitudes toward homosexual partners were carried over in relation to the heterosexual partner when the relationship became close enough, suggesting that these attitudes are an integral part of the character structure. It is of interest that these patients were able to marry at a point when neither the sexual nor the characterological problems were fully resolved. The marriage was a test not only of their ability to function heterosexually but also of their ability to make the adjustments and adaptations in living which are a necessary part of the continuing intimacy on all levels which marriage entails.

Female Homosexuals

As I have mentioned, Kinsey reports that only 3 percent of married females engage in homosexual activity, in contrast to 10 percent of married males who engage in such activity. According to Kinsey, the over-all incidence of homosexuality among females is about one-half of that among males. A psychoanalyst could expect, therefore, to see fewer female homosexuals as patients, and fewer married female homosexuals. My own experience is consistent with this expectation. I have direct knowledge of only one case in which a married female maintained a Lesbian relationship over a period of many years. This was a known, open relationship, carried on in defiance of the scandalized opinion of the entire neighborhood in which the woman lived. She had married a passive, unassertive man who permitted himself to be moved into a separate bedroom while the woman and her partner occupied adjoining rooms. She was active in civic and community affairs despite the scandal and even occupied a position of some prominence. There was a strong identification with her father, who had been much in the public eye.

On the other hand, I have seen several women who had engaged in homosexual activities at some time before therapy. They had had one or two partners in relationships which extended over a considerable period rather than the transient relationships so frequent among males. None of these women showed the kind of pressure toward the resumption of homosexual activity that characterized the males, nor were they beset by homosexual dreams or fantasies. They did not show any analogue to the male preoccupation with potency, but claimed rather that they experienced orgasm and were satisfied with their heterosexual relations. They were competitive and manipulative, but used feminine wiles to attain their ends. Under pressure, their usual reaction was not a turn toward homosexual fantasies or acting out, but inhibition and depression. Dependence upon the partner was a prominent feature, and loss of a partner was attended by suicidal thoughts or gestures.

One patient, during the time of her homosexual phase, had many homosexual male friends. After some years she found herself depressed by the termination of a Lesbian relationship and moved to another city. Here she avoided Lesbians, made male friends, and eventually married. She sought therapy not because of any recurrence of homosexual interest but because of depression. She had no homosexual contacts during the period of her marriage, but did have extramarital heterosexual relationships. She had one close friend, a confidante since college. This woman also had married. There was never specifically sexual dream or fantasy material relating to this woman. The husband of the patient was tall, good-looking, and "masculine." His attitude toward her was solicitous and motherly. In dreams she was frequently pursuing or looking for an ideal man who sometimes resembled her husband.

These contrasts between male and female married homosexuals are striking, but the interpretation of the differences is uncertain. Since the number of cases is small, more extensive sampling is required. Furthermore, it seems likely that homosexuals who marry differ in important respects from those who are, and remain, exclusively homosexual. The full range and significance of such differences remains to be determined.

Treatment

Certain problems in the treatment of married homosexual patients were encountered with sufficient regularity to warrant specific mention. Conflict was a prominent feature in all the cases. Those patients who were married when they entered treatment were for the most part led to do so by a marital crisis. The males who married during treatment soon found themselves embroiled in serious conflict. There was a marked tendency to convert outside problems into frictions with the spouse. The actual issues were rarely acknowledged and sometimes not recognized as such. The resulting quarrels were almost invariably marked by great bitterness and were accompanied by recurrences of anxiety and other symptoms as well as the homosexual fantasies and activities described earlier.

The patients usually tried to enlist the analyst as an ally against the spouse. They showed a general tendency to act out, avoided introspection, and resisted interpretations. The men, especially, made great demands for attention and reassurance, and needed much support for their shaky masculinity. It was often necessary for the analyst to take an active stand on matters at issue and make practical suggestions for handling the crisis. This necessity provided the basis for many ambivalent transferential reactions. Often, "submission" and "giving in" became the starting points for extensive interpretative ventures.

The tendency to act out was evident also in the work and social relationships of these people. Their subtle competitiveness and pronounced ambivalences often involved these patients in difficult situations which could easily bring them to the brink of disaster. Here, too, it was frequently necessary for the analyst to take an active stand.

These people were also prone to test the limits of situations. The testing process was specially marked in the transference, but was also evident in all relationships. The tests had to be met by firm, rational, and sensitive adherence to a sound therapeutic position, reinforced by a continued optimistic attitude on the part of the analyst. Individual patients showed particular characterological traits which served as major resistances.

Several of the wives undertook some form of psychotherapy. This proved to be a most salutary step. My experience with this group of patients suggests that it may be desirable to insist that the spouse enter treatment along with the primary patient.

Conclusion

In presenting this overview of married homosexual patients, I have tried to avoid the temptation to make generalizations based on what is, after all, a mere handful of patients. I have focused attention on the role of the homosexuality in the marital situation rather than on the genesis of the homosexuality. In these patients the homosexuality consisted of a constellation of attitudes and behavior toward the opposite sex, as well as the choice of an object of the same sex. The differences between males and females which I have summarized constitute impressions and obviously require confirmation in larger groups of patients. If substantiated, the differences may throw some light on some fundamental issues of masculine and feminine psychology, which in turn will have a bearing on problems of heterosexual marriage.

NOTES

1. A. C. Kinsey, W. E. Pomeroy, and C. E. Martin, *Sexual Behavior in the Human Male* (Philadelphia: W. B. Saunders & Co., 1948); A. C. Kinsey *et al., Sexual Behavior in the Human Female* (Philadelphia: W. B. Saunders & Co., 1953).
2. D. W. Cory, *The Homosexual in America* (New York: Greenberg Publishers, 1951).
3. I. Bieber *et al., Homosexuality: A Psychoanalytic Study* (New York: Basic Books, 1962).
4. *Ibid.*
5. *Ibid.*
6. Bernard S. Robbins, "Psychological Implications of the Male Homosexual Marriage," *Psychoanalytic Review*, XXX (1943), 428.

Marital Conflict, Analytic Resistance, and Therapeutic Progress

An individual has but one personality, and it is this personality which functions in all interactions, whether with man, woman, or child, with intimate or stranger, with spouse or analyst. The psychoanalytic process crucially involves defining the patient's interpersonal difficulties and evaluating the degree and manner in which the distortions within his own personality contribute to these interpersonal difficulties. Also included in the therapeutic process are the delineation and fostering of healthy resources. It is possible to observe the correlations of functioning, both pathologic and healthy functioning, as these are manifested in parallel fashion in marital and analytic contexts. An increase of dynamic understanding of the intrapersonal and interpersonal processes is gained by recognizing this parallelism, and, of greatest import, recognition of the correlations may be exploited therapeutically.

From clinical data I shall develop the two types of parallel, exploring first correlations between conflicts in marriage and manifestations of interpersonal pathology in therapy. The latter constitute the phenomena of resistance. Resistance may be defined as the struggle, specifically in analysis, to avoid constructive altering of pathologic functioning. Surrounding the serious conflicts of marriage, there exists the individual's struggle to preserve his interpersonal pathology; this struggle within marriage parallels resistance within analysis. Second, I will indicate the parallels of improvement in the patient's practices in marital and analytic interactions.

A brief introductory example of a pathological parallel is provided by a wife, a highly sophisticated woman with a frequently assumed ingenuous manner. This patient was exploring how her undermining of her husband contributed to the marital conflict. Near the end of a session she stated: "I don't know why I think of this now, but I feel anxiety whenever my husband boasts." I suggested that her anxiety might develop because, despite their concealment behind ingenuousness, there was danger that her derogations might be exposed. Her immediate association was an incident in which her husband was complaining to her about not having been given adequate and anticipated rank in his organization. Privately contemptuous of his overevaluation of himself, she asked him softly, "What made you think you were going to be given a vice-presidency?" As she posed the question, she had experienced anxiety.

I restated the possibility of a connection between her anxiety and the perhaps too thinly camouflaged undermining of her spouse and recommended as she was departing that she examine herself for such a connection in this and other instances. She smiled prettily, replied softly, "Yes, teacher," *blushed*, and departed.

How alike was her functioning with her husband and with her analyst. At home she was involved in a constellation of unrecognized behavior and felt anxiety when she undermined her husband's boasting. In my office there appeared the parallel constellation of the anxious blush I observed when, following not boastfulness but a professional recommendation, she was covertly pulling the rug from under her analyst. Definitions of her behavior, delineations of her emotion, and the establishment of correlations between her functioning at home and in the therapeutic circumstances served both her understanding and her personality change.

In another brief example, a husband lay on the couch giving obvious lip service to previous insights. In the same session, he spent most of the time bitterly and angrily condemning his wife for not believing in the genuineness of his efforts to deal with their marital problems. Then, as he left the session, he was in a fury at me for questioning the sincerity of his analytic explorations. Here the parallel was striking both in his pretenses in marriage and in analysis, and in his fury at being exposed in each of these interpersonal contexts. Again there proved to be substantial therapeutic value in establishing the correlations.

One may wonder, too, how consonant are the emotions when a spouse simultaneously considers plans to get a divorce and plans to give up analysis. It could be most inopportune clinically to regard these parallels as disparately evolved coincidence instead of a probably significant correlation.

The correlations that illuminate the personality are usually subtle, as with the wife who noted her anxiety when her husband boasted and who blushed when she slyly ridiculed her analyst. Occasionally, however, therapeutic-marital congruence is more explicitly expressed, as it was by a woman who started a session with the statement: "I was thinking that my feeling about analysis was like my feeling about love-making—it was like my husband having to force my legs apart."

The basic problem in marriage (one that makes so pertinent the parallelism with analysis) is the impact of interpersonal forces—forces necessitating change. The intimate relationship of marriage, for every individual a new and always more highly complicated kind of relating, requires alteration of personality in order to succeed. The success of analysis, too, requires personality change; the requirement of change in analysis, though more explicit, is not necessarily more drastic.

In the following case, the marital and analytic parallels were for a long time difficult to delineate clinically and were initially difficult for the patient to grasp or use. The patient was a woman who had given up an academic career to be a full-time housewife and mother and who came for treatment because her marriage was intolerable. Her husband's crass disregard for her needs and his patronizing attitude toward her in all areas of thinking and taste were insupportable, and she was heading for divorce.

Early in analysis it was suggested to her that in addition to feeling squelched and neglected, she herself had evolved great skills in self-effacement. Skillful self-effacing practices seemed to have the goal (though she was unaware of it) of proving to herself that she was really superior to all other human beings. Briefly: other people had needs—she was above having needs. Overtly she regarded and conducted herself as painfully modest. A large part of her marital problem was an unrecognized but definite collusion with her husband's disregard for her. The self-effacement on her part, moreover, was bad for everyone concerned: it supported her husband's grandiose myth of benevolence, and it encouraged in the children a false respect for their father while it also interfered with growth of genuine respect for their mother. Furthermore, through self-denial and self-effacement there was engendered an increasing bitterness in the patient. She was bitter because she continued to feel deprived of the comforts, self-expressions, and joys that she denied herself. In addition, she unknowingly felt contempt when she saw these ordinary elements of living enjoyed or striven for by others.

The gross subjugation of her own high-caliber judgment to the grandiose guidance of her husband and the inherent destructive influence of this behavior upon herself, upon the children, and even upon her husband were presented vividly in a dream six months after the beginning of analysis. In the dream the whole family was in a small boat, fishing. The patient hooked a large, vicious barracuda. She wanted to cut her line and let it go, but her husband called to her to land it in the boat; she deferred and landed the barracuda, which then proceeded to flail dangerously and snap within the boat—a danger to all of them.

Her subjugation of self prevented her from obtaining the ordinary emotional satisfactions most human beings need and want. What she looked for was something *extraordinary*, and she had married her husband in part because, in his courting, he had appeared to be extraordinarily kind and empathic and capable of providing unusual fulfillment for her without her having to seek for it. Not only did he fail of this unusual and seeming promise, but he also fell far short of ordinary considerateness. With an unrecognized but glorious sense of unique ability to rise above adversity, she endured excessive personal deprivation. She slaved, for example, without automatic equipment in her home, and was bitter but unprotesting toward her husband, who could well afford such equipment, yet delayed purchasing it.

This ostensibly humble woman's secret role of uniqueness was manifested in parallel fashion in the analytic relationship. It had been suggested very early, for example, that in this relationship too she would become angry, but she had thought inwardly, "Not *me*." It took a year and a half in analysis for her to acknowledge in herself and to express fury toward the analyst. Her fury, in turn, arose when it became clear that in spite of her truly extraordinary dedication to analysis, I considered her a patient. For her, this meant *just* a patient. For me, and it took some time for her to recognize the fact, it meant respecting her as I respected other patients. It was much later that she came to recognize my appropriately high regard for her exceptionally intense engagement in the therapeutic process. Shortly thereafter she gained some insight into her contribution in the analytic relationship to her feelings of rejection, deprivation, and bitterness. This came about through an incident at a theater party when I encountered her and a group of other patients whom she knew. My other patients and I greeted each other and chatted, but she shrank away and I had to seek her out to say hello. Next day she reported her feelings the previous evening in the theater lobby. She had sought to avoid me because she could barely keep from exposing what she called the "*extra* demands I wanted to make on you—I didn't want to be a peasant like the rest."

Only in this framework—that of accepting her role as my patient—did she begin to accept emotionally the necessity for struggling to achieve also a reasonable status as a wife, to demand and achieve ordinary rights and gratifications. (She stopped sacrificing so much for her children, too, and became less of a glorious and more of an ordinary good mother.) Basically, however, her progress in marriage resulted significantly from analyzing and beginning to overcome grandiosity in therapy, her striving for a role somehow "above" that of a patient. After understanding her resistance to overcoming grandiosity in analysis, she was then capable of realizing also how much she shrank away from being an ordinary wife and how much she did to foster the adversity she gloriously rose above—adversity in the form of painful exploitation of and disregard for herself in the marriage.

In analysis too, she manifested the pattern of fostering disregard for herself in order to rise above adversity. One day I failed to hear the bell when she arrived and offered to make up the lost time by meeting her twenty minutes early the following day. She spitefully replied, "I'll see you early and *pay* you for it." Then she volunteered, "I *wanted* to be angry—I wanted you to be a bastard," and as we talked about this she reported an association: "I just had the thought that I should be talking about my unwillingness to have a good relationship with my husband.

"I'm angry," she added, "because my husband's changing—not really, but enough so I can't feel justified in running away. I feel trapped." She had wanted some release from an intolerably painful marriage, but she also wanted to run away from her husband's decency in marriage, and from my decency in analysis. If husband and analyst were decent to her, she was threatened with the loss of both stoic and moral superiority and pressed with the rational necessity of accepting the roles of both patient and wife.

When she faced the problem of accepting wifehood, she was able for the first time to verbalize her negative and fearful attitude: "It frightens me. It's like decadence. If I sit back and enjoy being a wife, I'll deteriorate." It is important to record here that as she became willing to make substantial demands to be treated like a wife, her husband, after ferocious opposition, began to be more of a man, more responsive to her in all areas. He too had to make changes. He had to offer more, since she was no longer so collusive in his neglect of her. His rebellion gave her many opportunities to backtrack, but it was also a test of her commitment to change.

There existed for this woman, in summary, a dynamic parallelism between her marital and therapeutic roles. At home there was a subtle interweaving of behavior: utterly unaware of it, she painfully, contemptuously endured her husband's self-indulgence and vanity, while she gloriously rose above adversity; she maintained an unconscious disdain of any self-concept in the role of wife even while she was slavishly efficient in wifely performance; and she suffered continual deprivation and bitterness, engendered by her eluding gratifications of the marriage role. In like fashion, she applied herself most diligently in the analytic process while refusing (though unawares) the role of patient; instead of feeling the security, warmth, or self-respect engendered by her intensive therapeutic collaboration, she often suffered a sense of deprivation, frustration, humiliation, or bitterness. By struggling to overcome her resistance to being a patient, she opened the way to recognizing and combatting her self-destructive, unaware, parallel refusal of the role of wife. After many unconsciously self-glorifying but patently bitter married years, she began to build a marriage.

Earlier in this study it was observed that a basic problem in marriage is the impact of interpersonal forces necessitating personality change. Healthy personality development and change are achieved largely through cooperative activity with other human beings. A great deal of psychopathology arises, I believe, through the evolution of interpersonal functioning either designed to fend off being over-powered or designed to achieve power over others. It is unforunate (and this I believe lies at the core of most functional mental disturbances) that the competitive forces within our culture lead to profound and emotionally based confusion between the nature of any interpersonal influence on the one hand and specific interpersonal control and dominance on the other.[1] Much of what might be otherwise experienced as growth is instead felt as subjugation. *Marriage and analysis are potentially crucial growth experiences. In both, considerable emotional difficulty arises from misperceptions of domination by another human being and from struggles against being "forced" to change.*

In the following analytic experience with a depressive,[2] highly intellectual grandiose businessman whose initial chief complaint was anxiety attacks, a great deal of his problem turned out to involve avoiding mature responsibility. Taking responsibility meant giving others power to coerce him. Or it meant abdicating his power (largely through dependency) to control others. The basic functioning of his personality was found consistent not only in relation to spouse and analyst, but also in a wide spectrum of relationships, including those with his small children, with his business partner (a man), and with women friends. While these more broadly ranging correlations will be alluded to, the emphasis will be upon the parallels in feeling and behavior in marriage and in therapy. Spelling this out in his own clear, spontaneous words, the patient, after a weekend of depressive stubborn refusal to follow the analyst's recommendation to think over a problem, said: "*I just realized I'm reacting to you exactly the way I react to Lucy* [his wife]—I get all tied up in knots and get furious and won't do anything."

This man had always lived by two chief attributes—brilliance and pathos. He made an excellent academic record in high school and college but was unable to go into graduate work. The halt in his education was due only in part to the economic depression of the thirties, for he was in any case insufficiently motivated to move on into higher practical preparation for living. For twenty years he functioned on the fringes of literary, semiprofessional activities, free-lancing or ghost-writing some of the time, or keeping to such relatively menial activities as stock-clerking or filing. He read continuously, often abstruse material, and was a peripatetic encyclopedia of flashy facts.

He made a career of impressing friends and acquaintances, pursued no long-term job possibilities. When there were chances for meaningful advancement in a current occupation, he leached out his skill, his time, and his energy by meticulously carrying out clerical duties that might have been relegated to less gifted employees.

In his life with women, a similar pattern of underdevelopment was followed. He played the role of the lonely, pathetic, unappreciated man, confining himself to women who were responsive to this condition and demanded little of him. In the sexual realm, he cultivated those who, usually out of pity, permitted his feeling them, women who compassionately offered comfort by masturbating him. On one occasion, while actually participating in full intercourse, at the point of orgasm he had the sudden fantasy of being a tiny boy humping a three-year-old little girl.

Each maturing step in his life produced an anxious fantasy of arrest and imprisonment; the fantasied incarceration rescued him from maturity, but also frightened him with a loss of freedom to exercise control over others and to pursue his delusionally elite existence. He kept hoping that his unique qualities would spare him from descent into the mire of ordinary living, the mire of permanent and gainful occupation, a wife and children, a conventional role in an ordinary society.

Some years after my return from military service (he himself had received a neuropsychiatric discharge within a few weeks of induction), he returned for analysis, still showing the old pattern of grandiosity, pathos, sexual mendicancy, and occupational self-limitation. During the intervening years of sporadic jobs, however, there had been a rise both in the quality of his performance and in the demands for his increasing skills.

Shortly after resuming analysis, in his late twenties, he left his parental home with anguish and took a cheap room. Eventually he was able to work through problems involved in cultivating a relationship that gradually became intimate and meaningful and then culminated in marriage. He also achieved an occupational level at which he ventured with initiative and responsibility and established a good income. With each increment he panicked with the usual fantasies of arrest and incarceration, collapsed into helplessness and depression, and raged against life's (and his wife's and analyst's) demands. His analysis terminated approximately a year after marriage—he was refused analytic life tenure. Occasional consultations, however, continued through many years after termination.

Then a renewed period of analysis came when he was in his early forties. At this time he was capably managing a remunerative service, had some investments, and was the father of a couple of youngsters. His marriage was only rarely gratifying, and brief panics and depressive collapses continued to dog his progress. I offered him an inexorably final six months of intensive analysis. Throughout these valedictory six months, the dependent tyranny characteristic of depressives and his grandiosity were the prominent themes, while he railed both angrily and plaintively against wife and analyst. "I have," he stated during this new terminal period, "tremendous hatred against you and Lucy—I feel you have ruined my life," and then added: "If you act like a baby, you can get away with anything. If I can do things for myself, nobody will do them for me—I *can* do them, but when I start, I get scared."

Early during the renewed therapy he manifested a fairly consistent course of sad, ineffectual behavior and created a clear picture before both his wife and his analyst of a brave but hopeless outlook. Session after session in my office, and evening after evening at home, he revealed ineffective efforts to change or compulsive collapses that somehow defeated the most noble resolves. This consistent personality, his inwardly arrogant insistence on being served, was in fact reflected in relation to all who required his manly behavior.

With two months frittered away, I emphasized the immutable brevity of the remaining therapeutic time and stated that the only way he could deal effectively with his problems was to work intensively, including the intervals between sessions—and I emphasized that to insure his involvement he should actually sit and type out his pursuit of his feelings. The detection and delineation of his feelings were to be the focus of all his introspective and communicative efforts. He was furious at this limitation of time and the demand for initiative, but, in his own words, he nevertheless "started working on this shit!" Attacks of anxiety and episodes of anger became more frequent.

The generalized, persistent basis for the anger and the anxiety, for the resentment toward analyst and wife, was the necessity to change. Marriage had necessitated an increase of responsibility toward himself and his wife. The development of an independent business had increased his responsibilities for himself and toward others. The arrival of children further escalated responsibility. Resumption of regular analysis drew all these requirements of adult living into sharper focus and, instead of offering relief from his burdens, accentuated the necessity of dealing with them effectively. His wife embodied and intensified the necessity for change by her growing impatience with his complaints, by her resentment of his affectual parsimony in their marriage, and by her growing unwillingness to support the persistent heaviness of his moody demands. His analyst represented the pressure for change in two ways: by a continual investigation of the patient's part in producing his own difficult symptoms and by investigation too of the concrete *personal* resources upon which the patient could draw for relief. Wife and analyst were responded to as heartless, ununderstanding enemies seeking more from him than it was within him to deliver. Both were hated adversaries seeking to vanquish him and force upon him an unwanted way of life.

This man's anxiety, which accompanied his depression at home and in therapy, can be understood in terms to the threat of his sense of self. As a manipulative weakling he functioned effectively—was a "king." He felt powerful in terms of how he managed people by his own helplessness. As his practice of dependency became less effective with his wife and his analyst, he felt like a less effective total individual. The subjective sense of self that accompanies effective functioning was lost with each failure of his long-established pathology—he would feel disintegrated. The physiologic concomitant of this loss of functioning power, this lost sense of self, was the anxiety. The lost sense of self occurred and anxiety emerged also during the success of new healthy adult activity; with progress, his personality as expressed in dependent practice was threatened.

"Every time I do something positive," he said, "I have less reason to throw myself on people's mercy—ask for help." And a month before the end of analysis, when he found considerable evidence of a capacity for successful manly intimacy with his wife, he observed, "Every time I come closer to Lucy, I feel I will lose my wider powers." This would be echoed in business, where he inquired of himself, "Why do I prefer to call people on the phone rather than write? If I call, I can use my wiles on them, as a sweet, imploring baby." As a "sweet, imploring baby" he was functioning familiarly, effectively, and felt like himself. Writing like a businessman, he was unfamiliar to himself, and he became emotionally disoriented and frightened.

And likewise, becoming engaged in analysis through the pursuit and writing out of his feelings, associations, and insights—instead of collapsing on the analytic couch or on his living-room sofa—also, in addition to making him angry at his analyst and his wife, frequently tended to make him emotionally disoriented and frightened.

In spite of increasingly felt, enjoyed, and acknowledged gains, ambivalently he also resented his own constructive efforts, for they bore the hallmark of mediocrity. His intellectual excellence and his dependency techniques had always reinforced one another in maintaining his sense of eliteness, of being one who is served, not one who must strive. The requirements of struggle in marriage and therapy were threatening and infuriating. Concurrently, however, he searched honestly into his recalcitrant feelings and recognized clearly and freshly a part of his resentment, expressing it thus: "Effort is terrible —it is degrading—it's for slobs. Great men like me shouldn't have to do this." Simultaneously, with this expression, he associated to an old dream of being an Egyptian king with a whip and being borne by slaves. Shortly afterward he recognized his unwillingness to take initiative for the marital social life, musing, "I expect Lucy to provide interesting times and people." A week later he was depressed during a session and resented my not lifting him out of his mood. After leaving my office he became aware of his feelings toward me, which were much like those experienced toward his wife, much like his expectation that she "provide interesting times and people." Toward me the thoughts went: "I feel unhappy and bored—*Walter didn't jazz me up*—I hate him."

As he recognized his greater commitment to change, he experienced in his final month a typical depressive fantasy. It was a fantasy of competitive triumph, of outwitting those who would seemingly impose responsibility; he would escape responsibility and simultaneously punish those who refused to bend to his will, who refused to subsidize him. This fantasy involved wife and analyst. He pictured slashing his own throat in the bathroom at home, coming out to his wife drenched in blood, and in response to her horrified reaction he would say, "I did this because of what you and Walter have done to me. I want you to see this picture in front of you for the rest of your life."

Near the end of therapy, he had more and more accepted the need for continuing in his independent efforts to accept the necessities of ordinary adult living and had accustomed himself more to the leveling tendency of genuine intimacy. Concurrently he found his wife deliberately and wisely unresponsive to his attempts at reestablishing the effectiveness of his mournful or sullen appeals for sympathy and indulgence. On one such occasion, he recognized a series of thoughts that describe for us sadly, yet reassuringly, the victim of increasing health. It was two weeks before termination, and he wrote down: "Lucy showed no compassion. I want to be glamorous; I don't want to be just another schmo who sits around the house talking to his wife. Walter [analyst] is taking away all my props." And that night he had a nightmare in which there was anxiety, not from violence or catastrophe, but because of the presence of an individual who was a clean-shaven, manly father and husband and who represented himself. Much pathology had been overcome at home; much resistance had been overcome in analysis. He was living more fully as a father and husband, expanding his business, having more gratifying sex than he had ever offered or experienced; he had finally established a meaningful marital dialogue and was friendly, manly, and grateful to me. He was not just sullenly giving in to the triumphant forces of wife and analyst; he was enjoying using his capacities more fully. With some fear, sadness, and protest, this formerly angry, depressive, dependent prodigy was, in the crucial interchanges with wife and analyst, beginning to accept being an active ordinary man.

The case reveals the patient's parallel interpersonal functioning in marriage and analysis. This was manifested in the grandiose demands for deference, service, and immunity from responsibility, as well as in the anxieties and rages against wife and analyst when these demands were frustrated. *The pursuit of these parallels was valuable in the development of insight and in his employment of insight to effect change in himself.*

These cases have roughly sketched the parallelism between emotional, conceptual and behavioral processes in marital and psychoanalytic interactions.

Sexuality

During the presentation, relatively little has been said about sex. It is my belief that the individual's sexuality reflects more than it determines his personality functioning.[3] With regard to the patients described here, their sexual functioning did follow the pattern of other aspects of their personality, as already indicated in the dependent, begging, exploitative, and ungiving sexual behavior of the depressive businessman. Likewise, in the case of the grandiose non-wife-nonpatient, in her college days and early career she was promiscuous and compulsively went to bed with many men to maintain a self-image of superiority to other women, by never exciting a man without satisfying him. In marriage, her efforts always to rise above adversity included sex: she had a very lively appetite, but endured sexual deprivation from a physically highly adequate husband, just as she had endured deprivation of household equipment in spite of his financial adequacy. Her self-aggrandizement in enduring deprivation was, however, not an adequate substitute for the fulfillment of her physical needs. Some of her deepest bitterness toward her husband developed because he often avoided her in bed and thereby forced her, because of her strong appetite, to express and expose the existence of a need. She often yearned for the analyst to respond sexually to her so he then would not be so much a person she needed as someone who needed her. Jay Haley[4] in the following statement expresses well the distorted role of sex in marriage: "When a couple is in a struggle over who is in control of the relationship, the pleasure of sexual relations becomes a peripheral matter, if it is there at all. Sexual relations become merely a way of working out the conflict over the relationship." In parallel fashion, the sexual fantasy about the analyst is often an expression of resistance, an effort to divest him of influence over the patient, to reverse the situation and achieve influence over him.

Resistance

One of the theoretic and clinical considerations raised at the outset of this study concerns resistance. It was proposed that resistance is more clearly comprehended when regarded as the counterpart within analysis of interpersonal distortions found in other relationships. The assessment of resistance, as demonstrated by the foregoing cases, can lead to more effective therapy, especially when parallels with marital conflict are drawn. One genial husband often associated me with his wife, but, in his words, "didn't realize I *treated* you both the same way." After our achievement of any insight and his concurrent friendly recognition of the need for my help, there frequently followed a contemptuous aloofness that was entirely parallel to his treatment of his wife after emotional closeness with her. In both situations he was denying the need for another person, and escaping from the humanizing, deeply altering influence upon him of another individual. In the marriage it would be referred to as withdrawal; in the analysis it would be referred to as resistance. Delineation of the parallel more intensely illuminated the characteristic of the response and more fully opened the way to change.

Likewise with the unhappy wife who deferred to her husband: her holding herself above the role of wife and rejecting it would be regarded as unconscious grandiosity, while her struggling to hold herself above the role of patient would be regarded as resistance. Her manner of functioning in the separate circumstances was identical. Therapeutically, the important recognition was the peculiar manner in which she immersed herself in conventional activities (maritally and analytically), while neither accepting nor demanding the gratifications attached to these activities. Her subtle, unrecognized striving for self-aggrandizing, realistically unattainable satisfactions was at the core of much marital conflict and much analytic resistance. It left her constantly embittered and deprived in both analysis and marriage. By overcoming her resistance, the specific resistance of fighting against seeing herself as a patient, she was in fact preparing the way to seeing herself as a wife. One may learn about and detect resistance in studying marital conflict; one may learn about and detect forms of marital conflict in studying the married patient's resistance.

Therapeutic Progress

Regarding therapeutic progress, only a summary statement is in order, for its consideration has been implicit or alluded to in much of the foregoing. It has been indicated that particular distortions within the patient's personality are identical sources for conflict in marriage and correlative conflict, or resistance, in therapy. As insight and change occur, the interpersonal improvements within and outside therapy are also parallel, and the correlations of progress reinforce the patient's motivation for further therapeutic effort. The depressive, dependent businessman stopped resenting so deeply and leaning so heavily on both his wife and me as he began to experience self-respect and pleasure in independent functioning in domestic, therapeutic, and other spheres. The wife-patient who refused to acknowledge either role, by successfully accepting the patient role, laid the basis for her first and continuing efforts toward improving and enjoying marriage. She found through new kinds of satisfactions with both analyst and husband increasing encouragement to strive for a realistic role with each. In every case, explicit correlation of improvement not only sharpened insight but also generated reassurance within the therapeutic struggle and reinforcement of therapeutic commitment.

A particular and practical therapeutic aspect of recognizing the parallelism between the intimate analytic and marital interpersonal functioning arises especially when the patient is oriented toward divorce. It becomes important to sharpen the patient's comprehension of the ways in which he well might corrupt a relationship with any *subsequent partner*. By dealing with the patient's own distorting effect on relationships, documented in the marital and analytic dyads, one can sometimes help the patient to reorient toward both therapy and future life plans. Specifically, delineation with the patient of the marital-therapeutic interpersonal parallels may in some cases lead to a constructive approach to the present marriage, if the marriage still holds a potential; or, if divorce is inevitable, the impressiveness of the correlation can lead to the beginning of a salutary process of personality change that will make any sequential alliance more than a disastrous repetition.

Conclusion

In summary, analytic material has been offered to elaborate the clinical observation that the personality distortions of the patient are reflected in parallel fashion in the conflicts of marriage and the resistance of analysis. The essence of much of the emotional and behavioral disturbance in both situations is the individual's struggle to avoid alteration of the personality in response to interpersonal influence. It has been found in these and other cases that, when sought and recognized, the correspondences in the two crucial interpersonal milieus may generate valuable insights usable in the process of healthy change.

NOTES

1. See index references to "competitiveness" in Walter Bonime, *The Clinical Use of Dreams* (New York: Basic Books, 1962); also to "competition," in Rudolf Dreikurs, *The Challenge of Marriage* (New York: Duell, Sloan & Pearce, 1962).
2. For a discussion of the competitive aspects of depression, see Walter Bonime, "Neurotic Depression," in Silvano Arieti, ed., *American Handbook of Psychiatry*, Vol. III (New York: Basic Books, 1966).
3. This orientation is extensively developed and illustrated in Walter Bonime, *The Clinical Use of Dreams*.
4. Jay Haley, *Strategies of Psychotherapy* (New York: Grune & Stratton, 1963), p. 130.

The Role of the Psychoanalyst in Marital Crisis

Much has been written about the conscious and unconscious needs and emotional drives that impel people to marry, and much has been written about the conscious and unconscious needs and emotional drives that pull people apart, sometimes after long years of marriage. A discussion of the ingredients of a good marriage and of marital difficulties, predictions of whether or not a marriage will survive, cannot avoid being repetitious. Whatever one can say has, it seems, already been said, possibly in a somewhat different way. There are abundant data, collected by a number of therapists, psychiatrists, and practicing analysts who have attempted to salvage a troubled marriage or, failing this, tried to follow the usual therapeutic aim of salvaging the individual and helping him to reach a point where he could make his own decision regarding the wisdom of continuing in the marriage or of breaking it up and attempting to function alone.

One thinks of a "marital crisis" as a situation in which the marriage has become so untenable that one or both partners wish to dissolve it. In listening to the history of such couples, the psychiatrist soon discovers that there have been a number of critical situations during their marriage and that one or both partners had felt the breakup of the marriage to be imminent. However, both had—either on their own initiative or with some help—been able to find a solution that enabled them to continue. In the course of time, numerous smaller crises arose which were also weathered. By the time psychiatric guidance was sought, both partners were agreed on the necessity for a divorce, although neither partner felt quite able to assume responsibility for an irrevocable break.

Originally, it had appeared that a compromise could be worked out that would mitigate the severity of the "crisis." Finally, however, accumulated tensions, carried over from supposedly weathered earlier crises, reached such proportions that compromise solutions failed to achieve their patchwork aim. Both partners came to realize that further attempts would be futile.

The marital history of such people reveals an initial mutual attraction, love, and eagerness for a life of "wedded bliss." Both firmly believed that they were aware of the needs of the other and willing and able to gratify them. Thus they married and, in a number of cases, had children, who served to strengthen the tie between them. Eventually, however, the realization arose that they were no longer quite sure what they expected from the mate once a marital relationship had been established. It gradually dawned upon them that in evaluating their original expectations they had erred. Even when discord had reached monumental proportions, they could not, even when giving their history to a therapist, account objectively for this apparent error; their conscious reasoning could not rationally explain the severity of the difficulties they were experiencing with each other.

Early in the history-taking, the therapist gains insight into the many elements that entered into the original choice of a partner—elements over and beyond the conscious, objective, or logical; in other words, elements that exerted their influence from deeper strata of the mind, those dominated by unconscious drives and desires, which had an important influence on the decision to marry a particular person. Therapists usually refer to such elements as unconscious dynamics.

It is natural for unconscious dynamic factors to enter into the normal marital object choice; the problem revolves around the stength of the unconscious forces, the extent to which they lead back into the patient's developmental life, and the degree to which they influenced the choice of a marriage partner to the exclusion of "conscious" factors. In a normal marriage, one finds that every wife—to varying extents—represents a mother figure to her husband. This acknowledgment is quite conscious and may be seen in the common reference of a husband to his wife as "Mommy." It is equally common and accepted to hear a wife refer to her husband as "Daddy." But it is a conscious process having its roots in the unconscious, reflecting the earliest relationship with the parents and carried over into adult life in a normal way. When a woman feels the need to choose a husband whom she believes to be the direct opposite of her father, or when a man feels impelled to choose a wife who appears in every way the direct opposite of his mother, the basis for possible future marital difficulties is present.

In treating patients whose problems apparently stem from marital incompatibility, we find that there is a salient connection between the ability to adjust to the marital situation and the nature of the relationships with the patient's parents and siblings. In other words, the extent to which the husband and/or the wife is attached to each of his or her parents, brothers, or sisters is of great significance in evaluating possibilities for future marital adjustment. These early relationships very often, as we know, condition the choice of love object. Buried desires may be remobilized and appear in the marital relationship. Childhood affection for the parent—of the same and the opposite sex—and for brothers and sisters all help in forming harmonious marital functioning; conversely, these factors may be responsible for the discord that brings the patient to the therapist. The conscious and unconscious motivations that enter into married life and the choice of a partner will be the center of my discussion.

There exists in every marriage relationship a complexity of feeling, thinking, and action. People very often change during the course of a marriage; former compatibility may wane; new and conflict-causing factors may enter the picture.

One would ideally, of course, like to find a reliable tool for predicting the probable degree of marital adjustment. Psychiatric and psychological papers have been written purporting to set up standards for predicting marital compatibility. To my knowledge, however, there are no equivalent psychoanalytical studies. Nonetheless, based on an understanding of the dynamic structure of personality from a psychoanalytical approach, predictions of a general nature may be made concerning certain marriages. For instance, during the war years, I was consulted by many young people in their late teens or early twenties, or by the parents of one or both, concerning the advisability of marriage. In certain instances the parents wished me to convince the youngsters that marriage was inadvisable. I never gave direct advice but attempted to examine the situation, trying to ascertain exactly what the young people felt for each other and what sort of future they envisioned for themselves. In nearly every case I found that both youngsters had given thought to the possibility that the marriage might be of short duration—either because of the danger of the husband's being killed in the war, or else because of the risk of his becoming involved with another woman in a foreign country. Nonetheless, in most instances they were willing to gamble, hoping that, on the basis of a seemingly deep love between the two, the marriage would survive the dangers involved. They also felt that even if the marriage proved a mistake, it would not be a tragedy. My job, then, was to help the parents adjust to their children's decision. A young man who is old enough to fight, kill, and perhaps even die for his country can hardly be considered too immature to assume the responsibilities of marriage. In many such instances, I functioned more or less as a marriage counselor, seeing the young people once or twice and the parents once or twice, trying to help all concerned to evaluate the possible involvements of a marriage, helping the children to understand why they desired to marry, and helping the parents to understand why they objected to the marriage.

After the war, I had the opportunity to see some of these same young people. The pattern was similar: the young husband began to feel hemmed in; he was no longer part of the military world of masculine camaraderie; he now had many new and unwelcome responsibilities. I call these young husbands "bachelor husbands"—young men who wanted the best of both worlds. The young wife also contributed her share of vociferous complaints: she was alone too much in the postwar world, while her husband, to all appearances, preferred to spend his time at clubs, card games, football games, reunions, etc. At times the situation reached critical proportions, culminating in a divorce, which, had proper therapy been obtained, might have been avoided. The difficulties that manifested themselves in increasingly frequent flare-ups were directly attributable to the immaturity of both young people.

In analyzing married people, one is at times struck by the amount of energy the partners spend in devising ingenious and devious ways of torturing each other. One is impressed by the degree to which the

marriage is held together by mutual resentment and aggression, seemingly to the exclusion of love or any visible semblance of affection.
At times the therapist finds himself wondering how the marriage ever
came about in the first place, since it was a grievous error. Such cases
are not rare, and analysis may help both partners admit the feasibility
of divorce as the only workable method of solving otherwise insoluble
problems.

In two such cases in my own experience, in which both husbands
and wives were in therapy with different therapists, the marriages
were dissolved by friendly divorces that proved satisfactory to both
couples. In each case, both the husband and wife were involved in
intellectual pursuits. They had married because they had, at the time,
felt the need for a home. Both couples, however, were childless; they
felt that children would interfere with their careers. During years of
marriage, the couples became increasingly estranged from one another,
and the home for which they had ostensibly married ceased being a
"home" in any meaningful sense of the word. One or the other spent
days and nights away from home in research laboratories or on lecture
tours. Eventually, even their mutual scientific pursuits ceased to provide
a common meeting ground, and they found themselves with little to
say to each other. Since they were no longer even able to enjoy their
mutual friends, they found their social life becoming increasingly
limited.

The wife of one couple was in treatment with me, and it became
clear that the problems that led her to the choice of a husband originated in her early relationships and emotional ties to her parents and
siblings. All the male members of her family (she was the only girl)
were very ambitious, successful people, respected by everybody because of their accomplishments and positions in business and social
life.

She was the pet of her brothers and father. In her adolescence she
looked for ideals like her father and brothers, and her love attachments
at that age showed the influence of her positive Oedipal attachments
of childhood.

When it came to marriage, she chose, in many respects, the opposite
to her father and brothers. She could not be in real love with her
chosen husband; she could not be *really* married because that would
have been a realization of her early involvement with family members, and so her marriage was like playing house.

In the second case mentioned, the husband of the couple was my patient. His basic distrust of women, which was an outstanding problem, had its origin in his strong attachment to his mother. This attachment was consciously fostered by his mother. He was her only son, the eldest child, and he had four younger sisters. His father was actually always belittled by his mother, who was unhappy in her marriage. The patient was her only consolation.

The patient was always distant to his father. When he married, his own marriage represented to him unconsciously his earliest positive Oedipal strivings. So the wife could only be a mother substitute, not a woman with whom he could establish real closeness and for whom he could feel mature love. "His heart belonged to mommy," and he also was playing house.

Eventually and inevitably, they came to the conclusion that the marriage had been a mistake. What was lacking, however, was the courage to face the consequence of this admission—namely, a return to a single life. Nonetheless, the marriage was, in each case, inescapably a failure, and the initiative was finally taken by one of the partners—the wife in one instance, who was in therapy with me, and who felt more independent and less guilt-ridden about divorce. Both couples gradually learned to make their own decision: just as they had originally decided to marry, they were now able, in a more conscious and logical way, to solve their problem by dissolving what in this instance were truly the "bonds" of matirimony.

Another type of marriage that frequently winds up with one or both partners seeking psychiatric help is the one characterized by a desire to be married but an inability to *stay* married to the same person; there is often a compulsion to change mates repeatedly.

These people suffer from an inability to tolerate loneliness. Most often they function successfully in business or in professional work which keeps them in constant contact with people. However, when the day's work is done and they are faced with the necessity of returning home to an empty apartment, the fear of aloneness, which had been somewhat dissipated during the course of a busy day, returns in full force. They find the prospect of being alone in bed—even of being alone in the dark—insufferable; commonly, they have difficulty in falling asleep and are often hounded by nightmares.

Such people, one discovers, have an unconscious, insatiable need for love, for a sense of belonging, for a dependent relationship with a loving person who invariably represents primarily the mother and secondarily the father. Their life history reveals severe frustration and abandonment by the parents in early childhood, in some instances dating back to the age of three or four and sometimes even earlier. In analysis such patients experience difficulty in recalling these early years. However, since the same or similar familial conditions persisted into adolescence, they are able to recall clearly the painful feelings of aloneness endured at that time and the effort made to adjust to those feelings. As a result of inadequate emotional support, such patients commonly learn early in life to be independent to a certain extent. This ability later served as a source of pride, proving to them that they were able to manage their own affairs competently at an early age. This very independence, in fact, accounted, in varying degrees, for their successful careers, achieved at a relatively early age. Gradually, however, their private misery increased to the point where fears of being alone at night could no longer be minimized.

The patients still carry within them the seeds of their unresolved early childhood struggle. Although their need for a dependent relationship with a loving person is extremely acute, they are hampered by the fear of being disappointed were they actually to become involved with a member of the opposite sex. This fear is especially strong during adolescence. Eventually, however, they decided to marry in an attempt to fulfill the craving for a sense of belonging, of being cared for, and of caring. Unfortunately, the presence of unresolved childhood conflicts prevents the achievement of any fulfillment of this need for love, since what is being sought unconsciously is *parental* love and concern. And at the same time an ambivalent situation develops in which the provider of a loving concern is simultaneously seen as a potential rejector, capable of abandoning the patient, just as the parent of the opposite sex had done years ago. This already complex situation is further complicated by the unconscious problem of the incest barrier, carried over from infancy and childhood, which, in the case of the man, lends psychic reality to his desire for exclusive possession of his mother—a possession achieved, of course, by eliminating father as his chief if not sole competitor; and which, for the woman, lends psychic reality to her desire to be the sole love object of her father. However, when a woman marries, motivated primarily by her unconscious need to recapture the love of the father that she had once had, and when a man marries to pacify his inconsolable craving for mother love, the marriage will become slowly but inexorably intolerable, because gratification will be unobtainable.

But because the deep remnants of the past that have been reawakened in marriage remain in force and because consequently the fear of aloneness and the desire for a sense of belonging persist undiminished in intensity, a succession of marriages may occur. Some of the patients I have treated had a history of what might be called "serial" marriages, and finally had come for help on the advice of a friend or a physician.

It is characteristic of such marriages that the man or woman will choose a mate who is just the opposite of the parental image; that is, the man will tend to marry a much younger woman whose physical and mental attributes do not remind him of his mother. In so doing, he partially counteracts the unconscious incestuous involvement, saying: "Look, Father, I am not taking Mother away; I am marrying someone who is just the opposite—a mere youngster." Investigation revealed that the young wife of one of my patients not only represented the opposite of his mother but represented his sister, too. The incest barrier, then, was still present and gave rise to sexual difficulties in him. After three unsuccessful marriages, my patient married a divorcee— a woman closer to his ideal mother image, who had, moreover, been abandoned by her husband. This represented for him the abandonment of mother by father, thus freeing mother for him "on the square." Unfortunately, unconscious conflicts revolving around marriage, love, trust, sexuality, independence, competition with men, etc., led to the failure of this fourth attempt, following which the patient came for analytical treatment.

One of my female patients came to me after the failure of three marriages. She was a lovely, tender, well-liked woman with a tragic history. Her father had abandoned her mother before she was born, and so she had never known him. Her mother, of whom she did not remember much, had always been a cold, frustrating person, who tried to fulfill the role of a stern father instead of a warm, loving, and caring mother. In such circumstances my patient was forced to get along as best she could at a very young age—and her best was not very good. She did, however, choose a profession in which she became eminently successful. She, too, had an insatiable need for love and admiration, and she succeeded in fulfilling this aim in her professional and social life where she was well liked and the center of attention. As a result of her early miserable life experiences, however, she had a great deal of repressed aggression and resentment that manifested itself in the form of willful and stubborn defiance or, at times, severe depression, in her professional life. In her heterosexual life, she always became involved with married men and succeeded in marrying men who had been divorced. One of her husbands had to divorce himself not only from a wife but from a family as well. Although she could be exceedingly tender, loving, and gentle in her everyday relationships with her friends, she could—and did—become exceedingly willful, strong, and aggressive in her marital relationships. Although she was determined to get what she wanted—and the man she wanted—she suffered from unconscious feelings of guilt once she had succeeded. Her marriages did not last very long; she was dominating, impatient, and restless. She soon began to feel cheated in her desire for love. Her need for love was limitless and, by definition, therefore, incapable of fulfillment. When her sense of frustration and of being cheated reached a climax, she would go out to seek a new man to conquer—another father who might provide her with an unending, unqualified love. Consciously, then, she continued to seek fulfillment of her desperate need to belong, to be dependent on a loving man, for whom, in turn, she was ready to give anything demanded of her. Her unconscious hostility toward and distrust of men were, however, always lurking in the background. She saw every man as a potential abandoner, a frustrater of the need for love. She married impulsively and broke up the marriages impulsively. This was inevitable, of course, because of her inner confusion as to what she actually thought or felt about men. Deep at heart she felt lonely and abandoned. She married to ease this feeling. However, once married, she created the same situation by attempting to make her husband of the moment so lonely and so miserable that he would reject her, thus proving that her feelings of distrust were justified and leaving her free again to seek and conquer yet another father substitute. In the process of seeking a new mate, her need for love would propel her into marriage, but once she was married, her distrust and hostility gained the upper hand and the vicious cycle would be repeated once more.

The analyst's attempt to reconstruct the normal and pathological aspects of the premarital and marital problems of the patient, and his or her mate, may be resisted and counteracted by the partner not in therapy. The partner in therapy or analysis may consider the analyst an ally; the partner not in analysis may look upon the analyst as a rival or at the least a disrupter of the marriage relationship. The patient at times considers the analyst an ideal, supportive, omnipotent figure.

At other times he may become suspicious and believe that the analyst is allied with the family and with the partner not in therapy.

All these ambivalent, compliant, and antagonistic feelings are a natural result of feelings that were not adequately resolved during the developmental period of the individual—long before his marriage—which the transference situation revives. Understanding the sources of these feelings and the pattern of behavior to which they gave rise may bring about a reduction in their intensity, and so may lead to the patient's more harmonious functioning in all aspects of his life, the marriage relationship included.

The revival of the feelings mentioned above leads the patient to "act out" in the analytical situation, toward the analyst, feelings which belong elsewhere. One aim of therapy is to enable the patient—if so needed—to "act out" feelings in analysis instead of in the outside world and against members of his family. This is an important aid in helping the patient to establish a stronger sense of his own identity, which, in turn, will result in increased self-confidence and thus reduce undesirable behavior.

The degree to which therapy may be considered a "success" must be determined mainly by the couple themselves. In the most favorable circumstances, naturally, one would hope to see the establishment of a better relationship between husband and wife, an improved relationship with the children, and an increased ability to function effectively in social situations. Sometimes the therapeutic success of analysis will be manifested in a decision to divorce. Such a decision may result in more satisfactory functioning for each partner.

A number of people who believe in the efficacy of psychoanalytic therapy in certain neurotic difficulties doubt that psychoanalysis is really the proper treatment for marital difficulties. One frequently hears the accusation that such treatment eventuates in divorce. This is indeed possible; even, at times, probable. This is why the analyst has to consider very carefully the chances of treatment, whom he tries to treat, and what the possibilities may be for a divorce, either during the course of analysis or afterward.

The careful study and appraisal of the data that may reveal the causes of the onset of the crisis and the relationship between onset and causes of marital relationship difficulties and maladjustment of the couple in the years before the crisis will also reveal much of the background of the personality structure and character development of both husband and wife. In analytical therapy, constant history-taking—the pathology of both husband and wife before and after marriage, the strength or weakness of their egos, their functioning in reality problems—will help to give a clinical picture explaining how and why the marital crisis developed. This in turn will make the therapist aware of the inherent difficulties in the choice of therapeutic procedure.

It is obvious that one has to be careful in this respect because therapy always includes regressive process during analysis. In some critical situations, this regressive tendency may be fortified by the therapeutic pressure. As the aim of therapy of every neurotic difficulty is to stop the regressive process and help the patient to better emotional adjustment, therapeutic intervention can work in two directions. It can reduce the crisis and bring about a more stable adjustment in marriage, or therapy may, at least temporarily, exacerbate the assisting pathology in the patient.

I have had many experiences and varying results. I have had couples who came to me with a direct request for help. They wished to divorce, but they had children whose welfare they considered uppermost in importance, and they were in a quandary. In such cases, it usually turned out that family interaction improved during the course of analysis. As the analyzed parents became more aware of their various problems, and as their self-reliance and self-confidence increased, their relationship improved. Out of the improved relationship between husband and wife came a better relationship with their children and with the larger family group as well. Each partner, of course, underwent therapy with a different analyst.

The question one may ask concerning the published results of the analysis of marital difficulties is: What contribution has that knowledge made thus far toward the reduction of such difficulties? It is obvious that our present knowledge of the dynamics of marital adjustment and/or maladjustment is inadequate. Much research remains to be done; much research *is* being done, especially in the area of childhood education and indoctrination in methods of avoiding or minimizing conflicts between parent and child in early childhood and adolescence, covering such topics as disciplining children, methods for reducing frustration, and general ways and means of maintaining and strengthening friendly and loving relationships between parents and their children.

Psychoanalysis looks upon much of the family unhappiness caused

by marital discord as stemming from neurosis and therefore as an illness that can be treated and, hopefully, ameliorated. This necessitates
study and understanding of the individual's early environment—the
relationship between his parents and his relationship *to* his parents. In
other words, we must try to understand the intrapsychic processes
of the individual, all of which serve as a basis for later life adjustment,
including his ability to give or to receive love and to function with
normal harmony in a marriage situation.

Psychoanalysis of Marital Partners by Separate Analysts

The past decade has witnessed a notable increase in experimentation, innovation, and variation in psychoanalytic technique. These modifications of psychoanalysis derive from an admirable effort to make analysis more effective, more human, more widely available, and more in tune with our growing knowledge of sociocultural forces influencing individual personality. From the standpoint of the treatment of married individuals, particularly those with prominent marital problems, numerous studies have appeared advocating such techniques as simultaneous analysis or psychotherapy of marital partners by the same therapist,[1] group therapy and conjoint family therapy with married couples,[2] and an active consultation arrangement between separate therapists treating a husband and wife.[3] Several of these studies are part of this book and represent the conscientious efforts and experience of dedicated clinicians committed to increasing our effective psychotherapeutic tools.

We are told that these procedures can provide the therapist with a more balanced and realistic view of a marital couple in their unique interaction and can foster the therapeutic process for each spouse individually, while also working to correct the family neurosis, and thereby strengthen the healthy bonds of marriage. Many of the theoretical arguments and clinical reports that are advanced in support of concurrent therapy, joint sessions, group therapy, etc., are reasonably persuasive and indicate that such experimental work must continue and may prove to be of inestimable value. Nevertheless, it is my intention here to undertake a critical appraisal of these innovations, to report on and anticipate some of the pitfalls, dangers, and difficulties inherent in these new procedures, and finally to present a detailed discussion of the affirmative reasons for retaining the conventional psychoanalytic practice of having husband and wife treated by separate analysts.

Current Psychotherapeutic Procedures with Married Couples

The possible arrangements for treating both partners in a troubled marriage can be classified in the following manner:

1. Treatment of both partners by one therapist. This includes (a) individual treatment of both partners as if they were totally unrelated patients of the same therapist (Oberndorf, as far back as 1938, published a pioneering report on the concurrent analysis of married couples, emphasizing that the couple should be analyzed as though they were two completely separate individuals); (b) individual treatment of the partners with supplementary three-way or joint sessions in which specific marital problems are taken up; (c) a predominance of three-way sessions with occasional individual sessions. In all of the foregoing, there may also be group therapy where the couple participate in a larger group led by their individual therapist or by another group therapist.

2. Treatment by separate analysts who either consult with each other periodically or in some instances hold four-way sessions comprising both partners and both therapists.

3. Psychoanalysis of each partner by a different analyst where little or no attempt is made to have consultations between analysts.

It will be noted that I have used the term therapy or psychotherapy for the procedures that are included in the first two categories, and I have used the terms analysis and psychoanalysis for the third category of psychiatric intervention. This is admittedly quite arbitrary and will undoubtedly evoke some dissenting responses. I shall be criticized for arbitrarily distinguishing between therapy and analysis or for usurping the term analysis for my own preferred psychotherapeutic activities. It may also be alleged that I have designated classical psychoanalysis as a more "important" or "higher" order of psychotherapeutic procedure, thus downgrading other therapeutic procedures to a "second-rate" category.

Actually, I am not calling any procedure better or "higher" than any other. I utilize a variety of psychotherapeutic procedures in my clinical practice. The choice is dictated by the nature of the patient's illness, his therapeutic needs, the realities of his external circumstances, and the most reasonable goals that are consonant with the foregoing conditions. I am convinced that all these different procedures have therapeutic value, but they also have significant limitations and difficulties. Furthermore, I am forced to be consistent with my own personal experience, convictions, and definitions. For me, psychoanalysis refers to a specific psychotherapeutic process involving the development, interpretation, and working through of the transference neurosis. As I shall attempt to explain in greater detail below, this process, *when feasible*, seems to offer more enduring alterations in the individual patient's neurosis, and, as a secondary effect, there are more enduring consequences in the patient's marriage.

My emphasis on the distinction between psychoanalysis and other forms of psychotherapy is by no means a unique position. Among the most enthusiastic advocates of concurrent therapy and family therapy we find many who acknowledge that these procedures *are not equivalent to individual psychoanalysis*. Mittelman,[4] one of the earliest and apparently successful proponents of simultaneous treatment of marital partners, warned that in these cases "the accent is always on the current situation." Thomas[5] also supported concurrent treatment but acknowledged that "the transference situation between patient and therapist tends to become secondary and the emphasis to shift from the therapeutic situation toward the marriage relationship." Grotjahn[6] in his volume on family therapy conceded that "the statement that family therapy is psychotherapy and not psychoanalysis must be accepted gracefully and in silence." Most recently, Rodgers[7] discussed the value of concurrent therapy of spouses and acknowledged that such simultaneous treatment is always a "parameter," that is, a procedure "to be introduced only when absolutely necessary, kept to a minimum, and maintained only as long as is necessary." He emphasized that this parameter is never "a substitute for the working through of the transference neurosis."

Having established that a clear distinction must be made between individual psychoanalysis and the various concurrent, family, and group therapies, I shall devote the remainder of this chapter to a consideration of two major issues. The first involves all the reasons for not treating a husband and wife simultaneously. Much has been presented in this volume and elsewhere which stresses the therapeutic advantages that derive from simultaneous treatment of marital partners. It is not my intention to discount these procedures—indeed, from my experience with the simultaneous therapy of spouses I agree with the substance, if not with the enthusiasm, of some of the arguments for joint psychotherapy of married partners. But I feel it necessary to bring together here the arguments against concurrent therapy. I am also obliged to focus in detail on the pitfalls, difficulties, and therapeutic disadvantages of these simultaneous procedures, because I believe that these problems have not been sufficiently stressed by the zealous advocates of these methods. Obviously, in this first issue, the arguments against and the dangers of treatment of husband and wife by the same therapist are implicit reasons for the marital pair's being treated by two different therapists. The second issue is a more affirmative one and includes the distinct therapeutic advantages, to each spouse and to the marriage as a whole, that derive from treatment of couples by separate analysts and, more specifically, from the "classical" psychoanalytic treatment of the couple by separate analysts.

Problems Associated with Treatment of Couples

In the simultaneous treatment of the marital partners, there are several treacherous problems that ought to make the uncritical advocate of joint treatment somewhat more circumspect. In the literature we encounter several opposing views on what constitutes the proper (i.e., therapeutic) attitude of the analyst toward the patients' marriage. Kubie[8] wrote that the psychoanalyst treats individuals, not marriages, and "is not a marriage broker nor a marriage saver, nor yet a marriage wrecker." Friedman,[9] who has extensive experience involving joint treatment of marital partners, has indicated that for him the greatest risk ensues from the therapist's assumption that the marriage is a fundamentally "good" one and that it can and ought to be saved from dissolution.

A therapist's optimistic assumption may be based on his moralistic views that all marriages should be preserved wherever possible, and/or his optimistic, perhaps unconsciously omnipotent fantasy that *he* can help the couple overcome their neurotic difficulties and thereby convert a hopelessly incompatible couple into happy marital partners. This last fantasy by the therapist is especially likely when his own parents were divorced or when his parents remained married but openly miserable. Here, the therapist's optimism may be the result of a "rescue fantasy" whereby he, the child, will preserve and improve his parents' troubled marriage, not only for their sake, but more importantly for his own sake. (Every child's unconscious need to have happy, compatible parents in his early developmental experience has been rather neglected by psychoanalytic writers in the wake of Freud's monumental discovery of the child's more dramatic, unconscious wish to separate his parents, based on the Oedipus complex.)

The therapist may himself have failed in his marriage, and his unwarranted optimism about saving his patients' marriage may be an attempt to assuage his guilt or compensate for his narcissistic injury.

The consequence of the therapist's unwarranted optimism becomes obvious in those instances when the marriage finally "goes on the rocks" in spite of, and in some instances because of, the therapist's individual treatment of two partners. This is especially likely where one partner has made notably more progress and growth in his or her therapy and has come to realize that the marriage is hopeless. When this occurs, the other partner will often hold the therapist responsible. The therapist's initial optimism about saving the marriage will be thrown up to him as a broken promise or as a proof of his poor clinical judgment. In any case, the "injured" or abandoned partner may often lose trust in the therapy or in the therapist and terminate treatment when most in need of help. In such a circumstance, it is clear that one of the couple has had his therapeutic needs sabotaged by the initial decision to treat both partners simultaneously in a misguided attempt to save a marriage. As a side issue, it must be mentioned that the separation or divorce often calls for the transfer of one patient to another therapist and raises an immensely difficult question: With which of the couple does the therapist's loyalty rest? Is it the partner who first sought his help? Is it the partner who is making the most progress? Is it the sicker patient, who more desperately needs his help? I submit that whoever is chosen for transfer to another therapist is likely to feel rejection and distrust, with consequent interference with his indi-

vidual therapy. The fact that separation or divorce may be the outcome of any troubled marriage—indeed, the desirability of separation
or divorce may be apparent in some of these instances—appears as one
of the most cogent arguments against undertaking joint therapy of the
couple.

When the marriage is, in fact, salvageable, and separation or divorce
does not occur or even threaten to occur, there are still several serious
elements in joint therapy that can interfere with the therapeutic progress of either or both parties in the marriage. Kubie, who emphatically
criticized simultaneous treatment by the same analyst, said that the
task of the marital partners is harder, but alleged that there is no difficulty for the analyst who carries out the treatment. I must disagree
with this view and assert that the task is harder for all three, the married partners and the analyst as well. These difficulties derive from
the triangular relationship that is established between husband, wife,
and therapist. This triangle may serve all three persons as a platform
on which to act out conscious or unconscious neurotic conflicts
derived from current or earlier triangular conflicts.

1. Either or both partners may press the therapist into the role of
referee or arbiter of current marital problems. Minor as well as major
marital problems may be carried to the therapist for his solution. In
spite of his diligent avoidance of such a role, the patients often find it
irresistible to turn to the therapist for a decision just because they
know that he has heard both sides of the story. To avoid this trap,
the doctor may find himself unduly wary of taking any position in
the marital controversy, lest he be accused or accuse himself of taking
sides. Obviously, when the therapist treats only one partner and does
not have the "benefit" of hearing both sides of the issue, he is not
under pressure to be a referee and can proceed to treat his individual
patient more incisively.

2. Another pitfall of the husband-wife-doctor triangle is the creation of an outwardly "realistic" and often irresistible Oedipal situation
for any or all of the participants. I have already discussed the analyst's
rescue fantasy where he belatedly saves his parents' marriage through
saving his patients' marriage. Greenacre[10] has mentioned that in the
reanalysis of several analysts she has found that the strong wish to
analyze both marital partners represents "an unusual degree of unresolved primal-scene scoptophilia in the analyst himself." In the same
sense, the therapist must be more than ordinarily aware of his erotic

countertransference toward the wife and his rivalry with the husband. Such a transference may lead to his siding inappropriately with the wife against the husband. Then the wife's neurotic or unrealistic demands on the husband may be unwittingly supported by the doctor instead of being recognized and interpreted as irrational. Similarly, the husband's reasonable opposition to the wife's demands may be opposed by the therapist, who is enmeshed, to whatever extent, in such an Oedipal triangle.

When the wife has a prominent erotic transference toward the analyst, with the inevitable overvaluation and idealization of him, it may severely aggravate the husband's predictable and inevitable transference rivalry, which makes the delineation of the transferential origin of the husband's rivalry much more difficult. This real rivalry may interminably interfere with the husband's working through of his transference rivalry with the therapist.

Still another contamination arising from the Oedipal triangle of husband, wife, and doctor can be the result of the husband and the male therapist forming an unconscious homosexual alliance against the wife. Either of the men can have his unconscious fear of forbidden heterosexual impulses or his unconscious guilt over aggressive impulses toward castrating or binding females reinforced by the subtle communication of a similar feeling in the other man. In such a case, the husband's irrational attitude toward women is not clarified but is rather supported, and his neurotic behavior toward his wife based on this attitude will continue.

3. Sibling-rivalry problems may also be acted out in the therapeutic triangular situation. Either spouse may have such a transferential problem in relation to the partner and may vie for the favor of the therapist, who may represent either of the patient's parents. If the doctor has unresolved sibling-rivalry problems, he may identify with one or the other patient and in effect may make that patient his "favorite," thereby losing the clarity of perception that he has only when in the position of benevolent neutrality.

The circumstances whereby a couple come to be treated by a single therapist deserve attention. In many instances, one or the other partner has sought the therapist's help for various distressing neurotic symptoms that often, but not inevitably, include some difficulties in his marital adjustment. Sometimes, after hearing information that suggests that his patient's partner is also neurotic, the therapist suggests that this partner also needs help. If the doctor feels that he himself should undertake the treatment of both patients, he is well advised to make such a decision with some caution and only after he has considered his possible unconscious reasons for suggesting joint therapy, and after giving thought to the pitfalls which have been outlined above.

In many instances, too, the partner who is not in treatment may spontaneously express a desire for therapy and, indeed, may insist that the spouse's therapist, and no one else, will be acceptable. Again, the doctor must be wary of agreeing to such an arrangement. The prospective second patient may be trying to re-create a family situation for transference gratification or for acting out. Rivalry with the partner already in treatment may be prompting the other to "get in on the act," and ultimately to take over the therapist for himself or herself. These matters must be diligently considered before acceding to either partner's wish to have both partners treated by the same therapist.

I must add that consecutive as well as simultaneous therapy of a married couple may contain some of the elements of the triangular situation. On one occasion, I analyzed a young woman who, several years after the termination of her own analysis, referred her fiancé, later her husband, to me. After undertaking the second analysis, I found that several problems arose that are not unlike those of simultaneous analysis of marital partners. To begin with, the husband began analysis regarding me as *her* doctor. He saw me as oriented to her needs, intent on making him over into the man she wanted him to be rather than what he wanted or needed to be for himself. After their marriage, the wife felt the need for further analysis; and when I decided to refer her to a female analyst, in order to avoid their simultaneous analyses and also to facilitate the clarification and resolution of certain unresolved mother-transferences I knew her to have, the husband expressed a sense of victory in having me for himself, while the wife reacted with bitterness and resentment. I would add that my extensive knowledge of the patient's wife, derived from having analyzed her, was not of substantial help in carrying out the husband's analysis. I had constantly to guard against comparing the husband's perceptions of his wife with my own knowledge of her, which would have been a serious diversion from the analysis of the husband's transference neurosis, the central task of his analysis.

A similar situation arose in another case in which I undertook the analysis of a young woman who was referred by her brother several years after the termination of his analysis with me. The specter of the brother as an ally and confidant of the analyst was undoubtedly a complication of the sister's treatment. While these resistances were in fact analyzable in both instances, they represented a difficulty that would not have arisen had the second patient in each instance gone to a different analyst.

Some of the problems occurring when one therapist treats the married couple are also present when separate analysts treat the pair, have regular consultations with each other, and/or hold four-way consultation. According to Bird and Martin,[11] one of the major values of regular consultation by the therapists treating the pair is that such procedures will lead more effectively to recognition of reality distortions in each patient.

Such data are indeed of inestimable value in marital counseling and in brief psychotherapy, but they add little of value to a reconstructive psychoanalytic process. The same distortions will eventually emerge in the transference neurosis of the classical method. In this form, it is possible to trace the distortions to their infantile genetic origins and to modify them in the process of working through the infantile neurosis. In the less intensive procedures, correcting distortions is achieved through educative or authoritative influences by the therapist, and the infantile source and current transferential persistence of these distortions is in no way clarified or corrected.

Consultation between therapists treating a marital pair has also been urged by Alger,[12] to "cut through the fog of a psychiatrist's countertransference to his patient . . . [in] the light of his colleague's countertransference to the patient's marriage partner." This may well be the case, but I would warn that new countertransferences may be added by virtue of the four-way interaction among the marital partners and their two therapists. Each therapist may identify with his own patient and may find himself acting as advocate for his own patient's point of view. Also, one therapist may be unduly deferential or submissive to his colleague for any of the many reasons that may conduce to such a masochistic maneuver, and the patient of the submissive therapist may be the unfortunate victim of such complex countertransference acting out. Any unconscious professional rivalry between the consulting therapists, whether based on peer rivalry or Oedipal rivalry or both, may find its way into the joint therapeutic activities.

The foregoing discussion taken as a whole is aptly summarized by Rodgers's assertion[13] that the greatest obstacle to doing effective reconstructive therapy with both spouses "lies in the multivectored nature of the countertransference."

Reasons for Separate Analysis Using the Classical Psychoanalytic Method

The most compelling reason for the analysis of marital partners by separate analysts is to assure that each spouse be treated under conditions that are optimal for the achievement of an individual, reconstructive, psychoanalytic experience. Such a reconstructive psychoanalysis requires the most exhaustive exploration of unconscious psychodynamic and psychogenetic factors that have had a determining influence on the patient's character and neurosis and that continue to support the persistent character traits and neurotic symptoms. Obviously such problems are major contributing factors to the troubles in the marriage, but these neurotic problems more broadly affect the patient's entire life—his work, his recreation, his social and intellectual functioning—as well as his marriage.

The operating premise here is that if a reconstructive resolution of the patient's neurotic difficulties can be effected, it will have a salutary effect on the marriage. In this sense, it is wisest to treat the neurotic individual, not to treat a neurotic or troubled marriage. We must be prepared to accept the fact that the salutary effect of a reasonably successful analysis may be to make for greater harmony, gratification, maturity, and love between the marital partners. This is most likely to result when the healthy factors in the choice of mate are sufficiently enduring after the previously prominent neurotic factors have been substantially clarified and minimized. On the other hand, the beneficial consequence of analysis may be to lead to the dissolution of a marriage. This decision is based upon a recognition of the virtual absence of healthy interdependency and the fact that almost exclusively neurotic factors have brought the couple together and have kept them neurotically bound to each other.

To achieve the therapeutic goal, one must be free of the moralistic concept that the marriage *must* be saved if possible. Such sentiments—whether for the sake of the children, for religious reasons, or for financial or other "reality" reasons—are, in most instances, the very reasons or rationalizations that have been used by the partners to maintain the destructive "double bind." The analyst who supports such a view is immediately putting himself on the side of the patient's neurosis when he more properly should be allied with the healthy forces in the patient *against* the patient's neurosis.

Of these rationalizations, the one most commonly evoked is the concern for the children. This needs to be set straight at the outset. While divorce must always be regarded as an unfortunate event in the children's emotional development and will inevitably have some untoward effects on the children's mental health, these undesirable consequences may be considerably less damaging than the effect of being raised by parents who are living under the same roof but who expose the children to a continuing or recurring diet of arguments, recriminations, accusations of infidelity, emotional detachment, and minimizing or contemptuous behavior between them.

To return to the initial concept that the partners and their marriage are best served by the individual reconstructive psychoanalysis of two separate patients by two different analysts, the key to the stress on separate analysts is derived from an understanding of just what does constitute a reconstructive psychoanalysis.

This is a knotty question which is by no means settled at this time. Numerous papers, books, round-table discussions, and symposia have attempted to answer the question what is psychoanalysis as a therapeutic procedure. One always begins with Freud's definition that any procedure that concerns itself with transference and resistance may call itself psychoanalysis. Any attempt to outline the affirmations, variations, and dissents from this position would call for a much lengthier analysis than I am making here. I shall merely offer my own working definition of a therapeutic psychoanalysis in an effort to explain the stress that I have been putting on the necessity for separate analysts. This approach has been effectively summarized by Greenson[14] in his essay on "The Classical Psychoanalytic Approach." He says, "The aim of psychoanalytic therapy is to resolve the infantile neurosis which is the nucleus of the adult neurosis." I would add that resolution of the infantile neurosis requires that the observing and integrative components of the patient's ego have access to the previously unconscious infantile conflicts. These conflicts involve the adaptive ego functions that strive for both satisfactions and security. They also involve unacceptable instinctual drives as well as punitive prohibiting forces, both external and internal (superego). In effect, the infantile neurosis remains a kind of "unfinished issue." It persists and translates itself into neurotic, that is, transferential, character and behavior patterns, which are unconscious attempts to resolve or correct the infantile conflict. But these attempts are inevitably unsuccessful, because the present-day objects and situations are obviously inappropriate for solving the conflicts of a much earlier day.

One current situation that is inevitably drawn into the patient's transferential attempts to undo or correct the unresolved infantile conflicts and injuries is the patient's marriage. Every analyst is aware of the multiple transferences that each patient makes toward his spouse. The wife or the husband may be one or more transference figures— mother, father, or sibling—either alternately or simultaneously. Obviously these distorted perceptions and inappropriate expectations from the spouse will seriously interfere with the otherwise difficult challenge of functioning as husband and wife. It follows that the therapeutic goal of analysis is to perceive, understand, and gradually begin to liberate the individual from his compulsive transference distortions and expectations in all aspects of his life, including his marriage. To achieve this, the classical psychoanalytic approach is most effective, because as Giovacchini[15] has recently underscored, this method is specifically designed to encourage the development of the transference neurosis, which, more than any other experience, best serves to demonstrate to patient and analyst the substance of the unconscious infantile neurosis and its vicissitudes. The data about the infantile conflicts as observed in the transference neurosis are handled by interpretations, by clarification, and, where there is an effective therapeutic alliance, by working through both in the analytic session and outside analysis in daily living, most particularly in the patient's marriage.

It is clear, then, that anything which assists in the development and resolution of the transference neurosis, the central *modus operandi* of the analysis, is to be encouraged. This includes such arrangements as the use of the couch, free association, analysis of dreams, the analyst's relative anonymity and "benevolent neutrality." All other factors or parameters which dilute, obscure, or impede the development and resolution of the transference neurosis are in conflict with the foregoing strategy of the therapeutic process.

The treatment of both spouses by the same analyst, either individually or together, must be regarded as a parameter that tends to make the interpretation and working through of the patient's transference neurosis most difficult, if not impossible. To be sure, transferences do develop in each spouse toward the analyst, but they become merged with other responses to the therapist. His role as a referee, as a third party in the triangular situation, as a rival for the spouse's affection, etc., have substantial realistic bases and hence make the clarification of the infantile conflict in the transference neurosis very tedious and often very unconvincing.

The foregoing reasons for favoring individual analysis by separate therapists are not intended to minimize the value of other rational psychotherapeutic procedures, including analyses of couples by the same analyst, joint sessions, and group analytic procedures. At this time of great enthusiasm for innovation and new therapeutic technique, I feel that we must be reminded that some of our older procedures are still of enduring and inestimable value. In this vein, I have tried to emphasize the value of individual psychoanalysis of marital partners by separate analysts. When either or both partners would appear at the outset to be likely to be suitable for the classical psychoanalytic procedure (i.e., the patient has sufficient capacity for ego distance to permit an effective therapeutic alliance, which in turn allows him to see, understand, and eventually work through the transference neurosis), the classical psychoanalytic approach by separate analysts has the most far-reaching and reconstructive possibilities. Classical psychoanalysis is most likely to eventuate in either the cementing of healthy marital ties or the rational decision to terminate a hopeless marriage so that each partner can attempt, with greater insight and maturity, to make a new marriage with another person—freer from neurotic reasons for choosing the new mate and freer from unconscious infantile conflicts that have contaminated the marital relationship.

NOTES

1. Ian Alger, "Joint Sessions: Psychoanalytic Variations, Applications, and Indications," this volume; Bernard L. Greene and Alfred P. Solomon, "Marital Disharmony: Concurrent Psychoanalytic Therapy of Husband and Wife by the Same Psychiatrist. IV. The Triangular Transference Transactions," *American Journal of Psychotherapy*, XVII (1963), 443–

456; Bela Mittelman, "The Concurrent Analysis of Married Couples," *Psychoanalytic Quarterly*, XVII (1948), 182–197; Clarence P. Oberndorf, "Psychoanalysis of Married Couples," *Psychoanalytic Review*, XXV (1938), 453–475; Alfred P. Solomon and Bernard L. Greene, "Concurrent Psychoanalytic Therapy in Marital Disharmony," in Bernard L. Greene, ed., *The Psychotherapies of Marital Disharmony* (New York: Free Press, 1965); and Alexander Thomas, "Simultaneous Psychotherapy with Marital Partners," *American Journal of Psychotherapy*, X (1956), 716–727.

2. Martin Grotjahn, "Indications for Psychoanalytic Family Therapy," this volume; and Max Markowitz, "Analytic Group Psychotherapy of Married Couples by a Therapist Couple," this volume.

3. H. Waldo Bird and Peter A. Martin, "Countertransference in the Psychotherapy of Marriage Partners," *Psychiatry*, XIX (1956), 353–360.

4. Bela Mittelman, "Analysis of Reciprocal Neurotic Patterns in Family Relationships," in Victor W. Eisenstein, ed., *Neurotic Interaction in Marriage* (New York: Basic Books, 1956).

5. Thomas, *op. cit.*

6. Martin Grotjahn, *Psychoanalysis and the Family Neurosis* (New York: W. W. Norton, 1960).

7. Terry C. Rogers, "A Specific Parameter: Concurrent Psychotherapy of the Spouse of an Analysand by the Same Analyst," *International Journal of Psychoanalysis*, XLVI (1965), 237–243.

8. Lawrence Kubie, "Psychoanalysis and Marriage, Practical and Theoretical Issues," in Victor W. Eisenstein, ed., *Neurotic Interaction in Marriage* (New York: Basic Books, 1956).

9. David B. Friedman, personal communication.

10. Phyllis Greenacre, "The Role of Transference: Practical Considerations in Relation to Psychoanalytic Therapy," *Journal of the American Psychoanalytic Association*, II (1954), 671–684.

11. Peter A. Martin and H. Waldo Bird, "An Approach to the Psychotherapy of Marriage Partners: The Stereoscopic Technique," *Psychiatry*, XVI (1954), 123–127.

12. Ian Alger, "Joint Sessions."

13. Rodgers, *op. cit.*

14. Ralph R. Greenson, "The Classical Psychoanalytic Approach," in Silvano Arieti, ed., *American Handbook of Psychiatry*, Vol. II (New York: Basic Books, 1959).

15. Peter L. Giovacchini, "Treatment of Marital Disharmonies: The Classical Approach," in Greene, ed., *The Psychotherapies of Marital Disharmony* (New York: The Free Press, 1965).

Joint Sessions: Psychoanalytic Variations, Applications, and Indications

The inclusion of a chapter on joint sessions in a psychoanalytic book underlines the theoretical changes that have been rapidly evolving over the past three decades in the fields concerned with the study and influencing of human behavior. Psychoanalysis, which was born at the turn of the century, and therefore originally reflected the more mechanistic thinking of that era, conceived of the individual as a closed type of system, and understood neurotic symptoms as resultants from the disturbed equilibrium of an inner economy of instinctual forces. Interpersonal, sociocultural, and communicational theories have all emphasized the point that an individual cannot be understood apart from his relationships with other human beings. Indeed, communication theorists such as Haley have gone so far as to say that an individual's symptoms maintain the balance of his family system, and not the balance of his intrapsychic forces.[1] Regardless of the theories, the fact seems to be that psychoanalysts in increasing numbers are openly using the techniques of conjoint therapy of marital partners, as well as other methods which include the marital partner in the therapy plan. Conjoint therapy; concurrent therapy in which each spouse is seen by the same, or by a different analyst, but not together; and combined therapy, in which conjoint and individual concurrent sessions are both arranged, are all variations which take into account in a direct way the fact that the primary patient is a member of a family and that his behavior, whether or not it be labeled neurotic, cannot be understood in isolation from other people.

In his excellent book on the family neurosis, Grotjahn describes the historical development of family therapy,[2] as does Sager in a recent survey of the treatment of marital couples.[3] Reference is made to René Spitz's account in 1936 on "Family Neurosis and the Neurotic Family"; to a paper in 1934 by Oberndorf on *folie à deux*; and to the contributions between 1940 and 1952 by Mittelman, culminating in his paper in 1948 on "The Concurrent Analysis of Married Couples." More recent work includes contributions by Martin and Bird;[4] Thomas;[5] Jackson and Weakland;[6] Satir;[7] Grotjahn;[8] Ackerman;[9] Haley;[10] and Whitaker;[11] and as already noted, an increasing number of others.

During the time of these somewhat unheralded developments, however, the traditional and official attitude of psychoanalysis concerning contact with relatives of patients was supplied in 1955 by Glover, who found from questionnaires that all analysts questioned see members of families most unwillingly, and at the patient's request. The answers further revealed that a clear majority was against analyzing members of the same family, at any rate at the same time.[12] Greenacre has stated that exchange of information between the analyst and relatives endangers trust and confidence in the analyst, and may perhaps arouse prejudicial attitudes in the analyst.[13] Frequent mention has been made, in the literature, of the necessity of keeping the transference atmosphere clear, and this attitude is still widely prevalent.

A point made by Jackson and Weakland seems to provide perspective. They note that the treatment of a psychiatric patient *necessarily* involves dealing with members of his family, and with family relationships, either directly or indirectly. Therefore, the question at issue is not *whether*, in this case, a marital partner is to be dealt with, but rather *how* that partner is to be dealt with.[14] In other words, the traditional approach has been to exclude the spouse from the actual treatment situation and from direct contact with the analyst. However, this exclusion is in itself a method of dealing with the spouse. Nor does such a method mean that the analyst has been able to keep himself out of the marital interaction. The spouse will have reactions to the analyst even though he or she has never met the analyst, and all the information which the analyst can have concerning these reactions must come through the primary patient. Thus the analyst too is excluded from an opportunity to experience more fully the actual transactions involved.

An alternative method is to deal directly with the couple, both primary patient and spouse, or with the two spouses if they come as a couple with mutual concern about the state of their marriage. If a marriage is on the verge of breakup at the time one partner seeks analytic help, the likelihood of collaborative effort is lessened; however, hard-and-fast rules are not applicable, and most helpful results can occur even in a situation where separation has been sought and divorce proceedings are underway. This can be true because the objective in conjoint therapy should not be solidification of the marriage, nor should the objective be a divorce. Rather, the aim in conjoint therapy is to help each individual further his and her growth as a person so that each can be as capable as possible of deciding which course he genuinely wishes to follow.

One of the major advantages in dealing directly with the marital couple is that the possibility of obtaining objective data is greatly increased. In a later section of this chapter, clinical examples will be given illustrating the use of various techniques designed to increase the amount of available objective data. These methods include regular joint sessions, joint sessions with two therapists, and the use of videotape recordings with the marital couple. In this context, "objective data" means accurate observations of the actual transactions and interactions occurring in the session itself. There are various ways to understand the meaning of the behavior in the session. One can postulate a new transference family, with resultant multiple transference phenomena.[15] The behavior can also be understood in terms of game theory.[16] Another perspective, and one I have used extensively, comes from the application of communication theory to the understanding of the complexity of behavior in the joint session. The source of much difficulty in the marriage is the problem of one partner being misunderstood by the other. This problem has as one of its major roots the fact that communication is carried on at different levels of abstraction, and through different channels. For example, one message is conveyed by words at a high level of verbal abstraction, while a simultaneous message is conveyed by tone, and a third message is conveyed by the context of the situation. A second factor which adds to the problem of understanding is the fact that the various simultaneous messages may contradict one another and therefore may call for different and conflicting responses from the partner. For example, a husband may be aware only of the verbal content of the message he is giving. If his wife responds only to the critical tone with which he speaks, the husband may feel completely misunderstood and hurt, and react back to his wife with anger. Much effort in marital therapy is spent in attempts to identify and clarify the various messages being sent, so that development of mutual understanding can be encouraged.

Historical Reluctance to the Use of Joint Sessions

Following these introductory comments, there is a question on which I would like to focus my attention. It is a question which seems to me to have pertinent implications not only for conjoint therapy but for the therapeutic process in a two-person relationship as well. The question is: What has accounted in the past for the general reluctance of psychoanalysts to experiment with joint sessions?

As we try to answer this question, four pieces of information are pertinent. First, as already mentioned, early theory stressed intrapsychic process, and this emphasized the isolated individual. Second, the great importance of transference in the psychoanalytic treatment technique was underscored both by the early advice that the analyst should be a blank screen for the transference projections and also by the admonitions that no "outside" influences should be allowed to interfere with or dilute the transference reactions. The third piece of information to consider is the curious fact that until recently most of the work involving the inclusion of family members has gone on in an almost unnoticed and unofficial way, while the traditional psychoanalytic attitude has been much more publicized. Fourth, and finally, the open emergence of the psychoanalyst's interest in this type of therapy has been related to the appearance of several other developments both of an actual and of a theoretical nature; namely, the growth of the child-guidance movement in this country, which demonstrated the necessity of dealing with the parents as well as the child; the development of interest in group therapy, and in small-group dynamics; and the introduction of new theories and models of human behavior including interpersonal theories, transactional theories, sociocultural theories, and increasingly complex theories in the field of human communication.

How, then, are these four pieces of information related to the question of the usual analytic reluctance to utilize joint sessions? I suggest that the reluctance can be understood as a type of defensive maneuver to preserve more traditional concepts of transference, and its significance in the therapeutic relationship. If the analyst includes the spouse in the sessions, he now is involved in a three-way system, and both marital partners will have reactions to him. When the individual patient had a feeling, say of intimidation, it could be described as a transference reaction (after all, hadn't the analyst just been quietly aloof and giving no responses, so the reaction of intimidation couldn't be related to his behavior?). But when both partners in the same session begin to talk about feeling this way, it is much more difficult for the analyst convincingly to explain this as their transference reactions. Indeed, the possibility that both patients are reacting to something the analyst is *actually* doing which has the effect of intimidating them is such a good likelihood that even a highly polished mirror-of-an-analyst would have trouble reflecting it back on the patients. In other words, with more than one patient in the situation, the analyst has a more difficult time not including more of his own activity and feelings in the analytic situation, and once included, they must be dealt with in the analysis. The original premise that the patient's reaction to the analyst can be understood in terms of just a projection, because the analyst is an objective observer who does not provoke responses, is no longer tenable. As we better understand human communicative behavior, it seems clear that, as with other people, a patient's response to the analyst is related to the analyst's real behavior. The patient is responding to messages conveyed by the analyst's behavior, both verbal and nonverbal, and if the patient's response is similar to the type of response which that patient has developed over his particular life history to certain kinds of message situations, it is because some part of the actual situation with the analyst there and then is duplicating the original type of stimulus situation. It is certainly true that these messages being sent out by the analyst are not the only messages he is sending; and it is also true that very likely many of these messages will be outside the analyst's own awareness. And they may be out of the analyst's awareness no matter how thoroughgoing his personal analysis has been. That is to say, the problem of countertransference is a continuing one. In a previous paper on the topic of countertransference,[17] I suggested that the solution to the problem is not to hide the countertransference reactions behind a blank and very unreal façade, nor is the solution to attempt to achieve the state of "perfect" health in which the analyst is a person without distortions; rather, the solution, as I see it, comes from a willingness on the analyst's part to include any of his reactions openly in the therapeutic situation. This has a double benefit. First, it makes possible a genuine analysis of the analytic transactions while at the same time it provides a model of open inquiry for the patient to follow; and second, it has a very free-ing effect on the analyst, so that not only distorted reactions of his may be able to emerge, but also those spontaneous, genuinely warm reactions can be released which may also have been sealed behind the mirror façade. Suddenly the analytic situation becomes a much more human and I believe a more therapeutic one.

I know from my own experience that such an inclusion of the analyst's reactions and feeling can occur in individual sessions with the analyst and one patient. In order for it to happen, however, the patient must be extremely perceptive and persuasive, or the analyst must be particularly ready to experiment with the idea and to engage in this way with the patient. In joint sessions, however, the analyst need not be so willing, because in spite of himself he will be forced by one or the other of the two patients, or by both, to acknowledge some of his own behavior of which he has up to that time been un-aware, or which he has been unwilling to acknowledge, perhaps be-cause of his psychoanalytic belief that to do so would interfere with his role as analyst. These considerations, it seems to me, explain in some measure the reluctance of many analysts to try joint sessions, and further explain why so much of the experimental work on joint therapy continued in a kind of almost unrecognized state for so many years, because it went against such basic psychoanalytic tenets. It finally suggests a reason why more and more analysts are now emerg-ing with work they have done, and why so many others are beginning to try these joint techniques; by this last I mean that newer theories of human behavior have made such new experimentation more ac-ceptable to the field as a whole, and therefore less professionally ques-tionable for any one individual analyst.

Techniques and Clinical Examples

I would now like to present two clinical examples which demonstrate the application of the analyst's greater personal involvement in joint sessions, and one which also demonstrates the use of videotape recordings and playback. The first clinical example is taken from a conjoint session which included the husband and wife and myself. For the purposes of the illustration I want to make, most details of the history are not important. The wife, Marjorie, had been seen by me in individual therapy for over two years. The incident to be described occurred in the first joint session, which had been asked for by the husband after he learned that I was using this approach more and more in my practice. The husband, Brent, began talking in the session, and made it clear that he felt a great deal of anger toward Marjorie. She, for the most part, remained quite silent throughout the session, but would respond when questioned by either Brent or myself. Brent's anger reached crescendo as he screamed at her that he was goddam sick and tired of her lying in bed from eight to twelve in the mornings while their small son was left to fend for himself. Marjorie was silent in the face of the attack, but seemed somewhat frightened and hurt, and tears came to her eyes. What has just been reported is the necessary background for the specific interactions I want to focus on.

At the end of the session, I said that the time was up and that we would meet the following week at the same hour. I stood up, and Brent stood up. As we moved toward the door, I looked at Marjorie and realized that she was sitting on the couch with her legs tucked under her, staring up at me, and that she had not moved from that position since I had commented that the time was up. I became aware of an uncomfortable tension and at the same moment noticed the clock on the desk behind her. It read one minute after twelve. Smiling, I said, "Come on, Marjorie, it's twelve o'clock . . . time to get up!" Brent's laugh burst in my ear.

I was aware of an anxious feeling, and I turned and caught his look of amusement, mixed with what seemed to me a kind of incredulous amazement. Marjorie by this time was off the couch, apparently full of energy, laughing, and looking flustered. I joined in the laughter, with an uncomfortable feeling, and Brent went into the waiting room, while Marjorie entered the bathroom. The waiting room was empty, and I stood with Brent. The laugh he had given and the look of amazement on his face were still with me. I began to talk to him, in a way of thinking aloud. I told him I felt I had really given it to Marjorie and that I realized now that I had felt angry at her when I said, "Time to get up." I went on to say that as I had looked at her continuing to sit on the couch in the office, I felt that she was sending a message saying that I had to do something or say something before she could get up. I recalled feeling a little anxious as I had continued to look at her, and then I had felt angry at being coerced by her silence, and yet I did not know what to do or say anyway. I told Brent that it was at that point that I let loose my quip. Brent then remarked that it seemed to be effective, and I answered that it did but that I wanted to tell Marjorie about what I had just discovered, because I was sure that she felt badly at being knocked down that way by me at the end of the session. At that point, Marjorie came out of the bathroom, and I repeated to her just what I had told Brent. When I finished, Brent said, "You know, that is exactly the way I feel when she is lying upstairs in bed, and I feel she wants me to do something so that she can get up, but I don't know what it is." At this point, Marjorie said that she was certainly not aware of sending any such message. This, of course, is a crucial point, because the fact that she was unaware of the covert message that her behavior was transmitting is what makes such behavior so difficult for another person to deal with. This is the mechanism of the double-bind situation so clearly described by Bateson and his colleagues at Palo Alto.[18] I closed the post-session with the comment to Marjorie that if she wasn't sending that message, then there must be someone sneaking into her telegraph office after hours and sending out these messages without her knowing about it, and I just thought she should know.

In this example, Brent's raucous laugh and his look of amazement helped me to become aware of the effect of my needling behavior toward Marjorie. As a result, I was able openly to pursue an analysis of my own reactions and became aware of my anxiety and anger in response to her helplessly sitting on the couch and staring at me. The covert message in Marjorie's helpless behavior then became clear to Brent, and he realized that it was to this that he himself responded when she lay in bed at home. Finally, because of the exposure and clarification of these interactions, Marjorie was more aware of the impact of her behavior on Brent and on me, and although she still did not recognize the hidden message in her behavior, the possibility of understanding it further was opened up. This incident, then, shows how a countertransference reaction of mine was brought into focus by the husband Brent. It was a reaction that otherwise most likely would have gone unanalyzed by me, and the insights which developed for all three of us would have in this instance been lost.

Four-Way Sessions

The idea that adding the spouse to the usual therapeutic dyad can be useful has been expanded in four-way sessions involving a husband and his wife and the therapist of each of them. This method was described in 1961 in a paper by Hogan and Royce,[19] and during the past four years I have experimented with the technique and have come to use it more extensively since I have found it so useful in breaking through barriers that seemed resistive to other methods, including the usual conjoint session. In the four-way method, each analyst holds regular sessions with his own patient, but periodically all four persons involved meet together. The frequency of the four-way sessions can vary from once weekly to once a month, or at times even less than that, on a schedule dictated by the emergence of an impasse situation, usually between the marital partners, or between one of the analysts and his patient. Adding the spouse to the usual analytic session results, as we have seen, in the likelihood of greater clarification of what is really going on. Including another analyst as well can be of even greater help, for not only are his reactions and perceptions added, but his professional analytic skill and insight can be especially helpful in clarifying the situation, frequently for the other analyst in particular. Nowhere to my knowledge in the field of psychiatry do four people more clearly come to realize the truth of Sullivan's words that we are all more simply human than otherwise.[20]

The second clinical example I want to present is taken from one such four-way session in which I participated with a co-therapist, Dr. Peter Hogan, and with the married couple, Joan and Roger. The couple had been married for eight years, and Joan had been in individual analysis with me for two years, and Roger with the co-therapist for three years. During the year before the session here described, six other four-way sessions had been held. At the time of the session under discussion, the couple had been caught in an increasing impasse of distance between each other, and it was for this reason that the four-way session had been asked for by them. The incident to be reported was the crystallizing event in the hour, and only material that relates to it will be given here. Again, any detailed history about the patients will be omitted as not significantly contributing in this

presentation to an understanding of the dynamic transactions I want
to highlight.

About halfway through the session, Roger began to talk in a more
than usually animated way about his irritation at Joan when she
withdrew at home in a superior manner. With a tinge of disparage-
ment Joan said, "Oh, don't talk about it!" The fact that Roger became
subdued and didn't pursue his point any further lodged in my mind in
a dim way at that moment. Joan went on to say that she felt terribly
rejected when Roger came home and didn't seem interested in her.
She continued that in the evenings she felt very lonely even though
they were in the same room. As she described her lonely feeling, I
felt empathy for her, and I said that I felt like reaching out and touching her because she seemed so sad. She bristled, and with flashing eyes
and a somewhat imperious tone she said, "Don't you touch me!" I
drew back inside myself and felt like sinking deeper into my chair
as a kind of quietness crept over me. At that moment my mind came
up with the memory of Roger subsiding before Joan's earlier command for him to stop talking. I realized that I was behaving in the
same way and without question was accepting her order not to touch
her. I became aware of two things: first, that I didn't have to obey
her order; and second, that she must be very frightened when someone
moved toward her, whether in trying to reach her by expressing
feelings, as Roger had done, or in trying to reach her in an actual
physical way, as I had done when I felt like touching her arm in
sympathy. I stood up and walked toward her. She looked panic-
stricken, and cried out, "Don't you dare, don't you dare touch me!"
I said, "Yes, I will." She answered more desperately, "If you do, I'll
never speak to you again. I'll never see you again."

At this point I reached over and put my hands on her shoulders.
She cried out, "Ian, Ian, Ian . . ." over and over. I did not let go.
Tears came to her eyes, and she looked a mixture of defiance and
defeat as she began to cry. In a rather pathetic voice she called to
Roger to help her. He remained where he was, and did not answer.
She looked imploringly at the co-therapist, who also made no move
and said nothing. She said she hated me and told me again to let go. I
replied, "If you want me to let go, you'll have to do more than
just tell me to." She continued to cry and made no move to take my
hands away. I continued talking to her: "I wanted to touch you to
let you know I felt for your loneliness and sadness, and I don't have
to obey your order not to. But you are not helpless either, and you

can do something about it if you don't want me to touch you." At that point I let go and went back to my chair. Joan stopped crying almost at once. The co-therapist commented on what had happened and said that he realized that her imploring conveyed the message that he should do something to save her from me. He recognized, he said, that at other times he *had* responded to these subtle demands for help from her. Joan associated to past memories when her mother had responded to her looks for help. She felt betrayed by the co-therapist and spoke blamingly to him. He replied that he saw how angry and hurt she was, but that he also felt a response in himself different from what he had felt at other times. Now he no longer felt so trapped by her blame and feelings of betrayal. He felt he didn't have to retreat before them, and associated this directly to the fact that I had held on and had not retreated before her threats and tears. Roger broke in to say that he felt greatly relieved. He continued that at home he often became quiet and began to retreat when Joan gave some command, either overt or hidden, ordering him to stop the particular reactions he was having. He became aware of how angry he was when he did back down, and said that it was now so clear to him that he didn't have to obey her commands. Joan was listening to all this, and said finally that she felt she had learned something too, because now she could see how she ordered away the closeness she really wanted so much, and then felt angry and rejected when her orders were obeyed.

To summarize, then, I became aware of one type of interaction which was going on between this couple, and saw that I was beginning to respond in a similar way to Roger. Because of this awareness, I was able to act in a conscious manner, and with a primarily nonverbal mode of communication I was able to convey an insight to Joan. The technique involved in the nonverbal method of communication is incidental to the main point at issue here. In the previous clinical example, the husband's laughter alerted me to my countertransference reaction and resulted in new awareness for the husband, the wife, and myself; in this example, my consciousness of the significance of Joan's behavior, and my activity in interpreting and dealing with it, resulted in new awareness for Joan, and for her husband Roger, and for the co-therapist, as well as for myself. Joan recognized some relationship between her own sadness and withdrawal and the orders she was giving to other people. She also had to see that she would have to *act*, and not just give signals, whether overt or hidden, if she wanted things to happen. Roger became aware of his willingness to obey Joan's commands and also of his consequent resentment and feelings of alienation. And the co-therapist became aware of his tendency to respond to Joan's covert calls to be saved, and was therefore better able to hold firmly, even in the face of threats, while in addition he was better able to understand Roger's similar reaction.

Videotape Recording and Joint Sessions

In the previous two examples, the inclusion of the therapist's reactions was used to help validate perceptions that might otherwise have gone unnoticed by the patients or would have been very difficult for them to hold on to. The advent of videotape recorders has provided a new way to check and confirm perceptions, by the use of television recording and immediate playback of the videotaped portion of the session to the participants. The detailed use and rationale of this method with married couples has been described by Alger and Hogan.[21] The most significant advance is the immediate availability of hitherto unimagined quantities of objective data concerning the therapeutic interactions. Several effects of this are noteworthy. First, a patient experiences an "image impact" on first viewing the playback. This immediate reaction may be mild, or marked. A marked first reaction, whether positive or negative, seems in clinical work so far to be related to a higher probability that such a patient will be able to involve himself more intensively in therapy. One man, on first viewing himself, said, "I really am very pleased, and feel that I like that person." A woman commented, "Now I see why my children call me 'prissy.' "

After the initial impact has passed, the videotape method is most useful in clarifying the various channels and levels of communication. The fact that the partners themselves comment on what they notice seems to have a very positive result in terms of their motivation to engage more actively in the therapy, and in their understanding of the nature and complexity of their own behavior, and of the behavioral reactions of their partners. A "second-chance" phenomenon also is striking. An example of this is an incident that occurred in the tenth treatment session with a couple. During the early part of the session, the husband had been attempting to convey to his wife how troubled he was by her reluctance to have any dealings with his parents. In this original exchange, she maintained a rather cool and detached air, while the husband often seemed on the verge of tears. In the immediate videotape playback segment, both partners viewed this original section. As they watched the TV screen, the wife began to cry and impulsively turned toward her husband and said, "I didn't believe that you were really concerned when you said what you did at first. But now that I see the video playback I realize that you were really trying and really feeling very badly, and I'm sorry that you are feeling that way and that I missed it." This new understanding, which came about following a viewing of the replay of the original incident, enabled her to have a "second chance" to react in a different way with her husband. And her new behavior affected him, and he began to cry, because it was clearly not an intellectualization on her part but a feeling of genuine caring and regret. He felt understood, and they both felt more involved.

Conclusion

In review, then, let us draw some conclusions from this clinical material and consider some of the implications of joint sessions for psychoanalytic theory and practice. Nearly every clinician who has written on the subject of joint therapy has reported that the therapist becomes much more "active" in this type of therapy. In this chapter I have made the suggestion that traditional concepts of transference, and rules that prohibit the "contamination" of the transference, have actually operated to discourage earlier experimentation with joint sessions, and that this is why much of the innovation took place in a somewhat unofficial and unnoticed manner. Newer developments and theories have justified bolder experimentation, and the results throw new light on transference and countertransference reactions. This has had a freeing effect on the analyst and on the patient. When the analyst no longer feels the necessity of being inscrutable, or of being analyzed beyond the point of countertransference distortions, he can allow himself to be more open to the interactions that must necessarily take place in the complex transactions of the joint session. A word of caution might be sounded here, because the old attitude of not contaminating the field has crept into the area of joint therapy; for example, admonitions are made that the therapist must be sure to be fair and impartial. The point is not that one opposes fairness, but that the willingness to risk *being* exactly what you are with the patients is the most important element to insure the possibility of a thorough and genuine analysis of the relationships. This is not to be construed as in any way diminishing the necessity of the best possible training analysis for the therapist; however, the goal in the therapist's analysis is not to perfect all his imperfections, or to analyze away all his distortions, but rather to help him become liberated enough so that he can accept the reality of his own neurotic distortions when they do appear in the therapeutic sessions. In this respect, the use of videotape recordings gives promise of providing a new technological aid which functions to increase the validity and objectivity of our perceptions. This new tool is not in itself therapeutic, but it can be used to increase the capacity of the analyst's human potential, and when utilized in the analytic framework, it can become a potent factor in the therapeutic work .

When the therapist does become able to confirm the reality of his patients' perceptions, either through the use of videotapes or through the therapist's increased inclusion of his own reactions in regular therapeutic interchange, he is then opening up the way for his own and for his patient's further growth. In addition, this freeing process permits the analyst to be more open with those genuinely human aspects of his own personality which are so crucial to the patient's development as a person. This kind of analysis can go on between an analyst and one patient. But when a spouse is included, the likelihood that this kind of analysis will go on is greatly enhanced, to the benefit of all three, or all four, as the case may be. The work of understanding the feelings and inner reactions of each individual patient is still one of the important goals of psychoanalysis; but when this understanding takes place in a setting in which the accuracy of perceptions is confirmed, and the levels of multiple communication and interaction are clarified, then the entire therapeutic process has more chance of proceeding in an atmosphere of reality and genuine human relatedness and growth.

NOTES

1. Jay Haley, "Whither Family Therapy," *Family Process,* I (1962), 69–100.
2. Martin Grotjahn, *Psychoanalysis and the Family Neurosis* (New York: W. W. Norton, 1960).

3. C. J. Sager, "The Treatment of Marital Couples," in Silvano Arieti, ed., *American Handbook of Psychiatry*, Vol. III (New York: Basic Books, 1966).
4. A. P. Martin and H. W. Bird, "An Approach to the Psychotherapy of Marriage Partners," *Psychiatry*, XVI (1953), 123–127.
5. A. Thomas, "Simultaneous Therapy with Marital Partners," *American Journal of Psychotherapy*, X (1956), 716–727.
6. Don D. Jackson and J. H. Weakland, "Conjoint Family Therapy," *Psychiatry*, XXIV (1961), 30–45.
7. Virginia Satir, *Conjoint Family Therapy* (Palo Alto, Calif.: Science and Behavior Books, 1964).
8. Grotjahn, *op. cit.*
9. Nathan W. Ackerman, *The Psychodynamics of Family Life: Diagnosis and Treatment* (New York: Basic Books, 1958).
10. Haley, *op. cit.*
11. C. A. Whitaker, "Psychotherapy with Couples," *American Journal of Psychotherapy*, XII (1958), 18–23.
12. E. Glover, *Technique of Psychoanalysis* (New York: International Universities Press, 1955).
13. Phyllis Greenacre, "The Role of Transference: Practical Considerations in Relation to Psychoanalytic Therapy," *Journal of the American Psychoanalytic Association*, III (1954), 671–684.
14. Jackson and Weakland, *op. cit.*
15. Bernard L. Green and Alfred P. Solomon, "Marital Disharmony: Concurrent Psychoanalytic Therapy of Husband and Wife by the Same Psychiatrist (The Triangular Transference Transaction)," *American Journal of Psychotherapy*, XVII (1963), 443–450.
16. E. Berne, *Transactional Analysis* (New York: Grove Press, 1961).
17. Ian Alger, "The Clinical Handling of the Analyst's Responses," *Psychoanalytic Forum*, Vol. III (1966).
18. Gregory Bateson et al., "Toward a Theory of Schizophrenia," *Behavioral Science*, I (1956), 251–264.
19. Peter Hogan and Jack R. Royce, "Co-therapy in Special Situation." Presented at the 17th Anniversary Conference of the American Group Psychotherapy Association, 1961.
20. H. S. Sullivan, *Conceptions of Modern Psychiatry* (William Alanson White Foundation, 1947).
21. Ian Alger and Peter Hogan, "The Use of Videotape Recordings in Conjoint Marital Therapy," *American Journal of Psychiatry*, CXXIII, No. 11 (May 1967), 1425–1430.

Analytic Group Psychotherapy of Married Couples by a Therapist Couple

Therapy of married couples in groups is a relatively unexplored approach to marital disharmony. My training as a psychoanalyst was modified by the influence of analytic group psychotherapy, with its broadened focus on the interaction of the individual patient with persons in his milieu. Moreover, as a result of reading literally thousands of interviews with patients who had applied for treatment at a psychoanalytically oriented center, I became increasingly aware of the significance of pregenital influences in the primary family triangle as a source of inhibition of maturation. Almost invariably, the patient described manifestations of disturbance in the primary family marital couple, his parents. The most frequent observation was that "mother was dominant and father weak and passive." This finding led to the idea that married patients in individual therapy might be treated more effectively by dealing with the relationship to the spouse.

Like Boas,[1] I had been strongly influenced by orthodox psychoanalytic technique, which was opposed to contaminating the analysis by introducing other members of the family. Boas admitted that he had misgivings about starting a married-couples group, despite his conviction of the need to explore "the zipper reaction of the marital partners."

It is interesting that Perelman,[2] Boas, and I—all three of us with a medical background and with formal psychoanalytic training—had serious misgivings about working with the spouse of a patient or another member of his family. Yet the notion that simultaneous treatment of husband and wife is contraindicated had been challenged by reports of many successes, notably by Whitaker,[3] Solomon and Greene,[4] and Mittelmann.[5] It would seem that there is now a definite trend toward learning to understand and handle what Perelman referred to as "the triangular situation which dominates the therapy" and "which few therapists care to overcome."

I was encouraged in this new direction by the following experience with a married woman patient. After some five or six years in therapy she had improved considerably in her functioning, with growth in personal self-esteem, reduction of guilt inhibition, and new, rewarding experiences. A persistent area of difficulty was her sexual relationship with her husband. Anxious about her own adequacy, she made defensive projections of inadequacy upon him, and he in turn overreacted with anger and withdrawal or displays of exaggerated masculinity. Analysis of the interaction was achieved on an intellectual level only and to no avail.

I examined myself for countertransference, and it occurred to me that I was playing a role in a triangle consisting of the patient, her husband, and me. What was being "replayed" was the interaction between the patient and her mother and father. The patient had succeeded in getting my attention completely for herself, thereby displacing the father—a gratification of her unconscious homosexual wishes.

I made known my wish to see the husband. The individual interview with him went very well and resulted in a marked diminution of his feeling that he was playing second fiddle to the analyst. He became more accepting of his wife and more supportive and his acting out ceased. Meanwhile, the patient began to be aware of her negative feelings toward me, and eventually the therapy was terminated on a mutually acceptable basis.

After this experience I began to treat married couples concurrently in individual sessions, with encouraging results. The next step was to treat them in a group. A serious impasse had developed in the case of one couple as each spouse strove to form an alliance with the therapist against the other. Both related to the therapist through transference as if I were the mother and they the siblings vying for my approval and favor. At the same time my own countertransference contribution to the situation was not clear to me. In retrospect my interest and my desire to be helpful were so intense that I was not sufficiently myself and was not contributing enough of my own re-actions and feelings. Unable to break through the impasse, like Gottlieb,[6] I decided to place them both as a couple in a mixed therapy group. They were the sole couple although some of the other group members were married.

This move was successful in splitting the "ubiquitous" or omni-present mother transference and countertransference. The members of the group, feeling left out and indignant at the couple's focus on the therapist as the important one, reacted like an assertive father who will not accept exclusion and denigration of his family role by the mother-child symbiosis. They exposed the couple's jockeying for posi-tion, and reacted with anxiety and distress in the presence of the quarreling pair, bringing home to the couple the effect their quarrels had on their children. Like a wife not preoccupied by the halo of being a "good" mother, I was happy with the activity of this "father" (the group) and supported "him" whenever I could. The bickering which was being focused on the therapist lessened as each spouse be-came more involved with the group, and soon, like the others, they were focusing on themselves.

It is evident even from this sketchy review that the group was very useful in splitting the countertransference triangle and in providing an arena for diverse family interactions of a pregenital nature.

Theoretical Considerations

Group therapists have sought to explain the alterations undergone by the transference neurosis in the group situation. Some, notably Slavson,[7] have spoken of the "dilution of the transference." Others, such as Boas, feel it is more like a "splitting." It would appear to me that both take place. To my mind, dilution refers to the therapist's experiencing of a decrease in intensity in what Foulkes and Anthony[8] refer to as the "vertical transference" as a result of its splitting and the partial delibidinization of the therapist.

In the one-to-one relationship, the therapist is endowed with omnip-otent status—the "vertical transference." In the group, the transference tends to become more "horizontal." The therapist experiences himself as considerably "off the pedestal" and is related to more and more on a peer level—though he is still the object of distortion, often along more negative lines.

Jackson[9] postulated that, in the group, "patients reenact the primordial family in the unconscious." For example, the patient may at times relate to the group as the (primordial) mother and to the therapist (in the group) as the father. Feeling secure in the protection of the group (positive transference), the patient is less fearful of and freer to compete with the therapist (the father), and even contemptuous of him (negative transference).

I agree with Jackson that the "primordial family in the unconscious" is a useful frame of reference and would add the dimension of the "primordial narcissistic ego."[10] By the primordial narcissistic ego I mean the primitive ego state existing in infancy which subserves the function of self-preservation on the basis of the pleasure principle and corresponds to the "primary narcissistic state." Thinking is of primary-process nature, self-centered and magically self-fulfilling. Differentiation of self and object has not yet been achieved, and relatedness is of a positive and trusting nature. The narcissistic state is that described by Freud: "Narcissism is this sense would not be a perversion, but the libidinal complement to the egoism of the instinct of self-preservation, a measure of which may justifiably be attributed to every living creature."[11] A characteristic of this state is that the ego bestows upon the mothering object the full measure of its omnipotent expectations, so constituting the "primordial dyad." A further characteristic is a self-centered, subjective way of reacting emotionally to the object in terms of gratification or frustration of needs. The primordial narcissistic ego "loves" the object if it is gratifying, "hates" it if it is frustrating, without perception of its *separateness* and separate needs. Thus it fragments the object into a "good" part and a "bad" part, creating the prototype of the triangle.[12]

Object reaction at this stage is critical. Hostile parental corrective action, when the child expresses "bad" feelings creates threat and narcissistic injury. Primary narcissism may suffer inversion to the secondary type,[13] to self-glorification and a corresponding object glorification as a defense (grandiosity). Transference behavior can be seen as the expression of this narcissistic inversion. Now threatened, or made anxious, by its own hateful feelings (oral sadism) to the "bad" object, the now secondarily narcissistic ego defends itself by clinging to the aggressor, using repression and displacement of hostility onto the object of the "bad" mother's attention—a rival such as a father or a sibling.

Splitting of the transference can be more readily explained in the light of this pregenital defense. In the dyadic therapeutic relationship, the transference regression or return to the primordial hostility toward the "bad" object is frequently blocked to the point of impasse by powerful defenses which have as their purpose the denial of separation and its existential anxiety and a clinging to a perception of self *as being of central importance to the object.*

As in the first clinical example given above, clinging on the part of the therapist to the dyadic structure may be an indication of counter-transference—that is, the therapist's perception of himself as of central importance to the patient. By creating a triangle, the therapist loses his "all-good" status as anxiety is elicited in the patient, who now splits the therapist into "good" and "bad." A field of interaction is created in which such primary-process defenses as denial and displacement (as seen in sibling rivalry) are subjected to the test of reality and must be worked through as the strengthened ego learns to discriminate and achieve secondary-process thinking.[14] It follows, therefore, that the use by the therapist of himself in a triangle with the patient facilitates the elicitation and analysis of the fantasy of centrality. Thus, a therapeutic group is an excellent medium for encouraging growth from dyadic to triadic behavior.[15]

I do not mean that therapy in triangles or groups is more effective than therapy in the one-to-one relationship. I still do most of my work in the one-to-one framework. But I am aware that, in a group experience, previously unnoticed transference behavior can more easily come to light and is more readily open to interaction, to a reality-testing, and to being worked through. Moreover, the therapist can use triangular dynamics even when he is alone with the patient. For instance, if for some reason I cannot bring in the spouse of a patient, I am more likely now to include him by reference, through interpretation, or even by acting as his representative.

In my opinion, the persisting fantasy of centrality, reflecting secondary narcissism, underlies the Oedipal struggle, problems of sibling rivalry, and the like. It results in pathological adaptations geared to maintaining a favored position with the all-important object. In transference one can see the expression of such distorted adaptation, while resistance is related to a compulsively repetitive defense of the pathologic adaptation. Thus, the need for a meaningfully corrective experience becomes evident.

Persistence of the fantasy of centrality is the basic problem in disturbed marital interaction. There is a failure of maturation in each partner. The spouse "transfers" to the other a self-centered adaptational mode of behavior deriving from the pregenital period, when it was not only uncorrected but fostered by pathogenic parental interaction.[16] As a child, he most generally was the favorite of a parent, often the mother. The price he paid was the stunting of realistic self-esteem and of his capacity for autonomous behavior. Later he falls in love blindly, not with the other person as she really is, but with the fantasied re-creation of the idealized pregenital symbiosis. Marriage brings about an angry clash, the honeymoon is soon over, and a sadomasochistic struggle for dominance ensues.

The Therapeutic Approach

These theoretical considerations obviously apply to all analytic therapy. But we have learned that for a particular patient a different type of therapy, such as group therapy, may provide a helpful additional dimension. We who practice co-therapy have wondered if it might not be even more useful to have the negative transference displaced onto an individual who is more skillful and better able to deal with it, as presumably a trained co-therapist is.

Moreover, the natural tendency for primordial familial dynamics to appear more readily in a therapy group, and the group potential for therapeutic effect supports the conclusion that individual psychodynamics are created in a family group. Pathology arises in a family group and perhaps can best be treated through the artificial re-creation of such a group. It is also fair to speculate that treatment in the actual family group, if this is possible, could turn out to be the preferred form of therapeutic modality for reasons of therapeutic economy, to judge by the mushrooming growth of family therapy.

The deep resentment felt by patients for their fathers deserves careful study. The accusation that the father has been weak and passive is frequently not borne out as the real picture of the family is developed by the patient in therapy. Often the father is anything but weak and passive away from the family. But if he has been unable to diminish the child's perception of the mother as central and most important in the family structure, as the child may have secretly wished that he would, it follows that he would be perceived as "weak" and ineffective. The child thus identifies with the aggressor or omnipotent parent figure—namely, the mother. He learns to reflect and act out her basically competitive and contemptuous attitudes toward the father as his sexual development deviates toward homosexual rather than heterosexual behavior. In some way, then, the father *has* failed his children. What is not clear is how. My hunch is that the father's proper influence in the family is to correct dyadism for all family members, including *himself*. By reducing the centrality of the mother for all the family, he helps lessen the vertical transference and prevents or minimizes narcissistic injury. The son, retaining his primary narcissism while learning to adapt it to reality, comes to identify with the father. The daughter similarly identifies with the mother, who accepts and respects her husband.

When the mother competes with the father, she is encouraging the child to seek an alliance with her. The son, fearing to lose his favored position, cannot identify with the rejected father. The daughter, abetted by the father's resentment and counterrejection, identifies with her mother's distrust and competitiveness.

Our approach as co-therapists of a group of married couples is based on these considerations. In the group each patient re-creates his own childhood family configuration—which resulted in his pathological development—and projects it onto the co-therapists via transference. Our hope has been to effect corrective change through interaction with substitute parental figures. In addition, we would expect to develop our understanding of the dynamic factors involved in positive family interaction, which diminishes the centrality of the mother and promotes growth.

Experience with a Married-Couples Group

Asya Kadis had been experimenting with the treatment of married couples in groups since 1954 and was concerned about the lack of progress in some patients, which she began to attribute to her perception that there was inadequate "fatherly" influence in the group. Learning of my interest in co-therapy, she suggested I join her. We were both convinced that we would be able to work together well and complement each other. Our association as co-therapists began in 1962.

The group started with four couples, all strongly motivated to maintain their marriages. Three couples were K.'s, already analytic sophisticates, having had both individual and group therapy. The wife in my couple had had only two years of individual therapy. The husband was adamant in refusing treatment for himself, although he showed a marked willingness to come to the group to help his wife and his marriage.

The group met once a week for an hour and a half in the cozy living room of K.'s apartment office. We sat around a center table on which there was a jar filled with candy. Post-session meetings were held without the therapists from early on.

Both therapists were aware that the major family dynamic for both the men and the women was a close dependent tie with the mother, who was perceived as all-nutritive and nonsexual in relation to the father. The father was generally held in contempt (a fixated pre-genital attitude). It was anticipated that the patients would transfer these perceptions to the therapists. By splitting the transference one would be placed on a pedestal as the "good" mother; the other would be subjected to exclusion and derision as the "bad" mother. By displacement, the father figure would be endowed with the "bad" image. Since most of the patients had originally been K.'s, we suspected that I would be the target of the "bad mother" feelings.

This impression was confirmed in the first session. Right after K. welcomed me, giving me the most impressive chair in the room, the women led the attack. The predominant attitude was: Why in the world did they need me around? The purpose of the attack was to make "Papa" jealous of "Mama's" position, stimulate him to compete and thereby attack her, and so split the parents. Both therapists refrained from interpretation.

In the next session the gambit was reversed, with the attack taking the form of flirtation spearheaded by one woman and enjoyed by the others. The attempt again was to discredit the father in the mother's eyes by exploiting his masculinity as a weakness: to show him up as a seducer of his daughters, thus arousing the mother's resentment of him and winning her protection for them.

Before the fourth session began, K. informed me that the husband of the woman who had flirted with me had taken the chair K. had so ostentatiously given to me. I sensed the group's anticipated enjoyment of my inevitable humiliation, and I politely asked the "usurper" to relinquish my chair. Defiant at first and then angry at my insistence, he eventually gave up the chair, complaining to me that K. would never do such a thing to him and that he felt humiliated, that he had a pain in his chest. How dare I do this to him, knowing he was a cardiac—again an appeal for Mother's protection against Father.

There was general condemnation of me until K. pointed out that the "usurper," his mother's favorite, had in his childhood taken his own father's place strongly abetted by the latter's permissiveness. In this recreation, K. had not cooperated in protecting him as his own mother had, but rather supported the "father's" stand as rightfully aggressive. This incident was significant in that it established that I would insist on my place and that K. *recognized it too*. Mama showed she respected Papa's position in the family, even though she herself would not behave as he did. Had I offered an interpretation instead of taking action, it would have been rendered ineffective by being perceived as poor Papa's attempt to cover up his humiliation with complaints and attacks.

Subsequently the patient who had taken my chair worked through his compulsive pattern of dependency for self-esteem on his wife's approval—his seeking to be her favorite. He came to see his unconscious identification with his father's passivity, which played into his wife's neurotic passivity to her own mother. He had satisfied her neurotic need to be competitive and contemptuous of him as a sibling in her unconscious symbiosis with her mother.

Moreover, he had frustrated her real need for him to have the strength to help her free herself from that bind—thus doubly earning her contempt. He was her "weak" father, whom she could seduce, as she had acted out with me in earlier sessions. As the husband succeeded in giving up his masochistic behavior, he began to earn his wife's respect. Ultimately, after they left the group, he sent me an affectionate Christmas card drawn by himself, showing the "famous chair." Later he obtained a professorship in the art department of a well-known university—a "chair" of his own.

What is remarkable to me in the above-described interaction is that it could be elicited in so few sessions. It is an excellent example of effective and constructive use of triangular dynamics to achieve therapeutic breakthrough.

To reiterate, the cornerstone of these pathological dynamics is excessive libidinization in the mother-child dyadic relationship in which the father becomes an isolated point of the actual triangle. Mother's natural concern is distorted by the child's narcissism into a perception of himself as of central importance to her through which he achieves a fantasy of security. In the presence of healthy parental interaction such fantasy is soon corrected by reality. On the other hand, if parental discord is present, such fantasy is encouraged to the point of fixation.

The child, male or female, if fixated, develops a compulsive seeking for a position of centrality to the mother. His self-worth depends on the retention of the "high chair" position. He sits on this throne which no one else has and is catered to and hand-fed by mother as no one else is. He imagines that others, such as father or siblings, envy and compete for possession of the "high chair." As he basks in the security of the chair he also learns to feel anxious about its loss. The price of retention is all too often the renunciation of individuation and sexual maturation. Thus, the "centralizing" mother is "good" and loved; the potentially decentralizing one is "bad" and feared.

To use clinical illustration once more, in one group session Mrs. A. brought up her desire for closeness to and acceptance by her mother-in-law. Her own unconscious rivalrous attitude to her husband was latent in her associations to his sister's competitiveness with him. Mr. A. was shocked to learn of this. Mr. B. then associated the death of a male relative, a devoted father unappreciated by his wife and daughter. Mrs. B. elaborated on the symbiosis between the wife and daughter, the latter wanted father out, so mother threw him out. Her identification and reality testing were reflected in her feeling that "They were getting farther and farther out." Mrs. C. then told of telling her husband to get out and then regretting it. But she was unable to ask him to return because of her fear of what K. would think. "She is a black figure in my life." Note that she now specifies the mother figure as the "bad" one, not the father.

Each of the women contribute to the whole fabric of the dynamic. Mrs. A.: "I long for the high chair position with mother." Mrs. B.: "I have to drive out father [men] to keep the position. But I am too far out. I feel badly for the man." Mrs. C.: "I want to reverse this but am afraid of the retribution [loss] of mother." Mrs. B. and Mrs. C. are permitting themselves exposure of the wish to make heterosexual choice aided by the freeing effect of K.'s ability to do so in the session.

As for the men, compulsively competing for preference by women, they could not identify with their fathers whom they rejected as "weak." They habitually appeared almost eager to abdicate their maleness as they compulsively sought the favor of the "witch" mother. Their major defense against the pregenital anxiety was a false sense of security derived from the competitive rejection of the father by the mother, which they perceived as evidence of her preference for them. In this fantasy they experienced themselves as "winners" of a sort in the Oedipal conflict. They had fought for and retained the infantile "high chair" position of omnipotence, with mother's attention centered on them. Dreams of falling from high places and phobic reactions involving height reflect anxiety about the security of the "high chair" position. Reference to this in the session was made by Mr. B. when he said, "I went down a little bit here in the group." But the price paid for retaining the fantasy was enormous: subservience to feminine approval. Their covert passive resistance, even their helpless anger, served only to betray their basic attachment and susceptibility to manipulation by the unwilling "queen bee" they themselves had created.

Thus, in the session, the men too had begun to reality test. Mr. A. was shocked into realizing that he was not, as he had fantasied, the apple of his sister-wife-mother's eye. Mr. B., even more penetrated, exclaimed: "What god-damned fools we are—to kill ourselves for a woman." And Mr. C. to his wife, "Every fucking thing you say is derogatory. Don't talk for me. I can talk for myself."

As for the therapists, we were seeking to overcome the negative transference to me as the primordial father in the group. I was making some progress. I had to get the men to see how they were making fools of themselves. Ordinarily their competitiveness deafened them to my interventions, as they enjoyed making a fool of me, and they were more open to what K. had to say. Thus, K.'s astute and sensitive interpretation that it was understandable that men would not like to be made to look foolish by women opened them to recognition and exposure of their feelings.

The Role of the Father as Pathogenic Agent

On the basis of the above, a further word can be said on the question of "where father fails." He can be an effective and potent person everywhere but in the family. He fights for success realistically and achieves it. But at home he regresses to the "high chair" position: he transfers to his wife as to his mother and expects her to feed his ego with recognition and admiration. The strength he manifests elsewhere vanishes as he fails to perceive his wife as a separate person with needs and problems of her own and gives no room to their expression. Instead, he personalizes the manifestations of these in her as her finding fault with him. If she is unhappy, it is because he has been somehow "bad" or inadequate. His wife, who really needs him to have the strength to understand and react appropriately to her, is understandably chagrined at his failure. She comes to perceive him as a "little boy" seeking to trap her into the position of omnipotently "mothering" him at her own expense. In her feelings, he is equated with a brother or father who stood between her and her gratification from her mother. In other words, she now regresses to a competition with a sibling for her own "high chair." A viciously destructive pattern of competition for the position of favorite emerges, reactivating early homosexual strivings.

I have stated the notion that the proper function of the father is to relate to his wife so as to minimize her tendency to be central to the children. It is my conviction that Mr. B. weakened his function in the family by minimizing himself and aggrandizing his wife, putting her on an unrealistic pedestal. He maximized her as his source of narcissistic supply and minimized himself. He gave her a power and responsibility she did not need. Not needing to castrate, she did so anyway, compulsively, in the hope that he would stop her by asserting his separate integrity and his independence of her attitudes. This would be his own intact narcissism, which she could feel as his masculine potency. Thus, he could help his children learn to perceive their mother as fallible, rather than omnipotent, and himself as effective, rather than impotent, even though fallible.

My interaction in the group was both as a husband figure and as a father figure. For the most part, I did not allow myself to get involved, at the expense of my own self-esteem, in the manipulations of the members of the group. I felt positive toward everyone despite disagreements, hostility, and even contemptuous provocations. Too, I enjoyed being good-humoredly provocative myself. I knew as time went on that I would eventually earn the respect of the group. Most important was the tone of my relationship to K. At the beginning, I could see that her natural warmth and desire to help was the major factor predisposing to her being the central figure. This centrality was unintentionally but intrinsically seductive and double-binding as long as it was not counteracted. I set out, not to destroy it, for in its proper bounds I liked and admired it, but to add a dimension to it. If she taught reliance on her everflowing bounty, I would teach the value of self-reliance. I had confidence in her basic good will and her acceptance of me even when I would be tough, firm and frustrating where her natural impulse would be to fulfill. We complemented rather than competed with each other. In the final analysis, K. helped to reduce her own centrality as she willingly gave way to my role and participation. For the patients, it was experiencing Mama's primary loyalty to Papa that diminished her centrality for them and theirs for her. If she could choose heterosexuality, her "children" were released to do likewise. Two of the couples mentioned here (A. and C.) made a quick improved readjustment, the men growing separate and self-assertive and their wives growing too as women. There was evidence of growth and achievement in their various activities, and a new maturity as they "graduated" from the group. The B. couple are still in treatment but well on their way to its completion.

Results

Since at the time of writing (1965) we have had fewer than three years of experience with marital couples treated in a group by a heterosexual co-therapy couple, it would be premature to draw definite conclusions as to results. However, our experience may be summarized as follows. During this period we have treated fourteen couples and for some time had two groups in operation. We have observed to our satisfaction that couples can become involved in such a group, can make, analyze, and work through intensive transference in depth with extremely gratifying results for the marital interaction. This was so for at least eight of the couples treated. Not all couples have become so involved, however. Generally, the couples that did not become involved dropped out in the first three months. The reasons for this are by no means clear, but the following factors appear to be part of it.

Motivation. We have learned that it is extremely important to explore the motivation of each spouse to continue the marriage. If the partners are positively committed to the marriage and show loyalty to each other, despite the strains, the prognosis in a couple group is quite good. Infidelity makes the prognosis poor. The presence of children is a positive cohesive factor. Obviously, not all marriages are made in heaven, and the therapist should not commit himself to the preservation of any marriage.

Preparation. Couples should not be brought into the group right away unless they are intimately known at least to one of the co-therapists. It is important to establish some familiarity with the life history of each spouse, and to have some idea of the individual's capacity to make a transference relationship to one or both therapists. There may be special problems with couples referred by other therapists with whom they remain in treatment. In such cases there is negative transference to the new setting. Also, we have had a higher proportion of poor results with couples in which one or both partners were themselves therapists; competitive feelings play a large part here.

Selection. Selection is not always feasible in private practice, unless there are numerous referrals, and would probably be easier to practice in a clinic or agency. We do not include couples who are experienced by us as too detached to profit from involvement which we test interactively in the initial contacts. By and large the group welcomes new couples and they become part of the group very quickly. However, the emotional climate of the group at the particular time is important; the therapist must be sensitive to timing.

Countertransference. Self-searching on the part of the therapist is always necessary in regard to the omnipotent tendencies. A therapist may at times have an attacking reaction to a defense to which he is unduly sensitive. The co-therapist can be particularly helpful there. Undue commitment to the perpetuation of the marriage, we feel, is also a countertransference problem. Misperceived, it may reinforce masochistic commitment to the marriage in the patient.

Conclusion

Mrs. Kadis and I feel most encouraged about our therapeutic approach. We are quite certain of the validity of the theoretical thinking underlying it and intend to pursue and expand our activities along these lines. We feel that the treatment of married couples in groups is a fruitful approach to marital disharmony, and we are convinced of the added efficacy of heterosexual therapists working as a pair. In a "momist" culture, the importance of the father's role in the growth of children cannot be overemphasized.

In summary, the rationale for therapy of married couples in a group, including our own emphasis on the use of a heterosexual pair as co-therapists, is as follows: The psychopathology of the individual arises in the context of the nuclear family and its triangular interpersonal transactions. It is primarily determined by parental interaction, rather than attributable to one parent or the other.[17] Unresolved residues of a pregenital and Oedipal nature in both husband and wife stemming from their own parents' interaction find expression in character defenses and play a major role in neurotic adaptations requiring complementarity in the mate. The co-therapists provide a projection target that facilitates the drawing out, analysis, and working through of the unresolved residues.

NOTES

1. Conrad Boas, "Intensive Group Psychotherapy with Married Couples," *International Journal of Group Psychotherapy*, XII (April 1962), 142–153.
2. V. S. Perelman, "Problems Encountered in Group Psychotherapy of Married Couples," *International Journal of Group Psychotherapy*, X (April 1960), 136–143.
3. C. A. Whitaker, "Psychotherapy with Couples," *American Journal of Psychotherapy*, XII (1958), 19–23.
4. A. P. Solomon and B. L. Greene, "Concurrent Psychoanalytic Therapy in Marital Disharmony," presented at the American Orthopsychiatric Association Meeting, Chicago, 1964; "Marital Disharmony: Concurrent Therapy of Husband and Wife by the Same Psychiatrist," *Diseases of the Nervous System*, XXIV (1965), 1–8; "Marital Disharmony: Concurrent Psychoanalytic Therapy of Husband and Wife by the Same Psychiatrist," *American Journal of Psychotherapy*, XVII (1963), 443–456.
5. Bela Mittelmann, "Analysis of Reciprocal Neurotic Patterns in Family Relationships," in *Neurotic Interaction in Marriage*, Victor W. Eisenstein, ed. (New York: Basic Books, 1956), pp. 81–100; and "Complementary Neurotic Reactions in Intimate Relationships," *Psychoanalytic Quarterly*, XII (1944), 479–491.
6. Sophie B. Gottlieb, "Response of Married Couples Included in a Group of Single Patients," *International Journal of Group Psychotherapy*, X (April 1960), 143–159.

7. According to W. C. Hulse, "Multiple Transferences or Group Neuroses," read to the London Group Analytic Society, July 1960.

8. S. H. Foulkes and E. J. Anthony, *Group Psychotherapy* (London: Penguin Books, 1957).

9. J. Jackson, "A Family Group Therapy Technique for a Stalemate in Individual Treatment," *International Journal of Group Psychotherapy*, XII (April 1962), 164–169; and "The Transference Neurosis in Group Psychotherapy," *The Journal of Psychoanalysis in Groups*, I (1962), 54–61.

10. Max Markowitz, discussion of paper by J. Jackson, "The Transference Neurosis in Group Psychotherapy," *Journal of Psychoanalysis in Groups*, I (1962), 62–65.

11. Sigmund Freud, "On Narcissism: An Introduction," in *Collected Papers*, Vol. IV (New York: Basic Books, 1959), pp. 30–59.

12. In Paula Heimann, "A Contribution to the Re-evaluation of the Oedipus Complex—the Early Stages," in *New Directions in Psychoanalysis*, Melanie Klein, Paula Heimann, and Roger Money-Kyrle, eds., (New York: Basic Books, 1955), pp. 23–38.

13. Max Markowitz, "Narcissism and the Development of Self from Dyadic to Group Relatedness," in *Topical Problems in Psychotherapy*, vol. V (Basel: Karger, 1965), pp. 59–66.

14. Heinz Hartmann, Ernst Kris, and Rudolph M. Loewenstein, "Comments on the Formation of Psychic Structure," *The Psychoanalytic Study of the Child*, Vol. II (New York: International Universities Press, 1946), p. 20.

15. Markowitz, "Narcissism and the Development of Self from Dyadic to Group Relatedness."

16. Markowitz and Kadis, "Parental Interaction as a Determining Factor in the Social Growth of the Individual in the Family," *International Journal of Social Psychiatry*, First International Congress Issue, Special Edition, No. 2, Section K, pp. 81–89.

17. *Ibid.*

Indications for
Psychoanalytic
Family Therapy

When workers in the field of family therapy gather and exchange their views and experiences, they feel the relief of liberation from the narcissistic isolation in which we all work. After reassuring one another that family therapy is worth trying, we invariably proceed from the questions whether to do it and how to do it, to the questions when and where. The answers show considerable variation.

The Problem

All therapists agree with one aspect: any treatment that excludes the patient's family cannot deal efficiently with the patient's problems, conflicts, sickness, and health. This is also true for a patient in psychoanalysis. The time is definitely over when the analyst tries to stay outside the family circle and prefers not to become involved.

From there, opinions diverge in all directions. A man like Carl Whiteker[1] formulates five reasons for psychoanalytic marriage therapy: (1) interlocking psychopathology: (2) paranoid trends; (3) fragility of the marriage relationship; (4) bilateral emotional immaturity; and (5) the need for the marriage partner as a nonprofessional attendant for a psychotic or near psychotic partner. Andrew S. Watson[2] gives his view in his clear way and states that conjoint therapy is indicated in those families where reality distortions are so gross and so reality-disruptive that speed in checking family disintegration is a critical factor. Conjoint treatment offers an ideal way in which to slow down the destructive neurotic process and provides a chance to resolve problems of different levels of consciousness.

An excellent, comprehensive, and clear summary is given by Irwin Greenberg.[3] In the first place, he reduces the question of specific indications by stating that all psychotherapy is family therapy. In this sense, Sigmund Freud too practiced analytic family therapy, even if he limited himself to the introjection of the infantile family into the unconscious of the adult patient. Greenberg has seen especially good results of family therapy when the psychotic patient is torn in two directions by his family or when the phase of treatment is reached where it is contemplated to discharge the patient from the hospital.

Ian Alger's attitude as outlined in this book is similar to mine. He states that a neurosis cannot be explained, understood, or treated only as an intrapsychic phenomenon, but must also be viewed in its interpsychic communicative meaning. The therapist's countertransference helps indicate when it is time to ask to see the patient's marriage partner. The patient may give the clues himself by asking for a family interview or by complaining about actively or passively suffering under the influence of an unhappy marriage.

I myself have stated my position a little differently in my book *Psychoanalysis and the Family Neurosis*,[4] where I say that the person's neurosis may be anchored to a large extent in a complementary neurosis involving his marriage or his family. The unconscious communication or interaction between people can cause and maintain a neurosis just as another kind of communication can help to cure it. The family may thus both help and hinder growth and maturation.

I do not wait to start family treatment until I have failed or progress has slowed down or a therapeutic stalemate has been reached in individual therapy. Neither would I change a winning game; I would not change individual therapy if everything seems to be progressing well. In therapy that is going well I would, however, be aware that probably the patient himself is a family therapist who communicates insight and changes from the therapeutic situation in the analyst's office to his family at home.

The Problem Restated

For an analyst who uses family interviews as a parameter to analytic technique, the whole question of indications and counterindications is another aspect of psychodynamic reasoning applied to a technical question. I regard family interviews and treatment as another variation of psychoanalytic technique and relate them to the crucial concepts of psychoanalysis: transference, resistance, interpretation, integration.

Since I am always aware of the place and person of the therapist in the therapeutic process, I would like to add one more point of reference as to when to apply family therapy in analysis: the therapist's countertransference. I have found family interviews a most effective and perhaps consistently necessary control of countertransference distortions.

A therapist may not always feel like a scientist, but more like an artist; this may influence his approach to the problem of indications. Who can say when Picasso may transform a discarded wicker basket into a pregnant goat or into a dying man? Or what indications an artist follows when he chooses ink or oil, pen or brush, in order to create something he feels and wants to communicate to his friends? Are there indications and counterindications for an artist when he is creating which tell him when to change from painting to sculpturing, from bronze to terra cotta? Are there indications when Chagall turns from working on canvas to working on glass windows? Like the artist, the analyst also works and creates from his own unconscious. His spontaneous response to a therapeutic situation is as important as any conscious knowledge of indications or counterindications.

Getting involved with the family is regarded by me more and more as a part of the analyst's responsive action toward the patient's needs (as differentiated from his desires and wishes). If this is so, the question of indications begins to look quite different: it changes from the old-fashioned medical attitude of diagnosis-directed behavior to dynamically understanding action.

The Specific Situation of Psychoanalytic Family Therapy

Psychoanalytic family therapy implies a dynamic approach and a genetic understanding of a family. Such understanding must include the conscious and the unconscious of the individuals involved and the dynamics of their interaction.

This kind of family therapy is correctly called analytic because it takes into consideration the transference situation, which in everyday family therapy is so often overlooked in favor of interaction. It also takes into consideration resistance—even if a family's resistance differs from individual character resistance as it is known from psychoanalysis.

This approach to family therapy is explicitly analytic because the basis of therapeutic intervention is the interpretation of the unconscious and of the resistance against having it made conscious. Such interpretation aims at insight and integration. All such insight must be a part of an emotional experience. Psychoanalytic family therapy is an intensive, deep-going experience, and this fact—together with some specific features in the process of working through—makes family treatment so often effective.

Diagnostic Family Interviews

It is my experience that brief, diagnostic interviews with families may reveal family dynamics in a way that is more dramatic and convincing than any other conceivable method of teaching psychodynamic reasoning. Much can be learned from a well-conducted interview with an individual patient, from his behavior, his free-associative anamnesis, perhaps from a few dreams, and from his relation to the therapist. But our interpretation is to a large extent a matter of applied experience of preconceived concepts that make the patient and his unconscious understandable.

During a family interview, the unconscious dynamics of such a group of people become evident before our eyes—we only need to be able to see it. We actually see the interaction between a mother and her child; we see them getting involved or not involved; we see the relationship, perhaps the alliance, between father and mother, their relationship to the children, interaction between siblings, the transference of the family's past to the present therapeutic situation with the therapist. The learning experience becomes three-dimensional.

My experience also has shown me that such brief diagnostic interviews have some intrinsic therapeutic effect: the members of the family look at each other—so to speak—with the eyes of the therapist, but differently from the way they formerly interacted at home.[5]

A Special Aspect of Working Through in Psychoanalytic Family Therapy

Working through in psychoanalytic family therapy is different from working through in psychoanalysis or even group psychotherapy. The working through in psychoanalysis starts in a one-to-one relationship and is then internalized and continued within the patient, outside the analyst's office. In group psychotherapy, the process of working through is slightly different: insight is gained, felt, tried, and tested with the help of group interaction. After the end of the group session, the process of working through will be interrupted, perhaps stopped or internalized, approximately as in individual psychoanalysis. After the group session, each member of the group again becomes an individual patient, trying to deal with himself.

The family group will react quite differently, and this difference, so typical and significant, has not been sufficiently considered in psychoanalytic literature. The process of working through the family conflict (or the family constellation) will be neither interrupted nor stopped nor necessarily internalized; it will continue as in a group that meets in uninterrupted session for weeks and months of life and growth, of sickness and maturation, of constant interpretation of an existence together (special utilization of this aspect of family therapy has led to the technique of M.I.T., Multiple Impact Therapy, as developed by the Galveston team of psychotherapists).

Conjoint Interviews as Aid in Psychoanalysis

In *Psychoanalysis and the Family Neurosis*, I have described in detail the dynamics, the meaning, the technique, and the effect of conjoint interviews as a method of activating the therapeutic process in psychoanalysis and increasing its efficiency. I have seen my patient's partner either alone or together with my patient in analysis; I have seen them only once or occasionally, frequently, regularly, or not at all when that was indicated. I started additional therapy or did not do so; I employed these interviews as a parameter of psychoanalytic technique in the early stages of psychoanalysis, during the course of it, during the terminal phase, or even after years of having interrupted treatment entirely. If my patient's partner is in analysis with a colleague, I gladly see the colleague too—if he wishes to join us. I have also learned that two colleagues working in the same family may benefit from a conjoint conference with me—either simultaneously with the patients or without them. Such consultations may avoid countertransference battles, which always take place to the detriment of the patients. It sounds paradoxical, but it has been my experience nevertheless that, almost without fail, both analysts are justified in their complaints about the partners of their respective analysands. It is the beauty and the despair of work in our field that all embattled partners may be "right," but they may never meet on the same level of communication in order to work out their difficulties. As long as they try to communicate on different levels of a multilayered, complex system of communication, they need a therapist to guide them to successful in-fighting. In order to reestablish successful communication, the therapist must give insight into the multileveled nature of communications between human beings.

When I suggest a conjoint meeting, I immediately start working with the expectations of my patients. I work equally with the acceptance of my suggestion and with resistance against it. My main goal always has been, and still is, to gain insight into the unconscious meaning of my patient, his partner, and the complexity of the communication between them.

A part of this insight is the acknowledgment and discipline of my countertransference. Since my empathy and my responsive action use my countertransference as an essential therapeutic tool, I do not think that countertransference is a sign of the therapist's insufficient self-analysis or insufficient discipline. There is a great—and, to me, obvious—difference between the use of countertransference in therapy and its abuse. The first application asks for constant watching, and new insight will be gained; the second form asks for continuous analysis of the therapist.

In *Psychoanalysis and the Family Neurosis,* I have described one such situation: a patient turned to his (male) analyst in depressive despair, developed a strong, positive mother transference to him; at home his wife, in slowly deepening anguish, suffered nightmarish pain when the patient in a split transference treated her as if she were his bad mother. The analyst refused to recognize the wife's justifiable insistence on being seen and did not understand his patient's split transference neurosis.

I have emphasized—and have been misunderstood and criticized for it—that an analyst who turns from his patient to the patient's marriage partner is not becoming a prosecutor investigating truth or reality. The family interviews will give insight into the *dynamics* of such an unhappy marriage or into the complicated transference-countertransference situation.[6] It is not true that such interviews complicate matters further. Our patients show us the way if we understand their clues and the messages they communicate to us.

The Problem and "Responsive Action"

When I started to work with families, I followed approximately the outlines given here as guiding posts for my technique. I rarely doubted when to start or stop family therapy as an aid to psychoanalysis. I never rushed into it or procrastinated in hesitation. I followed my intuition exclusively. I took my curiosity as guiding motivation. First I asked myself: How does the wife of my patient look? talk? behave? How does the husband of my patient respond to the therapeutic situation in my office? Soon a family interview was arranged most naturally.

Later I learned to consider the whole problem not only in terms of transference and resistance but also in terms of countertransference. I realized this by observing myself and also by working with colleagues who consulted me. The difference between my expectations and my factual observation of my patients' partners or their families, when I finally was confronted with them, showed me the role of identification of the therapist with his patients and the blind spot that results from it.

In my third and present state of insight, I realized that indications and counterindications in psychoanalytic family therapy can best be understood as special aspects of the therapist's "responsive action" toward his patients.

This term was used by Joseph Natterson and me[7] in order to characterize the therapist's reaction to the patient's unconscious needs as different from his conscious wishes or desires. The therapist responds with understanding, with emotion, eventually with advice or action, always leaving to the patient the freedom to agree or to oppose.

The therapist's responsive action should be genuine and spontaneous: his technical skill should be expressed only in the degree and form in which he shows his responsive action—not in its emotional nature, which must be spontaneous and genuine. His response may vary between subliminal cues and clearly shown response.

Whatever he does (for instance, arranging for an interview with his patient's marriage partner or family) should be based upon the knowledge and general understanding of the issues at hand and an accurate, constant, and consistent appraisal of the transference-countertransference situation and the unconscious needs indicated by it.

Responsive action is particularly indicated in crisis situations, in therapeutic impasse, or when therapy slows down. Responsive action is often followed by a new burst of therapeutic work in which the therapist may resume a traditional, more distant, more interpretive attitude.

Because of its emotional nature and its intimate interplay between therapist and patient, responsive action cannot be defined to the last detail. Everything depends upon the emotional atmosphere in the therapeutic situation. This technique is based upon an inner attitude and upon being in tune with the patient. It is therefore similar to and different from any kind of transference gratification. It contains some countertransference expression, which shows to a certain extent the therapist's attitude, without, however, revealing the nature of his involvement in an exhibitionistic way. In no circumstances should the therapist do something in the presence of his patient that he should have done by himself or within himself outside the therapeutic situation. There is a great difference between the behavior of a responsive, sensitive, spontaneous therapist and masochistic, exhibitionistic indulgence.

Responsive action is also different from the corrective emotional experience or conscious role-taking. It differs by virtue of the therapist's emphasis on the patient's relationship to reality and interaction with the therapist. Responsive action (for instance, the suggestions for seeing the spouse) is reality-directed but grows out of the transference-countertransference situation. The emphasis is on response, not on interpretation, which will follow later. Such responsive action may be an essential part of every therapeutic experience, and it may contain an essential factor in the therapeutic situation as a human encounter, aiming at a therapeutic alliance in the interest of therapeutic progress.[8]

NOTES

1. Carl A. Whiteker, "Psychotherapy with Couples," *American Journal of Psychotherapy*, XII (January 1958), 18–23.
2. Andrew S. Watson, "The Conjoint Psychotherapy of Marriage Partners," *American Journal of Orthopsychiatry*, XXXIII (October 1963).
3. Irwin M. Greenberg, Ira Glick, Sandra Match, and Sylvia S. Riback, "Family Therapy: Indications and Rationale," *Archives of General Psychiatry*, X (January 1964), 31–47.
4. Martin Grotjahn, *Psychoanalysis and the Family Neurosis* (New York: W. W. Norton, 1960).
5. Martin Grotjahn, " 'Open End' Technique in Psychoanalysis," *Psychoanalytic Quarterly*, XXXIII (1964), 270–271; and "Clinical Illustrations from Psychoanalytic Family Therapy," in Bernard Greene, ed., *Psychotherapy of Marital Disharmony* (New York: Free Press, 1965), pp. 169–185.
6. Ian Alger, "The Clinical Handling of the Analyst's Responses," *Psychoanalytic Forum*, Vol. III (1966).
7. Joseph M. Natterson and Martin Grotjahn, "Responsive Action in Psychotherapy." Paper presented at the American Psychiatric Association Annual Meeting, 1965, in New York.
8. See further Theodore Lidz, *The Family and Human Adaptation: Three Lectures* (New York: International Universities Press, 1963); and Eugenia M. Huneeus, "A Dynamic Approach to Marital Problems," *Social Casework*, XLIV (March 1963), 142.

Sequential Marriage: Repetition or Change?

Sequential marriage—involving persons in their second or subsequent marriage—presents opportunities to evalute the effect on individuals of changes in spouses, in circumstances, and in intrapsychic structure. The subject of remarriage is especially valuable in providing insight into marital object relationships. In evaluating serial marriages, however, one encounters several difficulties: (1) the heterogeneous composition of the remarried population; (2) the lack of valid demographic statistics on successive marriages; (3) the many contradictions in the literature about the outcome of remarriage; (4) the unreliability of the retrospective data[1] obtained from oral and verbal reports; (5) the differences in the marriages of the divorced as compared to the widowed; (6) the limited experience of observers from various disciplines. These difficulties represent variables that make generalizations mandatory in evaluating sequential marriages. Further, Jessie Bernard[2] has pointed out that people who remarry have been filtered through three sieves: a first marriage, a relatively coarse sieve that admits almost everyone; widowhood or divorce, a finer sieve; and finally remarriage itself, an even finer sieve.

A study of remarriage is further complicated by the multiplicity of marital patterns, which results from the fact that the three marital types (single, divorced, and widowed) intermarry and that either party may show an individual history (once divorced, twice divorced, etc.). For example, Mr. and Mrs. Red, a couple in their late thirties, married for ten years, were referred for marital therapy. Mr. Red had been previously married at the age of twenty. After three years, he divorced his first wife, but remarried her six months later. This marriage ended in divorce after one year. The new Mrs. Red was first married at sixteen and divorced at eighteen. She remarried at twenty-three and was divorced six years later. Her third marriage, one year later, was to Mr. Red. The marital history of Mrs. Red's parents was also complicated. After fifteen years of marriage, her parents were divorced. Father remarried, but divorced after five years; then he remarried his first wife.

Attitudes toward remarriage are being reshaped step by step. This change is a response to the mobile, urbanized, industrialized society we live in, which facilitates divorce without lessening the instinctual needs that marriage satisfies. The frequency of successive marriages has given rise to a dual pattern of marriage, with "sequential polygamy"[3] being practiced by almost one-fifth of the population.

The impressions to be described in this chapter are based on four series of data: (1) the one hundred couples treated by me most recently, and consecutively, in which the identified patient is a sick marriage; (2) a hundred married patients admitted consecutively to a private mental hospital (Forest Hospital, Des Plaines, Illinois), in which cases the identified patient is a sick person; (3) a hundred families observed consecutively at the Irene Josselyn Clinic (Winnetka, Illinois), in which the identified patient is a disturbed child; (4) and, finally, intensive study of two couples who were divorced, and their ensuing object relationships (see Figure 21–2).

In this chapter I will present general concepts relating to remarriage, including a *nuclear dynamic model;* general variables influencing the outcome of a sequential marriage; specific variables effecting remarriage in terms of object relationships; some statistical observations on successive marriages; and, finally, clinical material illustrating the vicissitudes of two couples who were divorced and their ensuing choice of objects and object relationships.

General Concepts

The progressive evolution in our theoretical thinking on marriage can be traced in our previous articles on marital disharmony.[4] Our current theoretical position, recently published,[5] is as follows: "A human being may be regarded as incorporating three separate systems: an *individual system* composed of intrapsychic events, an *interpersonal system* involving transactions 'with significant others,' and a *social system* responding to an interplay of forces between the individual and society."

Some of the concepts of Eric Berne[6] have been most helpful not only in structuring a discussion on remarriage but also in developing a model of the multiple forces influencing such a marriage. This *nuclear dynamic model* (see Figure 21–1) can be visualized as a circle containing an enclosed smaller circle and thus having an internal and external boundary.

Nuclear Dynamic Model

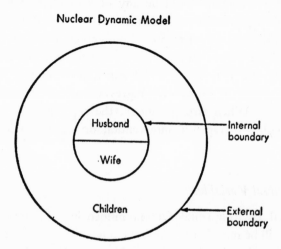

FIGURE 21–1

The external environmental factors influencing the outcome of a remarriage would be *outside* the external boundary and consist mainly of sociocultural forces. The internal environmental forces influencing the outcome of a remarriage would be those *within* the external boundary. These forces will be discussed further in the section on general variables. To explore fully all the external and internal forces would necessitate space beyond the confines of this chapter. When there is disruption of both internal and external boundaries, separation or divorce ensues. When only the internal boundary is disrupted, several outcomes are possible: emotional divorce, in which each spouse goes his separate way but maintains the façade of marriage; durable incompatible marriage, in which the system is maintained but the conflicting parties constantly take advantage of one another, playing the marital games as described by Berne; emotional break between the parents but coalitions with the children; and, lastly, a system maintained by means of an identified patient: a sick spouse, a sick marriage, or a sick child.

Other variables to be considered in evaluating a remarriage include the impact of psychotherapy, autonomous changes in the ego, and the impact of frustration on a spouse. Successful psychotherapy can lead to progressive structural changes in the ego, with acceptance of an inadequate marriage and no deleterious reaction to the treated spouse. Such acceptance may be based on any of a number of reasons; for example, children or socioeconomic factors. Or successful therapy may lead to legal divorce or separation. Autonomous changes in the ego, too, can produce progressive structural changes and likewise effect a remarriage. So can frustration, which can lead to positive progressive changes in the ego or to negative regressive changes to earlier levels of gratification. When strong enough, the repercussions of frustration bring either therapeutic intervention or separation in a remarriage.

General Variables

The external environmental factors influencing the outcome of a remarriage will be outside the external boundary (see Figure 21–1) and consist mainly of sociocultural forces. Norman W. Bell[7] has described how "disturbed families have a deficiency of family boundaries which leads them to involve extended kin in their conflicts and makes them sensitive to influence from extended kin." The influences of the extended family on remarriage are also important. However, since remarriages occur later in life, the extended family may by this time have accepted the situation, or they may be distant, and thus their influence may be negligible.

Other external environmental forces influence the outcome of a remarriage in various ways, among them the attitudes and reactions of children by prior marriages and the special custody and support arrangements for them, and the reaction of the new spouse to these children. In several instances, the solicitude of a parent for his children of an earlier marriage resulted in frequent quarreling, which led to divorce; or the former spouse either intervened directly or indirectly through the children, eventually disrupting the remarriage. In two couples involving a remarried widowed person, the deceased spouse was so idealized and the second partner so continuously and unfavorably compared that the marriage had to be terminated. In several other couples, the adverse reaction of friends led to divorce. On the other hand, many social activities require the participation of two people and this contributes to the maintenance of the marriage. So do financial considerations: the man is now better established and the new spouse knows what to expect; or the man is now established and has more time to devote to his marriage. These and many other factors are described by Bernard[8] and by Bell and Vogel.[9]

The internal environmental forces influencing the outcome of a remarriage will be exerted *inside* the external boundary (see Figure 21-1). Previous marital experience can be educational in a number of areas (e.g., sexual, housekeeping, tolerance). Remarried spouses are older, and with age not infrequently comes some growth and maturity. The self-image in older individuals is more sharply defined. The older bride is more apt to accept her new partner's identity and less likely to attempt to remold him. Moreover, the divorce and remarriage may have constituted such an emotional and financial strain that both spouses deem success in this marriage vitally necessary.

The intrapsychic forces operating may be multiple. Guilt feelings may greatly influence the outcome of a remarriage. The need for punishment on the part of either spouse may lead to masochistic provocation manifested in numerous and often remarkable ways. The guilt may be due to unconscious death wishes toward the former mate, or it may be conscious guilt at having forced a divorce on a spouse who is now unhappily married or not married at all. Conscious and unconscious homosexuality may be defended against by remarriage, a man entering into the remarriage because he needs a mate as a vehicle for his homosexual defense or as an alter phallus. On the other hand, a man may be attempting to conceal his inadequate sexual performance from himself and others by successive marriages with beautiful, seductive women. These and many other unconscious forces can influence the outcome of a remarriage and indeed, when one realizes the tremendous difficulties that remarried couples must solve, it is surprising that so many remarriages are successful.

Specific Variables

I will present sequential marriage in terms of object relationships, in keeping with psychoanalytic concepts of developmental stages. I have been influenced by Freud's concept of anaclitic and narcissistic object-relationships; Anna Freud's phase developmental stages; Therese Benedek's and George H. Pollock's proposals on symbiosis and symbiotic relationships; H. V. Dick's concepts of unconscious collusion and projective identification; and Peter L. Giovacchini's proposal of symptom and character object relationships.[10]

In man there is a progressive line of development from early physiological unity of infant and mother to a separateness that occurs in a "series of orderly sequential stages."[11] During this period of growth, many objects become significant, each being reacted to in a specific manner. These object relationships reflect their historical development, and although later derivatives may become important, their prototypes still exert some influence. Each transaction between the individual and the object results in the formation of an internalized mental representation (introject). Every individual has a library of introjects. Psychoanalysis with its strict adherence to psychic determinism suggests that introjects, with other variables both conscious and unconscious, determine the selection of one's spouse. Introjects can be unconsciously externalized onto an object, resulting in the phenomenon of projective identification.

Every person goes through a series of sequential object relationships. These relationships operate developmentally as well as currently; for example, couplings, intimacies, or antagonisms.[12] The newborn infant progresses from a stage of (narcissistic) parasitism, where it lives off mother, to one of symbiosis. Benedek[13] postulated an early neonatal stage of fusion between mother and child which she called "symbiosis." Husbands and wives are also bound to each other in a symbiotic fashion, but their bond is of a different order from that between mother and child because the needs of one partner for the other are relatively equal. This symbiosis is readily revealed in the multiple transference phenomena that occur during psychoanalysis, in which symbiotic elements at all developmental levels of the individual are displayed. Benedek believes that the fetus stimulates the receptive-retentive tenderness of the mother, and states: "After parturition the newborn remains the object of these instinctual needs. These drives constitute the psychodynamic source of the *symbiotic* [italics mine] need of the mother for her child." If unsatisfactory mothering occurs, this symbiotic relationship can reinforce the hostile-aggressive component of the ambivalent core of the individual. Inadequate mothering can later lead to serious problems in marriage, including a series of repetitive marriages in which one or both partners are seeking gratification of earlier needs that were never satisfied. Inadequate mothering can also lead to a series of marriages due to projective identifications that result in marital disharmony, in which the bad introject of mother is attacked internally as well as projected onto the partner, who is then attacked—thus setting off a series of provocative marital games.

Pollock[14] has proposed an interesting ecological approach as it specifically refers to the concept of human symbiosis along the developmental time-space axis. His thesis is that "during the unwinding of the transference neurosis evolving during the course of psychoanalysis, an understanding can be gained of the sequential ecological stages of development, as well as of the defensive compromises, resultants, compensations, adjustments, and adaptations that were instituted and subsequently internalized as part of the psychological apparatus. These symbiotic ties, if pathological, will be particularly in evidence during the psychoanalytic treatment." In a previous paper,[15] he described object choice and object relationships that are important in evaluating remarriage, as they appeared in the transference neurosis.

Mittelmann[16] has proposed that the neuroses of marital partners complement each other with dovetailing of conflictual and defensive patterns on both pre-Oedipal and Oedipal levels. Giovacchini[17] extended these conclusions and emphasized the mutually adaptive qualities of the mutual relationship. He has described these relationships as being symbiotic in nature to signify the mutual dependence of these transactions and has further concluded that the partners' needs for each other are equal. From his clinical observations, he has found their underlying personalities, their basic conflicts, their points of fixation and regression, and their general ego-integrations to be similar. Further, he has recently described[18] two types of marital object relationships, giving clinical examples, which are useful in understanding the phenomenology of remarriage. First, a *character object relationship*, characterized by a total characterological involvement between husband and wife. "The marital partner requires the total personality, including the specific character defenses, of the other partner in order to maintain intrapsychic equilibrium." Second, a *symptom object relationship*, which differs from the first group in that the marriage is transitory in nature and does not have the depth of involvement characteristic of a character object relationship. "The spouse does not require the total personality of the other; he needs only a particular trait or symptom, and the marital involvement seems only a partial one. Other objects with similar traits or symptoms, although differing in many respects, could serve defensive needs as well, and frequently such a patient had *several marriages* [italics mine] in which the spouses had a common denominator, so to speak, and also great differences." The defensive circumscribed meaning of the marital relationship leads to separation with repetitive marriages.

In conclusion, we note that different types of symbiotic bonds are present in all marital relationships, both healthy and unhealthy. There are many stages of healthy symbiosis along a developmental axis. The initial symbiosis undergoes a series of refinements and progressive developments. The elements of the earlier symbiosis continue to operate in so-called mature object relationships, but in healthy individuals they are expansive rather than constrictive because the symbiosis has undergone considerable reorganization. Pathologically we see fixations upon or regression to particular symbiotic states. These constitute the pathological symbiotic states and are attempts to relieve anxiety and deal with conflict. If a strong separation reaction occurs as a result of divorce or bereavement, the level of the previous symbiotic tie will be the important determinant in the new object relationship in remarriage. If the ego has not shown further maturation because of either regression or fixation upon a particular symbiotic stage, repetition in remarriage will occur. If, on the other hand, the ego has changed through psychotherapy, autonomous growth, or frustration leading to growth, then *change* for the better may occur.

Statistics

As stated at the beginning of this chapter, one finds that as a result of the large number of variables statistics cannot always be relied upon in the study of the outcome of remarriage. Thus, only impressions can be given. Until recently, it was the consensus that most divorcees did not remarry. Recently Thomas P. Monahan[19] has cited population surveys to support his view that "a large proportion of the divorcees remarry, perhaps as high as three-fourths." In an earlier study, Landis[20] gave the following figures: "At age 30, for example, the chances of remarriage for a divorced woman are 94 in 100; for a widowed woman, 60 in 100. The chances a spinster of 30 has of eventually marrying are only 48 in 100."

Another factor influencing the outcome of a marriage is the age at remarriage. Bernard[21] states: "Half the men who remarried in 1948 were more than 37 years of age; half the women were more than 31.3." She further notes that the remarriage rate for men past fifty-five is five times that for women of the same age.

Bernard[22] and others[23] suggest that remarriages are about as successful as other marriages. Bernard comments: "Perhaps the explanation for this seeming paradox lies in the final sieve through which the remarried population is strained—remarriage itself."[24] Paul Popenoe[25] studied 200 couples in which one partner had remarried his original spouse. He found that 48 percent were happy. On the other hand, Monahan, in an article published in 1958,[26] presented data gathered on a broad basis that indicated that remarriages have been less stable than first marriages. He stated: ". . . A divorce for one party weakens the strength of the marriage bond, and a second divorce experience greatly lessens the chances of survival of the marriage." He gives the following statistics: "*Primary marriages* [a first marriage for both parties] show a ratio of only 16.6 divorces per 100 marriages in that category. But where both parties had been divorced *once* before, the figure doubles to 34.9, and where both parties had been divorced *twice or more* times, the ratio climbs to 79.4." He assumes that divorce is a repetitive phenomenon.

Edmund Bergler[27] takes an even stronger position. He insists that the divorce-prone woman is essentially a neurotic who cannot be helped by repeated marriage. He asserts that divorce is futile and remarriages are only a repetition of the first; that only the partner is changed; that the basic marital problem remains; that nothing but death or psychiatric treatment can break patterns determined by infantile conflict. Recently Giovacchini[28] has expressed the same viewpoint of similarity of psychopathology and has given clinical data to support his contention.

Another factor to be considered in evaluating statistics on remarriage is that there are eight possible kinds of marital combinations: divorced man–single woman; divorced man–widow, etc. Paul C. Glick,[29] using data gathered in 1948, states that in 11 percent of remarriages one partner had been previously married and that in 7 percent both partners had been previously married. Thus, 18 percent or about one-fifth of all marriages involve remarriage. My statistics, gathered from three different sources, confirm these figures. The exact figures are 21 percent in my private cases; 20 percent of the couples in the Irene Josselyn Clinic group; and 18 percent in the Forest Hospital series.

Clinical Data

Through a most fortunate chain of circumstances I was able to observe not only the remarriages of two couples (see Figure 21–2) but also their prior object relationships. The first couple (the Whites) had only been married two years. The second couple (the Blacks) had been married fifteen years. Neither couple had children. My original association with the Blacks had occurred five years before the referral of the Whites.

THE BLACKS

Mr. Black, a handsome man of thirty-five, reported periodic quarreling because of his wife's disinterest in sex. Mrs. Black blandly complained that her husband was unfaithful. Her psychiatric evaluation revealed a borderline state with paranoid features. Refusing therapy, she divorced her husband and returned to live with her parents, who welcomed her home. Five years later she was still living with her parents, neither working nor going out socially. Mr. Black, outwardly aggressive and inwardly struggling with strong passive conflicts, could only receive psychotherapy because of his traveling work schedule. He was seen intermittently during the next five years. His therapy offered an opportunity to observe his sequential object relationships with Estelle, Esther, and Emily (see Figure 21–2). Each woman came to see me *at his request.* They were all of the same type: young, beautiful, and with the same complaint—constant quarreling because of his repeated questioning about their supposed unfaithfulness, which they denied as absurd. To my surprise, he came to see me with Mrs. White, now a divorcee. Her complaints were the same as those of her predecessors. In spite of my negative advice, they were married one month later and periodically consulted me because of their quarreling.

THE WHITES

Mrs. White (now Mrs. Black) had originally consulted me when her husband (fifteen years older than she) refused to cooperate in her request for a divorce. His reaction to her request consisted of threats of homicide and suicide. Mrs. White, an attractive twenty-

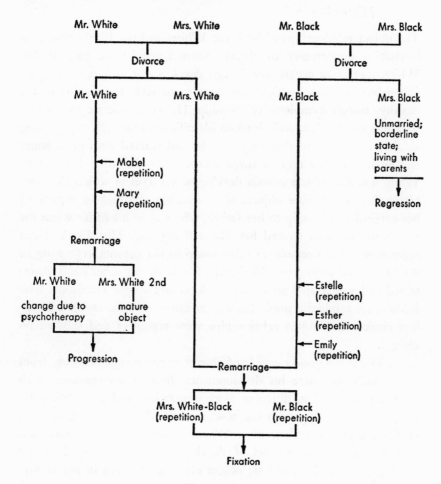

FIGURE 21–2

year-old woman, complained of her husband's indifference to her sexual needs. Their courtship had been stormy because of his periodic drinking and incessant questioning about her dating other men, which she strongly denied. Mr. White readily entered classical psychoanalysis. During his second year in therapy, he was twice involved with women who were the exact replica of his previous wife (Mabel and Mary; see Figure 21-2)—attractive, immature, dependent, clinging, and adolescent. Shortly before the conclusion of his analysis, he began to relate to a mature woman, whom he later married (see Figure 21-2).

Discussion

The object relationships of both the Whites and the Blacks afford an interesting opportunity to observe remarriages. In the case of Mr. White, there was *progression* in ego development as a result of psychoanalytic therapy, which enabled him to seek and finally find a healthy, mature symbiotic relationship. His symbiotic tie to his first wife was a narcissistic and vicarious identification (as well as providing an alter phallus), and thus originally he had reacted with great anger and anxiety to her request for a divorce. On the other hand, Mrs. White was *fixated* at a certain developmental level in which the symbiotic ties to her male objects were strongly anaclitic—a replica of her original relationship to her father, who was in his fifties when she was born and who treated her like a living doll. Mrs. Black shows *regression* in her later object relationship to her parents, regressing to the early child-mother symbiosis. Mr. Black, on the other hand, maintained and was fixated at the phallic level and sought symbionts who fulfilled his symbiotic needs (as well as other neurotic ones). His object choices and object relationships were repetitive and showed no change.

Mr. White is a good example of change in remarriage resulting from psychoanalysis, where his developmental fixation was undone, with further individuation, differentiation, integration, and progressive development occurring with the working out of his infantile neurosis in the analytic situation. Mrs. White, rejecting therapy, remained fixated at a dependent level of development and continued in her anaclitic narcissistic symbiotic object choices, and thus in her remarriage to Mr. Black there was no change.

NOTES

1. Reuben Hill, "Methodological Issues in Family Development Research," *Family Process*, III (1964), 186–206; and Marian R. Yarrow, J. D. Campbell, and R. V. Burton, "Reliability of Maternal Retrospection: A Preliminary Report," *Family Process*, III (1964), 207–218.
2. Jessie Bernard, *Remarriage: A Study of Marriage* (New York: Dryden Press, 1956).
3. P. H. Landis, "Sequential Marriage," *Journal of Home Economics*, XLII (1950), 625–627.
4. Bernard L. Greene, "Marital Disharmony: Concurrent Analysis of Husband and Wife. I. Preliminary Report," *Diseases of the Nervous System*, XXI (1960), 1–6; and Alfred P. Solomon and B. L. Greene, "Marital Disharmony: Concurrent Therapy of Husband and Wife by the Same Psychiatrist. III. An Analysis of the Therapeutic Elements and Action," *Diseases of the Nervous System*, XXIV (1963), 1–8.
5. Bernard L. Greene, Betty P. Broadhurst, and Noel Lustig, "Treatment of Marital Disharmony: The Use of Individual, Concurrent, and Conjoint Sessions as a 'Combined Approach,'" in Bernard L. Greene, ed., *The Psychotherapies of Marital Disharmony* (New York: Free Press, 1965), p. 136.
6. Eric Berne, *The Structure and Dynamics of Organizations and Groups* (Philadelphia: J. B. Lippincott Co., 1963); and *Games People Play* (New York: Grove Press, 1964), pp. 92–109.
7. Norman W. Bell, "Extended Family Relations of Disturbed and Well Families," *Family Process*, I (1962), 175–193.
8. *Op. cit.*
9. Norman W. Bell and Ezra F. Vogel, eds., *A Modern Introduction to the Family* (New York: Free Press, 1960).
10. Sigmund Freud, "On Narcissism: An Introduction" (1914), in *Collected Papers* (New York: Basic Books, 1959), Vol. IV; Anna Freud, "Psychoanalysis and Education," in *Psychoanalytic Study of the Child*, IX (1954), 9–15; Anna Freud, Introduction to Katya Levy's "Simultaneous Analysis of a Mother and Her Adolescent Daughter," in *Psychoanalytic Study of the Child*, XV (1960), 378–380; Therese Benedek, "The Psychosomatic Implications of the Primary Unit: Mother-Child," *American Journal of Orthopsychiatry*, XIX (1949), 642–649; George H. Pollock, "On Symbiosis and Symbiotic Neurosis," *International Journal of Psychoanalysis*, XLV (1964), 1–30; H. V. Dicks, see note 12 in Solomon and Greene, *op. cit.*; and Peter L. Giovacchini, "Treatment of Marital Disharmonies: The Classical Approach," in Greene, ed., *op. cit.*, 39–82.
11. George H. Pollock, "Transference Neurosis: Object Choice and Object Relationships: The Dyad and Triad," *Archives of General Psychistry*, Vol. VI (1962).

12. Pollock, "On Symbiosis and Symbiotic Neurosis."
13. Benedek, *op. cit.*
14. Pollock, "On Symbiosis and Symbiotic Neurosis."
15. Pollock, "Transference Neurosis."
16. Bela Mittelmann, "Complementary Neurotic Reactions in Intimate Relationships," *Psychoanalytic Quarterly*, XIII (1944), 479–491.
17. Peter L. Giovacchini, "Mutual Adaptation in Various Object Relationships," *International Journal of Psychoanalysis*, XXXIX (1958), 1–8.
18. *Ibid.*
19. Thomas P. Monahan, "How Stable Are Remarriages?" *American Journal of Sociology*, LVIII (1952), 280–288.
20. Landis, *op. cit.*
21. Bernard, *op. cit.*, p. 50.
22. *Ibid.*, pp. 112–113.
23. W. J. Goode, *After Divorce* (Glencoe, Ill.: Free Press, 1956); Harvey J. Locke: *Predicting Adjustment in Marriage* (New York: Holt, 1951), p. 302; Harvey J. Locke and W. J. Klausner, "Marital Adjustment of Divorced Persons in Subsequent Marriages," *Sociology and Social Research*, XXXIII (1948), 97–101; and L. M. Terman *et al., Psychological Factors in Marital Happiness* (New York: McGraw-Hill Book Co., 1938), p. 418.
24. Bernard, *op. cit.*, pp. 112–113.
25. Paul Popenoe, "Remarriage of Divorcees to Each Other," *American Sociological Review*, III (1938), 695–699.
26. Thomas P. Monahan, "The Changing Nature and Instability of Remarriages," *Eugenics Quarterly*, V (1958), 73–85.
27. Edmund Bergler, *Divorce Won't Help* (New York: Harper & Row, 1949), pp. 233–234.
28. Giovacchini, "Treatment of Marital Disharmonies."
29. Paul C. Glick, "First Marriages and Remarriages," *American Sociological Review*, XIV (1949), 727.

Marriage Terminable
and Interminable

The very words "marriage terminable and interminable" seem to suggest a question that is rarely posed as such in the mass communication media. But changes in the relationships between generations and in the sexual mores of the time make it timely to bring up for consideration. The question is: Has marriage as a foundation stone in the edifice of Western culture outlived its value? This question, once posed in this challenging manner, immediately suggests two subsidiary questions: First, if marriage is found to be based on anachronistic and unrealistic assumptions, what conventional substitutes might be considered as replacements? And, second, if it is to be considered a necessary foundation stone whose removal would lead to collapse of the social structure on which our culture depends for its equilibrium and survival, what, if any, are the symptoms that seem to threaten its continued health, and if such are found to exist, what are the causes of the disorder and what remedies might be considered worthy of application?

"Marriage terminable and interminable" is a phrase full of ambiguities and possible interpretations. Does it imply, for example, that there is such a thing as a marriage that is interminable? Obviously marriage is inevitably terminable in a realistic sense, no matter what the magical expectations to the contrary may have been. Death is the final dictator in such matters. His edict may leave a sense of bereavement, grief, and hopeless depression or, on the contrary, may bring welcome relief from what has been for years an intolerable servitude. Such, however, is the categorical imperative of human nature to seek survival at almost any cost that though the coming of death leaves the survivor with a confused medley of emotions, their balance being determined by the complexities of the relationship experienced during the lifetime of the marriage, the survivor eventually has to make some sort of peace with the situation. If we exclude death from our present concern, are marriages interminable in another sense? Legally, they are terminable in most jurisdictions, subject to the legal provisions for terminating the social contract. Spiritually, they may be interminable if a person holds to the credo of a religious faith, even though there is a *de facto* termination in terms of physical absence, cessation of marital intimacies, or legal separation. Psychologically, they may also be partially interminable, even though they have been physically terminated by the death of the partner, or legally dissolved, or though separation has reluctantly been agreed upon as the best method of avoiding intolerable tensions and conflicts of interest. Ambivalent feelings in such cases often lead to regrettable delays in effecting a resolution (painful though it may be) even when no economic threat is posed and no religious loyalties are involved.

It is with problems in this area that the psychoanalyst is most often called upon for help by one or both partners in a marriage. The "tie that binds" in marriages that fulfill or come near to fulfilling the expectations of both partners is the shared capacity to achieve ever sharpening sensitivity to the needs and feelings of the partner, combined with a freely felt and commanding impulse to respond in whatever manner such empathy requires. Such immediacy of perception and response does not, however, imply the loss of the self in the process, but rather its enrichment, signalizing the attainment of sufficient maturity to subordinate conflicting impulses to the achievement of a genuinely loving relationship with the partner. Marriages in which such a desirable mutuality has been reached reflect a progressive resolution in both partners of the original narcissistic requirements of the infant for the prompt recognition of every need and for its immediate satisfaction.

Failure of marriage partners to fulfill each other's original, somewhat magical expectations may set in motion other forces in the motivational system. If one partner fails to recognize or to respond to some need which has high emotional investment, the other feels hurt, angry, or frightened, or some combination of these. The emergency responses to feeling that the walls of the castle of security are cracking come into play. And then there is a quarrel. Already a new pattern of mutual response has made its appearance. Reconciliation follows and is celebrated by passionate reunion. The structure of security has been repaired, but quite possibly the essential weakness in the masonry remains.

If this type of stimulus-response becomes frequent, it becomes usual for one partner to feel put upon and the other not understood. Self-protective feelings become mobilized on both sides. In such circumstances, one of several patterns of maladaptive responses can come to characterize the relationship. One partner may become the aggressor—the one who complains, criticizes, blames, denigrates; and the other, the victim, the one who suffers unjustly, is not understood, is depressed, feels inadequate. There are marriages in which this becomes the chief idiom in the relationship, the so-called sadomasochistic compromise. For the "victim" and the "aggressor" alike, the failure to achieve the original magical expectations has left the field open for the appearance of self-protective emotions, and with their appearance, the damming up of the free exchange of affection. The need to reconstruct a more mutually pleasurable relationship, to repair the damage and strengthen the original structure, may, however, be sufficiently strong to bring one or the other or both to therapy.

Sometimes in the personalities of both partners there is a sufficient balance between aggressiveness and passivity in their approach to each other to lead to an alternation of roles: at one time the husband becomes the aggressor and the wife the victim; then after a quarrel and recriminations, the aggressor feels guilty and becomes the victim. A sort of obsessional stalemate is achieved. Neither has quite given up the wish to restore peace, yet both reserve the right to disrupt it whenever their specially required gratifications are denied. With this sort of compromise, couples frequently cannot separate, yet continue to berate or be berated. It becomes a kind of contest that has replaced for them both the values of a more peaceful exchange which their individual narcissistic requirements made impossible.

One such couple could not agree whether to spend their vacation in Europe or in South America—both wanted to visit both continents. They came to me complaining how bitterly they quarreled every year on the same question—where to go for his month's vacation. She liked to shop for clothes; he liked to play golf. They thought that perhaps their tastes were so different that maybe they had better separate. I refused to referee, of course, and soon realized that they were not seriously considering separation, or the therapy which I had suggested they might try. Some years later a friend reported to me that at a party at which they had both been guests, the husband had said: "You can tell your friend that even though he told us we had better separate, we are still together and glad of it!"

Terminable marriages, by contrast, are those marriages whose dissolution is made possible by legal means, where there is no spiritual reservation based on sacramental convictions or moral scruples, and where in the view of one or both partners the balance between pleasure and pain in their interpersonal exchanges of emotion has become so negatively freighted that one or both are now convinced that the point of no return has been reached.

In this rapidly changing, multicolored kaleidoscope of values to which the adolescent generations have been exposed during the past half century, it would indeed be preposterous to suppose that no changes would have occurred in the prevalent attitudes toward sex and marriage. Those of us who began life in the Victorian era have seen such vast changes in these phases of human experience that it is now hard to remember just how or why one felt and thought as one did during those innocent and romantic years. For the more fortunate among us, the idea of a family breakup other than by death was not even considered a possibility. There were rogues and vampires, of course, but they made their descent upon the families of innocent and loving people in some far-off community, mostly in the big cities. There was no thought of preparing children for the responsibilities of marriage. The sexes were kept separate for the most part after adolescence, except under the watchful eye of the girl's parents, and when two young people fell victim to Cupid's arrows, a simple kiss sealed the bargain, and next day the gentle swain presented himself before the young lady's father to ask for her hand in marriage.

It is not to be supposed that human beings in those days were any more virtuous than they are today. There was more hypocrisy, more intrigue, and numberless instances of loveless marriages. But the moral standards of the time, bolstered by the still considerable influence of the teachings of religion, provided safeguards against the sudden and impulsive rupture of the marital contract, and so favored the predominance of marriages that held together to the end, bitter though the struggle may have been.

Shaw's delightful satire on the sacred ties of marriage, *Man and Superman*, tells us that already there were underground rumblings in the British Empire at the time suggesting the inevitability of change in the conventional and hypocritical adherence to the rigid pretensions of men and women of fashion to virtues which they rarely exhibited except in the form of outwardly correct behavior. These attitudes did not permeate the entire fabric of society, however. Among the simpler folk of the middle classes—the bourgeoisie—and still more perhaps among the manual laborers, that a marriage might be dissolved was unthinkable. The relative number of successful, stable, mutually satisfactory marriages was probably not very different from what it is today. If there were a difference, it would probably be in favor of the Victorian or Edwardian partnership.

Just as the belief in romantic love and the patterns of religious and moralistic conformity characteristic of the Western world during the nineteenth century is for most of us associated with the name of Queen Victoria, so the break for freedom from hypocritical restraints was exemplified in the life and manners of her rebellious son and successor, Edward VII. The Edwardian era in England is known for the magnificent style in which the wealthy lived, for the last great displays of the glories of empire. In the United States, it saw the emergence of the great entrepreneurs: Carnegie, Morgan, Rockefeller, Harriman, Ford. We were still aping the social graces, the cultural mores, the educational methods of our British cousins. We still clung to the ideal of marriage that meant living happily ever after.

Bernard Shaw, who, I suspect, deliberately cultivated in his countenance that expression of ironical self-satisfaction which he attributes in his satire to the Devil, has much to say that bears on our task of evaluating the institution of marriage. Here are some comments on man's assumptions: "The Life Force respects marriage only because marriage is a contrivance of its own to secure the greatest number of children and the closest care of them." ". . . The confusion of marriage with morality has done more to destroy the conscience of the human race than any other single error." It is not that Shaw wishes to see the institution of marriage abolished, but rather he seeks to disabuse those who expect it to settle all men's wants and desires. Shaw's central thesis, of course, is that woman lures man to her purpose of propagation by arousing his desire, and that man has no choice but to accept the authority of the "Life Force." He implies further that man would really like to avoid the manifold ties and responsibilities which accrue to his position as father and head of the household.

Since Edward VII extended his numerous individual "ententes cordiales" to the international scene, thus laying the foundation for the Grand Alliance of the Western powers, Western civilization has been shaken to its foundations by the shattering of its moralistic pretensions through the revelations of psychoanalysis and the social upheavals occasioned by world wars and political revolutions. While the call to arms was the signal for a rash of impulsive marriages, the separations that followed, which in many instances went on to enforced absences of several years, led all too often to the abandonment of what fundamentally was a contract entered into under duress. Moreover, many marriages were dissolved by divorce when one or both partners came to realize that their ties of affection were not eternally binding and had found new anchorage. Divorce began to be an increasingly welcome solution to the ensuing conflicts.

Dr. Paul H. Jacobson,[1] in his exhaustive study of the history of marriage and divorce in the United States, quotes some interesting figures. Between 1922 and 1946 the rate of divorces per 1,000 existing marriages grew on an ascending scale from 6.6 in 1922 to 18.2 in 1946. Thereafter, there was a slow decline down to 9.3 in 1955. The most striking curve of frequency was that between 1943 (10.9) and 1949 (10.6), the greatest number of divorces occurring in the two years directly following the end of World War II. Another interesting curve of diminishing frequency in percentages of divorce is that relating to the number of years of marriage at the time the divorce was obtained. For 1946, the year of maximum frequency of total divorces, the figures were as follows:

0–4 years	35.5 (per thousand)
5–9	27.6
10–14	19.4
15–19	12.2
20–24	8.7
25–29	5.7
30–34	3.7
35–39	2.4

The remarkable increase in the birth rate following the end of World War II might be taken as an argument in favor of Shaw's contention. There has been such a manifest revolution in the attitude of young people to the free enjoyment of sexual impulses that it has become unnecessary to sacrifice the freedom of bachelorhood in order to enjoy the privilege of sharing sexual pleasure with an attractive companion of the opposite sex. In most cases, however, sooner or later these so-called "affairs," or, in a few instances, the more solid alliances known as common-law marriages, tend to be abandoned in favor either of a breakup or of matrimony.

In our culture we are still marriage-bound in our preferences. The questions we should ask ourselves, then, are: Is this continuing preference derived from tradition and maintained through fear of partial ostracism from society or of the tyranny of a punitive conscience? *Or* is the requirement for self-reproduction and for taking one's turn as parent instead of child the ultimate concern? In other words, are all previous adventures in sexual intimacy secretly regarded as preludes to a more mature close personal relationship in which full responsibility for the welfare of others is desired instead of the free and independent exercise of the capacity for sexual pleasure-finding? Are there any sure signs on which to base a forecast of the probable success or failure of this new undertaking? And if the answer is no, what seem to be the usual causes for broken marriages? What signs had been perceived, and by whom, when the decision to marry was hanging in the balance? Or what signs had been made under what seemingly was a sudden eruption in two breasts of the great Life Force?

The curious thing about the institution of marriage is that it embraces so many different patterns of mating that it takes a long article in any adequate encyclopedia to describe the various customs connected with it, the requirements of the participants, their respective duties and privileges after they have been joined together, and the legal rights conferred on them under the statutes or customs qualifying the union as valid. In ancient Turkey and in other Moslem countries, polygamy and the harem were the custom, and in China old farmers would frequently add an extra wife to their families. In the Hopi villages, the wife is the arbiter. If she is fed up with her husband's laziness or his unreliability, or something else, all she has to do is to put his shoes outside the door when he leaves for work in the morning. In many Latin American countries, the husband is the boss and the wife is expected to behave just as he says. In India, a little girl of twelve is considered ready for marriage and may be given in wedlock to a man of mature years. In France and Japan until recently, many marriages were arranged with little advance notice to the young people. Not all these customs seem palatable to us, preferring as we do the liberty to choose and take our own chances. There is one feature, however, that is common to all these customs: the union is arranged with a view to procreation. Viewed in this wider horizon, then, marriage as an institution seems to be a seasoned experiment in all societies, its variations in structure dependent on the customs and laws of the individual society.

It would seem that Shaw's views are not without evidence to support them. He also ventures the prophecy that couples will find a means to escape the trap set by the Life Force and the marriages that it engineers. Don Juan speaks: ". . . The day is coming when great nations will find their numbers dwindling from census to census; when the six roomed villa will rise in price above the family mansion; when the viciously reckless poor and the stupidly pious rich will delay the extinction of the race only by degrading it; whilst the boldly prudent, the thriftily selfish and ambitious, the imaginative and poetic, the lovers of money and solid comfort, the worshippers of success, of art, and of love, will all oppose to the Force of Life the device of sterility." Here Shaw seems to anticipate the population explosion, the increasing enslavement of married couples to their responsibilities, and the wide development and use of contraceptive devices.

Marriage as an institution in our society is here to stay, then, for it represents the surest way to promote the propagation of the race and the proper care of the young. Let us take a quick look, however, at other possibilities and consider what modifications of the customary plan have been considered or are in use. In the thirties, Judge Leonard of Cleveland made the headlines by proposing a system of companionate marriage that would permit couples to cohabit, postponing the goal of procreation, until such time as they were quite convinced that they were sufficiently attached to be formally married. This practice seems to have been wholeheartedly adopted by the new generation of adolescents, who often do not stop to wait for legal approval or the consent of their elders. These arrangements, however, are for the most part short-lived. Occasionally an unexpected pregnancy complicates matters, and the couple has to decide whether to seek an abortion—usually illegal—or get married.

Contraceptive devices have made possible these informal arrangements, thus validating once more Shaw's prophecy that man would find a way to dodge the unpleasant and seek the pleasurable. While we may by now be free of any tendency to moralize over such unconventional approaches to intimate living, we cannot but be appalled by the casual attitude youngsters so often seem to have to the possibility of an unwanted pregnancy and the dangers, both physical and psychological, presented by the inevitable search for a "reliable" abortionist. It remains for researchers to work out the significance of such experiences in the later lives of these youngsters. There seems to be a tendency too on the part of girls to assume responsibility for all the arrangements and not to expect the boy to shoulder any of the burden. From the number of such instances which I have seen, I am inclined to look on them as complicating rather than facilitating later adjustments to marriage and motherhood.

This more casual attitude to the biological demands of the Life Force has also influenced married couples. The mystical halo formerly assigned to the sexual relationship is now completely ignored, and if a sudden mutual attraction is experienced between opposite numbers, whether neighbors, acquaintances, or friends, there is apt to be less restraint on the free exercise of the right to sexual enjoyment than when reverence for the sacraments of religion and the sanctity of the marriage bond was more sincere and widespread.

Since the statistics indicate an increasing readiness to terminate marriages by divorce, we cannot escape the conclusion that marriage as a social institution in our culture is not fulfilling its allotted purposes with the success expected of it. It behooves us, therefore, as specialists in the understanding of the forces that motivate human behavior and of the disorders that result when these forces are not kept within the bounds of reasonable control and directed toward aims consonant with the needs of the individual and the demands of society, to scrutinize the symptoms that characterize marital breakdowns, to trace them to their possible origins, and to make use of the lessons gained thereby to postulate theories for reparative action aimed at improving the chances for satisfactory marriage and at reversing the curve of frequency of divorces.

First, then, can we begin to classify the symptoms of marital disorders in a readily available and clinically verifiable handbook for reference purposes? As psychoanalysts, our natural tendency would be to look to the authorities in our own field for a dynamic outline that would have ready clinical applicability. As I begin a review of my experience in practice, with special reference to the role of conscience as an aid to a successful adaptation in our culture, I have selected a number of marriages in which one or both partners consulted me and I have listed the symptoms of their maladaptive patterns according to the level of motivational organization whose dynamic influence seemed to have left a disturbing imprint on the course of their development. In psychoanalytic terms we would speak of this excessive influence as a partial fixation at one level or another.

Let us begin then with the (narcissistic requirements) of the infant and developing child as we see them reflected in the behavior of so many adults. What can we trace to this earliest of all sources of emotional investment? We have the spoiled darling who expects always to have his way. We have also the child whose narcissistic requirements were not adequately recognized or sufficiently gratified at the proper time. Such a person lacks the ability to feel sure of his proper expectation. He may develop into a tiresome self-apologetic creature or into an expert in making half-apologetic demands. We see the purest culture of unresolved narcissism in the gifted artist whose vision of the world is exclusively dependent on the images that his imagination creates. For him the impulse is the whole thing. Hence the childlike quality which endears the artist to women but which creates for a wife a very special sort of problem. And then there is the boy who is seized for the first time with the commanding excitement of a sexual infatuation and whose need to satisfy his own wishes is his only law of being, so he sweeps a young and immature bride into marriage. The usual aftermath is familiar to us all.

Next come the stages of (oral dependency) and (oral aggression.) With the studies of René Spitz, John Bowlby, and David Levy, so much has been learned of the importance of the way in which the child is handled during these critical stages in his development that it does not surprise us to find in so many marriages today an overwhelming dependency need providing the principal impulse for marriage. Such an impulse is all too often the source of competitive drives for attention and consideration and of the keenest disappointments, to the point where eventual disillusionment is inevitable. Often such derivatives of (unresolved dependency ties as depressive reactions, problem drinking, gambling, and extravagance become the symptoms that lead to dissolution of the marriage. It is easy, of course, to recognize, in the nagging wife and the hypercritical husband, the survival of unresolved problems going back to the oral aggressive period.

When we consider the phases of (anal pleasure)and (anal retention,) it is not difficult to see the difference between people who have worked satisfactorily through this stage of development, and have retained such benefits as pleasure in productivity and reasonable prudence in the handling and use of money, and those who exhibit acute anxiety over spending and are stingy with their wives and children, or who show such inconsistency due to conflict that neither wife nor children ever know whether daddy has a hidden treasure or is on the verge of bankruptcy.

During the period of genital primacy, the child becomes aware of his sexual being and sexual differences and of a variety of feelings toward his two parents. He enters the so-called Oedipal period, with its many possible complications. It is during this time that the foundation stones are laid for the eventual structure of object relationships. To the way children are handled during these years can be largely ascribed the later attitudes of the adult to persons of both sexes, whether the relationship involves problems of authority and conflict with those who exercise it, or is a peer relationship, or one in which sexual interest and gratification play the principal part.

It is now rather generally believed that most marriages come to grief on the rocks of sexual disappointment. Certainly this lies at the root of a great many divorces. It is, however, true that many marriages begin with what both partners regard in retrospect as a very satisfactory experience sexually and that the reasons for the divorce could then not be attributed to any difficulty there. Infidelity can of course signify many different things. It may be a natural outcome of abnormal absences such as are occasioned by war: it may be due to a man's continuing need to prove himself attractive to women. His narcissism is so insecurely attached to his image of himself as a competent male that the temptation is too great for him to forego. The shadow of a passive dependence resembling a compulsive hunger for acceptance may be behind his erotic adventures. Infidelity may also be an impulsive gesture of defiance or rage when relations between the partners have become murky. Above all, however, and on their most basic level, such wanderings from marital fidelity, except under abnormally trying circumstances, are evidence of an incomplete identification of the person with his or her sexual role, so that a lingering sense of inadequacy persists, interfering with the ability to keep the requirements for sexual satisfaction within bounds and to recognize them as part of a total strategy of motivational control rather than as the one primary aim in marriage.

Many marriages exist which are fully satisfactory to both partners although the husband is no great lover or the wife is inorgastic. There are also many enduring marriages in which one or both partners have not been strictly faithful in terms of sexual behavior. This is much more common in France than in the United States, where the tradition of suppression of wayward sexual impulses creates more of a conflict than in a culture in which sexuality is looked upon as a natural source of pleasure and is not too closely bound in the concept of absolute fidelity as the inviolable and only certain proof of love and respect between married partners.

The long struggle many marriage partners go through before finally deciding to separate is often endured for what is felt to be the best interests of the children. Exposure to chronic parental unhappiness punctuated by bitter quarrels or even by physical assault, however, is harmful to the development of a child's emotional health. Adolescent children seldom will beg their parents to separate; it is a more usual pattern for them to suffer in silence and take out their unhappiness in troubled relationships with teachers and their peers, or in the form of resistance to educational progress.

Economic factors and social status also play a part in determining married partners to stay together or seek divorce. As in many other aspects of our society, the economically underprivileged and socially depressed do not have the opportunity for obtaining divorces that is so easily found by members of the wealthy and middle classes. The legal expenses of divorce are considerable; and there is the added costs of travel to a state where short-term residence is required for the termination of a marriage contract. The economically less privileged have had recourse to desertion, entering into common-law relationships with other partners, or maintaining the formality of marriage while engaging in extramarital sexual relationships. On a radio program I happened to be listening to,[2] a lawyer who has made a specialty of marriage problems said that at one time in South Carolina there were more illegitimate babies than babies born to married couples. In New York State, where until recently adultery was the sole legally recognized cause for divorce, collusion in staging a faked episode of infidelity with hired assistance was frequently used to get around a law that no longer served a useful purpose. The increase in divorces on the national level and the general prevalence of various devices for evading the existing statutes are at last awakening the community not only to the need for revision of the laws pertaining to marriage and divorce, but to the equally serious problem of providing the adolescent with the sort of preparation for sexual experience and marriage which will serve to decrease disastrous premarital adventures and to make young people more fit and ready to undertake the very special responsibilities inherent in marriage.

Art Buchwald, the humorist, who comments in the country's newspapers on the current oddities in human attitudes and behavior, recently warned us that teenagers are themselves beginning to fill the gaps in preparation for marriage which their procrastinating parents have allowed to come into existence. He quoted a study by Lester Rand, of the Youth Research Institute of New York, which reveals that teenage boys are turning over their allowances and earnings to their "steadies," who have convinced them that they can manage the money better, in some instances even setting up joint bank accounts. The girls put their boyfriends on budgets, dictate their taste in clothes and haircuts, and even tell them what time they should put their lights out at night. The future looks bleak indeed unless parents are prepared to go into action. But what action?

Let me summarize here what seem to me the bare minimum of appropriate measures to supplement what the community presently has to offer.

1. Divorce laws need to be completely overhauled and brought up to date, so that they will be available to all segments of society, and adapted to the present imperatives of our culture.

2. Efforts should be made to develop interstate committees of top-level jurists to discuss approaches to consensus on uniform legislation for all states.

3. Education in the physiology and psychology pertaining to the sexual impulse and its expression in behavior should be a requirement in all schools, the basic minimum of the material presented to be approved by a committee of clergy, educators, psychiatrists, psychologists, jurists, and general practitioners in every community. The nominations to membership on these committees should be made by the appropriate professional societies in consultation with the local mental health authority, if such exists.

4. When the national plan for the establishment of regional mental health centers has been put in operation, one of the functions of these centers should be the establishment of seminars for parents: one for those who have children below school age, and one for those with children approaching adolescence.

5. All children entering school should be prepared for the experience not only by physical examination and the administration of various preventive inoculations but by a simple psychological screening,

possibly one conducted on a group basis, to determine any outstanding deviations from the norm. Parents would be interviewed by the principal after the results of the total health evaluation were tabulated, so that appropriate recommendations could be made. The parents would be held responsible for carrying out such recommendations.

6. In cases where the pupil's performance was found to deviate to a significant extent from what his evaluation seemed to warrant, in spite of efforts of the school personnel to help in its correction, the parents should be notified and a conference planned in which the situation could be explored with the school officials most immediately concerned with the child's progress. In the event that such a conference and the steps determined upon failed to provide a solution, the child would then be referred for more specialized evaluation to the proper medical or mental health agency.

I have outlined these proposals because they seem to me a step toward the solution of our present dilemma. The effort to bring marriage as an institution into a more effective medium for insuring the development of healthy and happy individuals is now going to be the responsibility and principal challenge of the adolescent generation. As things stand, the relationship between generations has reached a new low with the emergence of an angry, bewildered, and insecure generation of young adults. Juvenile delinquency, narcotic addiction, adolescent pregnancies, premature sexual adventures, reckless driving, alcoholic excesses, school dropouts—these and other less obvious signs of youth's discontent with life as they find it give little reason to hope that marriages between such individuals will prove stable or bode well for marriage as an institution. Our best chances lie in attempting to influence future parents in the direction of greater adequacy and lessened impatience, and in more thorough programs of preventive education, so that we may yet rescue matrimony from a declining reputation and restore it to its position as the most favored path to follow in man's search for self-fulfillment.

NOTES

1. Paul H. Jacobson, *American Marriage and Divorce* (New York: Rinehart & Co., 1959), p. 93.
2. Station WMCA, Barry Gray program, January 2, 1965.

Psychoanalysis and Divorce

One legal scholar describes divorce as ". . . a means of dissolving a valid marriage because of serious matrimonial fault or offense after the marriage took place."[1] Some psychoanalysts view divorce as one of the possible signs of successful psychotherapy which led to a more mature arrangement,[2] while others see it as still another more or less inept effort to resolve an interpersonal problem between a marital couple.[3] The last view seems the most valid to me: rather than serving as an end point, divorce is the rearrangement of forces in an ongoing struggle, especially in families where there are children.[4]

Most appellate court decisions regarding divorce cases strike one as being terribly remote from the issues being resolved in the trials. There is forceful demonstration that the real issues in contention by the parties lie obscured beneath the legal rubrics being debated. A psychologically attuned reader yearns for more information about the marriage in order to understand what is really happening. In short, it is like an elaborate mating dance of the swans: it's important—but it is only a necessary preliminary ritual. If the law is ever to resolve marital difficulties rationally, its processes must move toward making visible the significant tensions between litigating parties. Neither effective nor wise legal policies may be developed so long as crucial factors in problem matrices are kept obscure through manipulation of legal labels.[5] Such manipulation will "settle" (perhaps) a given case,[6] but it propagates and perpetuates policy confusion by effectively camouflaging factors that must be studied if we are to arrive at sound policy positions. Furthermore, it often lulls parties into the deluded state in which they believe they have resolved their problems through the divorce.

In an effort to explore the contributions and assistance that psychoanalysts might make in regard to the issues of divorce, Ploscowe's definition of divorce will be divided into its significant elements. These will be used to focus the knowledge and skills that psychoanalysts might, and in my opinion should, apply to the problems.

"A divorce, technically, is a means of:

1. *dissolving* a
2. *valid marriage* because of
3. *serious* matrimonial
4. *fault* or
5. *offense*
6. *after* the marriage took place."

Each of these elements may be considered from the standpoint of several psychiatric roles: (1) legislative or judicial consultant; (2) expert witness during trial; or (3) therapeutic assistant or clarifier. These roles will be examined and discussed in the context of what lawyers call *opinion testimony:* they will represent the personal views I have arrived at through clinical psychiatric experience and an extended study of legal problems about marriage and divorce.

Before beginning this exploration, it might be well to make some general comments about the nature of the legal process, so widely misapprehended by nonlawyers. Noncriminal trials always involve efforts to settle and resolve contested issues. They always involve two or more parties whose views of a given event are different, and the court must somehow arrive at a decision that will hopefully conclude the contention. In order to make the legal process work without the necessity of trying every issue in court, the law tends to follow a theory called *stare decisis*. This is the concept according to which prior holdings by judges become "precedent," and new decisions will be rendered in harmony with old precedents. Obviously this is not absolute or we would still be settling issues in the manner of the feudal tribunals of Henry II. The common-law system has, in fact, a delicate means for progressively updating itself in the face of new information. This need for new information is the central reason why contemporary psychoanalytic (or, more accurately, psychodynamic) theory should be brought into juxtaposition with the legal process.

In the whole fabric of the law there is no more tangled or confused area than that of family law. This is, in my opinion, due to the fact that until recently courts had no adequate theoretical concepts around which they could organize ideas about family relationships. Only with the advent of "psychoanalytic theories" has there been any substantial framework that could be utilized to integrate complex legal problems involving family life. For this reason, when we look at the law of divorce, marriage law, and problems of child custody, we see legal doctrines that evolved during medieval times to meet feudal conditions. In fact, some legal procedures derive from the time when divorce was strictly an ecclesiastic procedure.[7] This brought to the fore such notions as marital "fault" and made it a crucial determinant of whether or not a marriage could be disrupted. However, as the crown courts progressively took over settlement of property rights, they developed a second set of procedures akin to contract law.[8] Thus, marriage came to be seen as a contract in which contracting parties enjoyed certain legal rights. Coming up to the present, we see courts expressing another old doctrine in an entirely new garb, whereby they take an interest in the children of a marriage through the doctrine of *parens patraie*.[9] This doctrine sets forth the notion that the state has a right to regulate family life, especially in regard to children, because of its vested interest in their welfare. In medieval times this reflected the concern of feudal lords for maintaining their military strength. Now it mirrors the concern of the state that its citizens grow to maturity in order to make responsible contributions to society as well as to enjoy the benefits of citizenship.

These contending policy views are to be found throughout the area of family law. Since they often reach in opposite directions, judicial opinions may make little sense to a psychologically sensitive observer. Yet they reflect present realities in the law of the family, and, as such, they must be dealt with. With these preliminary comments, let us turn to the questions of divorce.

The Dissolution of the Marriage

When a couple decide to dissolve their marriage through a divorce action, they generally have ideas about the procedure and its results that verge on the fantastic. This is especially true when they have children. The dissident couple approach divorce with the hope of resolving the tensions and problems that have plagued them over an extended period of time. One or both feel that divorce not only will give relief from past difficulties but will provide access to new relationships and experiences that will be the antithesis of the former marital tensions. This may include finding a new mate who will "love" them. It may mean new opportunity that might fulfill prior and grossly distorted notions about what marriage can provide.

When children have been born to a marriage, such a reversal of field is only rarely possible. Because most parents *do* care about their children (though the "caring" may take varied and weird forms), many of the psychological impasses that deadlocked the marriage will persist after the divorce in the form of arguments over child rearing. Decisions still have to be made jointly, and it is virtually impossible to escape from the need to arrive at these joint decisions. Where shall the children go to school? What church should they attend? What clothes should they wear when Dad visits? How should their allowances be handled? With whom shall they play? These and a myriad of other questions continue to press. The parent who has custody of the children usually has to take into account the attitudes of the non-custodial spouse, or battles ensue. Whether or not these battles precipitate legal consequences will be regulated largely by economic factors. Fighting a former spouse through legal counsel takes money.

A lawyer, confronted with a spouse who wants a divorce, should at least raise questions about whether or not it is a bona fide desire. Recently developed theory regarding the interlocking psychology of marriage partners permits one to assume that there are many positive forces in a marriage regardless of the presence of powerful animosity.[10] Adaptive necessity forces the parties to resolve progressively the negative factors in the relationship, and indeed a successful marriage is one in which the inevitable differences are resolved. Mere presence of differences is not evidence of a poor marriage. (Failure to work out the differences is.) For these reasons it is always appropriate for counsel to wonder if the parties really want a divorce.[11] A lawyer may be approached by his client with the underlying and unconscious hope that somehow, through the magic of his role, the lawyer will bring about some restitutive change in the marital balance: perhaps counsel will use the imagined power of the law to bring a reluctant spouse to "understand" or "behave" better and then harmony can be restored or achieved. These and other covert goals may enter the office in company with the divorce-seeking client.

This is a point at which a psychiatrist might be helpful in a potential divorce action. I hasten to add that not *all* psychiatrists will be useful here. Many psychiatrists believe that they cannot and should not intervene in the life-space of their patients because that would interfere with therapeutic goals. Though I do not agree, this view will often inhibit useful intervention by a psychiatrist and blunt any potential influence he might have. If it is available, a dynamically trained psychiatrist's knowledge about human behavior and the distorting potential of a psychic defense system *is* something that can help a client and his lawyer to understand the factors that raise the issue of divorce. Ideally, some of the techniques of family interviewing,[12] or the "conjoint interview,"[13] can be used to broaden the scope of the psychiatrist's observations, increase comprehensions, and effect greater psychological leverage in the consultation. Regardless of the outcome of the marriage, clarification of issues cannot but help the warring spouses. All too often, their mortal struggle may be characterized by its lack of focus. Both parties struggle with issues they cannot define, and thus they cannot bring to bear any rational resolution of the tensions. Illumination of the shadowed areas in the marriage relationship could be the principal contribution that psychoanalytic observation brings to the divorce deliberation.

It is commonly stated by lawyers and judges that psychiatrists are of little help in the legal resolution of marital difficulties.[14] I would have to agree that all too often this is true, but the main reason is failure to communicate rather than failure to perceive the issues. It is regrettable when so much potentially useful information is not brought into the context of such an important social decision. While marriage counselors know many techniques for effective communication, they often lack the kind of psychological sophistication which could make their communications most meaningful. Psychoanalysts could be useful in training the marriage counselors who do so much of the divorce consultation work and will do more in the future. Learning may also take place in the opposite direction. We can learn from marriage counselors that active interpretive intervention can be very useful in situations of marriage stress.[15] There is surely sufficient evidence derived from recent studies of the therapeutic process to make it clear that a psychotherapist can become more involved with patients than was believed possible in the past and still maintain his objectivity and effectiveness. It has been argued by some (myself included) that dynamic intervention in matters such as this will even improve the effectiveness of the therapeutic involvement.[16]

Regardless of the success or failure of the marriage per se, effective psychodynamically-based intervention can at least help the parties to "break clean."[17] As noted above, one of the most debilitating aspects of divorce is the continuation of the battle. If the couple has children, they will often be used as pawns in this battle, and any means that can effectively terminate the blind and symbolic fighting between the former spouses will be all to the good. For this reason, clarification even of a dissolving marriage will be useful.[18]

Many psychiatrists fear involvement with marriages that are breaking up, because they may be drawn into court as partisan witnesses. The adversary process currently used in divorce procedures makes this a very real possibility. However, a search of case law (those cases which went to appeal and thus produced an appellate opinion) revealed few examples of actual psychiatric testimony during trial.

Often, when there was psychiatric testimony, it involved an "insanity defense" (the "grounds" for divorce were caused by mental illness and thus were invalid; see below), such as in *Schuler v. Schuler* [290 S.W.2d 192 (1956)]. Also, the defendant might plead incompetence to defend his action, as in *Box et al. v. Box* [45 So2d. 157. 283 Ala 297]. Psychiatric testimony may be used as evidence in predicting the future course of such factors as homosexuality [*H. v. H.* 175 A2d. 721. 57 N.J. Super 227. (1959)]. Finally, child-custody decisions are the most likely to involve psychiatric testimony. (For an example, see Goldstein and Katz.[19])

Judges who call upon psychiatrists or marriage counselors in an attempt to handle these difficult cases generally recognize the necessity for the counselor to be covered by what the law calls *privileged communication*.[20] In most states where statutes establish marriage counseling in domestic-relations courts, the counselors are covered by privileged communication. This means that the counselors may not be drawn into court without permission of the parties. While there are some technical problems in relation to the issue of privileged communications, they will not be discussed at length here.[21] It is sufficient to note that a therapist should make his position very clear to the marital couple if there is any possibility that an effort will be made to cause his involuntary participation in divorce litigation. I have made it a practice to tell couples that under no circumstances would I be willing to discuss their case in the adversary context of a divorce proceeding. Though in my own jurisdiction (Michigan), this treatment is covered by a privileged-communication statute, the technical nature of such a statute would permit both parties to waive their privilege and a doctor could then be subpoenaed to testify. More often than not, if the treating psychiatrist describes to the warring spouses the information that would be revealed in testimony, they are not eager to force the doctor into court. The logic of the adversary-trial process makes this procedure work most of the time. In the last analysis, however, if both parties wish to waive their privilege, the therapist would be forced to make an ethical decision. If he refused to testify on grounds that it would disturb his therapeutic relationship to the patients, he might be cited for contempt of court. Although there is no support in law, many judges would be sufficiently aware of the reasons for the doctor's decision to forego contempt proceedings.[22]

Occasionally, information that is adverse to a therapist's patient will come into an adversary-divorce proceeding. The therapist will experience frustration in such a situation, knowing that he possesses data that would clearly rebut the negative impact of such information. However, consideration of his therapeutic goals with the patient or the couple will make it necessary for him to stay out of the procedure. Here the psychiatrist engages in the same logical balancing that lawyers do when they weigh competing strategies of procedure and arrive at a choice. The over-all needs and considerations of treatment necessitate such occasional frustration and perhaps even some injustice. The doctor must simply, and perhaps painfully, make the decision that his continuing usefulness as a therapist to the party has far more importance than his occasional value as an expert witness. This line of reasoning must be made clear to the parties involved before the therapeutic process has gone very far. In this way, there will be no question about the therapist's intentions or his reasons for not participating in the litigation per se.

On some occasions the psychiatrist may be involved in a purely diagnostic capacity. Here values run in a different direction and participation in the divorce proceeding may take place without conflict. In this instance, the psychiatrist would function solely as expert diagnostician and expert witness for the court or one of the parties. This situation is most likely to occur when disposition of children arises as an issue. Even in this role, however, the psychiatrist must clarify his relationship to the couple so that he will not compromise any imagined relationship of professional confidence. When a report is to be rendered, it is a good idea to discuss its content in advance, so that no unnecessary anxiety will be caused in the persons described. This gives the couple an opportunity to prepare themselves for the inevitable stress created when certain information is revealed.

Marriage Validity: The Rationality of the Contract

In our society a decision to marry is generally evolved by the potential partners in the context of a free choice of mates and on the basis of "romantic" love. Such "contracting" is not only carried out in full flush of a traditionally poetic atmosphere, but it brings with it a multitude of illusions about the nature of the married state.[23]

Historically, marriage contracts were relatively unbreakable because of their ecclesiastical nature.[24] The principal way such a contract could be terminated was through a finding of some initial fault in the contract. For example, one of the partners might be in an unmarriageable condition, such as when there was a prior and still existing "valid" marriage. Similarly, a woman might be incapable of having children, and this broke an implied condition of contract. These defects would be viewed as breaches of contract, and the marriage would be declared null in the ecclesiastic court. This procedure provided a technique for disrupting the otherwise undissolvable marriage.

Since stringent divorce laws still exist in many states, couples must often resort to annulment as the means of terminating a marriage.[25] Though annulment provides a means for ending an unsatisfactory relationship, it is often grounded on specious presumptions. In light of contemporary theory about interpersonal communication between marriage partners, it is most unlikely that there will be many bona fide "contract frauds" in marriage. Though one or the other partner may find it psychologically desirable to be "defrauded," at some level of awareness they "knew" what they were getting into. Continuing to employ these archaic procedures to resolve marriage problems can only result in a progressive discrediting of law by the public. This is a point at which psychoanalytic theory could help bring about changes in legal procedures so they would reflect more accurately what people know and believe. If we do not wish to permit divorce, we should say so.[26]

As psychiatrists well know, people embark upon marriage for many reasons. These may include psychological escape from family, from group pressures, or from undesirable images of the self.[27] These conscious and unconscious motives may cause persons to marry when they do not have the emotional capacity to involve themselves freely in the intimate interpersonal relationships of marriage. These marriages, "legally valid" though they may be, contain all the corrosive ingredients that can destroy marital harmony (if it ever existed) and necessitate its ultimate termination. At present, the law will only rarely recognize such reasons as justifiable grounds for terminating marriage, even though these factors may ultimately create the "grounds" for the divorce.[28] The psychiatrist's skill in clarifying the underlying causes for a failing marriage may help bring about their resolution or bring the couple to a less stressful termination by divorce.

Hopefully, one day this kind of information about marriage will become sufficiently well understood and accepted by the community so that the grounds for divorce may be broadened to include psychological incapacity, especially if there are no children. Although this is not likely to occur immediately, psychiatrists as a professional group should strive to educate the community about the existence and the importance of these emotional factors. (This book would appear to be a helpful step in this direction.)

As legislators formulate statutes which regulate marriage contracts, they raise certain barriers to the contracting that hopefully screen out some inappropriate marriages. For example, there may be a waiting period of several days between the application and the granting of a marriage license. This is an attempt to force at least several days' glare into the starry eyes of those who impulsively decide to marry in order to gain some immediate pleasure.

Similarly, marriage statutes set a minimum age for the nuptial pair. These laws, however, take into account the biological and social fact that many sexual unions occur before the marital bonds are tied, and so the statutes make exceptions to the age limit for marriage. Society goes to great lengths to legitimize any biological union likely to bring forth children. In its pragmatic way, law has bowed to the inevitable.

Marriage statutes also contain prohibitions against consanguinity, reflecting efforts to reinforce ancient taboos against "incest." Incest is defined in many ways, however, and the varied definitions mirror widely varying social attitudes about family structure. Usually, marriages that fall outside the defined limits are declared void, notwithstanding what may happen to children of the voided marriage.[29]

We should note that appellate opinions in divorce cases reveal very little about the circumstances in which the cases arose. Often one suspects that the appeals were brought in order to readjust or alter some economic factor after the death of a spouse. For example, a man married to a woman not legally available to him as a spouse might will his property to her. After his death, some collateral member of his family, who technically could be a possible heir at law, might contest the will on the grounds that the marriage was nonexistent. Other instances occur among the poor. While in this group illegal family relationships are usually ignored, an employer may question a marriage to avoid an obligation to pay a widow under workman's compensation laws. City or county welfare departments also make challenges as they attempt to shift financial responsibility under ADC (Aid to Dependent Children) or welfare laws.[30]

Though psychiatrists will not often be involved in this kind of case, their insights can be useful at a legislative level. Every effort should be made to bring laws into rational relationship with the psychological facts of life. As I said earlier, any statute which does not do this encourages nullification and loss of respect for the law.

"Seriousness" of the Problem: A Question of Prediction

The law, always reflecting a conservative position, will generally not permit a divorce unless some serious problem is present. This reflects the view that society has an interest in keeping marriages intact. Minor differences of opinion between marriage partners will not be accepted as serious enough to justify disrupting the relationship that society has deemed so valuable.

If a person petitions for divorce, there is explicit or implicit legal demand that evidence be presented to show there is little chance for repair of the relationship. Often psychiatrists will be asked to provide information on this point, and this necessitates utilization of their clinical ability to make predictions. Needless to say, this gives us pause, and we often attempt to avoid the invitation in order to escape the risk of demonstrating real or imagined lack of skill. When psychiatrists do perform this function, they utilize such concepts as repetition compulsion, Benedek's "parenthood as a developmental phase,"[31] and other psychodynamic theory. These dynamic concepts must be presented to the court in clear and non-technical language.

Perhaps the most reliable psychiatric data for predicting the outcome of marriage difficulties come from the "trial of therapy." Though the predictive techniques mentioned above leave much to be desired, after an individual or a couple has been in treatment for a while, there will be more reliable evidence upon which to base judgments. This will be especially important when the disposition of children is in question.

In most legal situations the "weight of the evidence" question (the legal counterpart of scientific "validity") will arise. It is here that psychoanalysts, aware of the vulnerability of their science, often hedge their comments in testimony and reports in a way which makes them difficult to comprehend. While the desire to be right makes psychiatrists and psychoanalysts like all other human beings, it produces confusion when it appears in the context of expert opinion. It reflects doubts about the *role* of expert witnesses, which could be eliminated readily if the details of the role were known.[32] Lawyers, masters of logical analysis, swiftly discover efforts to camouflage and circumvent. They properly judge that such efforts reflect concern and defensiveness. If psychiatric experts fail to acknowledge the realities of their science and art, lawyers will likely dismiss their opinions. It is important for psychiatrists to remember always that when lawyers ask for our views, we are giving merely "opinion evidence." This is viewed by the law, and should be viewed by ourselves, as just *opinion*. Opinion need not be validated data; it merely reflects the best judgment of the expert. Though few psychiatric theories have high validity at present, our opinions about human behavior have demonstrated value and can be of great assistance in the resolution of many complex questions about divorce.

The Fault Concept: Who's Good and Who's Bad

Marriages originally were virtually indissoluble. A few narrowly defined faults could lead to annulment; and it took difficult-to-get ecclesiastical approval to obtain a termination. As the crown's courts during the twelfth century slowly gained power and began to influence marriage dissolution,[33] the concept of fault was extended in the canon law.[34] Divorce would be granted only when one party had committed a fault, and these faults were equivalent to sin. The earliest fault that would legitimate divorce was adultery. If it could be proved that one party had engaged in adultery, that party was vulnerable to divorce, with the legal disadvantages that accrue to the party at fault.

With the passage of time, various forms of brutality and deprivation also came to be viewed as "grounds for divorce." The party seeking the divorce had the burden of proving these acts on the part of the spouse. A corollary to this concept was the idea that the petitioner had to have "clean hands." Traditionally and even today, one available defense against a divorce action is to prove fault in the petitioner (the doctrine of "recrimination").[35] A "cross petition" is filed. The result, if each succeeds in his argument, is that there is proof that neither party is an "innocent" spouse, and neither can get a divorce. The presence of marital virtue in the petitioner, at least, is necessary to obtain a divorce.

Contemporary psychodynamic theory would vigorously challenge the idea that "fault" is an appropriate and useful concept for understanding marital discord. More and more evidence is accruing to demonstrate that the actions of one spouse are closely interrelated with, if not aided and abetted by, the other spouse.[36] Thus, an adulterous husband may be pushed into adultery by a rejecting wife, who in turn is responding to his emotional insensitivity regarding her problems with the children. There is circularity. Lawyers will wonder why, if this is true, the wife raises the issue of divorce. Our clinical observations lead us to believe that the divorce will be sought when some emotional factor of importance reaches disequilibrium, and the legal move is an attempt to reestablish some kind of harmony. Often the divorce will not accomplish that goal, providing only an inappropriate solution. A lawyer, to be effective, would need to know how to elicit or secure the necessary information so he could help his client avoid this situation.

If this theory of marriage is true, it would suggest that the concept of fault should be eliminated from consideration in marriage terminations. Other criteria, such as whether or not the couple can live together with more advantage than disadvantage, would be more useful. The farcical situations that now exist in jurisdictions where many divorces are obtained by "collusion" should be acknowledged and eliminated.[37] When it is necessary for the parties to carry out such a complicated and specious procedure to achieve their legal goal, the only result will be the progressive depreciation of the public image of law. There may also be damage to the individual who is sensitive to such issues and who is forced to "lie" to get a divorce.

In summary, psychiatry has much to offer of a substantive nature regarding the concept of fault in divorce actions. Our theories of marital psychodynamics make the traditional logic of the law obsolescent in this area. Every effort should be made to bring this knowledge before legislators so it may be utilized as statutory revisions are considered.

"Offenses"

If a spouse commits certain kinds of offenses, they will provide grounds for divorce to the other party. For example, in many jurisdictions, if a husband (or a wife) is convicted of a crime and imprisoned, his (or her) marital partner may, after a certain length of time, automatically receive a divorce. Thus, the criminal act is grounds for a divorce. One party commits fault, the other is faulted, and the dissolution may be carried out.

Similarly, certain sexual acts that psychiatrists view as appropriate sexual foreplay remain in the statutes as criminal offenses. They may be used by warring couples as levers for divorce, if not legal blackmail. If a complaining spouse wished to reveal these facts to the prosecutor, it could result in prosecution, and a conviction could then provide grounds for a divorce action. Though these statutes are only rarely invoked, they are on occasion utilized for coercion during divorce negotiations.

Another interesting "offense" is that of becoming "insane." In some states (Michigan is an example), if a person becomes mentally ill, he or she may not be divorced at all. In other jurisdictions, mental illness over an extended period of time may be grounds for divorce. Whichever way the law puts it, this factor raises logical dilemmas in the light of contemporary knowledge about family behavior. For example, in one case,[38] during the trial there was proof that all the "grounds" for divorce were "caused" by mental illness. This should have eliminated the basis for divorce, under the law of the state. The appellate court, however, responding to the obvious fact that the couple could not get along, by-passed this proposition of law and simply stated that since the parties could only live in misery, the law should not force them to stay together. This upheld the trial court and nullified the statute, at least in that case.

The concept of "offense" is another form of the fault notion and cannot logically remain in our divorce laws. It does great harm to the image of a rational rule of law and for this reason should be eliminated.

Problems of Timing

When a divorce is granted (in contrast to an annulment), it always relates to something that has occurred after the marriage. A condition that existed prior to the marriage, provided it was known to both parties, may not be used as grounds for a divorce action. The legal theory is that if the marriage "contracting" took place in the presence of a known undesirable attribute or disability, then there was acceptance of it by both parties.

There is a similar legal concept in regard to "faults" arising during the marriage that are apprehended and then *tolerated* by the spouse. For example, if a husband finds out about his wife's adulterous action and continues the marriage (more particularly the sexual relationship), this "condonation" will be viewed as erasing that particular "ground" for divorce.[39] Such magical manipulation by legal policy-makers is an attempt to view the marital state as a system of shifting balances of goodness and badness. Divorces may only be granted when there is a one-sided negative balance that runs against the defendant.

One important aspect of timing (and condonation) relates to reconciliation attempts. Under the law of some states, if a reconciliation attempt were to be made and it was at least temporarily successful, the parties might "give away" their grounds for divorce. When this is so, therapists cannot properly urge reconciliation unless their patients are fully aware of, and willing to take, the legal risks. This illustrates the importance of knowledge about divorce law to psychotherapists who treat persons in marital difficulty.[40] Failure to have such knowledge might cause serious misunderstanding as well as legal disability, if one or both spouses are receiving advice from a lawyer will also reflect the active involvement of psychoanalysts in the area of family-law research.

Another place where our knowledge can be valuable is in the law schools. Law students, who in their professional practice will have to cope with couples in trouble, should acquire some psychodynamic knowledge. In the past, lawyers have had no tools with which to approach the difficulties of family disharmony, and it is no wonder that they have resorted to the magic of legal formulations. Many experimental efforts are being carried out in American law schools to increase lawyers' skills in dealing with interpersonal relationships.[43] This is all to the good. Psychoanalysts should seek opportunities to assist in such efforts and to expose their theories to both the criticism and the exploration of the bar. This surely will be mutually advantageous. Our analyst colleagues have made many brilliant intuitive leaps toward understanding human behavior, and some of these ideas have been progressively raised to a higher level of validity. However, we may well use the analytical skill of good lawyers to help us gain greater understanding of our own concepts. In my experience, intimate contact with law professors, law students, and members of the bar and bench has been of great value.

Domestic-relations law is probably one of the most controversial insofar as expert testimony is concerned. If there is any place where the decision to testify for a patient will be difficult, it is here. If reconciliation efforts through therapy are to be made with those who may potentially be divorced, there must be no risk of having these efforts brought into the limelight of a public trial. Hopefully, procedural techniques will be found to minimize this risk, without losing potentially useful information.[44] At any rate, little improvement will be made without our active participation. These questions do not resolve themselves in the abstract, and only experience and experimentation can demonstrate difficulties and suggest modifications for better functioning. We owe it to the community to help in any way our competence permits.

In conclusion, let me say that the analysts who participate in these kinds of legal settings will have a most rewarding intellectual experience. The many complex and fascinating problems found in the law of the family lie fallow and waiting for our involvement.[45] Until we do become involved, we cannot legitimately complain about the foolish and meaningless maneuvers that are currently carried on by courts as they struggle to deal with problems of the family.

regarding their "case." "Resistance" to treatment may
of legal reality.

This surely is another place where expert opinio
rected toward legislative change in the statutes. It
that reconciliation efforts should jeopardize the par
The result of such legal policy runs counter to the
conserving salvageable marriages.

General Considerations

As psychoanalysts and psychiatrists explore problems in
partners who are in trouble, several considerations come
their minds. First and foremost are questions of ther
competence can make one of its main contributions at
vided it is applied in the reality context of divorce l
acteristics of the law (for example, regarding condonat
that psychiatrists deal with the reality problems that
they consider divorce. Psychiatrists must understand
that therapy raises and perhaps modify therapeutic st
ingly. If the therapy cannot be modified (which is un
the risks may be openly faced and realistically interpret
of the instances in which it would seem impossible fo
to make accurate and apt interpretations without know
of the reality involved. This last point runs counter to so
theories (the notion that the therapist deals with the m
transference); these theories will probably have to give

Psychiatric knowledge may also be highly useful in
modification of statutory language. Our profession sho
an ongoing education of the bar and the public to hel
needed changes in the direction of rationality. When N
action in Marriage appeared in 1956, it represented or
explorations of marriage psychodynamics.[41] Those pape
as they were, made a valuable contribution to legal
they are often quoted in the literature of family law. A r
of the widening scope of legal literature on this subject
and the Law by Goldstein and Katz.[42] This is a major e
psychiatric and other behavioral science materials more
able to law students and lawyers. Other books nearin

NOTES

1. M. Ploscowe and D. Freed, *Family Law* (Boston: Little, Brown & Co., 1963), p. 145.
2. Norman Reider, "Problems in the Prediction of Marital Adjustment," in Victor W. Eisenstein, ed., *Neurotic Interaction in Marriage* (New York: Basic Books, 1956), p. 324.
3. Robert Redmount, "An Analysis of Marriage Trends and Divorce Policies," *Vanderbilt Law Review*, X (1957), 536–545.
4. Lawrence S. Kubie, "The Challenge of Divorce," *Journal of Nervous and Mental Disease*, CXXXVIII (1964), 511–512.
5. For those who wish to read a legal work with treatises on the various issues in family law, see *Association of American Law Schools Selected Essays on Family Law* (Brooklyn: Foundation Press, 1950).
6. Goldstein and Katz, in their book *Family Law*, have done follow-ups on the divorce cases they discuss in the book. They find that more than 95 percent of the plaintiff parties proceeded to put into operation *their* wishes regardless of how an appellate court may have ruled (personal communication with Dr. J. Katz). See J. Goldstein and J. Katz, *Family Law* (New York: Free Press, 1965).
7. Theodore Plucknett, *A Concise History of the Common Law*, 5th ed. (Boston: Little, Brown & Co., 1956), p. 304; and Redmount, *op. cit.*, pp. 528–534.
8. Plucknett, *op. cit.*, pp. 547–548.
9. Orman M. Ketcham, "The Unfulfilled Promise of the American Juvenile Court," in M. Rosenheim, ed., *Justice for the Child* (New York: Free Press, 1962), pp. 22–27.
10. John G. Howells, *Family Psychiatry* (London: Oliver & Boyd, 1963); Jules H. Masserman, *Individual and Family Dynamics* (New York: Grune & Stratton, 1959); Virginia Satir, *Conjoint Family Therapy* (Palo Alto, Calif.: Science and Behavior Books, 1964); Andrew S. Watson, "The Conjoint Psychotherapy of Marriage Partners," *American Journal of Orthopsychiatry*, XXXIII (1963), 912.
11. The lawyer as counsel is often put in this kind of role and therefore should develop counseling skills. See Andrew S. Watson, "The Lawyer as Counselor," *Journal of Family Law*, V (1965), 7–20.
12. N. W. Ackerman, *The Psychodynamics of Family Life* (New York: Basic Books, 1958).
13. Satir, *op. cit.*
14. For a typical complaint, see the well-articulated comments of Judge Victor J. Baum, "A Trial Judge's Random Reflections on Divorce: The Social Problem and What Lawyers Can Do About It," *Wayne Law Review*, XI (1965), 462.
15. This kind of collaborative teaching is, in fact, being carried out in such places as the University of Pennsylvania and Bowman Gray Medical Schools. See Emily H. Mudd, "Marriage Counseling Instruction in the

School of Medicine Curriculum, University of Pennsylvania," in E. Nash, L. Jessner, and W. Abse, eds., *Marriage Counseling in Medical Practice* (Chapel Hill: University of North Carolina Press, 1964), pp. 319–327; Ethyl M. Nash, "Marriage Counseling Instruction in the Bowman Gray School of Medicine Curriculum," in *ibid.*, pp. 328–338.

16. Watson, "The Conjoint Psychotherapy of Marriage Partners," pp. 916–917. Also see Andrew S. Watson, "Reality Testing and Transference in Psychotherapy," *Smith College Studies in Social Work* (June 1966), pp. 191–209.

17. Some courts would say that helping the parties separate cleanly should be the limit of the intervention. See Maxine Virtue, *Family Cases in Court* (Durham, N.C.: Duke University Press, 1956), p. 219.

18. Kubie proposed a novel "committee" to help parents settle matters of child care after divorce, when the parents are unable to do so. See Lawrence S. Kubie, "Provisions for the Care of Children of Divorced Parents: A New Legal Instrument," *Yale Law School*, LXXIII (1964), 1197–1200.

19. H. Foster and D. Freed, "Child Custody: Part II," *New York University Law Review*, XXXIX (1964), 615–630.

20. Baum, *op. cit.*, p. 472.

21. See "Confidentiality and Privileged Communication in the Practice of Psychiatry," Report No. 45 (New York: Group for the Advancement of Psychiatry, 1960), pp. 101–109.

22. This happened to Dr. Roy Grinker, Sr., in Chicago. *Binder v. Buvell* (Circuit Court of Cook County, Ill., No. 52C2535, June 24, 1952).

23. O. English, M. Katz, A. Scheflen, E. Danzig, and J. Speiser, "Preparedness of High School and College Seniors for Parenthood," *A.M.A. Archives of Neurology and Psychiatry*, LXXXI (1959), 469–479; M. F. Ashley Montagu, "Marriage: A Cultural Perspective," in Eisenstein, *op. cit.*, pp. 3–9.

24. F. W. Maitland, "Magistri Vacarii Summa de Matrimonio," in *Association of American Law Schools*, pp. 104–113; Fernando Henriques, *Love in Action* (New York: E. P. Dutton, 1960), pp. 257–261.

25. This occurred, for example, in New York State when the only ground for divorce was adultery.

26. Litwak in a paper on divorce asks: ". . . To what extent can divorce laws be used to *prevent* [italics mine] de facto family breakup?" See Eugene Litwak, "Divorce Law as Social Control," in N. Bell and E. Vogel, eds., *The Family* (Glencoe: Free Press, 1960), pp. 208–217.

27. Ludwig Eidelberg, "Neurotic Choice of Mate," in Eisenstein, *op. cit.*, pp. 57–64; Watson, "The Conjoint Psychotherapy of Marriage Partners."

28. In a small but increasing number of jurisdictions, courts are beginning to allow divorce when there is mutual incompatibility, without need of finding one party at fault. See Ploscowe, *op. cit.*, pp. 222–225.

29. In law, a *void* marriage never did legally exist. A legally defective

marriage may also be found *null*, but it takes some initiative by one of the parties to nullify. See Redmount, *op. cit.*, p. 536.

30. Current legal studies under the War Against Poverty program are focusing on these kinds of problems and will go far toward clarifying our knowledge in these matters. See "The Extension of Legal Services to the Poor" (Washington, D.C.: U. S. Department of Health, Education and Welfare, 1964); Patricia M. Wald, "Law and Poverty: 1965" ("Washington, D.C.: National Conference on Law and Poverty, 1965).

31. Therese Benedek, "Parenthood as a Developmental Phase," *Journal of the American Psychoanalytic Association,* VII (1959), 380–417.

32. Andrew S. Watson, "Communication Between Psychiatrists and Lawyers," in *International Psychiatry Clinics,* Vol. I, No. 1 (Boston: Little, Brown & Co., 1964).

33. Maitland, *op. cit.*, p. 108.

34. In England, the ecclesiastical court had complete control over divorce until 1857. See Ploscowe and Freed, *op. cit.*, p. 136.

35. *Ibid.*, pp. 217–218.

36. Don D. Jackson, "Family Interaction, Family Homeostasis and Some Implications for Conjoint Family Psychotherapy," in J. Masserman, ed., *Individual and Familial Dynamics* (New York: Grune & Stratton, 1959), pp. 122–141.

37. "Collusion" in a divorce action is always illegal, even if it seems to be a practical necessity. See Ploscowe and Freed, *op. cit.*, pp. 229–230.

38. *Vial v. Vial,* 120 N.W. 249, 369 Mich 534 (1963).

39. Ploscowe and Freed, *op. cit.*, pp. 240–242.

40. Henry H. Foster, "What Psychiatrists Should Know about the Limitations of Law," *Wisconsin Law Review,* No. 2, Spring 1965, 189–239.

41. Eisenstein, *op. cit.*

42. Goldstein and Katz, *op. cit.*

43. John Suarez, "Reciprocal Education—A Key to the Psychiatrio-Legal Dilemma," *Journal of Legal Education,* XVII (1965), 316–328.

44. Through the creation of family courts, with their adjunctive services, these goals are being met with increasing skill and success. See Judge Paul Alexander, "The Family Court—An Obstacle Race?" *University of Pittsburgh Law Review,* XIX (1958), 602–618; Jacob Isaacs, "The Role of the Lawyer in Representing Minors in the New Family Court," *Buffalo Law Review,* XII (1963), 501–521.

45. Andrew S. Watson, "Family Law and Its Challenge for Psychiatry," in Y. Koskoff and R. Shoemaker, eds., *Vistas in Neuropsychiatry* (Pittsburgh: University of Pittsburgh Press, 1964), pp. 157–169; also *Journal of Family Law,* II (1962), 71–84.

Dynamics of Growth and Maturation in Marriage and in Psychoanalysis

S ex, marriage, and the family are not the same as they were yesterday. Originally the family was formed not around the Great Father but around the Great Mother. This knowledge goes back beyond what Sigmund Freud presented in his book *Totem and Taboo*. Although he was vaguely aware of the matriarchy, Freud emphasized the patriarchy. However, symbols of the matriarchy had been studied in almost analytic fashion by J. J. Bacchofen, who was not recognized at the time of Freud. He had described early matriarchy, which changed to patriarchy in the second millennium B.C. for reasons that we do not know.

Since the establishment of the patriarchy in the Jewish family, the woman had had little influence outside the home. Inside the home she retained a central position, symbolized in her ritual blessing of the Sabbath candles.

The patriarchy came to full flower in the Greek culture and especially in the Roman civilization. It is symbolized in the birth of Pallas Athena from the head of Jupiter. This myth, like so many others, indicates well the creative anxiety of the man who cannot produce life in the manner of women. The story of Eve's birth from Adam's rib seems to express the same anxious envy: "We men can create life, too, as the woman does." It conceals the man's anxiety about being a drone.

In the Christian family, the depreciation of the woman went somewhat further than in Greek antiquity. It was symbolized in the Catholic dogma: "Women will have to be silent in matters of the Church"—which sounds somewhat more civilized and diplomatic in the canonical Latin: "Tacit Mulier in Ecclesia."

The patriarchal character of the Jewish-Christian family is perhaps the greatest contribution of the Jewish people to the cultural development of the last two thousand years. The Jewish family has always offered a haven of rest from the storms around it during centuries of persecution, and a retreat from life in the ghetto. The Jewish home was a place where Jewish culture and the Jewish person became visible in their brightest light. Heinrich Heine describes it with these words: "In the marketplace, the Jew was perhaps hard and sometimes ignoble; in the world, he helped his judges to misunderstand him; in the home, he was himself."

The family of today—perhaps the family of tomorrow—in the Western world tries to do something new in history: the modern family tries to establish the equality of man and woman in the home and outside it. Even children have their rights—that is, the rights of children as different from those of adults.

At the present time, the American family is getting stronger, which seems to contradict our doubts and some of our statistics. The increasing strength of the Western family is not necessarily a sign of growth, maturation, and wisdom; it may also be regarded as a sign of the ever deepening alienation of modern man from everyday life, from professional work, from science, art, and religion. The world around us becomes more and more threatening, frightening, and alienated, and we retreat from it into our families. There we find relative freedom from the cruel reality around us.

The Western family is one of the few remaining islands of freedom. There we need not conform—or at least not to the degree in which we must outside the family. The intimate climate of the home safeguards us to a certain degree from the ever increasing powerful threat of having to submit to the rapid spread of uniformity. The family is the last stronghold of individuality in our time.

The Human Need for a Creative Challenge
and the Sense of Mastery

In the present time, man faces a double dilemma. Ahead of him lies a time offering a way of life in which practically every wish can be fulfilled—and at the same time he faces the possibility of total destruction. A second dilemma is somewhat less discernible: the offer of effortless living conflicts with the human need for challenge and with the need to be creative.

Tomorrow is almost here, and in the near future nobody will envy anyone his money or his luxury. People will envy the few who have something to do that makes sense, that is needed, that is outside automation, and from which they do not feel alienated—something that may be creative, some work that must be accomplished and is meaningful. Without creative challenge, we would live a life of agitated boredom, which camouflages depression. The cult of effortless living fails to satisfy human needs.

In this dilemma, modern man makes the mistake of hoping that sex offers the answer to all questions. Sex certainly cannot be made by machine—it is something which must be made by hand (if that is the right word). It is based upon a creative effort, as the words "making love" indicate. At the same time, sex is not the answer to the existential despair of our time. When all else is in doubt, making love remains something from which people are not yet alienated; but love is more than sex, as it is more than refuge: it is a part of man's creative need.

This is also the point at which the therapeutic analytic situation is similar in its dynamics to the marriage situation. The therapist will take anxiety as a sign of the place where work is required. In marriage, with its intimacy, anxiety cannot be concealed and has to be worked out; if not, disaster will occur.

The Dynamics of the Family and of
the Psychotherapeutic Situation

The key to the study of similarities and differences between psychoanalysis and marriage lies in the role that transference plays in both situations. (The infantile past is transferred into the present of both. This means, for instance, that the eldest of three sisters will behave differently in her marriage than will the youngest of six siblings. Both women will transfer their experience from the infantile past into the present of their respective marriages. Or a twin brother will have to make more difficult adjustment in marriage than a younger brother who may have learned from an older sister how to work toward being loved. People bring into marriage their past in order to repeat it; it is their assignment, their duty and fate, to try to master it. They may fail or they may win, but they must fight for it, respond to the challenge. In psychoanalysis, essentially the same has to be tried as in marriage. Sigmund Freud once asked Franz Alexander, while discussing an especially difficult patient: "Where and when did your patient say 'No' to further growth and maturation?" There the transition must be made from interpretation to insight to responsibility for change and progress.

Residuals from the difficult stages of the development of the past, which lead to sex and love and their fulfillment in marriage, may be seen when studying the dynamics of family life. From the early oral level we retain the desire for a Utopian state of effortless bliss: the eternal hope of finding peace and fulfillment, of enjoying dependence and passivity without guilt and threat. This is also the time when we build our confidence and faith in our ability to master inner and outer reality. It is a time of narcissistic fulfillment. As we once felt sure that we could dominate the mother and her milk-giving breasts with our magic omnipotence, we cling in later life to this hope. We spend much time and effort in our later life reestablishing this dominance over inner and outer worlds. Deep down in our heart or in our unconscious, we still hope and wait for the blissful existence to return to us. We find it only in death and perhaps in addiction or in deep sleep. Otherwise, the absent mother at first—and reality later—forces us to recognize reality and to submit to the reality principle, which corrects the dominance of the pleasure principle. We must accept it even if we do not like it, as we silently protest against it.

The experience of weaning is the first trauma with which we must deal. It will be repeated endlessly in all forms of separation and will be felt with anxiety. The last form of separation-anxiety is the fear of separating from this life, which has to end in death.

From the anal stage, we retain the idea of private property and possession. This stage also gives us the ability of symbolically mastering the loss of the mother, who is now recognized as no longer being a part of the mother-infant-baby unit, but as a part of the outer world, which could be separated from the baby. This early mourning for the loss of the mother gives us an acquaintance with the first reality—leads us to the first testing use of symbols in the form of introjection, projections, splitting of objects into good and bad parts. The outer world finds its reflection in the inner world, and symbol formation begins. Anal training sets the pattern for later sexual attitudes. Virtue and cleanliness are equated symbolically, as are sin and dirtiness. This leads to the frequent splitting of love and sex, which may decide the fate of a love and marriage in later life.

The prolonged infancy that is so typical in the development of the human person causes an increased need for dependency, which in turn has to be fought bitterly by us. Man suffers under the curse of deepened separation anxiety. Men are happy in their infantile dependency on their mother's love. In order to become adults, they must accept the necessity of no longer desiring the woman who nursed them. Were this not so, then there would be the danger that all of us would remain children—or animals, neither of which knows sin.

Perhaps all anxiety stems from the ego's incapacity to accept separation which equals death. For the infant, to be loved by mother means life; to be deserted by mother means death. To experience separation means to experience deepest death anxiety. It is a hard time when the infant must learn how to accept separation and how to live between dependency and death.

It is essential to know that at this point of development a child will experience even the best, the most devoted and deeply loving mother as bad (or as partially bad). The child must realize that he and mother are different people, as he must later realize that he and the world are different (and that is why the world must later be changed symbolically and perhaps realistically).

All drive to mastery aims symbolically at the restitution and reparation of the child-mother unit, which the child feels he has demolished by his destructive rage at mother's leaving during weaning or later toilet-training. He bemoans the loss of the mother and the loss of his narcissistic belief in himself and his magic-mystic omnipotence. This he attempts to restore with the world of the symbol.

Only the repeated experience that the mother who could get lost is also the mother who may return can restore the health and happiness of the infant.

To a certain extent, the human family offers freedom from reality and freedom from death, because it counteracts separation anxiety. The return of the mother offers reassurance. Sheltered from reality and with enough parental care and the lust of infantile narcissism, the infant conceives a dream of narcissistic omnipotence in a world of love and plenty and pleasure. Then comes the insight that mother is not always there. A great amount of early hostility and destructiveness and aggression is released—followed by guilt and fear of retaliation. With the help of the symbol and the help of a kind object in reality, the child comes to terms with inner and outer reality. The mother keeps us from despair and keeps us alive; she gives us our ideas of love. In the last analysis, the incest taboo can be explained by a desperate last effort to fight dependency on the woman who once had complete power over us.[1] Never again will we dare to desire that person upon whom we were once so totally and helplessly dependent. This struggle from dependency to independence and final interdependence is the most difficult balancing act that human beings must learn to perform. His marriage is the stage upon which to train, to succeed, to fail—but always to work in order to muster the transference of the past into the present.

Only after the role of pregenital developmental stages has been acknowledged can the Oedipal situation be understood, and the Oedipal situation is of critical importance in the development of sex and love, of marriage and of family life. In marriage, people finally try to work out the residuals of the Oedipal situation that they had not previously worked out in their lives. We work on unconscious relationships partly with our wives and partly in later family life with our children in the "reversed Oedipus situation." With all due respect to the therapeutic efficiency of psychoanalysis, we must realize that there is such a thing as a natural maturation, a working through of unconscious trends in love and marriage as part of life. Attempts to solve this Oedipal situation keep us busy the rest of our lives. Sigmund Freud himself knew about the possibility of working through in daily life, and he hoped for what he called an "analytic atmosphere" to help in the further progress of mankind.

The inner drive that leads man to continue to learn was called by Sigmund Freud the repetition compulsion, which he related to the death instinct. This may be true, philosophically speaking. For the clinical observer, it is easier to say that we are driven to repetition by a healthy striving for mastery. Our narcissism drives us to mastery—at first by magic-mystic means; then by realistic attempts at changing our environment for the better; finally, with the help of symbol creation.

The infantile past reflects in many ways upon the marriage situation. A man finds his mother, his mistress, his daughter, and his sister—in his wife. He also must see in his wife what she really is: not only a screen for his transference feelings, but also this person here and now. Not only is she an imagination and transference figure, not only a screen, but she has her own wishes, her own desires, and her own responses. This constitutes a difference from the analytic situation in which the analyst, through his training, his technique, and his style, has learned to show impassive loyalty to the study of his patients' unconscious needs. He is also a living person and will have reactions divergent to the associations of his patients. He is supposed to consider the analytic situation, however, mostly as a one-sided relationship—from the patient to the physician—whereas the marriage relationship is a two-sided relationship. Whether the analyst chooses to show his reactions to his patients, and to what degree, constitutes his technical skill and style and tact. The analyst reacts with interpretation; the marriage partner, with understanding and responsive action.

It is the intent of working through to free us from our transference illusions and still tolerate and perhaps even love our partners. The aim is to bring the desires of childhood and the needs of adult reality into harmony. This is not easy—either in psychoanalysis or in marriage. That it can be accomplished at all is one of the miracles that everyday life presents to the person who appreciates witnessing a miracle.

The woman may want to find in her husband her father, lover, son, and brother. There are other transference images too that lead to an even more complex situation. For instance, a man also finds his father again in his wife; and most important and mysterious, a woman also sees a mother in her husband. Before the man realizes this, understands it, and, by satisfying his wife's needs, leads her to the understanding of her relationship with her mother, much trouble can be caused. By working on it, much trouble can be avoided and much happiness may be given. Happiness in marriage depends upon the harmonious integration of man and woman with their unseen host of images from their respective pasts transferred into the present. This does not imply a destruction of the past; even if this could be accomplished, it would lead to emotional impoverishment. It implies insight and knowledge of the unconscious, which speaks to us through the symbol. In analysis, the pathological influence of the past must be analyzed and perhaps eliminated. In the life situation, the knowledge of the symbol will lead to insight and understanding of the symbol, which combines the past with the present; it should lead not to therapeutic intervention but to maturating, responsive action.

A child must have a model of how this has been done by his parents in order to continue where his observations of his parents' marriage left off. The model may be found in the "nuclear" family. A child must see and feel that his parents have formed a stable coalition, a kind of alliance. Parents must maintain well-marked lines of demarcation between the generations, and they should emphasize appropriate sexual identities. Only then can we expect children in later years to apply to their own marriage situations what they learned by observation from their parents.

In all this, it is neither possible nor advisable to draw lines between conscious and unconscious. This is one of the differences between therapeutic situations in an analytic office and the life situation in the parental home. The life situation is replete with subliminal cues that we both give and receive and use constantly and consistently for insight, action, and maturation. Only when this perception is disturbed can analytic interpretation restore this ability to learn from life again.

The problem of man's biological bisexuality must be solved with mechanisms different from those of transference in marriage. A person has to employ the mechanism of "projective identification," as Eduardo Weiss described it first and as Melanie Klein later named it. The projection of a man's femininity upon a woman is a normal procedure in the development of the ability to love. The man projects his femininity upon the woman and loves it there, while she does likewise with her bisexual, masculine component. It is probably this procedure of projection which stands at the cradle of the belief that love cures all. Love does not cure all—but it certainly helps. Without it, nothing helps. Without the projection of one's own bisexual part, a person remains at the level of self-love, and we need for our happiness that kind of emotional interchange of give and take which we experienced when we were infants.

Trouble and danger are connected with this kind of projective identification: besides this normal procedure, there are pathological forms. We project all kinds of undesired, unacceptable trends upon our partners, sometimes upon our children, and then either we try to enjoy these trends vicariously or we fight them viciously. Most confusing: we may do both simultaneously. We seduce our partners in love or our children into doing what we dare not do; then we punish and torture them for having done it.[2]

The Process of Working Through in Relationship to Growth and Maturation

Marriage offers a fresh start to the solution of old problems. Psychoanalysis often continues where marriage fails—and a marriage may take up again where psychoanalysis left off. It is even possible that psychoanalysis may start with one partner and shift and continue with the analysis of the problems of the other partner.

Marriage partners continue from approximately the point at which respective parents left off. The new family continues where the infantile family left off. This is one of the reasons that started me investigating the potentialities of analytic family therapy.

Women have perhaps a better gift for spontaneous working through. In the care of their babies, they are closely connected with reliving long-repressed stages of their own development. This is a chance that men do not have or carefully avoid. A woman is also by destiny more insight-directed. A woman marries a way of life—which is an invitation to contemplate; a man is more future-oriented. A woman creates life within herself, while a man tries to create life outside himself. He loves a woman for what she is—and a man is loved for what he promises.

A man experiences sex first and discovers love later—if he discovers it at all. A woman is different: she experiences love first and discovers sex later. For both, the sex experience is of such maturational value because it shows how much joy and happiness can be derived from love and from one's own body. It is the final reward for having relinquished the hope that mother's love is the only love. It contains the final fulfillment of that narcissistic trend in us which we need to live.

The "natural superiority" of woman is debatable—Freud certainly doubted it—but it is an observational fact that women are closer to being mothers and therefore have a better chance for maturity. It is the natural fulfillment of their narcissism in the best sense of the word—in the sense of pride and love and satisfaction—or of freedom and mastery over oneself, as the Greeks developed it.

Men, on the other hand, are more closely related to being boys in need of being loved. Perhaps it is more natural and easier for women to become mothers than for men to become men. Women identify early and easily with their mothers, while boys tend to remain boys. Women often solve their conflict with their mothers by identification, while men have to separate more deeply from their mothers in order to grow up. A feminine identification in a man has to be sublimated and disguised to a high degree before it becomes acceptable.

It all goes to show that it is the woman's task to bring up her man—which we the men love, need, resent, and often hate.

To become a man, a boy must relinquish his mother; to become a woman, the girl does not really have to renounce her mother. She can solve this problem by identification. She may even remain faithful to her father with the help of this introjection of her mother. This explains why women never really believe in the incest taboo—neither insofar as the father is concerned nor insofar as their own sons are concerned. As long as she feels like her mother, she may also act like one—and accept her privileges in the bargain.

To seduce is the mother's destiny. If anyone prefers not to believe this, he has only to look at Harlow's monkeys. Without sexual training by their mothers, these monkeys never get acquainted with the facts of monkey love and life.

The potentialities for working through in marriage are also the best defense of monogamy. The monogamous arrangement is a life-long pressure for working through and not avoiding it. Naturally, there are exceptions. There are marriages which do not work out and must be dissolved, just as there are sometimes realistic factors between patients and analysts that may lead to a therapeutic impasse and require dissolution by changing analysts.

It is equally true that a love affair sometimes can be of great maturational value. I once observed this in a patient who had to be hospitalized with a severe asthma attack. Within a few critical days, this patient improved remarkably. The internist thought it was his cortisone which helped; the psychoanalyst thought it was his silent visits that reassured the patient's separation anxiety and his cry for love; the wife hoped it was her demonstration of her love and concern in watching at the patient's bedside; the hospital's social worker thought it was the hospitalization and the change of environment, the turning toward the powerful hospital-mother, that brought about the change for the better. The attractive, young, and willing nurse's aid who attended the patient had her own thoughts—and so did the patient, as he later revealed in analysis. True working through can take place outside the analytic office.

A man may realize that his wife's masochism permits him to enjoy his own sadistic behavior without guilt. Such insight may lead to deep and lasting behavioral changes in a marriage. We have no right to say that psychoanalysis is the only way to communicate with the unconscious. It is only a special therapeutic approach, similar in its dynamics to other maturing events that take place in a creative life.

The legitimate aim of psychoanalysis is negative: the removal of resistance against correcting distortions and illusions. The aim is to enable the patient to learn again. The aim of analysis is not the full and complete knowledge of a human being, not the setting of values or the finding of the meaning of human existence. Freud never considered himself a philosopher. He considered himself an observer— hoping to become a healer. The therapeutic situation conceals what the life situation reveals, namely, that men are not only driven by their pasts but also guided by their futures and their ideals. The joy of mastering life is the main force that keeps people at the task of constant working through.

The main difference between psychoanalysis and the process of working through in the life situation—especially in a marriage—leads to the discussion of negative transference, hostility, and the resistance which they cause in the process of working through. The necessity of having to work through hostility toward the love partner explains the sad fact that a certain amount of in-fighting is inherent in a creative marriage. It has to be expected and must be accepted. A marriage that is not worth fighting for is not worth being maintained. Happiness is not found but fought for in marriage. Happiness is the result of hard labor and sometimes of intensive fighting. Albert Einstein put it well when he once said: "Happiness is for pigs." When I once quoted this statement to a patient in analysis who was reluctant to fight his wife any longer, he promptly answered: "Then I want to be a pig."

It is, of course, a special kind of fighting that is needed. In family therapy, the fight is never avoided—but neither is it enjoyed. The normal marriage fight does not lead to insight because it is waged to win, not to understand. The partners are out to hurt and not, as they claim, to convince. They approach each other on different levels of communication and will never meet. They bypass each other. The therapist is not a judge in such situations: he is more an umpire who tries to show the combatants that they are bypassing each other, that they are moving on different levels of communication, and that understanding is possible only if they find the underlying conflict. It is amazing to behold how little else is needed in therapy other than understanding. Everything else starts from there and is easy.

The psychoanalyst is a specialist in the handling of negative, hostile feelings—whether they are consequences of a negative transference or are based upon some realistic event. To deal efficiently with his patient's hostile feelings is also the true reason for the analyst's distance from his patient. In this way, he himself is less involved with his patients and therefore less exposed to painful injury. In love and marriage, the partners are much more vulnerable and need that kind of patience and tolerance which only love provides.

A marriage partner has to learn how to meet hostility and not necessarily how to accept it, but how to understand it. At first the partner must withstand it so that he can finally understand it. An analyst is trained in the consistent interpretation of resistance, which prohibits the emergence of unconscious material. How could true working through of resistance occur in a marriage of two people who are utterly inexperienced in the technique of psychoanalysis?

Two sets of answers are possible. At first, intellectual interpretation of resistance in analysis is probably without much therapeutic value either. Such interpretations must be related in word and emotion to the human interaction between patient and therapist. Many facets of human experience are shown in the therapeutic situation: love, patience, trust, hope, faith, devotion, the will to help and to be helped, endurance, determination to work through hatred and hostility and anxiety. If these emotions are not embedded in mutual respect, in some kind of basic trust, then the therapeutic process will reach a standstill.

Psychoanalysis is not a love affair, but so far as intimacy of relatedness between two people is concerned, it finds its counterpart only in
the intimate relationship between two marital partners. There is
perhaps only one other human situation that is more intimate, and that
is the early infantile mother-child relationship—which seems to be
the model for love, marriage, and psychotherapy. All three situations
contain symbols of death and rebirth. The patient with his unmastered
past has to die so that his rebirth at the present may be possible and
so that changes may prepare for a better future. This symbolism of
death and rebirth is common to the analytic situation, to initiation
rites, and to marriage.

There is a second answer possible concerning the changes of
spontaneous working through of unconscious material outside the
analytic situation. Anyone who observes families in health, happiness,
crises, sickness, growth, and maturation gains new confidence in the
resources of sick people when they have group support. There are
strength-giving factors in the group, e.g., in the family, which may
not be fully available in the unique one-to-one relationship of the
analytic isolation. This seems to be confirmed by animal observations:
the most severe, psychotic-like disturbances in Harlow's monkeys
could be avoided when monkeys were exposed, even for short periods
of time, to a group of peers. The most pathogenic influence of
schizophrenogenic monkey-mothers can be compensated by the healthy
influence of playmates.

The responsive action between members of a family who are
attuned to each other's conscious and unconscious can lead to mental
disaster when abused and to mental health when applied with mature
love. Responsive action probably plays a much greater part in all forms
of psychotherapy than we therapists wish to acknowledge. With our
responsiveness, we do not fulfill our patients' desires or wishes, but we
respond spontaneously, freely, and naturally to their unconscious
needs. The family is poor in interpretation and rich in this responsive
action. The family therapist will aim to restore this interaction when
it is disturbed in a sick family. After such interfamilial communication
has been restored, a process akin to therapy goes on uninterruptedly—
because a family continues its therapy outside the office to a much
higher degree than does the individual patient who leaves his analyst's
office.

The Marriage and the Future

The future is no longer what it used to be. Our dreams, and to a certain extent our insight into the future, have changed. The greatest difference lies in a peculiar assignment that man has to accept, one that is complex and difficult to describe: it concerns the integration of psychoanalytic knowledge and insight into our lives.

Further progress in automation and technology is almost unavoidable: it is almost automatic. For the first time since man became human, people will be free from want. It is a great temptation and a great challenge to walk through the open doors to Paradise on earth. The horrible failure to utilize such great inventions as television and automation and atomic energy is a warning that it is possible to miss this great moment in history. Henry David Thoreau, when told that it was now possible to telephone all the way from Maine to Texas, sadly asked: "And what has Maine to say to Texas?" With all the wealth in our hands, what are we going to do with it?

The future that makes us free from work should give us the freedom for communication between our conscious and unconscious. This is the one thing that will not happen automatically; we have to establish it by an act of creativity and of effort. The gap between mastery of outer reality and mastery of inner reality must be closed. It *can* be closed if we integrate psychoanalysis.

The Greeks developed a high level of cultural achievement; they delayed the invention of the machine because they could not give up their narcissistic pleasure in their bodies and the narcissistic enjoyment that they derived from their minds. Out of this narcissism, in the best sense of the word, was born the idea of individuality and of freedom, and it constituted the Greek miracle.[3] Their narcissism did not allow Greek scientists to project bodily functions upon the lifeless machine. Only after the naïve narcissism of antiquity had been destroyed through the influence of Judeo-Christian philosophy could mankind take the next great step in the Renaissance, which was the transition to the Machine Age. A new sense of mastery replaced the Old World's sense of pride.

What we must do now is achieve a similar conquest of our narcissistic involvement in what only yesterday we called with such pride our "soul" or our "mind," what we now, since Freud, call our unconscious. For the Greek, the knowledge of the unconscious had to be expressed in poetic form in the great truth of the Greek singers, poets, and philosophers. Replacing this insight through scientific knowledge derived from Freud would have shattered the Greeks' eternal hope of becoming divine and challenging the gods.

For us today, such integration of the symbol cannot be described in terms of "adjustment" or "maladjustment" or in terms of health or sickness. All these terms are outmoded. The only way into the future would be an acceptance of our unconscious—not as divine, not as animal-like either, but as what it is: developed from most particular and primitive ways, almost embarrassingly unscientific beginnings following natural laws that can be investigated, understood, and controlled through the human gift for integration and the need for mastery.

Such insight will lead to levels of maturation that we have seen in only a few human beings commonly called "genius." Whether such a culture development can be a mass culture—or whether it must undergo a time of restraint in generativity—remains to be seen. The Greeks showed such restraint because they knew that the price for inner freedom must be paid with a sense of responsibility. We, too, will have to pay the price for freedom. It is possible that any mass culture demands such a high degree of mechanization and automation that individuality must die. It is conceivable, therefore, that the threatening population explosion must be fought not because of the inability to provide adequate nourishment—this will be child's play—but because the kind of education that this kind of cultural development demands cannot be provided for an unlimited population. Not even the Greeks could do that, and they carefully restricted their democracy to the male citizens of the city of Athens.

Picasso spoke well in a remark to Cocteau: "One starts to get young at the age of sixty—and then it is too late. Only then does one start to feel free; only then has one learned to strip oneself down to one's essential creative simplicity." In the words of a great artist, this is what I meant by "symbolic integration." This is where the experience of working through joins the experience of artistic creation.

Paradoxically, this new analytic attitude toward problems of living of today and tomorrow is similar to the religious attitude. It is an attitude of love, patience, tolerance, understanding, and insight.[4]

NOTES

1. Adrien Turel, *Zur Emanzipation des Mannes von Reich der Mutter* [Concerning the Emancipation of the Man from the Empire of the Mother] (Bern: Hans Huber, 1939).

2. For more about the past and present, see Edith Hamilton, *The Ever Present Past* (New York: W. W. Norton, 1964); Erich Kahler, *The Tower and the Abyss: An Inquiry into the Transformation of the Individual* (New York: George Braziller & Co., 1957); Carl Jung, *Man and His Symbols* (New York: Doubleday & Co., 1965); Herbert Marcuse, *Eros and Civilization: A Philosophical Inquiry into Freud* (Boston: Beacon Press, 1956).

3. On this topic, see Hanns Sachs, "The Delay of the Machine Age," *Imago*, Vol. XX (1934); also printed as Chapter 4 in *The Creative Unconscious* (New York: Sci-Art Publishers, 1942).

4. On the topic of growth and maturation, see also Martin Grotjahn, *Psychoanalysis and the Family Neurosis* (New York: W. W. Norton, 1960); Martin Grotjahn, "The Untamed Analyst," in *Psychoanalytic Pioneers*, Franz Alexander, Samuel Eisenstein, and Martin Grotjahn, eds. (New York: Basic Books, 1966); Theodore Reik, *Voices from the Inaudible: The Patient Speaks* (New York: Farrar, Straus & Giroux, 1964).

INDEX